HERDER

Aesthetics against Imperialism

GERMAN AND EUROPEAN STUDIES

General Editor: Rebecca Wittmann

JOHN K. NOYES

Herder

Aesthetics against Imperialism

UNIVERSITY OF TORONTO PRESS
Toronto Buffalo London

Toronto Buffalo London
www.utppublishing.com

ISBN 978-1-4426-5038-1

(German and European Studies)

Publication cataloguing information is available from Library and Archives Canada.

University of Toronto Press acknowledges the financial assistance to its publishing program of the Canada Council for the Arts and the Ontario Arts Council, an agency of the Government of Ontario.

Canada Council for the Arts
Conseil des Arts du Canada

Funded by the Government of Canada
Financé par le gouvernement du Canada
Canada

For Sascha, Anjou, Indra, and Sheba

Contents

List of Illustrations ix

Acknowledgments xi

Introduction: *Postcolonial Theory and Herder's Anti-Imperialism* 3

1 From Epistemology to Aesthetics 23

2 From Organic Life to the Politics of Interpretation 60

3 From Human Restlessness to the Politics of Difference 95

4 From the Location of Language to the Multiplicity of Reason 135

5 From Human Diversity to the Politics of Natural Development 191

6 The Aesthetics of Revolution and the Critique of Imperialism 246

Conclusion: Herder, Postcolonialism, and the Antinomy of Universal Reason 297

Notes 313

Works Cited 371

Index 389

Illustrations

0.1 *Johann Gottfried Herder*, painting by Johann Ludwig Strecker, 1775 5
3.1 William Hodges, engraved by W. Watts, *Matavai Bay*, 1773 98
3.2 *Vorstellung der Europäischen Handels Plätze in Asien*. Engraving, anon., ca. 1770 102
3.3 William Hodges, engraved by J.K. Shirwin, *The Landing at Middleburgh*, 1784 104
3.4 John Webber, engraved by William Sharp, *Inside of a House in Nootka Sound* 105
3.5 Giovanni Battista Casanova, *Apolito Sauroktonos*, 1821 132
4.1 Frontispiece to Guillaume Thomas François Raynal, *Histoire philosophique et politique des établissements et du commerce des européens dans les deux Indes*, 1781 184
5.1 Eberhard Zimmermann, *Tabula mundi geographico zoological*, 1760 228
5.2 Zimmermann, *Tabula mundi* (detail) 231
6.1 Frontispiece to *Briefe zu Beförderung der Humanität*, 1793 271

Acknowledgments

This research was supported by grants from the Social Sciences and Humanities Research Council of Canada and the Joint Initiative in German and European Studies at the University of Toronto. I am also grateful to the Cornell Society for the Humanities for a fellowship that allowed me to explore some of these ideas in their early stages. An early version of the Conclusion appeared in the *Journal of Postcolonial Literary Inquiry* (2014).

HERDER

Aesthetics against Imperialism

Introduction: Postcolonial Theory and Herder's Anti-Imperialism

When I began writing this book, it was my intention to explore the way writers in Germany in the late eighteenth and early nineteenth century were responding to the expanding world, to the first signs of globalization, and the way this was affecting their work.[1] I was intrigued, for example, by scenes addressing this topic in Goethe's *Faust* (1829) or the *Wilhelm Meister* novels (1796, 1829), in Schiller's *Love and Intrigue* (1784), in Kleist's *Betrothal in St Domingo* (1811), and many other important works. It was clear to me that the writers of the time were almost without exception fascinated by the rapidly changing political and economic landscape of the world outside Europe, and were posing difficult questions about how these changes affected the lives of Europeans. Not only were the effects of the changing world economy being felt increasingly at home in Germany, the rapid expansion of the European world was also calling into question some of the most fundamental assumptions about living in the world. As I delved deeper into the writings of some of Germany's most prominent intellectuals of the time, I discovered the works of Johann Gottfried Herder, and soon realized that to understand Herder's position on imperialism alone would require a book-length study. My intention here is to trace the threads that connect his Kant studies to his innovative philosophy of language and history, and to his condemnation of imperialism as it appeared to a mid-eighteenth-century German intellectual. The key lies in Herder's epistemology, which shifts philosophical analysis towards aesthetics, anthropology, and cultural history. The critical literature acknowledges this shift, but ignores the fact that, in doing so, Herder was investigating – perhaps for the first time – how anti-imperialism can be not only ethically but above all epistemologically grounded. This makes his work not only of historical interest. It connects directly to some of the most pressing questions that have been facing theories of aesthetics and imperialism over the past few decades.

Herder was born in 1744 in the small town of Mohrungen in Prussia, the son of a schoolteacher and church cantor. He was a student of Kant, a Protestant theologian and one of the first modern writers to recognize the need to protect cultural diversity and to foster the plurality of cultures. He was also remarkably prescient when it came to the threats which unchecked commercialism posed to the global environment – whether we take this as the environment of cultural and linguistic diversity, or that of biodiversity.

Like so many German intellectuals at that time, Herder avidly followed the latest discoveries of men such as James Cook and Georg Forster, and he made an effort to understand the way their explorations were changing the picture of the world and its inhabitants. He read widely in a number of the latest scientific fields, including history, anthropology, ethnography, geography, and biology. Herder's theoretical project was formulated at a pivotal time in the long process of globalization. The second half of the eighteenth century was the time when, to speak with Dimas Figueroa, the three structural conditions that make it possible to speak of the beginnings of globalization were in the process of being fulfilled: the experience of the planet as a unitary whole, a real relationship between all regions of the planet, and "the inadequate regulation of this relationship by way of moral or political norms."[2] This is the moment when the markets and trade routes established in the sixteenth century are being expanded throughout the world, while in the popular imagination the thread that ties them to the conquests which originally established them is growing ever fainter.[3] This period has been described by Immanuel Wallerstein as "the second era of great expansion of the capitalist world economy."[4] It marks the transition between what is often referred to as the first and second phases of globalization. However we parse it, the result is more or less the same: The brutal conquests of previous centuries are making way for new forms of economic and political interaction, with their own characteristic modes of exploitation. The discovery of the world is rapidly approaching completion, and the conquest and enslavement of other cultures is meeting with ever more vociferous opposition, while at the same time the world market is becoming increasingly consolidated, and the diversity of world cultures is rapidly becoming a fact of life. As early as 1959, the renowned historian of the Enlightenment

0.1 *Johann Gottfried Herder*, painting by Johann Ludwig Strecker, 1775. Hessisches Landesmuseum Darmstadt.

Reinhard Koselleck began his book *Kritik und Krise* (Critique and Crisis) with the observation that, in the eighteenth century, the modern subject became increasingly defined as encompassing all of humanity, and its "field of action was the unitary world of the globe."[5] This new global awareness was not an idealist development, and Herder went to great pains to show that he had not arrived at his critical position through idealist postulates. Eighteenth-century global consciousness was a response to the changing world economic and political order as it presented itself in the everyday lives of writers, and the changed imaginary relationship to the world as a whole was based on the changing structures of everyday life.[6] While the everyday lives of many writers were slowly becoming influenced by the new economic world order, the confrontation with a new, globalized subjectivity was sudden and radical, and it affected the imaginary relationship between local and global phenomena. As a result, it is possible to speak of a crisis in the imaginary geography of subjectivity, or, to use Istvan Hont's words, the beginnings of a "permanent crisis of a divided mankind."[7] Viewed in this way, we begin to see the strong impetus for reading the literary and philosophical writings of this age as an ongoing exercise in crisis management related directly to globalization.

Herder's writings can be read as a direct response to this restructuring of the world. He took careful note of debates concerning world trade and imperialism, weighing the criticism of older forms of imperialism and the defence of newer forms, and asked what the changing world order means for a philosophy that wishes to address the politics of inequality. He saw that there were two sides to the economic restructuring of the world. World exploration brought a remarkable explosion in scientific knowledge about the world and its inhabitants. World trade brought luxury goods to the houses of those in Europe who could afford them, and with these goods came a general sense that living standards were improving. But there was a dark side to this process, exemplified by the Atlantic slave trade and the decimation of indigenous populations throughout the New World.

The European discourses that fed on the expansion of knowledge generally saw themselves as contributing to the wisdom of humanity as a whole. But the study of other cultures began to drive home the problem of cultural relativism in the pursuit of wisdom. Herder's corpus can be read as a sustained engagement with the problem of cultural relativism. Seen through the lens of cultural relativism, the great scientific explorations of the eighteenth century were looking increasingly like a new form of European imperialism. At the same time, the knowledge they yielded was beginning to unsettle the ideas supporting imperialism – ideas such as the superiority of European civilization, the primacy of reason, and the progress of mankind. Imperialist expansionism revealed the world as a place of infinite diversity, but the world's diversity was in turn threatened in many ways by the ideology of imperialism.

Although he is often read as a cultural relativist, Herder was careful to consider the pitfalls as well as the benefits of relativism.[8] The result was a critical examination of what it meant to pursue knowledge within the context of a culture, a linguistic group, a nation, but also as a species. In this way, Herder was able to ask what forms of knowledge enabled imperialism, and what forms best revealed its deception. In his works it is possible to trace precisely the path that led from the experience of living in a world structured by expanding capital, uneven development, and imperialism, to the idea that the aesthetic project is also a project of anti-imperialism.

When he began to link the question of knowledge to that of form, Herder found himself engaging with the intense debates in the middle of the eighteenth century on the epistemological status of art. The claims made on art at the time were large, regarding not only the production but also the appreciation and critique of art. As Robert Norton has shown, Herder came to see aesthetics as "a descriptive, explanatory science" aimed not at telling artists how they should produce art, but at tracing the historical genesis of individual art forms and art works.[9] There was a specific and a general aspect to this project. Aesthetics should be universal enough to explain the role of artistic expression in all of human life, but should also be able to explain why artistic expression is culturally – and often individually – specific. It is in artistic expression that human life shows itself most clearly to be a specific actualization of a universal potential. The proponents of imperialism either misunderstand or wilfully falsify the nature of knowledge and artistic expression. The idea that artistic expression can be universalized, reduced to a set of a priori rules, is intimately related to philosophical rationalism, the academic school that dominated German philosophy at mid-century. And this is intimately related to the idea that a dominant culture can impose its own sense of social form, its own value system and its own economy on another. Herder's remarkable response to the increasingly tenacious ideology of empire was motivated by his attempts to reformulate the questions posed by rationalist philosophy, shifting them into the domain of aesthetics, anthropology, and history. This also meant that aesthetics cannot be reduced to either art production or art criticism; it is an extended field in which philosophical analysis is intimately related to artistic expression. In order to do justice to this insight, I will be using the term aesthetics in this book to describe the alliance that art forges with philosophy in Herder's work. Aesthetics as Herder practises it explores the dialectic relationship between universal principles of thought and their specific expressions. It examines how universal expressions of human life are always restricted by the cultural context in which they are produced; but it also pursues the universal quality at the heart of culturally determined forms of expression.

In understanding anti-imperialism to lie at the heart of Herder's writings, I will show how the problems he faces are inherent in the project of opposing imperialism with aesthetics. As anyone who has read Herder knows, he made no secret of his opposition to imperialism. You don't have to read very far into his work to discover a deep-seated aversion to any form of exploitation or domination of one culture by another, but Herder nuanced this in a way that spoke specifically to European imperialism. There are several dimensions to his anti-imperialism. The most important arises out of the conviction that all cultures need to develop in the manner that is appropriate for their own particular environment, their history, their traditions, and their understanding of the world. This is an idea Herder began to develop early on, as he began to think about how the experience of living in the world varies according to the environment, language, and traditions of any one culture. Seen from this perspective, Europe's forays into the New World look like violations of the natural law of development, which requires that each culture should be allowed to actualize its full potential without interference from or subjection to any other culture. This is why, in an early poem, Herder calls Columbus an "assassin," who has "destroyed with poison our world and all its beauties, its charms, its customs and, alas, its life and youthful vigour!" (*HSW* 29, 426).[10] The natural constitution of this world with its single humanity and its diverse customs provides the lens through which he will develop his critique of imperialism. His own particular moment in history sees Europeans inventing "*means* and *tools* to subjugate, to deceive, and to plunder other parts of the world." But he also foresees a time when (addressing the subjugated world) "it will one day be precisely your turn to *triumph*! We affix chains with which *you* will pull *us;* the *inverted pyramids* of our constitutions will turn *upright* on your ground; *with us you will* ... Enough, it is evident that everything is tending *to a larger whole*! We embrace the circle of the earth – whatever we may do this with – and what comes next can probably never any longer *narrow* this circle's *foundation*!" (*HPW* 352).[11] As he will state later, "nature is everywhere a living whole, and it wants to be gently followed and improved, but not violently dominated" (*HSW* 13, 288).

Although Herder does not use the word imperialism, it is clear that he is talking about what Christopher Bayly calls the "first age of global imperialism," beginning around 1760, that is, around the same time Herder started to write.[12] In order to understand what imperialism looked like to Herder, I believe we have to adopt the broad perspective taken by Barbara Bush, who sees it as an "expansion of states outside their territory, a widening of geographical space, either by land or by sea, extending boundaries of power and influence," inscribing "social, cultural and political relations of power between the empire and its subordinated periphery,"[13] that is, uneven power relations mapped onto territory.[14] This is also the gist of V.G. Kiernan's even more succinct description: "The most elemental definition of imperialism might be the uninvited presence of armed men from outside; their very multifarious motives, and the consequences, still await classification."[15] This also keeps the term vague enough that it can serve as an umbrella concept for the various expansionary policies Herder sees at work in Europe in his time. He pays careful attention to the mechanisms of subjugation he sees when he looks at the foreign policies of the European nations and their trading companies. His aim is not to theorize the economic and historical links that tie imperialism to the monopolies established by the trading companies. Instead, he adopts a critique of commerce similar to that sketched out by Montaigne in the late sixteenth century, whereby the excesses of Europe drive the sacking of the New World. Herder writes: "The gold of royal diadems, the delicacies of our tables, all the appurtenances of splendid display and luxury, concealed beneath the mask of convenience, all these are the pillage of distant worlds. The dearer the booty becomes, the higher rises its value; and the *raison d'état* of commerce thus masters languages, so that other nations may at least be deceived in words of their own tongue" (*HEW* 30). And: "If each nation were to enjoy, within the confines of its frontiers and attached to its soil, nature's gifts from the womb of the earth without asking illicitly for tribute from other peoples' riches, perhaps no one would need to trade the citizen's birthright of his fatherland for foreign advantages" (ibid.). Instead, when he looks around him, he sees "the unnatural expansion of States, the savage mixing of humanity's types and nations under *one* scepter" (*HSW* 13, 384), a situation that causes him to ask: "Has not Europe been troubling itself and the world for long enough? Has it not for long enough waged senseless wars of religion and hereditary succession? Is not every continent dripping with the blood of those whom it slaughtered? with the sweat of those whom it tormented as slaves?" (*HSW* 17, 108). And furthermore, what is to be said of "the culture that the *Spanish, Portuguese,* English and *Dutch* brought to the East and West Indies, to the Negroes of Africa, to the peaceful Islands of the South Seas? Do not all these lands cry out – some more, some less – for revenge?" (*HSW* 18, 222).

What Herder is describing is how the growing interconnectedness of the world economy implicates all Europeans in the injustices committed in the name of trade. "From ancient times the East Indian trade was a rich one; the industrious, modest people served other nations at sea and overland generously with many of its continent's treasures and remained on account of its remove in a relatively peaceful state – until finally Europeans, for whom nothing is too far away, came and bestowed upon themselves kingdoms there. All the news and goods which they send us from there are no compensation for the evil they visit upon a people who committed nothing against them" (*HSW* 14, 32). These Europeans "roam through the whole world as merchants or robbers" (*HSW* 14, 37). Politically, the world is structured increasingly according to the principle "divisum toto orbe Britannum"; but the "monarchic merchant" begins to establish an independence from political structures, and need not have a "fatherland" at all.[16] Not having a fatherland is, in this reading, not being subject to the natural rules of growth that govern (or should govern) all life. Once this step has been taken, Europeans are acting as if nature's laws have no sway over them. "What right," he asks, "did you monsters have even to approach the land of these unfortunates, let alone to tear it away from them through thievery, deception and brutality?" (*HSW* 13, 263). Viewing European politics and commerce from the point of view of the world's natural development, Herder states that "our continent ought not to be called the wise, but the *presumptuous, intrusive, manipulative* part of the earth; it has not cultivated, but destroyed the germs of other peoples' cultures, wherever and however it was able" (*HSW* 18, 222–3).

Imperialism is built upon and fosters this arrogant, self-serving misunderstanding of natural principles. This applies in equal measure to the subjugation of other peoples and the destruction of their environments: "*Let it not be imagined that human artifice can with blusterous capriciousness transform a foreign region at once into another Europe* by cutting down its forests and cultivating its soil; for all of living creation coheres in a nexus which responds only to careful modification" (*HMA* 3/1, 256). It is no surprise that European arrogance gives rise to violent resistance. Speaking of the Native Americans, Herder observes: "The wars of the savages for their country, or on account of its children, their brethren, torn from it, or degraded and oppressed, are extremely cruel. Hence, for instance, the lasting hatred of the natives of America toward Europeans, even when these behave to them with tenderness: they cannot suppress the feeling: 'This land is ours; you have no business here.' Hence the treachery of all savages, as they are called, even when they appeared altogether satisfied with the courtesy of European visitors. The moment their hereditary national feelings awake, the flame they have long with difficulty smothered breaks out, rages with violence, and frequently is not appeased, till the flesh of the stranger had been torn by the teeth of the native. To us this seems horrible; and it is so, no doubt: yet the Europeans first urged them to this misdeed: for why did they visit their country? why did they enter it as despots, arbitrarily practicing violence and extortion?" (*HRP* 12). Similarly, the craving for excesses that drive the world economy will exact its own revenge, ensuring that "the poisons we have stolen cause us to die a disgusting, slow death, impoverished amidst the greatest wealth by our restless, infernal activity, tormented by desires, enervated by luxurious sloth" (*HSW* 18, 224).

In making statements like this, Herder is aware that what is at stake is the correct perspective on nature and on history, and that this perspective stands in direct opposition to the ideologies of imperialism. Imperialism rests on complicity with a secularized faith in progress, with the belief that it is providence and industriousness that has granted Europe "the power, the cunning and the tools to become the thieves, intruders, agitators and destroyers of all the world" (*HSW* 18, 223). This is why the "written histories of the wars and conquests of peoples" cannot legitimately be used to derive the "principles according to which they acted and wrote." Wherever it is tied to a legitimation of power, history will present a false moral code to posterity. "Violence and despotism can command the things they have power over, but not the *principles of rights and their infringements* [*Grundsätze des Rechts und Unrechts*] *in the history of humanity*" (*HFA* 7, 708). At the same time, Herder understands that the expansion of European interests throughout the world is, paradoxically, providing him with the evidence he needs to argue in favour of preserving humanity's cultural diversity.[17]

One of the reasons I wanted to write this book is the continuing uncertainty in the critical literature about how to evaluate Herder's opposition to imperialism. Is it structurally intrinsic to his theories of culture and language, or is it simple moral outrage? Did his epistemology lead directly to anti-imperialism, or was it an opinion he added on at a later stage? How does imperialism relate to the development of collective identities and the self-determination of individuals? Herder's opposition to imperialism has been commented on repeatedly in the literature, though it is my contention in this book that so far Herder scholarship has failed to understand why his anti-imperialism forms a necessary foundation of his entire philosophy, and how it mirrors the central problems of his thought. There has long been consensus that Herder opposes imperialism. As early as 1976 Isaiah Berlin spoke of Herder's "passionate anti-racialism and anti-imperialism." Herder, he observes, "dwelt on the folly and cruelties of imperialism all his life."[18] Berlin claims that "there is nothing against which he thunders more eloquently than imperialism – the crushing of one community by another, the elimination of local cultures trampled under the jackboot of some conqueror."[19] The well-known Herder scholar F.M. Barnard observes that Herder was "fully awake to the dangers of racist variants and ethnic imperialism."[20] In reading Herder's "Negro Idylls," Ingeborg Solbrig speaks of an "attack against colonialism," which is "forthright and consistent with his central concern for the dissemination of humanistic thought."[21] John Tomlinson extends this to cultural imperialism, observing that modern discussions of cultural imperialism can be traced back directly to the close linking of the concept of culture to the idea of cultural pluralism introduced by Herder.[22] For Tod Kontje, in Herder's eyes "modern European imperialism is only the latest chapter in the history of injustice."[23] Michael Frazer speaks of "Herder's liberalism and anti-imperialism – his opposition to the remarkable cruelty of the empires of his day."[24] Sankar Muthu refers to Herder's "anti-imperialist political philosophy."[25] He calls Herder an "anti-imperialist" whose concept of *Humanität* (humanity) was intended to theorize "international justice and a world beyond empire."[26]

Over the years, a number of attempts have been made to gain a more nuanced view of Herder's anti-imperialism. In a perceptive article of 1989, which found remarkably little resonance among scholars of anti-imperialism and Herder scholars alike, Samson Knoll discusses

Herder's "nascent condemnation of the economic system upon which colonialism was founded."[27] Knoll correctly understood Herder's anti-colonialism not as a sentiment, but as a scientific position "based upon lessons drawn from a lifelong study of history."[28] This led him to an intensifying opposition to colonialism during the course of his lifetime, strengthened by "a growing awareness, not common in his days, of the economic roots of the colonizing urge. His anticolonialism became, in fact, an attack upon the commercial capitalism of the age and its tragic impact upon the peoples whose welfare it pretended to promote."[29]

In a recent book on Herder's political thought, Vicki Spencer notes that "throughout his life, he is a strident critic of imperialism," which relates to "both economic and cultural imperialism."[30] She even goes so far as to claim that Herder's "opposition to European imperialism can also be seen as providing encouragement to post-colonial nationalist movements."[31] Spencer sees the key to this anti-imperialism in a pluralist conception of culture that is founded on "his expressivist theory of language."[32] I will be arguing that this is indeed the case, but that we need to dig deeper into his epistemology in order to ground this in an aesthetics of human nature. By doing this, I hope to show that, while the expressivist theory of language is important in understanding Herder's politics, it is not necessarily the decisive point in translating his ideas into today's theoretical attempts to ground anti-imperialism. Instead, I will show how anti-imperialism and the expressivist theory of language both arose from attempts to think through fundamental contradictions in the nature of human life. Spencer makes a convincing argument for the continuing relevance of Herder's thought within the context of political theory. As she shows, many of his ideas prefigure the current debates in interesting ways. But if this were Herder's claim to relevance, his importance would be largely historical, and there would be no real need to engage with his work as a challenge to current discussions around globalization and imperialism. My argument is that Herder's relevance is largely methodological and has to do with his attempts to shift questions of political conflict into the sphere of epistemology and aesthetics. Beyond describing the affinities between Herder's political thought and current debates, we need to examine the methodological challenges that arise from Herder's writings and to reflect on the way these persist in a number of debates today. I will address these issues in the conclusion to this book.

Nicholas Robinette argues convincingly that Herder arrived at his anti-imperialism via "a theory of the sign that accounts for the importance of human labor in producing language. Though it has received little attention, the emphasis he placed on language labor lead Herder to a bold, economically oriented critique of empire."[33] This was possible because Herder recognized the link between language labour as an essentially human capacity for cognizing existence, and colonial labour, which essentializes cultural difference in order to maximize profit: "Herder saw the creation of signs as an essential drama of existence, one that is shared among the variety of languages. The dignity of language labor stands in stark contrast to the depravity of colonial labor. Thus the most unexpected development follows on these claims: understanding language as a common human labor led Herder to a heated critique of empire."[34] Robinette argues that Herder's radical attempts to link semiotics to materialism have had far-reaching consequences. He cites Raymond Williams's historicist approach to language as well as the ideas of language relating to labour as set out by Ngugi wa Thiong'o, and he claims that these attempts to link labour, language and history show that "the main points of argument have changed less in two hundred years than we might expect."[35]

In her insightful and nuanced study, Sonia Sikka points to Herder's condemnation of "the emptiness and hypocrisy of the rhetoric of universal brotherhood that he hears around him. Underneath this rhetoric, he suggests, lies imperialism – economic, political and cultural."[36] Sikka traces this condemnation to a complex position on morality, which Herder never explicitly and systematically develops, and which must be reconstructed from disparate comments throughout his work. Herder's ethics represent an attempt to weave a path between a relativist position (whereby "in the sphere of morality cultural conventions fully determine truth")[37] and a commitment to a collection of values whose universality has to do with the structure of social relations and the constancy of human nature.[38] "Only because Herder posits human flourishing as a goal, and thinks that some things genuinely contribute to this goal while others do not, can he pass critical judgement on the societies he considers."[39] While, in the course of his life, he becomes increasingly committed to a universalist view on the shared organic nature of human development, he never loses sight of the fact that this is expressed in an endless variety of ways. Even when he speaks of shared humanity, his universalism "coexists with the same kinds of relativism about different societies" that one finds in his earlier works. As Sikka observes, the crucial point here is that "all peoples are *human*, expressing distinct ways of being human."[40] As I will be arguing, Herder understood the study of specific forms of human expression – the realm of the aesthetic – as a way of working out the tensions between universalism and relativism, thereby enabling a critical position on imperialism.

Sikka demonstrates clearly how "Herder's profound anti-imperialism – intellectual and cultural as well as political – contains lessons from which there is still much to be learned."[41] The assumption underlying the pages to follow is that, in broad terms, anti-imperialism today is still trying to learn the lessons that Herder was working through. One of the reasons I believe Herder has not succeeded in providing a lasting model for anti-imperialism is because he himself did not put forward a clear theory of anti-imperialist aesthetics. His ideas are scattered and unsystematic– to the point where at times he gives the impression that he himself does not realize completely what he was doing in his political critique. Sikka is correct in pointing out Herder's strong critique of a Eurocentric universalism, on the basis of which he criticizes his contemporaries "for the cultural partisanship and prejudice that underlie their unthinking Eurocentrism, and their ignorant condescension towards non-European peoples." And I agree with her when she points to the "serious flaws in Herder's writings," but I am not convinced that these result from "his failure to live up to this insight, in that he often commits the sins of which he accuses his contemporaries."[42]

This seems to represent the consensus on Herder's anti-imperialism: that he gained valuable insight which he himself could not fully realize. Reading the current state of the scholarship on Herder's anti-imperialism, one can easily gain the impression that the problems he confronted and the answers he provided – as well as the shortcomings in his positions – are due to his inability to do justice to his most innovative ideas. Sikka may even be right in calling this his most serious flaw. But Herder saw this flaw, and what's more, he saw the difficulty in avoiding it, since it emerged in his thinking as a systemic failure in the critique of imperialism. There are other, equally interesting flaws in his argument which he himself sees, and which he tries his best to repair. As I will show, these flaws and the suggested solutions make him topical. Even with regard to his apparent lapses in insight, close readings often reveal an irony or a tongue-in-cheek presentation of the contradictions in what he is trying to achieve. This is perhaps nowhere more apparent than in his confrontation with imperialism.

As I worked my way through Herder's writings and through the literature, I found myself looking for better explanations for the contradictions in his position on imperialism, explanations that go beyond an inability to heed his own insights. What I found was that these lapses open onto a number of more fundamental contradictions in his work, all of which impact on his writings on imperialism. Why exactly did he criticize imperialism? Was it a vague sense of moral outrage at the injustices associated with European expansionism? Did it have to do with his ideas on self-determination, on cultural diversity? If so, how is it possible for him to speak of the common development of humanity? And why the occasional slippage into what looks like racist and Eurocentric dogma? Why does he sometimes write as if none of his ideas on imperialism really matter? As I will argue in this book, Herder's importance today lies not in a set of correct insights which he himself could not adhere to. Instead, the insights themselves must be viewed as inherently contradictory, ideas about the nature of the political that in themselves cannot be lived up to – not by Herder, perhaps not at all. But – and this is what I aim to show – this is where the task of aesthetics begins. And Herder knew this. Pointing to the limits of both universalism and relativism, he demonstrates why attempts to think cultural diversity together with common humanity continue to encounter such intense conceptual difficulty to this very day, and why they continue to be of importance.

What I am proposing is that the anti-imperialist project itself, whenever it is framed as a problem of critique, of reason struggling with its own claims to universality, is subject to a series of inherent contradictions, and that these contradictions are best understood in the way Herder presented them. They pit some of the founding ideas of idealist philosophy against the insights of history, biology, and anthropology, as they were understood in the eighteenth century. This understanding of those sciences and the relationship they have to idealist philosophy has coloured the way critiques of imperialism have been formulated over the past decades. And it has also had an important effect on what aesthetics is thought to be capable of achieving.

This book is not only about Herder's path from a critique of epistemology to a project of aesthetics against imperialism; it is about deep systematic problems inherent in the project itself. It is intended as a foundation for anyone wishing to navigate the various debates that regard the aesthetic as the appropriate realm for opposing not only discourses of imperialism but also imperialist politics. Over the past decades, these debates have come to be known as postcolonial theory, and while I will not be addressing these theories (I prefer the plural) directly, I will uncover some of the core assumptions that are historically embedded in the project of aesthetics against imperialism, but that tend to be obscured in current debates. These assumptions are not only philosophical, historical, and even theological in nature, they also have to do with the biological and social constitution of human beings, as well as the difficult idea of common humanity. This book is not about postcolonial theories, but it is about a set of problems that are all too familiar to the readers of these theories, problems that arose in the midst of Enlightenment debates on aesthetics, knowledge, and the nature of human life. To be more exact, it is about Herder's attempt to formulate and resolve some of the problems that continue to haunt postcolonialism. These problems gave rise to a great deal of debate in Enlightenment Europe, and many attempts to theorize imperialism today have been impaired by tendencies to caricature the Enlightenment as a wilful subjugation of the non-European world in the name of science and profit, a self-congratulatory objectification of nature.

There is a general undertone of accusation against Enlightenment in the field of postcolonialism, according to which (in the words of Lynn Festa and Daniel Carey) Enlightenment appears as "irremediably Eurocentric." Festa and Carey describe the main tenets of this widespread misreading of Enlightenment:

> In its quest for the universal, Enlightenment occludes cultural difference and refuses moral and social relativity. Inasmuch as its values are identified as coextensive with modernity, the Enlightenment naturalizes a teleology in which all roads lead inexorably to an episteme associated with the West. Frozen in the dark backward and abysm of the "primitive" or "savage," non-Western populations are stripped of the agency and historicity that underwrites civilized advancement. The doctrine of progress, in turn, legitimates imperial conquest under the guise of the civilizing mission, while the celebration of reason disqualifies other belief systems as irrational or superstitious.[43]

They then go on to competently outline the difficulties arising from this dismissal of Enlightenment.[44] For one, the stereotyping of Enlightenment as a one-sided pursuit of power and knowledge is too simplistic to be of much interest. Much of what postcolonialism objects to in Enlightenment thought was itself the subject of intense criticism and debate at the time – to the extent that we need to ask how useful it is to continue speaking of *the* Enlightenment.[45] As Sankar Muthu observes, not only were there multiple claims on universalism in the Enlightenment itself, there was also a strong anti-imperialism at work within Enlightenment thought.[46] Nothing is gained by setting up a straw Enlightenment only to knock it down with the same arguments that were raised by many writers at that time. Furthermore, the conceptual tools of postcolonialism are themselves derived in large measure from the philosophers of Enlightenment Europe. How is a critique of European imperialism to deal with this? Dipesh Chakrabarty put it well in the introduction to his 1992 book *Provincializing Europe*:

> Concepts such as citizenship, the state, civil society, public sphere, human rights, equality before the law, the individual, distinctions between public and private, the idea of the subject, democracy, popular sovereignty, social justice, scientific rationality, and so on all bear the burden of European thought and history. One simply cannot think of political modernity without these and other related concepts that found a climactic form in the course of the European Enlightenment and the nineteenth century. These concepts entail an unavoidable – and in a sense indispensable – universal and secular vision of the human. The European colonizer of the nineteenth century both preached this Enlightenment humanism at the colonized and at the same time denied it in practice. But the vision has been powerful in its effects. It has historically provided a strong foundation on which to erect – both in Europe and outside – critiques of socially unjust practices.[47]

This is why Spivak proposes reading the great critical philosophers of the late Enlightenment (she focuses on Kant, Hegel, and Marx) as "remote discursive precursors, rather than as transparent or motivated repositories of 'ideas.' I keep hoping that some readers may then discover a constructive rather than disabling complicity between our position and theirs."[48]

But with this discovery come new problems. As postcolonialism's relationship to Enlightenment comes increasingly under scrutiny, it becomes clear just how problematic and unresolved this relationship is. A telling example is Pheng Cheah's *Spectral Nationality* (2003), which argues that the "decolonizing nationalist discourse" out of which postcolonialism grew is indebted to debates in German idealist philosophy. Cheah is thinking above all of idealist attempts to understand freedom as both a transcendental project of "rational purposive endeavour" and as associated with "the causality of culture and organic life."[49] For postcolonial theory, the problematic ambivalence of Enlightenment's transcendental project of freedom is well understood. Cheah's book provides an important corrective to the one-sided understanding of Enlightenment as built upon this project. As he shows, freedom could not be conceptualized in idealist philosophy without thinking its relationship to the organic. Out of this arose the "organismic metaphor of the social and political body inaugurated by German idealism."[50]

Cheah is quite right to trace this project back to Kant's critical philosophy, but by refusing to look further back to the roots of the problem Kant was attempting to solve, he introduces a number of misconceptions about what freedom and the organic meant in the eighteenth century. It may be true that, in the wake of Kant's critical philosophy, the organic had to be thought of as a metaphor, and that this introduced a fundamental problem into any attempt to think of how freedom relates to the organic. But this metaphorical understanding of the organic was gained at the price of turning away from the questions that Herder (and the pre-critical Kant) had posed for rationalist philosophy. Cheah is correct in pointing out the common engagement with what he calls an "organismic ontology" that is shared by the universalist and particularist positions. But he ignores the way Kant's struggle to wrestle the universalist position out of this ontology was at the same time a struggle against Herder. What this means is that, by asking us to reconsider the persistence of this ontology in Kant's critical philosophy, he is asking us to engage with Herder's objections to Kant. Sikka puts this well when she notes that Herder understands the importance of reason in "the fulfilment of the human essence, but he does not see this faculty as isolated – or isolable – from perception and feeling. He also does not conceive of it as the sole thing in the world that has intrinsic worth, in part because he does not conceive of it as a 'sole' thing at all."[51]

Drawing heavily on Leibniz and Spinoza, Herder sought to grasp the organic not as a metaphor but as the material expression of nature's force.[52] In consequence, he pursued a developmental theory that provided a real alternative to the (extremely narrow) understanding of development, or *Bildung* described by Cheah, who sees it as the "creation of an object corresponding to an ideal model."[53] To see *Bildung* this way encapsulates all that Herder finds wrong with idealism. This has important consequences both for freedom and for culture. Culture, for Herder, cannot be conceptualized as the "incarnation of human ideals," which is how Cheah thinks the Enlightenment saw it.[54] Herder's idea of culture is diametrically opposed to the "philosopheme of culture" that "articulates the formative power over nature that co-belongs with humanity, not only as an animal capable of rational contemplation, but as a purposive being with the ability to shape its natural self and external conditions in the image of rationally prescribed forms."[55] Nor could Herder have ever adopted the cosmopolitical stance that saw "the nation and its culture as the most effective actualization of universal ethical ideals," as Cheah claims.[56] To argue the view of nature and culture imputed here to Herder is to make the same fundamental mistake Herder rails against when reviewing the ideas of the rationalists. Herder's question to the rationalists also has to be posed to Cheah: how can culture possibly incarnate human ideals? Because he saw the difficulties in this claim, Herder had to talk about freedom in a completely different way to that identified by Cheah. Freedom becomes the mind's capacity to grasp and to represent organic processes in a different register from the natural forces these processes express. This is the significance of language and the aesthetic – it promises Herder an alternative to the dualism of the organic and the will, and to the dualism of particularity and universality. The aesthetic is the realm of freedom in so far as it represents the actualization of the will, in the context not of moral certainty, but of cultural self-formation.[57] As Vicki Spencer observes, the principal function of government is to act in accordance with the aesthetic balance of the particular and the universal.[58] With this realization, the postcolonial project faces Adorno and Horkheimer's penetrating analysis of the dialectic of Enlightenment.[59] How do the humanities speak against the alliance of truth and power in the language of that alliance? Or is there perhaps an alternative language?

Herder was well aware of the problems posed for aesthetics by the fact of imperialism. The most important dimension of this for him was, as mentioned above, the recognition that thought is always embodied thought, and thus located in time and space. Thinking can never be transcendental, since it is informed by the body's sensory relationship to the world. But more than this, language embodies a culture's specific conceptual engagement with its own history and geography. Language is a cultural negotiation of the forces of nature both within and outside the human organism. As a result, any given culture is engaged in a constant negotiation of its own representation, a politics of interpretation. If such a politics of interpretation is to be effective, philosophy needs to stop pretending that it has access to a privileged realm of logical thought that can be radically severed from the experience of cultural location. This means that philosophy needs to retool itself in order to fulfil its anthropological obligations. It needs to historicize embodied thought. How is this to be done? In asking this question, Herder is laying the groundwork for a philosophically founded anti-imperialism.

The thought experiments of postcolonial theory were already being conducted two centuries ago, and in the case of Herder, they were being pushed to their limits in ways that remain instructive to this day. It is within the context of this realization that my book unfolds. My aim is to explore the struggle at the heart of Enlightenment Europe to describe common human development in a way that will not fall prey to those claims to universality that were – even then – understood to be in league with European imperialist interests. My intention is to resituate the unavoidable split that has opened within postcolonial theory – the split between acts of theory that understand themselves as a continuation of the Enlightenment project and those that attempt to uncover the irresolvable contradictions within this project. This split runs right through the centre of theory today – not just theory that calls itself postcolonial. Donna Haraway addressed it, for example, in her famous "Cyborg Manifesto" as a problem facing feminist and post-feminist critique. When she stated that the "transcendent authorization of interpretation is lost, and with it the ontology grounding 'Western' epistemology," it is understood that the establishment of a transcendental authorization of interpretation is part of the Enlightenment project.[60] And yet, as she goes on to explore, oppositional politics appear to need political agency to be authorized in this way – resulting in her cryptic suggestion that the "acid tools of postmodernist theory and the constructive tools of ontological discourse about revolutionary subjects might be seen as ironic allies in dissolving Western selves in the interests of survival."[61] If a vision of justice is to be in any way politically effective in the world today, it needs to come to terms with the fact that it is just that – a vision. And as such, it is a representational device that threatens at all times to draw on transcendental concepts – thereby repeating the moves the postmodernists found most objectionable in Enlightenment philosophy; even to the point where, if the political desideratum is for oppressed subjects to "speak for themselves," the very nature of representation introduces uneven power relationships into political life.[62] Is it possible then to develop an aesthetic practice (and theory) that enables political action while at the same time sidestepping the seemingly natural alliance of representation and power? This question has been a huge challenge to postcolonialism. Witness the strong critique expressed by one of the founding members of the Subaltern Studies Group, Sumit Sarkar, of what he called "Saidian frameworks" in historical analysis, which homogenize postcolonial situations and underplay material culture and political economy.[63]

This is the matter at hand in my book. If we understand the acidity of postmodernism to be its relentless questioning of the representational devices that create a sense of subjective integrity, and if we understand the constructive work of ontological discourses as enabling political action in the name of human rights, then their oppositional movements were the topic of a great deal of debate in Enlightenment Germany. And much aesthetic production was intended to set up an "ironic alliance" between them. What is more, the methods that were employed to investigate the apparent impasse of political agency, the answers that were suggested, the aesthetic experiments, the failures in finding viable solutions – all of this prefigured the trajectory of the postcolonial schism. What I am suggesting in the pages that follow is that postcolonial theory and its legacy can learn a lot through a careful reading of the exemplary attempt to resolve its core problems in the second half of the eighteenth century, the writings of Herder.

1 From Epistemology to Aesthetics

Herder in Königsberg: The *Essay on Being*

During the time Herder was studying with Kant at the University of Königsberg, he set out to record his enthusiasm for his teacher's philosophy, but also to raise some profound concerns regarding what he saw as a fundamental contradiction in Kant's method. The *Versuch über das Sein* (Essay on Being)[1] was most likely composed in 1764, on the impulse of Kant's lectures on metaphysics.[2] Like Kant, Herder examines Being as a concept that cannot be further analysed, and he follows his teacher in denying the status of a predicate to Being: nothing is explained by stating that an object is existent, or has existence. Herder also rejects any attempts to explain either Ideal Being (*Idealsein*) or Existential Being (*Existentialsein*) on the basis of the other, as Descartes had done by declaring *cogito ergo sum*, or Crusius in asserting the existence of the self on the basis of self-consciousness.[3] Herder refers again and again, both directly and indirectly, to Kant's publications of the years 1762 and 1763, such as *Die falsche Spitzfindigkeit der vier syllogistische Figuren* (The False Subtlety of the Four Syllogistic Figures, 1762), *Versuch, den Begriff der negativen Größen in die Weltweisheit einzuführen* (Attempt to Introduce the Concept of Negative Magnitudes into Philosophy, 1763), and, above all, *Der einzig mögliche Beweisgrund zu einer Demonstration des Daseins Gottes* (The Only Possible Argument in Support of a Demonstration of the Existence of God, 1763).

The general philosophical problem Herder addresses is what Wolfgang Pross calls the "crisis in causality and the problem of evidence" (*HMA* 1, 844), which, in the wake of Locke and Hume, had split the philosophical debates of the Enlightenment, forcing writers to think about how best to use the rules of logic or observation and experimentation to explain the workings of the natural world. The point of departure, and the guiding principle of the essay is stated clearly in the Prolegomena, where Herder declares his adherence to a philosophy that follows the "*human* paths of attention, abstraction and reflection" (*HMA* 1, 576) – a position held also by Kant in his writings of the 1760s.[4] The human dimension of thought is characterized by the specificity of sensory experience, on the one hand, and the universality of logical thought, on the other. Herder links the two through innate cognitive processes. Attention is the capacity of the mind to focus on the information imparted by the senses, and the processes of abstraction and reflection are the cornerstones of the analytic method, which Herder recognized as the cognitive distinction that sets humans apart from the rest of creation. With this declaration, Herder is announcing his philosophical lineage, and he opens the Prolegomena with reference to the "well known truth, which suddenly issued forth long ago from the grey beard of Aristotle, and which, since Locke extolled it once again, has been recited over and over again – that all our concepts are sensory, that there are no innate truths" (*HMA* 1, 575). By mentioning Locke, Herder is invoking the philosophical problem of how cognitive processes are able to develop abstract and generally valid principles from the raw data of the senses, which furnish the mind with the experiential content of knowledge. This in turn raises the problem of philosophical method.[5] In the wake of Descartes, philosophy had to decide whether truth in human knowledge could be arrived at following the synthetic principles of mathematics, that is, by identifying universally valid laws and axioms then asking how they apply in each individual case, or whether it required an analysis of individual events, in order to arrive through abstraction and reflection at the general principles underlying these events. Just how the method of philosophy was to be distinguished from that of mathematics, and how it could provide proof and certainty in knowledge was debated by the most prominent philosophers around mid-century, including Condillac and Voltaire in France, and Christian Wolff and Alexander Gottlieb Baumgarten in Germany.

Kant himself formulated his pre-critical philosophy in dialogue with these ideas, which led him to take the position that the analytic method is the one proper to philosophical inquiry.[6] But more than this, he was opposing the rationalists with what Zammito calls the "unprovable givenness of the real."[7] In this, he had an immediate and lasting influence on Herder. His lectures on metaphysics in the 1760s took as their starting point Baumgarten's *Metaphysica* (1739), which was written in the rationalist tradition of Leibniz and Wolff. Wolff and his school had dominated academic philosophy in Germany for decades, and Baumgarten was one of his most influential students. Kant chose Baumgarten as his point of reference, since, as he told prospective students, the *Metaphysica* demonstrated a "wealth and precision" that, with "a little manipulation," could be brought into line with Kant's own ideas (*KAA* 2, 308–9).

Kant's essay on the existence of God provided the starting point for Herder's *Essay on Being*. Here, Kant showed how the grounds for proof of the existence of God are to be sought not in abstract concepts, but in the limit concepts of understanding, those concepts which prove irreducible or inexplicable through analysis – at least through analysis as the rationalists understood it. Such concepts provide a different kind of certainty from those that are analytically reducible. Analysis as the method proper to philosophy is dependent on the principle of agreement between the subject and predicate of a sentence, the Leibnizian predicate-in-notion principle (*predicatum inest subjecto*), whereby for a proposition to be true, the predicate must be contained in the subject.[8] The objective certainty of analytic concepts derives from principles of logic (Wolff stated in 1719 that "something cannot simultaneously be and not-be"),[9] and analytic method consists in demonstrating through a reduction of concepts the truth of a proposition or concept.[10] But can this apply to Being?

In *The Only Possible Argument*, Kant proposed that Being cannot itself be a predicate, since the subject would have to be assumed to exist in order to be given the attribute of existence (*KAA* 2, 74). What this means is that reality external to the mind provides the irreducible framework within which thought becomes possible, since this level of reality provides the material of thought itself. Kant presents this as an a priori affirmation of external reality. Taking this argument further, he then shows how a proof of the existence of God will be possible through what Gaier calls a combination of elements from the cosmological proof (derived from the very fact of existence) and the ontological proof (based on logic) (*HFA* 1, 846). Out of the logical possibility of thought, Kant derives the fact of real experiential existence, and on the basis of reality thus conceived, he arrives at the necessity of thinking a supreme being grounding this reality.

In his *Essay on Being*, Herder enlists Kant's own methodological premises in order to reject Kant's conclusions. Herder sets his criticism at a number of points in Kant's essay. The first concerns the structure of Kant's ontological proof, in which he works his way through the logical possibility of Being. Herder argues that it makes no sense to speak about the logical possibility of Being as if it could be removed from what he calls Real Being (*Realsein*). In order to make this point, he begins with the concept of possibility itself, arguing its supplementarity to the concept of Being. Attempts to base the reality of Being on an "obscure concept of possibility" are bound to fail (*HMA* 1, 581). Possibility is either logical or real, and these relate to one another according to the hierarchy of abstraction and Being. The concept of Being precedes that of possibility, and real possibility precedes logical possibility. The distinction between Being and possibility gives clarity to abstraction, and it forces an explanation of cause and effect, but when philosophy identifies the sequence of relationships between Being and possibility, or speaks of cause and effect, this is not the same thing as providing an explanation of Being. Being has to be assumed before these philosophical conversations can take place. Being is a concept of experience (*Erfahrungsbegriff*), whereas abstractions are random logical hierarchies of concepts (*HMA* 1, 581–2).

Next, and most important, Herder objects to the mixing of logical conceptions of Being with the concept of real Being. In *Concept of Negative Magnitudes* (*KAA* 2, 202), Kant had distinguished logical foundations (*logischer Grund*) from real foundations (*Realgrund*), arguing that the former permitted the logical connection to conclusions according to the principle of identity, whereas the latter gave rise to conclusions which formed part of a person's true concepts, but cannot be subjected to judgment.[11] In his reading of *The Only Possible Argument*, Herder believes Kant is working against his own method and, in using the logical concept of Being to found real experiential existence, forgetting the lesson he had learned from Christian August Crusius, whose insistence on the priority of experience attracted Kant's attention in his early writings.[12] Crusius, a student of Leibniz, had criticized Wolff for attempting to subordinate the principle of reality to that of logic. The distinguishing feature of human consciousness is self-consciousness, but this does not mean that self-consciousness is capable of giving rise to the contents of consciousness.[13] In an open jibe at Kant, Herder declares himself to be "still in agreement with the Crusians, who hold that the concept [of Being] cannot be explained" (*HMA* 1, 583).

The purpose of his essay, Herder tells us, is to establish as fact the irreducibility of Being. It cannot be explained and it cannot be further analysed (*HMA* 1, 579). Real Being is the primary, absolute concept. It is the foundation of all possibility, both real and logical (*HMA* 1, 583). This is very close to Kant's own position in *The Only Possible Argument*, when he speaks of Existence as one of those concepts which are "almost unanalysable" (*beinahe unauflöslich*).[14] But in Herder's conception of Being, this *almost* is inadmissible. In fact, the dispute over the *almost* in this sentence is the first sign of the deep and ever widening rift that will open up between Kant and Herder for the rest of their shared lives. For in speaking of Being as a concept that is almost unanalysable, Kant is opening the way for his later understanding of Existence as a limit concept of human understanding, and thus (as Gaier observes, *HFA* 1, 850) one that can be enlisted in logical processes. Herder insists that *Being* is not a logical category; it cannot be understood or explained, it is not subject to analysis, and cannot be proven. It is the most abstract of concepts, but it can be experienced as the most sensory of all concepts (*den allersinnlichsten Begriff*, *HMA* 1, 577–8),[15] and for this reason it provides the foundation of all certainty (*HMA* 1, 585–6).[16] The conceptual apparatus of human understanding is built upon the certainty of Being, and it establishes an order that relates subjectively to the thinking individual as a sensory being. Herder describes this order of understanding in terms that will continue to hold great importance for him in the years to come. First there is *astonishment*, which is an initial mediated experience, an event based on sensory perception; then comes *observation*, a temporally conditioned realization that the event occasioning astonishment repeats itself (and with this comes the attention to form as the vessel in which repetition is held); this is followed by *consideration* of the possible causes that may have given rise to the event; next, the unidentified aspect of causality is *named* as force (*Kraft*); and finally, the relationship between force and the effects of a cause is called *possibility* (*HMA* 1, 582). This order of understanding grounds logic so firmly in the initial experience of the most sensory of concepts, that any attempt to conceptually sever logic from the senses, to divorce thought from the body, does violence to the human condition, to the extent, as Barnard argues, that the concept of mind in Herder encompasses the entire body.[17]

It is part of the human condition to employ a specifically human mode of thought – logic – in order to approach that which can never be fully grasped – Being. The resistance that logic meets as it approaches the limit concepts of Being or God results from the disconnect between logical processes and Being. Logical being is only a copy of real Being, and the logical processes that give currency to thought are already a step away from the most sensory of experiences. Human beings are already a step away from the Being that cannot be explained. Not only is it the case that "Being cannot be demonstrated," but there is "no Being of God that can be demonstrated" (*HMA* 1, 585). The fact that God's existence is not subject to proof is not inherent in Being, nor in God, and it is not a shortcoming of language. It is inherent in the nature of human life. But this is not to disparage the quality of human Being. On the contrary, it is to realize the wealth of thought, manifested in culture, that opens between sensory experience and logic.

The Importance of Aesthetics

With the proof of God and the certainty of absolute truth removed, the task of philosophy becomes an examination of the order of certainty grounded in the senses. As he explores the consequences of this realization, Herder will understand the destabilization it brings to the idea of universal truth. As Sikka has shown, the concepts with which philosophy deals do not address the truth of things, but the relationships humans establish with things.[18] And since these relationships are built on a system of sense perception and linguistic formation, philosophy needs to understand that truth can only be negotiated aesthetically. To understand this is to do justice to the realization that the workings of logic will always refer back to the experience of the senses and the forms of phenomenal repetition. In making this distinction, Herder is following what Gaier calls a characteristic move in eighteenth century philosophy – the shift in focus from "the aporia of philosophy to aesthetics as a metatheory" (*HFA* 1, 857). Philosophy is not in a position to add to the store of existing knowledge. It can only provide a better understanding of knowledge through relating concepts to experience.[19] This meant taking up the project of Baumgarten, who is generally accredited with having founded the study of aesthetics with the publication of *Aesthetica* in 1750.[20] While Herder, following Kant, is openly critical of Baumgarten's metaphysics in the *Essay on Being*,[21] his position on the latter's aesthetics is more ambivalent. Baumgarten wanted to show that the realm of the sensory is not closed to cognition, but that it could be studied as an object of philosophy, using the methods of Wolffian logic.[22] Herder read Baumgarten as undermining the strict separation from the realm of aesthetic experience which grounded Wolffian logic, and he felt that Baumgarten had understood that the ultimate goal of aesthetic investigation could not be to reduce the aesthetic object to the rules of logic.

The purpose of aesthetics, as Baumgarten saw it, was to establish poetry as an alternative discourse of truth, but one that was accessible to the operations of logic.[23] In consequence, aesthetics was aimed not "at the objects of fine art but rather *through* them at the mysterious nature of human subjectivity."[24]

Herder saw great potential in Baumgarten's revaluation of poetic discourse and the establishment of aesthetics as a field of inquiry – what Herder calls "the *science* that *Baumgarten* invented, and that no-one has fully realized" (*HFA* 1, 659). Herder viewed poetry as an earlier and more essential communion with the nature of experience than rational discourse, prose, and philosophy, and so any project that elevated it to the status of an essential object of investigation was praiseworthy. In the various fragments on the ode, which Herder worked on in 1764 and 1765, he defines aesthetics as "the metaphysics of the fine *arts*," noting immediately that Baumgarten only provided an imperfect supplement to this with his "theory of the fine *sciences*" (*HFA* 1, 78). And when, in a later revision of this paragraph, he calls Baumgarten the "true *Aristotle* of our time," he again notes Baumgarten's failure to provide a metaphysics of the fine arts (*HFA* 1, 97). Baumgarten's attempts to understand poetry through the tools of Wolffian logic result in a method that provides "nothing more than *theories* of the fine *sciences*, of *rhetoric* and *poetics*; *all the fine arts* are absent" (*HFA* 1, 659). Wolffian formal logic may suffice for this project, but it cannot explain the true nature of poetry, which, as Wolff himself realized, had to be approached as a formal attempt to mediate general and specific applications of reason.[25] The true nature of poetry is to be grasped epistemologically, through the sequence of cognition Herder outlined in the *Essay on Being*, but also historically and anthropologically as the expression of the possibility of humanity's wholeness and fulfilment as it announces itself at any one moment in human imagination. The poetic expression of reality is not something that can be brought within the fold of logical method and subordinated to it, but has to be studied in its own right as an expression of those experiences that provide the foundation of logic. This is why, in a later sketch on Wolff's writings, Herder differentiates between poetic knowledge, whereby "I feel in all its light the sensory which I recognize," and intellectual knowledge, whereby "I recognize only the One within it [the sensory] according to how I feel" (*On Christian Wolff's Writings*, *HMA* 2, 11). Poetic knowledge reproduces experiences of beauty, whereby emotion is aligned with the unity of creation, and this gives it the distinction of holding closer to actual experiences of reality, upon which intellectual knowledge is based. Furthermore, it is more appropriate for representing the organic nature of Being, since it serves to enhance the inner life of objects, rather than forcing them into a predetermined mould.[26] This is why so much more is at stake than "just" poetry. Poetry is the expression of what Adler calls "a gnoseological desideratum, which was initiated by a change in the conception of humanity," and which grounds Herder's aesthetics.[27]

The very fact that it is possible to make the kind of errors Herder identifies in Baumgarten testifies to the specifically human constitution that anthropology needs to address. We are, as Herder states in the *Essay on Being*, hybrid beings, *Zwittermenschen*, capable of experiencing the certainty of Being, but also of establishing independent systems of coherent thought outside of experience (*HMA* 1, 577). This leads to the two extreme philosophical positions regarding Being, that of the idealist, propounding a logic of understanding, but viewed sceptically by common sense, and that of the empiricist, putting forth a logic of affect doubted by the idealist.[28] Either of these systems is able to establish certainty on the basis of its own premises, and neither requires the other to uphold its own particular brand of certainty. Herder wants to bypass the resulting split in discourses on the human, establishing instead a holistic science of cognition. Only by viewing the whole human being can science overcome partisan philosophical discourses and investigate the integrative cognitive processes that found human beings as creatures of understanding and affect. In making Real Being the basis of both ideal and existential Being, Herder is "postulating an originary unity of Being and consciousness" and is grounding it in the senses (Gaier, *HFA* 1, 858). Poetry points to this unity, and its affective power comes from its engagement with beauty.

When Herder addresses questions of beauty in art, he thinks of beauty as an object-subject system that is historically and culturally determined. Like Diderot, he was convinced that the eye and the ear are accustomed to the art products of an individual's own culture, and that differences in taste between individuals, or between nations, derive from the different development of processes of accustomation.[29] In the fourth of the so-called *Kritische Wäldchen* (Critical Groves, 1769), Herder's remarkably original, unpublished statement on aesthetics, he points to the endless variations in judgments of beauty and grace given by the multiple relationships in which the sensory powers develop. It follows that the sensibility of human nature "is not exactly identical in every region of the earth" (*HAW* 200). Herder never denies that there is such a thing as universal rules of beauty; he simply believes that the nature of their universality is misunderstood both by the Wolffian rationalists and by those who believe to provide an empiricist alternative.[30] In order to demonstrate the falsity and the dangers of the rationalist position, he criticizes the writings of Friedrich Justus Riedel, then professor of philosophy in Erfurt. He begins the *Fourth Critical Grove* with a sharp rebuttal of Riedel's naturalization of judgment. In his study on aesthetics, *Theorie der schönen Künste und Wissenschaften* (Theory of the Fine Arts and Sciences, 1767), Riedel had asserted that for each of the three "ultimate goals" of human life – the true, the good, and the beautiful – "nature has given us a corresponding basic affinity: *sensus communis* for the true, conscience for the good, and taste for the beautiful." He then goes on to claim that these internal senses for truth, morality, and beauty are innate, or as he puts it: "internal feelings of the soul."[31] These internal feelings possess the power of direct conviction, so that those experiencing them will know without further mediation that what they have experienced is true, good, or beautiful.

In his discussion, Herder immediately seizes on the primary fallacy of this claim. Experiences of beauty, goodness, and truth entail judgments and conclusions. A simple sensory experience cannot hold the power of conviction in determining beauty, not to mention goodness or truth. These are abstractions, and they are arrived at in the manner Herder had already outlined in his *Essay on Being*. In the first section of the *Fourth Critical Grove*, Herder explains the psychological processes of habituation whereby epistemological, moral, or aesthetic judgments are naturalized and come to appear spontaneous and unmediated by critical processes. "From our earliest childhood we have grown accustomed to thinking and to all the different modes of thinking and to all of these different modes of thinking working in harmony, so that, as with all habits, it ultimately becomes difficult to observe and distinguish the partial actions [*Teilhandlungen*] that we habitually perform" (*HAW* 180; translation modified). This is where the task of the philosopher begins. Like Newton, the philosopher should employ analytic method to distinguish these partial actions, and to fill in all the various procedural stages that lead from the sensory awareness of an object, a situation, an event to judgments about its beauty, goodness, or truth.

The reason why Herder is so vehement in his attack on Riedel's method lies in the understanding that it precludes critical analysis in judgments of goodness, beauty, and truth. It is a naturalization, a reification of object experience, to the point where there is no room for critical inquiry into the conclusions about the world of experience. The "essence of philosophy," Herder declares, "is to entice forth, so to speak, ideas that lie within us, to illuminate into distinctness the truths that we knew only obscurely, bringing them to clarity, to develop proofs that we did not grasp clearly in all their intermediary steps" (*HAW* 182). This places Riedel's fundamental goals of human existence outside the range of philosophical method, for an "immediate feeling without rational inferences cannot be illuminated, cannot be developed; and if it could, what purpose would this long and pointless detour serve?" (*HAW* 183). If we possess unmediated knowledge of truth, beauty, and goodness, then the pinnacle of human thought can only lie in the blind assertion that something is beautiful, good, or true. Riedel's empiricism leads directly to dogmatic assertions that are not open to critical analysis. Again, the proof that Herder draws upon lies in uncovering the genesis of those processes which Riedel naturalizes. Against the reification of experience, Herder draws on analysis, psychology, and historical anthropology.

Universal rules of beauty are not innate in the human constitution. They develop out of the sequence of cognition Herder had described in *Essay on Being*. And as a result, the evaluation of taste is still open to critical analysis, and can be negotiated as a component part of the underlying basis of cultural interaction. Human culture in its diversity obeys the rules of beauty, and in doing so, individual cultures create variations on the manifestation of these rules, which all point to the universal. The nature of the human soul is that it possesses "unity in its foundation, thousandfold diversity in its development, perfection in the totality! ... Everything is formed a single unity and raised to the most manifold perfection" (*HAW* 198). Seen in its multiplicity, a judgment of taste is like Proteus: it "transforms itself under every new sky, in every foreign clime wherein it draws breath." Herder asks: "Does not this diversity of taste itself prove, by the causes of its transformation, that beauty is one, just like perfection, just like truth?" (*HAW* 202). Herder had been thinking about this from the time he wrote the *Essay on Being*. In an essay on diversity in taste written in 1766 he stated: "As soon as it is proven that what I consider with good reason to be true, beautiful, good, pleasant is considered by another – also with good reason – to be false, ugly, evil, unpleasant, then truth, beauty and moral value become phantoms that appear in different guise and in a different way to different people. A true Proteus which is ever changing and appears through a magic mirror, never in the same form" (*HFA* 1, 149).

Herder seems to think that the timeless ideal of beauty exists as a relationship between culturally and environmentally determined limitations on aesthetic production, on the one hand, and, on the other, the products that emerge from within these limitations. A gifted individual can rise above his or her own cultural specificity and enjoy the ideal. In doing so such individuals are exploring the infinite taste of humanity and the history of the forms of expression of humanity. It is possible, he states, "to extricate oneself from the irregularities of excessive singularity and ultimately, unguided by the taste of a particular nation or age or individual, to savor the beautiful wherever it manifests itself, in all ages and in all peoples and in all arts and in all varieties of taste, to taste and experience it in its purity, freed everywhere from all foreign elements" (*HAW* 202).[32] But how, we might wonder, will the individual thus elevated be sure that the universal experience of beauty is founded on analysis and not on a priori concepts? The answer is to be found in examining the genesis of concepts of universality.

When he demonstrated in the *Essay on Being* that experience becomes increasingly inaccessible to the operations of logic as it comes closer to the saturated fullness of unmediated sensory perception, Herder felt that he had also shown the error in the founding premise of Baumgarten's aesthetics. Baumgarten followed Wolff and Leibniz in regarding sensory cognition as taking place on a lower order than rational cognition, but he applied their concept of rational analogy – which they had used in order to compare the cognitive faculty of animals to that of humans[33] – in order to argue that there is a science of sensory cognition, just as there is a science of rational thought, and that this science can serve as a guiding principle in making true judgments about sensory experience, and in the production of objects of beauty.[34] The problem with this approach to aesthetics is that it applies the same formalism that undermines the effectiveness of logic,[35] and it consequently prescribes artificial rules to artistic production, thereby inscribing them with the limitations of rational thought. Rational thought needs to confine itself to the sphere of cognition, where it remains effective. Aesthetic experience, as it comes closer to the experience of Being – the "most sensory of concepts" – recedes from the grasp of logic, and no attempt to bring it back will succeed. What remains for the philosopher is to investigate the genesis of concepts and the factors influencing aesthetic experience. This is what Marion Heinz and Heinrich Clairmont call the "anthropocentric turn" in Herder's epistemology, whereby "pointless attempts to solve the problem of truth as the central task of classical epistemology are to be renounced in favor of meta-reflection on which kind of certainty is possible for which kind of subject."[36] The experience of universal ideals of beauty has to rest on the human path from the senses to cognition. In this way truth becomes a matter of aesthetics.

In turning the philosophical pursuit of truth to an aesthetics of human life, Herder is pushing the philosophical project in the direction of an anthropology of cognition, which will ask questions about the material factors influencing the subjective processes that lead from experience to a world view. Aesthetics as a "science of sensory cognition," which is what Baumgarten wanted, has both a subjective and an objective dimension. As an objective science, it is a "philosophical investigation of sensory cognition," the science Baumgarten invented. But Baumgarten's failure to understand the relationship between subjective aesthetic experience and its recreation in objective works of fine art had caused him to confuse the subjective and objective dimensions of aesthetics, with its two very different methodological implications (*HFA* 1, 659).[37] In his critical notes on Baumgarten's *Aesthetica*, written in the years 1765–7, Herder differentiates "natural aesthetics" from "artificial aesthetics." Like logic, the latter is a science – it seeks "to *instruct and convince* through *propositions* and clear *concepts*." Natural aesthetics is "always *habitus*," and it "*has effect* [*wirkt*] through *sensation* and *dark* concepts" (*HFA* 1, 660). This is not a distinction of degree, but of essence.[38]

Baumgarten's confusion between the epistemology of lower cognition and reasoning by analogy also prevented him from recognizing that the human dimension of aesthetics – natural aesthetics – takes precedence over the logical dimension, just as Being takes precedence over possibility, and real possibility takes precedence over logical possibility. The purpose of aesthetics is, as Herder writes in 1769, to reveal how "the beauty I have felt, whose phenomena I analyze both in the object itself and in my sensation" can be made to approach "the distinctness of truth" (*HAW* 187). Aesthetics thus applies the method of philosophy in order to grant insight into those cognitive processes which are not accessible to logic (*HAW* 192). Herder is quite explicit on this point: aesthetics

> chooses the method of philosophy, that is, rigorous analysis; it examines as many products of beauty of every kind as it can, attends to the whole, undivided impression; it returns from the depths of this impression to the object itself; it observes its parts both individually and working in harmony; it does not compromise on a merely beautiful half-understood idea;

> it brings the sum of the ideas rendered distinct under general concepts, and these in turn under their own general concepts; finally, perhaps, there is a general concept in which the universe of all beauty in both arts and science [*Wissenschaft*] is reflected. (*HAW* 188–9; translation modified)

The abstractions of beauty in art and science are derived analytically from the experience of objects, making beauty a philosophical encounter with human nature.

As Herder writes in his Baumgarten studies, "*artificial aesthetics* arose out of *natural aesthetics*, and it must be possible to explain it on the basis of the human condition [*aus dem Menschen erklären*], as a *unique* and *important* natural *phenomenon*" (*HFA* 1, 660). In other words, the foundations of conceptualization can be investigated, but only in terms of the human condition, which is one of embodied thought. Herder seeks ultimately to ground aesthetics in human physiology and the nature of the senses.[39] He draws here on the empirical psychology of Locke, Berkeley, Condillac, and others.[40] Later, in the Fourth *Critical Grove*, he will write that "the whole ground of our soul consists of obscure ideas," and thus "the integral parts of the human soul" must be conceived of as bodily. In other words, the soul "has been given to a human body [*sie ist einem Menschlichen Körper beschieden*]; it is a human being" (*HAW* 193; translation modified). As a result, the "true philosopher" has no general and abstract concepts, except those "that appear to him in one of the senses. There he apprehends them and pursues them through all the subtle bifurcations of the nerves up to the point where they reveal themselves to other senses, then finally to the soul." For the philosopher, "this physiology of the senses and sensuous concepts" amounts to everything (*HAW* 212). By focusing on the subjective processes of aesthetic experience and tracing the orders of logic that build upon them, Herder aims to present a more accurate picture of how not only aesthetic experience, but also logic itself is possible. In this sense, Baumgarten's apologetic attempts to raise aesthetics from its lower status to the level of philosophy are misguided. Aesthetics cannot be seen as "beneath the dignity" of the philosopher, when in fact it is itself "the most rigorous philosophy concerned with a worthy and very significant conspectus of the human soul and of the imitations of Nature; it is even a part, a significant part of anthropology" (*HAW* 191). The resultant dialogue between the aesthetic and the philosophical becomes, as Gaier observes, the core of Herder's anthropology (*HFA* 1, 1237).

The Question of Force

With this move, Herder is signalling the direction his philosophy will take in the decades to come, and is laying the foundations of the ideas that will be the focus of this book. What began as a position paper on Kant's ability to adhere to his own premises conceals within its argument a set of ideas, some of them radical, others more or less in currency at the time, which taken together shift philosophical analysis in the direction of aesthetics, anthropology, and cultural history. In doing so, Herder is laying the groundwork for a philosophically founded anti-imperialism. When, in other essays, he begins to confront directly the effects of imperialism in his time, he takes as his (often unspoken) point of reference the primacy of Being as the foundation and limit of all that can be said about human life. In this respect, he is laying bare the philosophical assumptions that will, in the subsequent course of European imperialism, serve to anchor various positions among its critics or proponents.

Once Herder takes this move, he is preparing the way for the shift in the focus of his writings which will come in the following decade. He will hold his early ideas on epistemology and aesthetics in reserve, using them as the more or less unexamined premises on which to develop his studies in language and his philosophy of history. The significance of the *Essay* for the later direction of his studies lies in Herder's belief that the aporia of philosophy can be sidestepped by reformulating philosophical questions as anthropological and historical ones, while at the same time providing a philosophical justification for the way he structures these questions.[41] The anthropological and historical turn in Herder's work is a convenient point at which a discussion of his aesthetics could be concluded, as Norton does, but it is important to retain Norton's insight that Herder's historical and cultural studies are built upon the understanding of the analytic method as he developed it in the 1760s.[42] In fact, Herder's politics are also built upon this turn, as he himself observes in his essay of 1765 (published posthumously), *Wie die Philosophie zum Besten des Volks allgemeiner und nuetzlicher werden kann* (How Philosophy Can Become More Universal and Useful for the Benefit of the People). Herder sees his shift in focus as a continuation of philosophical discourse on different ground. He does not intend to abandon philosophy for anthropology, but instead to revitalize and humanize philosophy, giving it political relevance in the lives of the people. When he writes of the need to "incorporate philosophy into anthropology," what he means is that "if philosophy is to become useful for human beings, then let it make human beings its center" (*HPW* 21). To change the perspective of philosophy in this way amounts to a similar paradigm shift as the move from the Ptolemaic to the Copernican system (*HPW* 29). In this essay, Herder also explains (or at least sketches out) the parameters of this kind of history and why it is necessary. The history of the human species (*Geschichte der Menschheit*) is not to be a history of human beings as the agents of politics or the actors in a fragmented play of great events.[43] It cannot be the history of the rules and principles established by society (*nicht der Regeln der Menschheit*), nor of the products of human enterprise (*nicht der Werke der Menschheit*). The history of the human species is the history of nature itself and it works via the psychology of the individual, while at the same time unfolding within its own "grand theatre" (*der große Schauplatz, HFA* 1, 131–2).

In the *Essay on Being* we can pinpoint the moments where Herder's discontent with the idealism/empiricism discussion together with his reliance on analytic method cause him to turn his attention to the developmental, anthropological, cultural, and historical problems that will in turn frame his understanding of imperialism. One of these moments has already been noted – the commitment to the "human path" (*HMA* 1, 576), the process of abstraction built upon sensory cognition. As Herder comes to investigate the human path as the genesis of concepts of logic and the concealed origin of a priori judgments, he becomes increasingly interested in uncovering the origins of concepts in sensory cognition. This pushes his investigations in the direction of historical analysis, and it will at the same time beg the question of the analogy between the genesis of individual cognition and the historical development of shared concepts within a culture or a nation.

There is another, stronger moment forcing Herder's turn to history and anthropology but also his understanding of the place of literary criticism within philosophical inquiry. This concerns the central importance of time, space, and force (*Kraft*) as grounding human experience. Herder describes how, as analysis moves closer to Real Being, to those aspects of human experience that are not analysable, it encounters limit concepts that define the place of human experience in relation to Real Being. These limit concepts mark the difference between Being or God, which cannot be positioned in time and space, and the being of bodies, which can be located and described in terms of Crusius's *ubi* (where) or *quando* (when).[44] Mediating between God and bodies is *per* (through, my means of), corresponding to the concept of force (*HMA* 1, 586).

As always, Herder developed these ideas on the basis of a startlingly wide reading in contemporary science and philosophy. The concept of force (*Kraft*, or the Greek δύναμις) was of great importance in the eighteenth century, which saw it expanding in application from purely mechanical explanations of motion and inertia to the realm of the organic, from physics to psychology. Force also became the focal point of the growing tensions between "inherited metaphysics and the results of the scientific experimentation of the seventeenth and eighteenth centuries."[45] In this way, it problematized the body-mind distinction (how does the force that moves a body by the power of will relate to the force that moves a body through contact with an exterior object?); and also the question of causality as it had been highlighted by Locke and Hume (if force is only apparent through its effects, how can force be known?). What's more, "force" paved the way for the centrality of *Bildung* by relating it to Aristotle's discussion of entelechy (εντελέχεια), the actualization of potentiality as it resided in force (δύναμις). And so it became a touchstone in some of the most controversial philosophical questions of the time.[46]

As he begins to place *Kraft* at the centre of his philosophy (causing Sommer to describe it as "pan-dynamism"),[47] Herder's most immediate points of reference were Locke, Wolff, and Reimarus, but above all Leibniz. In understanding force as substantial force (*vis primitiva*), Leibniz followed Aristotle, who saw it as inherent in matter itself and thus the proper object of metaphysics. In this view, philosophy can properly aspire to describe the workings of force a priori according to its inherent laws. However, Leibniz also recognized what he called derivative forces (*vis derivativa*), which Edwards describes as "laws of action that are known not only by reason, but are proved by the evidence of the senses."[48] The consequence of this distinction is to give force a "mixed epistemic quality" that "effects the transition from metaphysics to nature." What this means is that there is no break "between the metaphysics of corporeal nature and physics as an empirical science."[49] The forces at work in nature that are accessible to empirical study are themselves related to the forces that express the plan on which the cosmos rests. This seemed to provide a strong alternative to the Cartesian duality of thought and matter, and it held lasting appeal to Herder.

In Leibniz, the reasoned plan for nature continues to work on nature from within, as it were. Herder wanted to extend the Leibnizian continuity of nature and metaphysics to internal organic and cognitive processes, in a way that would allow him to speak of these processes as part of the divine plan for humanity. And he wanted to understand natural forces at work in the mind in a way that would bypass the rationalism of Wolff, who relied on his own particular theory of force to explain how the mind's representation of the world could form the foundation of knowledge.[50] In the discussion around force, Herder correctly understood the damage Wolff had done to Leibniz's recognition that empirical science demonstrates and rests upon the infinite diversity of phenomena by abstracting general representations in the mind and giving them priority.[51] Herder also saw that Wolff's rationalism rested upon the scholastic distinction between superior and inferior faculties of the mind (corresponding to the power of reason and sense-based representations respectively). In keeping with the latest scientific advances, Herder wanted the analysis of force as manifest in human life to be founded in the biology of the organism. This could not be achieved as long as investigations were driven by the false distinction between superior and inferior faculties.[52] What was needed instead was a psychology capable of explaining how the force of nature that Leibniz described at work in the interaction of inanimate bodies had a direct correlate in organic processes of the mind.

It is here that the animal psychology of Reimarus seemed promising to Herder, since it shows how Leibnizian force can be understood as working on organisms from within, psychologically.[53] In 1760 Reimarus had published *Allgemeine Betrachtungen über die Triebe der Thiere, hauptsächlich über ihre Kunsttriebe zum Erkenntniss des Zusammenhanges der Welt, des Schöpfers und unser selbst* (General Observations on the Instincts of Animals, Chiefly on Their Instincts to Artifice, for the Better Understanding of Connections between the World, the Creator and Our Selves). Herder would return to Reimarus again and again throughout his career, building on his differentiation between humans and animals and their connectedness. Reimarus developed a subtle set of distinctions between different kinds of instincts or drives found in animals, including those that enabled fundamental organic processes, as well as responses to the environment, culminating in the drives that are capable of modifying the environment, such as a fox might do when it constructs a lair or when a spider builds a web. The capacity for artifice separates human life from the life of animals, in that in humans it is no longer a drive or an instinct. Instinct is a "determinate force," which is to say it is "a blindly determined inclination toward a certain effect, in which all animals indulge with pleasure and industry."[54] Humans possess the capacity for analytic reason, which allows them to step above instinctual responses.

According to Reimarus, "processes in the material world" are governed by natural forces (*Naturkräfte*) working according to intrinsic principles. According to these principles,

> all the individual bodily changes must occur naturally in accordance with the fundamental rules of their forces at this time, at this place, in this manner, and in this amount. They cannot simply fail to occur, nor can they occur in a different manner. The consequent degree of this determination consists in the fact that these forces are specifically determined to call forth a particular kind of action in a particular manner. This nevertheless takes place in a way whereby what is individual about the action is not yet determined in the fundamental rules of the force, but instead can be determined in various ways according to circumstance.[55]

One of the most important aspects of this idea was Reimarus's insistence (founded on Leibniz) that there is a gradual continuity, involving infinitesimal organic distinctions, between animals and humans. In this way, animals represent an intermediary stage between objects, which are subject to mechanical laws only, and humans with their powers of volition. But how exactly does volition separate itself from natural force? In answering this, Herder turns once again to aesthetics.

According to Pross, Herder saw the revolutionary implications of Reimarus's work, and regarded it as a possible model for how natural force works in human life (*HMA* 3/2, 213–20). As early as the *First Critical Grove* (1769), Herder is attempting to think through the implications of Reimarus's theories for his own ideas on aesthetics. Here, as Clark shows, he discusses poetry as "the art of 'Kraft' – power, or energy. Music exists in time, formative art [*bildende Kunst*] in space. Poetry, the linguistic art, is the communication of 'Kraft,' that is, it resembles the flow of a potential, taking place only through the channel of language from one pole to another."[56] Herder believed that Reimarus's model of the organic determination of forces was a sound one up to a point – which was the fact that, as Clark notes, animals do not symbolize. Furthermore, because the path from sensory experience to logical thought and symbolization is so various, there is a developmental principle that works together with natural force to multiply the aesthetic expression of force infinitely. As a result, "the only way for an aesthetic method to come into being would be through a historical analysis of the different ages of the various human cultures, always preserving the integrity of each culture, each age, and each personality."[57] The question of free will thus is referred to that which can be reclaimed, through aesthetics, from the symbolizations of past moments.

In the further course of his writings, Herder would increasingly use the manifestations of *Kraft* not as a marker for the inexplicable nature of causality, but as the means of expression of nature's vitality, and thus of God's creation. In Sikka's words, "life is itself an expression of the 'divine forces' giving rise to all that exists."[58] In his essay on Spinoza, *Gott. Einige Gespräche* (God. Some Conversations, 1785), Herder stated that all forces of nature "work organically. Every organic structure [*Organisation*] is nothing but a system of living forces, by which eternal rules of wisdom, goodness, and beauty serve one main force" (*HSW* 16, 569).[59] And at the end of the second book of *Ideas on the Philosophy of History*, in which he moves from a description of the earth as the site of organic life in its diversity to the place of human beings therein, he states categorically: "It is therefore true, anatomically and physiologically, that the complete creation of our world is defined by the analogon of *one organic structure* [*Organisation*]" (*HFA* 6, 76).

That said, *Kraft*, as a limit concept, will continue to resist analysis. In 1775 Herder will state (in the essay "On the Human Soul's Cognition and Sensation"): "I do not say that I hereby *explain* anything; I have not yet known any philosophy that explained what *force* is, whether force stirs in a single being or in two beings. What philosophy does is to *observe*, *order* together, *elucidate* after it always already *presupposes* force, irritation, efficacy" (*HEW* 194). As Herder develops his idea of force, as well as of time and space, these emerge as the limit concepts that connect bodies to Being, since their further analysis yields nothing but the unanalysable concept of Being. The effect of this realization is to ground cognition in the historically and geographically located body, since geography is the spatial coordinate of bodily life and history is its temporal coordinate. Thought itself is historical and geographical, since, as Herder puts it, "one has to *really exist* if one is to think" (*HMA* 2, 11). And to really exist is to exist in time and space. Philosophical inquiry has to confront the fact that the concepts it uses have a history, a genesis within the thought processes of the perceiving subject, in the same way that they have a geography, a location in the natural world. This idea of a located genesis that follows natural rules, the geography of becoming, will assume central importance in Herder's work.

Geographical Diversity and Shared Human Nature

Here, too, Herder is building upon the teachings of Kant. In his pre-critical writings, Kant was exploring empirical models for explaining how individuals relate to their environments and their cultures, and he drew extensively on the wealth of geographical, anthropological, and cultural information from Africa, the East, and the New World that was flooding Europe at the time. The topics of Kant's lectures were wide-ranging and included physical geography, which he was later to declare as the cornerstone for an understanding of humanity's place in the world.[60] One of the reasons why geography assumed foundational importance in Kant's thinking was that it had already been prepared to a certain extent by philosophers such as Hobbes, Spinoza, and Leibniz, as a discourse that could treat the distribution of bodies in space mathematically.[61] As such, it provided Kant with the grounds upon which the various other aspects of human life and thought that escaped the mathematical could be situated.[62] It formed the basis for what he called a general pragmatic anthropology, the study of the self-apprehension of human beings in their relationship to the natural world and to their own human nature. This meant that the view of physical geography Kant imparted to his students placed it on the interface of nature and human life.[63] Geographical knowledge points to the diversity of the human condition. It presents philosophy with a set of problems that are closely related to the problem of Being. In Herder's anthropology, as Menges notes, dissemination and dispersion become "the point of departure, and the description and historical grounding of its diverse manifestations becomes Herder's 'great topic.'"[64]

The grounding of history in geography suggests that the story of humanity's development through the ages derives in some as yet unexplained manner from experiences of geographical diversity. But how can geographical location ground human diversity while at the same time enabling the story of humanity's common development? Herder seeks the answer in the way aesthetics unifies diverse phenomena. The priority of geography as the "real foundation" of historical narratives indicates a collective experience of geographical Being that has, through time, been translated into various collective narratives of historical becoming. So there must be something in these stories that harks back to the common forms of the sensory cognition that makes the experience of Being. Geography does not secure the truth of history in contradistinction to fairy tales, as Kant had hoped. Instead, history is itself grounded in and merges with a more fundamental discourse of Being, and this discourse is aesthetic in nature.

In Herder's opinion, Baumgarten was right in identifying poetry as a pure discourse of the experience of Being, but he was mistaken in his attempts to explain poetry in terms of Wolffian logic. Poetry, like the other art forms, is an aesthetic expression of aesthetic experience, whereby the first two moments in Herder's sequence of human conceptualization are activated: *aisthetic* perception is subject to *aesthetic* reflection.[65] Artistic products testify in different ways to what it is like to be located in time and space, and to what kind of models of force can be used to link the spatial and temporal aspects of embodied being. To draw up a catalogue of the different genres that does justice to the complex poetic reflections on time, space, and force would be to draft what Herder calls a "map of the human soul" (*HMA* 2, 11). This map would show how the different sense perceptions of time, space, and force give rise to different forms of artistic reflection.[66] Here, literary criticism is forced to engage with the fundamental problem of philosophy.

The challenge facing literary criticism is to write of poetry in a language that does not supplant the immediacy of originary experience with the "totally univocal language" towards which philosophy strives.[67] Instead, the descriptive language of criticism needs to trace the self-understanding that arises from the apprehension of the world. History works together with philosophy and aesthetics in providing the theoretical framework for this project. As we have seen, Herder called this project *Anthropology*, and "he pronounced it philosophy's legitimate successor,"[68] since any philosophy which was to be for humanity[69] will have to re-centre scientific inquiry on its real object – humanity, in all its manifestations. As Elias Palti has observed, in the 1770s Herder came to see history as analogous to cosmology,[70] a view that would prove increasingly important in explaining the connection between universal and particular phenomena, or between the unity and diversity of phenomena. Already here, it is apparent that what cosmology promised Herder was a model for thinking about changing perspectives on that which cannot be seen: in the case of Copernicus and Kepler, the force at the centre of the universe that determines the motion of all heavenly bodies; and for Herder, the force that determines the concerted development of all organisms.

Herder found these ideas invaluable in thinking about the different ways Being can be conceptualized. The awareness of geographical diversity meshed with his epistemology, challenging him to explain how diversity relates to the unity of Being. The philosophical formulation of this coincidence of the individual with the species will lead Herder to take the position that Marion Heinz calls "sensual idealism."[71] According to Heinz and Clairmont, this position is first taken in the essay *Plato sagte* (Plato Said, 1767), which describes the soul as a finite force that enters into dialogue with the body via "a specifically organized body-soul constitution produced by itself."[72] What is being described here is not only the psychological genesis of concepts in a particular individual or a particular apperceptive event, but a fundamental quality and a central process of human nature. It is part of the objective constitution of human beings that cognitive faculties of the soul point to Being, which they cannot grasp, while our physiology organizes sensory concepts according to the concepts of time, space, and force. Out of this objective constitution arises the possibility of speaking about common humanity.

Starting with *Plato Said,* Herder begins to address the paradoxical position of the mind or soul (*Seele*) with respect to Being. Here, "representations mediated through external sensory perception are considered as consequences of inner thought occasioned by the perception of objects."[73] This appears to invite Descartes in through the back door by assigning primacy to the mind in grasping Being, while time, space, and nature's force are concepts relating to bodily experience. What Herder is in fact trying to do – and what he will continue to attempt in his subsequent writings – is to find a way to describe the conceptual unity that resides within the infinite variety of phenomena and experiences. The assumption that there is such a conceptual unity grounding creation is central to Herder's theology and cosmology. It contains the idea, as Pross shows, that the infinite diversity of creation only makes sense if we think of it as preceded by the "purely intellectual anticipation of their unity." Furthermore, this is built into the diversity of nature as a structural potential for unity, and natural as well as historical development is motivated by a drive to realize this potential. In the realm of thought, the progression from the physiological apprehension of time and space through to thinking about Being follows this structural potential, and it leads to the realization that thinking about Being is "purely symbolic" and that it is "the opposite of sensory representation" (*HMA* 3/2, 347–8). Symbolization is what Heinz and Clairmont call a "spiritualization of nature" and a "naturalization of spirit."[74]

Because Herder understands himself to be speaking not only of unique individual psychological processes but of human nature, the objectivity of knowledge can be thought of not only in epistemological or psychological, but also in anthropological terms. Representations of the world are not only individual, they are shared, and they have a shared history. In approaching the concept of Being through the concepts of time, space, and natural force, the body represents its environment to the mind – and here Herder was thinking of Spinoza. But in the shared genesis of these representations, and in the shared medium of their communication (language and art), the individual appropriates the world and the culture in which he or she lives.[75] This is why the philosopher in pursuit of the essence of human life cannot begin by tracing human expression back to an act of divine intervention (this conviction forms the backbone of Herder's later essay on the origin of language). Instead, he has to take account of the fact that, in acts of linguistic creation, human expression understands itself as working in analogy with and according to the same laws as the divine force at work in nature. The essence of divine force causes it to manifest itself as a diversity of cultural expressions, which themselves retain structural traces of the idea of their unity. For Herder, language could not be traced back to a single, ideal purpose that might be named divine. Language is a social arrangement that expresses the diversity of human life. Writing in 1766, he asked what would remain for him the fundamental question of linguistic diversity: "Are there not a thousand indications in one language, and in the diversity of languages millions of vestiges, of how it was precisely through language that the nations gradually learned to think, and through thinking that they gradually learned to speak?"[76]

In pursuing this program of research, Herder had to start with history and language, since the thrust of his argument was to try to think about imperialism's expanded world as a place of natural diversity and conceptual unity. In Herder's analysis, nature's force reveals itself in the relationship between various unifying and diversifying impulses, each of which requires a corresponding conceptualization on the part of the philosopher – to the point where philosophy needs to take on board the various other discourses aimed at understanding human life: psychology, biology, physiology, cultural anthropology, and so on. This division of the disciplines corresponds to modes of experience that are all just as important as philosophical systems in shaping human life. In fact, their proximity to lived experience threatens to undo the dominance of idealist philosophy with its preconceived structures of life.

Herder began early on to think of aesthetics as an inquiry into the common foundations of this process, but at the same time he saw the endless possibilities for studying the historical development of shared representations in specific cultures. Any such study would have to remain grounded in the essential insight into human nature, that "all human beings have *aestheticam connatam*, since they are *all born* as sensory animals, and since they are more animal than spirit, the aesthetica connata is *necessarily* greater than innate logic ... Here lies the origin of the *sensory* sensibility for beauty, which all humanity has in common" (*Plan zu einer Aesthetik, HFA* 1, 660). This idea of an aesthetic drive will remain of central importance.

Poetry and the Quest for Historical Origins

In 1764, at the same time that he was working on the *Essay on Being*, Herder drafted a study of poetry as evidence of this single human drive to expression. In his posthumously published *Versuch einer Geschichte der lyrischen Dichtkunst* (Outline of a History of Lyric Poetry), he ties the problem of formal multiplicity and unity of purpose to the question of the origin of things, and the genesis of the world. "One of the most pleasant fields in which human curiosity can stray," he tells us in the opening sentence, is the recognition of "the origin of that which exists" (*HSW* 32, 85). This study of origins is even more appealing when it is concerned with the products of human artifice, for all the reasons outlined above.

In the opening paragraph of this essay, it becomes clear that Herder is already trying to relate the origin of an individual's knowledge in sensory concepts to the origin of human knowledge in the depths of prehistory. He speaks of the drive to knowledge (*Wißbegierde*), which "pushes forward, unsatisfied," following a path "into the darkest times, in order to experience historically the beginning of things, or else to explain them philosophically, or to speculate on their possibility" (*HSW* 32, 85). These darkest times are like the Leibnizian obscurity of the sensory.[77] In the *Essay on Being* Herder declared that "all my representations are sensory – they are dark; sensory and dark have been synonymous expressions for a long time" (*HFA* 1, 11). The darkness in which historical knowledge merges with oral tradition, myth, and the unknown is like the place where truth slips from the discourses of rationalism, and enters the domain of poetic language, the form of expression that is both epistemologically and historically prior to the language of philosophy.[78] And so the natural drive to seek origins leads directly to a history of humanity. This, he continues, is the reason why "we take such pleasure in reading the poetic or philosophical hypotheses on the origins of familiar objects"; and here he cites the opening chapters of the Bible as presenting "the oldest reports on the childhood of the world" (*HSW* 32, 85).

In formulating the challenge facing the study of origins in poetry or philosophy, Herder emphasizes how all nations have responded to this historicizing explanatory drive in a similar manner, with the development of "cosmogonies that contain the grounds of their wisdom." The diverse forms of these cosmogonies cannot themselves be traced back to a single origin, although their form of expression may point in that direction. Herder rejects from the outset the possibility that "all nations appropriated these treasures from a single people; that everything has to be traced back to the lands of the East, that all streams arise from a single spring." Instead, he insists that it is more helpful "to seek within each people itself the seeds that were capable of giving rise to the arts and sciences" (*HSW* 32, 94–5). This is not to deny the common ground of poetic expression, but to shift it away from facile models of geographical origins in favour of the common anthropological condition – an idea that Herder will soon address in his defence of monogenesis.

The project of a history of the forms of expression of humanity in all its diverse manifestations is itself like the cosmogonies of the nations. In taking cognizance of the single drive to expression that unites all peoples, such a history must at the same time recognize that the more we study the origin of this drive, the more it fades away into the far distant past, becoming ever more fictional as its recedes. In its place, we are left with the certainty that all people share an intense desire for knowledge, an epistemological drive, as well as a form-giving drive, an aesthetic drive, and that the forms of expression of these drives are infinite in variety. The historian of humanity is like the poet – he responds to a desire for knowledge by creating aesthetic products that mark the limits of this knowledge. And if there is such a thing as a single origin of human expression, its traces lie in the multiplicity of poetic form throughout the world. The diversity of expression is like a mosaic image of humanity, a composite picture of that which each nation can only dream in its cosmogonies.

By outlining the historiographic challenges of poetic expression in this way, Herder is setting the markers for his future aesthetic project. Pross speaks of a "program of research" that sets itself the goal of grasping the universal nature of the human being in its anthropological constitution while "taking account of the legitimacy of the divergent historical forms of this constitution" (*HMA* 1, 649). One of the earliest attempts to do justice to this program of research was the essay *Über den Fleiß in mehreren gelehrten Sprachen* (On Diligence in the Study of Several Learned Languages, 1764), and it marks the point where Herder's epistemology first leads him to confront some of the contemporary effects of European imperialism. Here he will argue that the fact of linguistic diversity forces modern society to choose between the exploitation of other cultures by the imperialist trading nations and their integration into a broader human community. The linguist who discovers the world of diversity also discovers a world of uneven cultural development. And it is diversity that provides the key to overcoming inequity: "Here we will find gaps, there superfluity; – here riches, there a desert; and we will be able to enrich the poverty of the one with the treasures of the other" (*HEW* 33). The distinction Herder outlines here between an enriching spread of culture and economic exploitation of other peoples remains central throughout his writing.

On Diligence was one of the last essays Herder wrote before leaving Königsberg for Riga. It was published in the *Gelehrte Beiträge zu den Rigaischen Anzeigen* in October 1764, but was composed in the form of a speech earlier in the year.[79] On the surface, it addresses the question of priority in the teaching of the mother tongue and foreign languages in schools, a matter that was much debated in Herder's day, and that continued to occupy him in the years he spent in Riga.[80] As Michael Morton has shown, there has been a recurrent tendency to read the essay on this surface level, and to derive the interesting but not particularly surprising position Herder takes: that the mother tongue will always have priority over acquired languages, since "nature imposes upon us an obligation only to our mother tongue," but that, in the developmental history of humanity, the learning of foreign languages plays a key role (*HEW* 30). However, reading this essay within the epistemological framework Herder developed in *On Being*, it becomes clear that much more is at stake.[81]

The opening paragraphs of the essay are built upon a number of assumptions that relate directly to *On Being*. The first of these concerns what we have seen to be the central task of Herder's anthropology, bringing philosophy into dialogue with history and poetry in order to gain insight into the genesis of humanity. In order to clarify what exactly the terms of this dialogue should be, he begins the essay by setting himself apart from the view that it might be possible to revitalize the originary and divine language of nature. The most important proponent of this view for Herder was his Königsberg friend Johann Georg Hamann, who believed that philosophy should strive to counter any artificial divisions that human thought introduced into the world, such as those between reason and revelation, spirit and nature, matter and form.[82] Hamann was intent on demonstrating the importance of sensory experience and, above all, of feelings and emotions in the life of the mind, since "nature works through the senses and the passions."[83] Language for him was the key to unity in human life, but the consequence of this is, as Katie Terzakis observes, that we live in a world "not of unconditional presence but of mediated existence; we deal not in divine abundance but in human language."[84] In its dependence on logic, philosophy is but another language which is attempting to speak in a divine tongue it can never completely master. This grants poetry and the poetic arts a special place, since they provide a form of expression that pushes beyond the mistaken conviction that it is possible to speak about truth in the register of logic. Furthermore, they allow specific cultural experiences to be expressed in accordance with the unique qualities of a specific language. In his *Aethetica in nuce* of 1760 Hamann wrote that poetry is "the mother-tongue of the human race; even as the garden is older than the ploughed field, painting than script; as song is more ancient than declamation; parables older than reasoning; barter than trade."[85] This historical priority of poetic language has an epistemological correlate, since poetic language focuses on and reproduces the imagery of the senses and the passions. Nature is to be read as a compendium of signs, and the key to human happiness lies in the correct deciphering of nature's signs. "The senses and passions speak and understand nothing but images. The entire wealth [*Schatz*] of human knowledge and happiness consists in images."[86] The imagery of poetic language is thus one step closer to originary experience than the concepts of logic.

Hamann's ideas on the history of expression connected well with Herder's conviction that the poetic expression of individual cultures cannot be evaluated in absolute terms, nor measured on a scale given by European culture. In fact, there is something that might be called innocence in the lives of many cultures (Hamann speaks of "the heathens") that allows them, in their "blindness" to recognize "the invisibility which humans [*der Mensch*] have in common with GOD."[87] The underlying assumption of this recognition of linguistic diversity together with the belief in a common human communion with God and Nature, is that there is a single unidirectional movement of human development, which issues from some primary divine or natural force, or some primal creative event.[88] Not only did Hamann believe that poetic language could transport humanity back to its childhood, where the communion with divine creativity had not been tarnished by the rational mind, but he felt there must be other cultures who were closer to this process than his own. When he wrote *Aesthetica in nuce*, he was beginning to explore tentatively the idea that other cultures held the potential for reinvigorating what had ossified or decayed in the European context. He asked himself how it would be possible to "raise the defunct language of Nature from the dead," suggesting immediately that the answer was by "making pilgrimages to the fortunate lands of Arabia, and by going on crusades to the East, and by restoring their magic art. To steal it, we must employ old women's cunning, for that is the best sort."[89] The terms in which Hamann imagines this process are still rudimentary to say the least, still rife with imagery borrowed from popular tales of crusade, conquest, and plunder, but his ideas on poetic language and on cultural cross-fertilization provide Herder with a pressing question: if poetry is the mother tongue of the human race, how well do we still speak it?

Herder was to take a plain stance on this in his essay on Hamann, *Dithyrambische Rhapsodie über die Rhapsodie kabbalistischer Prose* (Dithyrambic Rhapsody on the Rhapsody of Cabalistic Prose), written in early 1765, where he stated: "If poetry is the mother tongue, then ours is prose" (*HFA* 1, 31). Similarly, the earlier, unpublished version of *On Diligence* begins with the words: "It has vanished, that flourishing age …" (*HFA* 1, 22). Herder casts this age irrevocably into the past even while retaining Hamann's understanding of what the poetic age looked like: it was a "golden age," when "our earliest ancestors dwelt round the patriarchs like children round their parents," and when "all the world was of one tongue and language" (*HEW* 29). Like Hamann's "mother-tongue of the human race," the language of Herder's golden age is poetic in the sense that it presents the imagery in which the senses and the passions speak and comprehend.[90] And it is the language of nature, since "nature acts [*würkt*] through the senses and the passions."[91] And like Hamann, Herder registers the chasm that separates this language from our own, which is marked with "the burden of our learning and the masks of our virtues" (*HEW* 29). But unlike his friend, Herder sees no point in sustaining the rhapsodic evocation of the lost language of a lost age: "But why do I sketch a lost portrait of irreplaceable charms? It is no more, this golden age" (*HEW* 29). What Herder wishes to investigate is the problem of social cohesion and social representation in the present, not as a lost opportunity that can never be regained.[92] We may be able to comprehend the fact that poetry was once our mother tongue, provided we do so via the critical analysis of the present, and in the medium of contemporary critical language.[93] "Philosophers came forth quite late in time; they themselves hailed from poets; they spoke in the language of poets; they derived their wisdom from poets and from common life" (*HEW* 81). In a prosodic age, philosophy can attain its goals only by drawing the full methodological and topical consequences of the impossibility of analysing Being.

In beginning *On Diligence* with a critical nod to Hamann, Herder is once again raising the problem of philosophical method. Herder's rejection of the rationalist school's attempt to apply mathematical method in philosophy and transfer this to aesthetics was in agreement with Hamann.[94] But the methodological consequences he drew were quite different. In the *Essay on Being*, Herder had stated that idealism cannot be refuted on the basis of that which is logically possible.[95] Logical possibility is embedded in a certain use of language, where it serves to link concepts to one another through the rules of grammar. Since logical possibility and grammar mutually guarantee the validity of propositions of Being, the Being of which they speak cannot be proven or disproven using logical possibility. Similarly, common sense shows that no experiential concept can be proven a priori (*HMA* 1, 584).[96] What this means from a methodological point of view is that the idealist position must be unmasked by demonstrating, using the method of analysis, that its claims to make meaningful statements about Being are all based on the unspoken assumption of Being's unanalysability. Once analysis has pointed to the moments where idealism is built upon the knowledge of Being as its own unanalysable foundation, it can be shown how grammar hides its founding premises. This is the point at which Herder solicits poetic language. As a formalization of Being's nonanalysability, it speaks within, not outside of philosophical language.[97]

On Foreign Languages and the Mother Tongue: Against Imperialism

When Herder begins *On Diligence* with an imaginary foray into mythological time, he is asking to be read in this way. The opening images of a golden age, followed by the whirlwind tour from the Tower of Babel through the Greeks and Romans to present-day Germans, Spaniards, and Africans is intended to present the process whereby knowledge of history becomes possible. When it confronts the origin of things, historical discourse devises stories about the Being that has enabled it, and that will forever escape its grasp. Only after Herder has uncovered this process does he begin to speak of the mother tongue as the material perpetuation of one particular way of moving from prehistory to history, and from Being and sensation to consciousness. Once we see it in these terms, another methodological question presents itself, and this one will prove to be much more problematic for Herder: What is the principle of the analogous development of individual language speakers, of individual linguistic communities, and of humanity as a collective language-speaking organism? This is, as Morton observes, "a key element of Herder's thought."[98] With his image of "our earliest ancestors" placed in juxtaposition with the image of children in the presence of their parents, Herder is establishing the link between species and individual as one of the most important assumptions of his essay. He uses it not only to describe the initial poetic communion with nature, but also the growth out of this condition and into maturity. In doing this, he sets himself the task of explaining how the processes that shape individual life are different from, and how they are similar to, the processes at work in the development of the species. In *On Diligence* Herder begins to sketch one of the most important aspects in the coincidence of individual development and the development of the species: the role of language. Language mediates the individual's experience of the world and the collective thought processes that make sense of the world. And it also provides the building blocks for repeating this mediation on a collective, perhaps even a species, level.

Herder embeds the question of language learning in the context of the historical development of humanity out of mythical origins into its current state. Herder's age is characterized by a multiplicity of languages and cultures scattered across the earth, each with its own set of traditions and a distinct relationship to its specific environment. Each of these has its own national characteristics, interpretations of the world, and characteristic sets of skills. After the failed Tower of Babel, humanity began to split into "families and dialects" that were "transplanted to various points of the compass; and a thousand languages were created in tune with the climes and mores of a thousand nations" (*HEW* 29). It is only natural that languages and cultures drift apart in the course of history, since they are acted upon from without by the different environments in which they take root (*Clima*, climes), and from within by the perpetuation of tradition and shared memory (*Sitten*, mores). This becomes increasingly pronounced throughout history.

Herder's early observations on history and anthropology are closely related to his encounters with current theories of climate and milieu.[99] Herder's use of climate as the prime geographic force of expression for nature's diversity is in keeping with a long ethnographic tradition reaching at least from Hippocrates through to his eighteenth-century contemporaries, which I discuss in more detail in chapter 6.[100] But it raises another problem that will occupy Herder for years to come. As the languages and cultures drift apart, on what basis and in what language can their unity be described? And how do we imagine the many cultures of the world developing into an organic whole, without imposing our world view and value system on them? Already in *On Diligence* we see that this is going to be a problem for Herder. It erupts symptomatically when he speaks of the national languages and national character in the crudest of stereotypes: the emotive speech of the Orient, the sensuous mildness of Greek, the forcefulness of Latin, masculinity of German, the "gibberish" of the "Hottentot" (*HEW* 29–30). Taken together, he hopes, these diverse cultures with their national languages provide a snapshot of the current state of humanity. But viewed individually, they look strangely distorted when seen though his European eyes.

But even here, we have to be careful. According to his own theory, Herder's prejudice and stereotyping is itself enacting a natural law, and I will have more to say about this later. Within the life of an individual, there are various forces at work to create a tight bond between psychological development, the development of the mind, and the cultural context in which development takes place. This tight bond ensures that the individual experiences culture as possessing a natural dimension, since culture mediates the effects of climes, and a historical one, since culture appears as a collection of historically transmitted mores. Within this cultural context, the most important force at work in the psychological and cognitive development of the individual is the mother tongue, since "it is perhaps better attuned to our character and coextensive with our way of thinking" (*HEW* 30). In describing the primacy of the mother tongue in human development, Herder is careful to emphasize the blurry line between historical and environmental factors. The language of the fatherland forms a cultural bond that ties its members together, while at the same time creating an inner drive that presents one's own language as the most attractive one of all. In using the word *Reiz* (attraction, allure, stimulus, charm) to describe this attraction, Herder is also blurring the line between those emotional and psychological forces that may be subject to critical reflection and those which express themselves involuntarily. This is because it is the experience of attraction that bonds the individual to his language and gives preference to the mother tongue as part of the developmental psychology of the human being. The early experiences of pleasure in the mother tongue "impressed themselves upon us first and somehow shaped themselves together with the finest fissures of our sensibility" (*HEW* 32). But they are also part of the individual's physiological constitution, since, as he argues in *On Being*, the mental life of the individual is grounded in the senses. It follows that not only the organs of sense themselves, but also the regime of concepts built upon them have a particular affinity with the language into which an individual is born. In Herder's words: "Our mother tongue really harmonizes most perfectly with our most sensitive organs and our most delicate turns of mind" (*HEW* 30). What this means is that the mother tongue "is the instrument with which the child collects a world of images and concepts into his or her soul by means of words; the specific ways and methods of thinking characteristic of a people are as it were planted in its language, and the learning child forms soul, ear, and organs of speech synchronically."[101]

In acquiring a mother tongue, a person is shaped, developmentally and physiologically, into an individual who is also a member of a group, who exists in time and space, and is subject to the forces, both environmental and social, that make up their culture. The experience of becoming human means confronting one's own Being as it is moulded by the forces associated with the Crusian *ubi* and *quando*, which amounts to confronting the forces of history and geography. But it also means striving to live in the consciousness of one's historical and geographical determination, and to understand how the organism one has become is a result of these forces. This is why the limits of cognition Herder described in *On Being* also mark the limits at which one is able to confront one's own cultural, historical, and geographical determination as something external to oneself or, better said, as a material extension of one's own organic condition.

Why, then, would a person ever choose to learn a foreign language? In asking this question, Herder is introducing a theme which will remain of central importance in his anthropology, the distinction between the forces that work on the individual to perpetuate the specific culture into which he is born and those that work to ensure communication between cultures. In describing the communication between cultures, Herder will have no choice but to confront the problem of imperialism. And this is precisely what happens in *On Diligence*, when Herder looks around him and notices that one of the prime reasons for learning another language has to do with the commercial interactions of nations. "If each nation were to enjoy, within the confines of its frontiers and attached to its soil, nature's gifts from the womb of the earth without asking illicitly for tribute from other peoples' riches, perhaps no one would need to trade the citizen's birthright of his fatherland for foreign advantages" (*HEW* 30). The key word here is "illicitly." Herder is describing a form of communion between cultures that is motivated not by a sense of shared humanity, but by greed. This has set in motion a regime of commerce whose effects are seen as detrimental to all parties concerned, and ultimately to humanity itself. If each nation could sustain itself (both physically and spiritually) within the confines of its own territory, as he describes above, there would be no need to "ape the gallantries and ambiguous courtesies of others, and no city would become a hodgepodge of ten languages of commerce. But how much do our glittering needs of today not require that we move in both worlds? The gold of royal diadems, the delicacies of our tables, all the appurtenances of splendid display and luxury, concealed beneath the mask of convenience, all these are the pillage of distant worlds. The dearer the booty becomes, the higher rises its value; and the *raison d'état* of commerce thus masters languages, so that other nations may at least be deceived in words of their own tongue" (*HEW* 30).

These are harsh words for an essay on the learning of foreign languages, and they could easily be read as evidence of xenophobia or, at the very least, protectionism, and that Herder's project is one of nationalism and isolationism. He precludes this in the very next paragraph, where he notes that it is through commerce that "state policy links languages together into a universal chain of peoples, and precisely in that way they also become a great bond of learning" (*HEW* 31).[102] Herder is overlaying Hamann's story of a lost communion with nature with another story about the positive and negative potential for communication between cultures. Read in a certain (Hamannian) way, the Tower of Babel has brought confusion and conflict to humanity, but read a different way, it provides a myth of the necessary diversity of humanity, and it documents the starting point for imagining how the different cultural manifestations of Being can be united into a common project of humanity. The fact of linguistic diversity begs the question of how to conceive of what motivates cultural difference, but also how to understand humanity's common ground. The anthropology of human diversity is incomplete without asking what forces are at work compelling individuals and their cultures to act in accordance with humanity's common causes.

Of course, multilingualism can foster harmony of cultures and traditions,[103] but Herder's observations are intended to go deeper than that. His point is not that the learning of another language is a matter of choice, and that it will somehow give an individual a more rounded personality. It is that there is a developmental principle at work in the emergence of the world's languages, "a kind of organic entelechy,"[104] and that this principle involves not only the communication within languages, but also among them. The developmental principle governing one language is the same as the one guiding the development of humanity as a collection of cultures speaking different languages. Herder speaks of the collection of human languages as a plant that "transformed itself according to the soil that nourished it," so that it became "a Proteus among nations" (*HEW* 30). In speaking of the collection of languages in this way, Herder is pointing to the single developmental principle underlying the different forms of expression this principle acquires in different times and places.[105] On the face of it, the diversity of languages may look like an "indispensable evil," but seen from the perspective of humanity, it is "almost a genuine good" (*HEW* 31). True progress is only possible through the sharing of insights and achievements across linguistic barriers, and since Herder dismisses the possibility of a universal language enforced by authority, just as he dismisses translation as a solution, the only path to progress is the learning of foreign languages. Because language is embodied knowledge and embodied thought, it cannot be regarded as an empty vessel for bearing ideas. It is an appropriation and confirmation of one's geographical and historical being. As Russell Fox puts it, "No real sense can be made of being with others (politically or otherwise), whether intimately or internationally, if one is not simultaneously with that communal space which through language has been embodied as one's own."[106] The monarch who would enforce a universal language cannot enforce the intimate link between the refinement of the senses and the development of the mother tongue. And translations can never bear the colour, the harmony, and the rhythm of embodied language (*HEW* 32).[107]

Learning foreign languages is therefore an exercise in the internalization of diverse world views that have grown organically as possible manifestations of the growth of humanity. To learn foreign languages is to "encompass the spirit of each people in my soul!" (*HEW* 32). It is important to understand that Herder is not simply advocating the broadening of one's horizons through acquaintance with another world view. What is at stake is the self-realization of Being. In the terms put forward in *On Being*, different languages can be seen as incorporating different regimes of possibility – both logical and real. The real possibilities expressed in any language are a response to the specific environmental and historical factors out of which it arose. Each language is an encounter with the limit concepts of human life: time, space, and force, and thus a unique constellation of ideas arising out of the most sensory of concepts, Being. On the basis of this dialogue between the manifestation of Being and the language of real possibility, there emerges the wealth of logical possibilities upon which the conceptualization of life depends. The process of this genesis is the process of language learning. "Whoever masters the entire scope of one language surveys a field full of thoughts, and whoever learns to express himself precisely in it thereby gathers for himself a treasure of clear concepts. The first words we stammer are the foundation stones of our knowing, and our nursemaids are our first teachers of logic" (*HEW* 33).[108] And by exposing oneself to other languages, the realm of logical possibility and the extent of its application are expanded to the extent that they begin to point towards the underlying unity that binds all the languages.

By stepping outside of one's own language, a person learns to re-enact the conceptualizations that belong with another language. This amounts to an augmentation of a local world view with another one, in the very real sense that one gains access to the sequence of cognition that a language community has made its own. This means not only sampling the sensory perceptions privileged by that community in its own particular environment, but also positioning oneself within the tradition of interpreting and explaining these sensory perceptions. This ensures that any one language community will not remain isolated, but will become a piece in the puzzle or mosaic of all possible human experiences. In stepping across linguistic boundaries, conceptualization itself contributes to the development of humanity. The conceptualization of the world embodied in the mother tongue provides a stable base from which this process may be launched. In the learning of a foreign language, "our mind clandestinely compares all tongues with our mother tongue, and how useful this can be! Thereby, the great diversity of languages is given unity; our steps exploring foreign regions become shorter and more self-assured, when the goal of our fatherland remains steadily before our eyes; in this way, our diligence is facilitated; I am afloat on a bark which carries me" (*HEW* 32–3).

In all of this, Herder has explained the usefulness for humanity arising out of rootedness in the mother tongue, combined with the learning of foreign languages, and he has shown the necessity of this dual linguistic growth for the development of humanity. But he has not answered the question of how this usefulness and necessity announces itself in the life of the individual. And he has not explained how he intends to grasp the development of humanity as self-generated, and not preconceived by the workings of logic. His arguments are convincing in themselves, but it would contradict his stance against idealism if he were to suggest that the growth of humanity depends on certain privileged individuals having logical insight into this usefulness and necessity, then acting on this insight for the edification of humanity. If the development of humanity follows an organic principle, as Herder wants to suggest, it remains to specify not only the nature of the principle, but the mechanism by which it works to affect and determine the actions of individuals. On the first point, Herder is only just beginning to embark on a long study of possible scientific models for explaining the genesis of human history. And on the second point, he is taking steps towards naming the principle that forces the encounter with alternative conceptualizations embodied in foreign languages. In *On Diligence*, Herder is not yet explicit on this point, but he closes the essay with a preview of how he will formulate the problem in the years to come. The essay ends with lines from a poem by the popular poet Ewald Christian von Kleist:

> Often, when departing from home, we must take measure of the bees
> – who in scattered swarms
> whisper through the air, and fall upon clover and blossoming plants,
> and then return to the hive burdened with sweet booty,
> and bring us the honey of wisdom! – (*HEW* 33–4)

In the speech version of *On Diligence*, Herder introduces the poem with the words: "When I take leave of the land of my home [*Heimat*] and explore the fields of the languages, I imitate the bees" (*HFA* 1, 28). The drive to learn foreign languages is like the drive that sends the bees out into the fields and brings them back again to produce the honey of wisdom. Since the principle driving encounters with alternative conceptualizations of the world is part of the organic principle of development governing humanity, it must be conceived of organically. Here Herder begins to conceive of human restlessness as a drive that has important effects on the lives of individuals, and that is of decisive importance for what he will have to say about imperialism. If we look back from the vantage point of the closing lines of *On Diligence* to the paragraph where the essay raised the topic of imperialism via the detrimental effects of commerce, we can see why Herder felt it necessary to problematize commerce at the same time that he introduced the theme of learning foreign languages. The argument that foreign languages are necessary because they foster commerce is like the rationalists' attempts to understand reality on the basis of logical possibility. Of course, one conceivable use of language competence is to promote trade, but there is nothing about trade itself that gives it priority in the crossing of linguistic boundaries, and there can be no philosophical justification for making this argument. Any claims for the usefulness of commerce that are based on logical possibility, and not on the principle of human growth, are missing the point, and dangerously so, since they risk perpetuating their own false analysis by justifying practices that are ultimately detrimental to the growth of humanity. This is the problem that Herder is initially staking out with his early critique of imperialism. In opposition to the false argument of commercial advantage (the *Nützlichkeitsdenken*, or instrumentality argument, which would see increasing opposition as the century progressed), he raises the possibility of an organic drive that pushes the individual to expand the horizons of his experience, while at the same time contributing positively to humanity's development. This is why he is so critical of how, in the way it structures relations with distant nations, unbridled commercial greed destroys not only local civic community, but the community of humankind.

2 From Organic Life to the Politics of Interpretation

The Organic Principle and the Problem of Writing

The development of Herder's initial critical statements on imperialism out of his epistemology and his aesthetics is dependent on his proposed alternatives to Baumgarten and Wolff, but also to Crusius and Kant. European imperialism becomes problematic in the same way that philosophy's difficulty with sensory experience is problematic, and the methodological challenges posed by the fact of imperialism begin to reveal themselves as the same as those posed by current debates in philosophy. Once Herder had established that philosophy had not paid sufficient attention to the fact of Being as the foundation of knowledge, the methodological problem of how to explain the correspondences between Being and knowledge becomes inseparable from the pursuit of adequate models to explain the historical genesis of Being itself and of knowledge, that is, to explain how the history of humanity has led to Europe's domination of the globe, and how European knowledge naturalizes European domination. Herder's quest for alternative knowledge systems was closely related to his rejection of Baumgarten's attempts to formalize the chaotic impressions of the senses by assuming an *analogon rationis*, which assumes that the realm of sensory experience is accessible via a predetermined logical formalism.[1] Instead, knowledge has to be explained on the basis of its foundations in bodily experience and its organic genesis. This means understanding that the diversity of experience (whether on an individual or cultural level) is not something that can be assessed and evaluated according to a priori universal principles. Instead, the universality of thought will have to be sought in common organic principles guiding both human experience and human thought. In consequence, Herder takes the position (which Heinz and Clairmont call "thoroughly original") that the acquisition of new knowledge in apperception is guided by "organically determined" schemata, and that individual cognitive processes are "to be regarded as a result of bodily organization."[2] The connection between knowledge and Being is secured in the preservation of memory, a process that takes place both individually in the body's organic constitution,[3] and collectively, since language – the actualized medium of cultural transmission – embodies shared knowledge (*HEW* 31). Individual and collective processes of memory are in this way guided by a common principle of development. Herder examines this process repeatedly in various early writings, where the path to the world view embodied in the contemporary European languages follows the historicization of the cognitive processes Herder outlined in the *Essay on Being*. This is possible only because Herder assumes that the developmental principle at work in individual cognition is the same as that governing a common store of knowledge in a linguistic community, possibly even in other forms of political community. This assumption of a common principle forms such a powerful framework for Herder's historical speculation that he can move at will between its various manifestations with the utter conviction that he is dealing with the same fundamental process.

Out of his conviction that language cements communities by mediating between the organic development of the individual and that of the group, Herder developed his ideas on the growth of nations. As Morton puts it: "Languages and the people that speak them develop in concert with one another. As 'dialects' become 'languages,' so 'families' grow into 'nations.'"[4] With this realization, Herder set himself the task that would continue to occupy him for the rest of his life: how to think of the development of individual organisms, which contain intrinsic rules of generation, while at the same time explaining the general course of history, in which the same developmental principles are at work, but are equally occult. His life's work reads as a tireless investigation of potential models for this parallel development, and a series of thought experiments in which he attempts to apply these models.

When Herder moved to Riga in November 1764, the framework of this extremely ambitious project was already staked out, and it involved the epistemological insights into Being and logic, the central role of aesthetic theory, the extension of philosophy into anthropology, the holistic view of human development, the need to rethink the meaning of national identity, a revised theory of language, and a critique of imperialism. In Riga, Herder also began to think of his intellectual project as what he calls a *Demopaedic* project: a philosophical writing aimed at mediating these insights for the betterment of humanity.[5] Riga was a former free Hanseatic city, and at the time Herder lived there, the corporative participant structures of self-government persisted. Herder's relatively privileged position in this society made him aware of the potential for acts of thinking that might combine his identity as a citizen of a local community with an identity as a member of the community of humanity. To be human, to occupy a human body as a thinking, philosophizing being, is to occupy a place that is at once abstract and concrete, cosmopolitan and local – it is, as Herder repeatedly noted, to be an in-between creature.[6] And the place of communal identity had to be grasped as ranging across the narrow confines of the immediate, while stretching out to a public comprising the imagined communities of all humanity. The contradictions and tensions between these two understandings of subjectivity played an important determining role in Herder's thought throughout his life. Time and again, we find him asking questions concerning the relationship between local experience and universal ideas, up to the point where this relationship will become the defining feature of his work, taking the shape of his much-discussed model of diversity in unity or unity in diversity, and offering a new angle on the Presocratic problem of the One and the Many.

The negotiation of the local and the global also led to conflicts of interest, primarily with some of the other intellectuals who dominated the cultural landscape of the German-speaking world – people who have since faded into obscurity, but who were at the time formidable adversaries with whom the impulsive young man could hardly avoid locking horns. These conflicts initially focused on the anonymous publication of *Fragmente: Über die neuere Deutsche Literatur* (Fragments: On the Most Recent German Literature) in Riga in 1766 and 1767.[7] This collection of essays was, as the subtitle indicates, intended as a supplement to the weekly *Briefe, die neueste Litteratur betreffend* (Letters Concerning the Most Recent German Literature, 1759–65), the groundbreaking series of meditations on the current state of literature edited (and in large part authored) by Friedrich Nicolai, Gotthold Ephraim Lessing, and Moses Mendelssohn. The *Letters* were responding to a wide-felt rethinking of the role German culture played and could play in a rapidly restructuring Europe.[8] As the Seven Years' War (1756–63) progressed, it became increasingly clear to the German-speaking public that literature should be considered in relation to the power struggles defining Europe's relationship to the rest of the world.[9]

The *Fragments* were Herder's first major work, and the reception they met had an important influence on his understanding of how language relates to territory, and how both determine the shape of the reading public. When Herder sought to publish his *Fragments*, Nicolai offered him access to his journal, *Allgemeine Deutsche Bibliothek*, ensuring him the attention of a wide reading public. His work was positively received in the Berlin circle around Mendelssohn, who reviewed the *Fragments*, and the Königsberg circle around Kant, who personally congratulated Herder on his achievement once he found out that his ex-student was the author. They were also praised by Lavater in a letter from Zurich. In Morton's words, the *Fragments* immediately propelled Herder "to the front rank in the increasingly animated discussion of fundamental questions of poetics and aesthetics in Germany in the 1760s."[10]

This response made it clear to Herder that, writing anonymously, his voice could reach out from the confines of his narrow Riga life into the wider world, where it would speak to the German public. And yet, it was this initial experience that introduced a fundamental discontent with modernity's public into Herder's thought. One focal point of this discontent was the question of how to take responsibility for authorship, when the act of writing – and in particular anonymous writing – addresses a different level of experience, and in fact a different spatial scale, from that in which the writer lives his everyday life. Anonymity for Herder was a tool for transcending locality and entering the space of modernity's new, problematic public.[11]

Herder's pursuit of anonymity in the *Fragments* was not long successful. An altercation developed with Christian Adolf Klotz, professor of philosophy and rhetoric in Halle, and editor of the *Acta litteraria* (1764–72), and the *Neuen Hallischen gelehrten Zeitungen* (1766–71). In his newly founded *Deutsche Bibliothek der schönen Wissenschaften* (1767–72), Klotz and his followers took pleasure in unmasking Herder, and in denouncing him as a follower of Hamann and a member of the "Königsberg Sect"[12] – a label that must have appeared quite derogatory to them. Herder insisted repeatedly that he was not the author of the *Fragments*, and the attacks coming from Klotz's circle became more vehement. Herder was beginning to realize first-hand how print culture related to the physical act of writing, and how problematic the idea of presence in writing would prove to be.

After the bitterness ensuing from his altercations with Klotz caused him to cease work on the *Fragments*, Herder's next project was the *Critical Groves*, commenced in 1768. The title is intended to evoke a walk in a forest, where direction and purpose cannot be mapped from the outset, but must be negotiated empirically by the existing trees, the towers of strength that make up the cultural landscape – the Lessings, Winckelmanns, Abbts, and Kants. The analogy to his epistemological model in the *Essay on Being* is clear. Herder conceives of the project of the *Critical Groves* as *Gedankenspaziergänge* – mental ambulations through an obstacle course of fixed positions, stubborn in their inflexibilities like the tree trunks in a forest. In the second and third *Critical Groves*, Herder continues and intensifies his polemic against Klotz, while again insisting on anonymity.[13]

If Herder's position is anything other than disingenuous, it is because he understands the nature of authorship as straddling the spatial scales of modernity. The self that produces critical documents, sent anonymously into the world, is indeed a different self from the "I" that enters into local dispute with other (provincially minded) critics. One cannot help but read a certain irony – mingled with an unfortunate measure of naivety – in the stubborn insistence on the non-identity of these two selves. And yet, this insistence is indicative of the same fundamental problem that refuses to go away in Herder's early writing – the gap between experiences of Being and their conceptualization reappears here as the problem of reconciling abstract performances of the self in writing with the cultural location of writing and the fact that writing always issues from a specific individual.

The *Fragments* reveal this through their framing in an encounter with the territoriality of literary production. Herder opens the preface to his first set of fragments with an image of his position as a writer straddling the boundary marker laid by the closing volume of the *Letters*. He sits "like Marius upon the ruins of Carthage, contemplating the fate of Rome and Phoenicia, or like an honest German margrave of old, contemplating his German fatherland" (*HEW* 87–8). The public contemplation of the German fatherland through German literature is for Herder the vehicle for understanding community in terms of a common history and a common language – but he requires a territorial image to formulate it. And he requires a transnational perspective to perform it. Herder's radical and innovative claim that the genius of a nation's literature is its language dovetails with the problem of speaking about the proper place in which the common history of a linguistic community can unfold.[14]

The Development of Languages: A Political Poetics

Already in the *Prologue* to the *Fragments* Herder's imagery indicates that he is drawing on his geographical studies to think about the extended community he wishes to address. He uses metaphors of travel to describe the authors of the *Letters*, and he likens his work to that of contemporary ethnographers and scientific explorers. Herder makes a tongue-in-cheek reference to the Enlightenment propensity for equipping travellers with questionnaires for the inhabitants of distant lands, with the purpose of expanding the knowledge base of their own country:

> I see [in the *Literaturbriefe*] a company of travellers, with unpronounceable names, with great commentaries upon the principality called German literature!, with recollections that I would like to see transformed into a history of literature. My mania for doubting, to question and explain – or to speak in more complimentary terms, my patriotic curiosity that urges questions to them upon my lips – questions perhaps like those of a German Arab, which here and there should not, and will not, be answered. (*HEW* 88)

As Menges and Menze observe, Herder is making elliptical reference to a questionnaire published in 1762 by the Orientalist and Professor Ordinarius at the University of Göttingen, Johann David Michaelis, under the title *Fragen an eine Gesellschaft Gelehrter Männer, die auf Befehl Ihro Majestät des Königes von Dännemark nach Arabien reisen* (Questions to a Society of Learned Men Who Are Travelling on Command of His Majesty the King from Denmark to Arabia).[15] Michaelis became known throughout Europe when he conceived of this scientific journey to the Orient and later managed to solicit the patronage of the king of Denmark.[16] Using the work of the French Academy as a basis, Michaelis had listed a set of questions aimed at illuminating the history, chronology, geography, law, religion, and culture of Yemen.[17] The underlying idea had to appeal to Herder: in order to understand the cultures of the Near East, it would be necessary to present them with questions, not preconceived answers. And in order to understand his own culture, he would have to imagine an ethnography from the outside, not unlike that popularized by Montesquieu's *Lettres persanes* (1721).[18]

And yet, Herder was also aware of the problems in this approach. Imagining himself in the position of those who are supposed to answer the questions of the travelling scientists, he notes that some questions are unanswerable. With his reference to the refusal of the "German Arab" to answer Enlightenment's questions, Herder is providing us with an important clue to understanding how he intends to relate the study of individual cultures to the place of humanity in the history and geography of the world. In the context of the changing world order, scientific questions need to be contextualized, evaluated, and answered (or not) from the particular cultural perspective in which they arose. One nation's scientific questions cannot necessarily be answered by another culture, but it is the cultural location of questions that enables the de-located science of humanity. Curiosity must be recognized as "patriotic curiosity," and only then will it be possible to write a "history of literature." The perspective afforded by patriotic curiosity enables a history of literature as a history of culture, since it points to the common principle of development Herder was pursuing.

The first collection of his *Fragments* of 1766 contains a clear statement of this common developmental principle, with the essay "Von den Lebensaltern einer Sprache" (On the Stages of Life of a Language). Here Herder speculates on the development of languages as expressions of the same "single law of change" that applies to each and every family and nation, as well as to "the entire human race, indeed the inanimate world itself" (*HFA* 1, 181). The task of the historian, as Herder understands it in the *Fragments,* is to grasp the "spirit of changes" that is the "core of history," to "isolate this spirit, to compose in one's mind the taste and character of each age, and to journey through the various periods of world events with the penetrating gaze of a knowledge-hungry traveller" (*HFA* 1, 158). The principle of development driving the spirit of change is not unilinear, but cyclical, propelling individuals as well as collectives "from the bad to the good, from the good to the excellent, from excellent to worse, and to the bad: this is the cycle of all things" (*HFA* 1, 181). In the *Fragments,* Herder is also beginning to consider how the place of language and of writing in the developmental system of individuals, nations, and the world impacts on the responsibility of the writer. The cycle of development Herder sees in all things applies equally to the arts and sciences: "They germinate, bear buds, blossom, and fade" (*HFA* 1, 181). Where then does that leave writing in his own day?

The "Stages of Life" essay is primarily concerned with how a single discourse – poetry – can blossom and fade, while the prosaic discourses gain in prominence, resulting in the current situation in Europe, where language is given over to philosophical reflection and speculation. In German, prose has become "the only natural language," while poetry has ceased to be the primal expression of the experience of Being. Instead, it has become "the art of beautifying the nature of language, in order to have a pleasing effect" (*HFA* 1, 186). In outlining this process, he is attempting to position the German language historically, as belonging to the European propensity for contemplation, as opposed to living in direct expression of the senses and the imagination. But any attempt to conceive of the history of language in this way begs the question of the apparent meaninglessness of this endless cycle of growth and death.

Herder responds by turning from the development of a single language to that of human language itself, which he describes as parallel to the development of human culture, and analogous to the growth of a child to adulthood. In Herder's view of history, everything will come to rest on the status of analogy in this assertion, about which I will say more later. For the moment, let us see how he develops this analogy.

Herder begins his fragment on the life cycles of languages with the observation that the passage of time affects all things, "in the same way that the human being appears at various stages of life" (*HFA* 1, 181). Although the force of time is truly universal, Herder is primarily interested here in language. In its childhood, a language "sputters out monosyllabic, raw and high-pitched sounds" (*HFA* 1, 181). And the childhood of a language is by necessity also that of a nation: "In its initial wild origins, a nation stares at all objects like a child; terror, fear, and then wonder are the only feelings of which both are capable, and the language of these feelings are sounds, – and gestures" (*HFA* 1, 181–2). Herder then goes on to describe how, with the parallel maturation of child, nation, and language, there is a progressive development, whereby unmediated responses to sensory impressions give way to increasingly differentiated articulation and reflection. The earliest communion with sensory experience remains obscure in the same way he had described in the *Essay on Being*. Just as we cannot gain knowledge of our earliest childhood through memory, we have no historical access to the earliest stages of human language. In the same way that he had described how the analytic method approaches the moment where experience becomes unanalysable, he is now describing the psychological moment where the analysis of events preserved in memory becomes lost to the prehistory of the growing child's consciousness. And the historical and anthropological correlate of this is to be found in the prehistory of nations. The gap between historical recall and prehistory is indicated by changes in the medium of memory – language. "Just as the child or the nation changed, language changed with them" (*HFA* 1, 182). Herder is using an amalgam of psychological speculation, epistemological theory, and historical conjecture, together with his extremely wide reading in the latest ethnography, in order to assemble a picture of the earliest phases of human development. His evidence lies in the language in which ancient peoples have preserved their memory of their own encounter with Being: in legend, myth, and folk songs,[19] but also in the fact that, in Herder's day, Europe is discovering communities in the New World that seem to have retained this moment in their primary forms of expression: "People sang in the same way that many peoples still do today, and in the same way that the oldest historians tell us their ancestors did" (*HFA* 1, 182).

As he continues to describe the developmental stages of languages, Herder observes how poetic language reaches perfection: the poetic use of rhythm is accompanied by a sensual wealth of powerful images, the language of passion. This is accompanied by the emergence of conceptual language, the language out of which philosophy will be born. This is where the importance of the Greek language for Herder's study of history becomes apparent. It provides an example of the natural emergence, development, and eventual decline of a historical language. In describing this process, Herder uses his favourite metaphor for natural growth, the tree: the Greek language is "like an independent tree, emerging slowly from its roots in beautiful earth. Its noble nature gave birth to noble shoots, healthy leaves, invigorating blossoms, perfect fruits. No matter how many different kinds of plant and fruit it received, all its juices remained related to one another and refined into its nature. No aspect of it was smothered by the dominant shadow of a taller tree nearby, and nothing acerbated by nearby growth. Nothing was forced to rot in air that was too close. It spread out all its branches and became the crown among its neighbours and the mother of so many offspring" (*HSW* 2, 59). In this context, the poetic age is the first phase of linguistic development that Herder identifies concretely with a historical period, namely, the ancient Greeks – or, to be more specific, as he wrote in 1768 in the revised version of the *Fragments*, the "pupils of Socrates, Xenophon and Plato" (*HSW* 2, 85). This is the age of the καλός καγαθός, the complete and harmonious human personality, "for whom wisdom has not yet become science, writing is not yet learned artifice, and both appear together as a work of nature" (*HSW* 2, 86). This age is followed by the age of prose, the "manhood" of language (*HSW* 1, 154), characterized by the first tendencies to separate poetic language from the denotive language of prose. Grammatical rules begin to impose upon descriptive language the reduced use of inversion and idiom, those characteristic constructions that mark individual statements as belonging to a specific speaker and situation.[20] Herder sees inversion and idiom as the chief markers of poetic language, corresponding to the sensory experiences of an individual. In this way, the development of language and grammatical rules prepares the way for the split between idealism, with its privileging of the universal, and empiricism, with its emphasis on the particular. At the same time, private uses of language begin to depart from public uses.

As Karl Menges points out, this moment in language development is of such importance to Herder, since it pairs together a cognitive and a socio-historical moment. "*Individuum est ineffabile*: with that concept medieval philosophy adopts the Platonic dualism of the universal and the particular, of idea and matter, while retracing the boundary between what can be said and what resides in the margins and remains beyond articulation."[21] The social expression of this division leads to the point where the extreme of private speech is the idiotic babbling that a disturbed person speaks in response to an individual passion, and the extreme of public speech is the erasure of the presence of the speaking body under the imposition of universal discursive laws.[22] Herder's epistemological pursuit of an alternative to the dualism of idealism and empiricism now reappears as a sociological quest for an alternative to the split between public and private language. As I shall discuss later, this becomes a defining imperative on the writer of critical prose.

First, let us continue to follow Herder as he expounds on the maturation of language to the point where it has come of age and become philosophical language, the language of modernity and of contemporary Germany. The philosophical age of language is one where grammar begins to function as the arbiter of logical possibility, both enforcing and confirming its own priority. It "places inversions in chains," and the philosopher "attempts to discern or discard synonyms" in order to "introduce authentic words in the place of inauthentic ones" (*HFA* 1, 184). From this perspective, poetic language, the language of the senses and the passions, appears imperfect.[23] But if one takes account of the genesis of philosophical language itself, poetic language appears as one of the conditions of its possibility. In fact, as Herder will explain in the *Fourth Critical Grove*, it is only through the habituation of thought that we forget how, in the earliest, low-level abstraction out of which language first emerges, complex philosophical work is already being performed (see *HAW* 194–5). What writers like Breitinger are forgetting is how all language use, poetic as well as philosophical requires the work of abstraction if it is to move beyond somatic reactions to sensual stimuli and enter the realm of communication. This appreciation of abstraction in pre-philosophical language will in turn have far-reaching consequences for the understanding of the thought processes of societies generally regarded as primitive, savage, or wild.

The other mistake Herder targets in the *Fragments* is the trend towards linguistic engineering (*Sprachverbesserung*), which he notes in a number of current authors. If we accept, as they do, that poetic language is nothing but a language of unnecessary embellishments and misleading concepts, whose only function is to provide arabesques for the pleasure of some readers, the next logical step is to ask how philosophy would profit from programs of linguistic purification.[24] Such proposals are driven by a fundamental misconception about the nature of thought. Human beings are not pure spirit, and so we cannot speak pure concepts. We are sensory beings whose language is grounded in sensual experience (*HFA* 1, 189). As a result, what the language engineers regard as unnecessary adornment is in fact the fingerprint of a language, its history. This means not only its cultural history but its political and economic history as well (see *HFA* 1, 194–6). And what they see as contingencies or impurities arising from practice are in fact a flexibility geared to the needs of individual speech acts (*HFA* 1, 216).

What gets lost in language purification is what Gaier calls "the poetic and mythopoetic mother tongue" of humanity. In the modern world, "conditions of climate, topography, neighbors, and so on" have shaped this mythopoetic language into "the language and mythology of a nation."[25] In modernity, myth becomes a form of heuristic thinking – "the best possible and most probable conjecture of an earthly human being" concerning not only the afterlife or prehistory, but basically "anything that is impossible to know."[26] Myth needs to be studied anthropologically and historically, as a record of a nation's consensus on the status of the unknowable, but also as a vision of human completeness. This is why, as Menges observes, true poetry "is not above the world but engaged in the political process."[27] It is part of the response to the modern loss of the "idea of complete humanity, as opposed to the Enlightenment tendency toward professionalized activities in which a person is engaged only partially."[28] The erasure of poetry from a purified language is like the erasure of embodied speech in the anonymity of writing. A political poetics will set itself the task of recovering the strategies of erasure that point to the presence of the body in language.

Herder sketched out some of the foundations of this political poetics in 1764, in the address "Haben wir noch jetzt das Publikum und Vaterland der Alten?" (Do We Still Have the Public and Fatherland of Yore?) – a commemorative piece written on the occasion of a visit to Riga by Catherine II of Russia to dedicate the city's new courthouse.[29] The central question Herder wants to address in this essay is whether there are political practices that are capable of bonding a nation that has lost the public institutions which provided social cohesion in antiquity. He begins by listing the institutions that might potentially make a people into a public by providing shared experiences. These may be spiritual (temples and schools), educational (churches and schools), philanthropic (churches and houses of mercy), or political (courthouses, which provided the link to the context of the address). However, such institutions alone are not sufficient to create a public. The decisive difference between the modern public and the public of yore is the loss of public space. The public of antiquity had its origins in the extended family and in a shared place: "The patriarch who first gathered his family in a circle of tents and surrounded them with a fence was the first king who founded a *public*" (*HEW* 55). Modern life has become more complex, and society has become more stratified by class (*HEW* 56–7), with the consequence that the modern public cannot be localized.[30]

This also has repercussions for democracy, since "under the institutions of the modern state *democracy* as such and government by the people is no longer possible" (*HEW* 55). What we call "the people" have themselves changed: "Even *the people* [*das Volk*] are no longer the same" (*HEW* 57). In a modern state, the people have become degraded to the status of "the masses," and what was once the citizenry has become "the *mob* and the riffraff" (*HEW* 57). The body politic has become differentiated and specialized within itself, and it has become distinct from government. What Herder is describing is, in the words of Menges, a "transformation of *Volk* into Nation," reflecting "the relentless modern trend toward division of labour and the attendant process of social stratification. The end result of this process is modern statehood, which Herder defines in terms of artificiality and mechanical functioning."[31] The state has supplanted an organism of collective life with an abstract machine. How did this come to be?

The Public Intellectual and Institutional Space

In addressing this question, Herder turns to the question of institutional space. The institutions of antiquity were physically located in space and supported public expressions of opinion in a physical location. This is no longer the case. Herder asks: "For, where did the Demosthenes and Ciceros have their beginning? In the public forum! And where is that now? ... Where would the public today decide upon an important undertaking on the basis of the wilfulness of the moment?" (*HEW* 57). Modern Europe has replaced the open forum of public decision-making with private spaces (where decisions are made, but are not open to widespread debate), and marketplaces (where the people gather and intermingle openly in order to purchase commodities, but where no political decisions are made). Herder's comments on the modern state do not really amount to a political analysis, and this is not where his interest lies.[32] Instead, he is concerned with the vision of social cohesion he attaches to antiquity, and which he sees undermined in modernity, and above all is concerned with the cultural institutions and forms of communication that might contribute to reform. History is, in his view, "made not by politicians but by poets and priests," whose effectiveness issues from their organic belonging within the modern community.[33]

What has been lost with the disappearance of the public of antiquity is not only an open and accessible space of persuasion, but the art and language of persuasion itself. This is why Herder states that not even the English parliament can be seen as an institution of public decision making (*HEW* 57). Not only is parliament architecturally separate from the eyes and ears of the people, its exercise of rhetoric is no longer dialogue but oration. In modernity, a rhetoric of persuasion has given way to one-sided discourses of reason, law, and spiritual edification, whose medium is not dialogue, but a private experience of communion with an author's concepts or an authority's dictates. Herder sees in the rise of print media the demise of public dialogue and with it an acute threat to democracy. Herder's public has been ruptured by the spatial structure of modernity and by the role of print media, and this rupture is felt within the life of the writer as a destruction of the public forum, and an imprisonment in the medium of writing:

> When I enter a library in which spiders have lined velvety strands around the books, my author's eye is often melancholic like that of Darius beholding his army: miserable folios full of wisdom, all of you scribbled, sweated, and

> smeared for the public. Who is your public? The quiet, learned moths who call themselves literary critics? Is it not merely a compliment made in jest, to say that each author encloses his spirit within his book …? (*HEW* 58–9)

Herder does not openly say so, but we know from his other writings of these years that, in his view, the effects of this imprisoned spirit were to remove conceptualization from its localized embodiment. With the *Fatherland* essay he is now beginning to explore the political ramifications of this distinguishing feature of modernity. In doing so, he asks whether, in an age that has lost its public and its democratic government based on open dialogue and a shared rhetoric of persuasion, there are still shared experiences of community that constitute a functional self-governing community. This is the point of the second half of the essay, which in the printed version of 1765 is titled "Do We Still Have a Fatherland?" The categories Herder suggests for posing this question are religion, courage, freedom, usefulness, and honour, and the answer he arrives at is, yes, there are shared experiences of self-determining community, but they need to be examined using different measures than those of antiquity, and they pose different political (and philosophical) challenges. Religion was once a political matter, meaning that it was localized within a community, and retained its value "only as far as the walls of the city extend," changing "with the air of another region" (*HEW* 60). With the discussion around the separation of church and state, political theory is disavowing the fact that such a separation can only be conceived of with a particular understanding of religion – as the "pure and reason-based religion" (*HFA* 1, 49) upon which the community of the state is founded. This brand of religion has also subjected tolerance to the forces of the market and international commerce. The question of courage, freedom, and honour (that of usefulness fades away in the course of the essay) is intended to address the passions – is there a concept of community strong enough that it can move an individual to sacrifice his life for it? Or as Herder puts it: "Do we yet have the fatherland, the love of which will move us to the unselfish sacrifice of our selves; do we yet know the passion of the ancients to court the fatherland's love, its honour and reward, as the patriot's finest garland?" (*HEW* 61). In answering this question in the affirmative (which, given the context of the address, he had more or less forced upon himself), Herder is not solving the problem, but sidestepping it.

The open question at the end of this essay is where, in the age of the modern state and its institutions, the forces of patriotism, tolerance, and a shared vision of human life, all of which are the underpinnings of a functional democracy, are to be located. *Fatherland* offers Herder a concept for thinking of community in modernity as what Barnard calls "a novel conception of integrative pluralism within an essentially undifferentiated or horizontal sense." This involves "advocacy of multiple affiliations, where individuals can move between, or belong to, a diversity of groups."[34] The documentation of this process is of vital importance, since community is forged by organic – that is to say, authentic – experiences of belonging and growth. The historian, like the poet, studies the traces of a people's mythology, its original voices, which have become submerged in the discourses of modernity. In this way, the aesthetic process becomes a means of negotiating the multiple affiliations of modernity.

Language anchors the abstract in bodily experience, rendering it intelligible and meaningful for individuals.[35] In this understanding, the body of the speaking and writing subject is first and foremost a place where a lived locality enters into a dialectic with an imagined community. As Menges notes: "Herder perceives nations not as immutable entities but as living organisms, and in a very modern sense as something similar to Benedict Anderson's concept of imaginary communities."[36] And like Anderson's imaginary communities, Herder's nation is bound together by print media. Print media allows the lived locality of readers and writers to engage with the imaginary public that transcends locality. There are many dimensions to this process. At times Herder seems to be interested in the locality of reading in opposition to the community of writers. Or the expressions of displaced linguistic groups opposite the traditions of a cultural heritage. Or the locality of action and the indeterminate de-localized sphere of its effects. In Riga, the discrepancy between these localized actualizations of print media and their abstract de-location appeared as the distance between Riga's German-speaking community and the still nascent idea of a German public with its institutions of collective expression. Writing to Nicolai in 1768, Herder speaks of the "aides to self-formation [*Bildung*],"[37] such as "the world-register [*Weltton*] of literature, good manners in social interactions, amicable consortium in one's studies, libraries, art galleries." And then he asks: "Without these, what am I doing here among all the dead books?" (*HBG* 1, 125). Herder could only develop the dialectic of imaginary community and lived locality by virtue of his decentred position with respect to the German public.

A central theme begins to emerge here that is important for understanding Herder's politics. He is trying to conceptualize self not only as a place, but a place that can be worked upon, inscribed, and read within the physicality of a body: a corpus, a work. Self reveals itself to the inquiring mind as a system of traces whose legibility is of the same order as the writing in books. For Herder, experiencing the feelings of restlessness and discontent in his own spirit meant accessing this regime of legibility, this system of traces that properly resides in books. But books begin to emerge as a problem themselves. In Herder's view, the intellectual mired down in book-learning is the opposite of the public intellectual. The book-learner is cut off from the practical proximity to life, and thus hampered in the work of spreading improvement. This was not simply a concern that book-learning confines intellectuals to ivory towers and renders them unsuitable for facing the practicalities of life. Their fundamental remove from practical life prevented them from engaging with the needs of their readers. But over and above this, books were seen to be chasing practical circumstances that were themselves in flux. The task of the public intellectual was to play a guiding role in this process, and this amounted to a political intervention.

In Riga, the political imperatives on the public intellectual soon revealed themselves as the need to make choices on concrete political issues. Some of these issues must have driven home to Herder the fact that his ideas on humanity and cultural diversity are also a matter of human rights in the world economy.[38] When he arrived there in 1765, the local government was in the process of formulating reform proposals aimed at dissolving the old practices of *Leibeigenschaft*, or chattel slavery.[39] This was part of a pan-European Enlightenment move to do away with practices seen as barbaric affronts to human dignity. Almost at the same moment Herder arrived in Riga, the provincial parliament, the *Landtag*, had opposed these proposals, claiming that the practice of chattel slavery did "not derive from barbarism, but from the natural genius of the ethnic Lettic nation, and is perfectly suited to prevail alongside humanism [*Humanität*]."[40] Where the European cosmopolitan writers abhorred slavery, Livonia's provincial parliament could argue that it was a regionally specific, ethnically established custom, and thus had the status of legal right. This was a direct challenge to Herder's belief that local custom should be defended in the face of abstract preconceptions concerning human rights. This challenge was more or less eclipsed by Herder's impassioned anti-slavery rhetoric, which, in the ensuing decades, was to join an increasingly widespread criticism among intellectuals of all forms of slavery and serfdom throughout Europe.

The question of serfdom and chattel slavery in Europe was easily transposed onto that of slavery outside Europe,[41] and Herder saw both as extreme examples of the domination of one people by another more powerful one. More importantly, this critical position was not based on a priori moral principles – at least not as he understood it. His opposition to slavery was justified not on universal moral grounds, but because the science of human development demonstrates that slavery is unnatural, perverse. Herder will go on to develop this idea via the economic connection between European serfdom and international slavery. There is no doubt in his mind that slavery in the non-European world is a product of the expanding world economy, a displacement of the slavery that Europe requires economically, but morally cannot tolerate to witness at home. And yet his position was more complex than might at first be apparent. Herder was experiencing on his own doorstep the contradictions between shared human values and local traditions and the need to weigh the legitimacy of each in terms of his own understanding of humanity. The Enlightenment reforms that were sweeping Europe could not do so without upsetting local custom, itself entrenched in economic relations. And in the eighteenth century, Latvia already had a long history of German colonization suppressing local customs and exploiting the local peasant population.[42] The reform movements in Latvia pushed by German-speaking cosmopolitan intellectuals like himself would have looked to Herder like both a colonizing and a civilizing project, and he experienced directly the practical difficulties involved in such a project in his capacity as a teacher and preacher in Riga, but also as a member of the colonizing elite. These difficulties underlined the duplicity involved in supporting both Enlightenment reform and the expansion of the world economy.

It is around this time that Herder's later, highly critical position on slavery began to take shape, and that slavery becomes a marker of the failure to reconcile the dictates of local custom with the need to promote humanity. The outspoken condemnation of slavery will continue to mark his project of humanity throughout Herder's life. In one of the final letters of the *Briefe zu Beförderung der Humanität* (Letters for the Advancement of Humanity, 1793–7), he imagines how a "history of the trade in negroes banned and of slavery abolished in all parts of the world," will form "a beautiful monument in the entrance to the temple of universal humanity [*allgemeiner Menschlichkeit*]" (*HSW* 18, 244). On the question of slavery, the moral idea related directly to the project of extended human improvement, education, and the respect of other cultures. But this was not possible without facing the inherent contradiction between development as formation of the human race, as facilitation of humanity's organic growth, and development as self-expression of local culture, as facilitation of the organic growth of one sector of humanity. This contradiction was the inevitable political consequence of his epistemology, and it forced the question: What exactly is development?

The Developmental Problem in History

If we read Herder's initial explorations into the individual and socio-historical development of language against the backdrop of his epistemology, we find an attempt to describe the self-realization of the individual and the collective alike as the expression of a natural force. The cognitive event itself, whose sequences he described in the *Essay on Being*, and which he named the "human path," is seen as an expression of this natural force. In his subsequent writings, he then raises the developmental principle behind cognition to the status of universality. Herder sees the progression from sense perception to imagination to reason not only as a single, multilayered cognitive event. It is also a description of the learning process whereby children come to intellectual maturity, and of the process of self-discovery and self-realization whereby a community finds its collective identity. He also sees this developmental process at the base of the growth of cultures, languages, and nations: the self-formation of nature itself. In reframing his epistemological theory to include history and anthropology, Herder was, as Menges notes, opening himself up to what appears to be a "conceptual contradiction." If "every entity, individually as a person, or collectively as a nation, is centered in itself, the stipulation of a general unifying process toward humanity seems contradictory. Individual history can hardly progress toward a universal goal when it is stuck in a self-referential loop."[43] The only way to solve this contradiction for Herder was to demonstrate that there was a common principle underlying the growth of the human organism and the organic development of humanity as a species. But what exactly is the nature of the developmental principle? And if there is indeed such an organic principle of development in the individual organism, how is it possible to speak about the community of organisms as if it too is driven by this principle? Finally, how can we be certain that our attempts to specify it are not simply another imposition of an idealist form upon the chaos of nature? In attempting to answer these questions, Herder finds himself embarking on a search for the appropriate scientific model for the development of the human organism and of humanity itself.

It is evident at an early stage in his writing that he is aware of the challenges facing him in finding an appropriate model for development. In the *Versuch einer Geschichte der lyrischen Dichtkunst* (Essay on a History of Lyrical Poetry, 1764),[44] he observes that thinking about the origins of things is not simply an amusing pastime, it is "also necessary to search for the origin of matters that one wishes to understand with a measure of completeness." The scientific pursuit of origins is coupled to the study of history, and together they make up a scientific method for pursuing the genesis of humanity. In the study of human genesis, the origin is the "most important part of history, from which, in the end, everything is derived" (*HEW* 70). And yet, the origin of human culture and its products is "cast in darkness, and we grope nowhere as blindly as when we pursue the question: *How and in what manner did something come to be*?" (*HEW* 71).

It is here that he begins to understand the historical method as tied to the other sciences that study genesis. Botany is one of his most important references,

> for, as the tree may be derived from its root, the progress and flowering of an art must be derivable from its source. Just as the seed contains, concealed within itself, the entire plant with all its parts, the source of an art contains within itself the entire essence of its product; and it will be impossible for me to derive from the *subsequent* shape the degree of elucidation [*Erläuterung*] that would be required to make my explanation *genetical*. Since my object [*Gegenstand*] is always changing, I do not know where I shall find oneness; as often as I place the creature into the field of the magnifying glass, it appears in another shape. Should I take account of only *one* stage, my observations would doubtless be too fragmented and incomplete; should I take one after the other, but miss the first one, I would indeed miss the clew [*sic*] from which I may unravel those that follow. (*HEW* 70; translation modified)

With this, Herder has pinpointed his methodological challenge for the scientific study of organic development. The genesis of history is like the genesis of plants – not in terms of any metaphorical similarity, but in terms of the methodological problems facing scientific explanations of their development. Both history and biology require a different kind of explanation than the mechanical cause-effect model, since no original cause of an organism can be identified in biology, just as (as Herder observes) the origin of historical events is obscure.[45] The darkness which logic finds as it approaches Being is analogous to the obscurity of historical origins, but for different reasons. First there is the problem of causality, which epistemological obscurity shares with its ontological counterpart: "The fact that we cannot mechanically trace a formative process, going from one cause to the preceding one, and thus traverse the causal chain back towards its source" is the same problem of causality that Hume had raised, but compounded by the problem that "true evolutionary developments were not produced mechanically."[46] Second, a complete picture of humanity's development cannot be obtained, since there can be no privileged position outside history from which its totality can be observed: "Always already-inscribed within the circle of their own culture, human beings had no way of 'composing' the different possible views of history in a single image."[47] Third, the medium of observation at our disposal may be adequate to observing and describing causal sequences, but it cannot apprehend origins. This applies to the biologist's "magnifying glass," just as it applies to print culture, the medium of observation the historian uses to delve into the past. Information about past events requires a technology of writing that preserves this information in a reliable and durable medium, in other words it needs what Herder calls "one of the most difficult and most recent inventions" (*HEW* 71). This is "the artifice that enables writing, writing everything one wishes, as much as one wishes, and in the manner one wishes; and that enables a kind of writing that will provide continuity and last forever" (*HMA* 1, 11). And finally, historical origins are subject to what might be called historical *Nachträglichkeit*: the origins of things are only recognized as significant once the things themselves have disappeared, and in disappearing have acquired their historical significance. If we try to identify the origins of "the greatest of things," we find that they began as "miserable experiments, shabby games. Much later, they became specific abilities (*Handgriffe*), which then became, even more slowly, the arts. Much later, rules were derived from the arts; these rules, again, only after many intervals, were elevated to the status of science; and now, in order to practise this science, an overview of the whole is striven for – but, where is the origin? The thread is lost" (*HEW* 71; translation modified). The pursuit of historical origins will always come up against their epistemological and ontological obscurity, and it will be compounded in a number of ways: by the fact that the scientist's perspective is itself a part of the phenomenon under investigation; by the problem of writing, which cannot represent humanity's earliest experiences; and by the fact that origins are always culturally named and invented after the fact.

In the fundamental obscurity of historical origins, Herder will encounter the problem of monogenesis. In the 1770s, he will begin to grasp what Palti calls "the irreducible peculiarity of every national and cultural formation [*Volksgeist*]" as "a meaningful whole that, like Leibniz's monads, formed a closed universe realizing by itself the entire biological cycle of growth, development, decline, and death."[48] And yet, cultural/national entities are not windowless. They relate to the world in the same way Herder understands organisms relating to their environment, and their development can be described along these lines. This causes him in *Lyrical Poetry* to reject the hypothesis that all culture can be traced back to a common origin in a single people, "that everything must be derived from the Orient, that all streams issued from the same spring. This hypothesis is marked by too much arbitrariness; everyone leads the stream in the direction they desire. They cross one another to the point of utter confusion. So much learning comes from the migration of the arts and sciences that we will do better to assume no origin and to seek within each people itself the seed that had the power to bring about the arts and sciences" (*HEW* 76; translation modified). As Herder illustrates with these images, the principle of development involves a degree of chance, of randomness. This is driven by the specific environmental circumstances and traditions of different cultures, but also by the fact that an innate drive to restlessness causes humans to propagate their own cultural achievements beyond their geographical boundaries. But chance is not what he wants to talk about. The genesis of history is driven in large measure not only by chance, but by the fact that the human being lives, as Herder frequently observes, "in contradiction with himself and with the earth" (*HMA* 3/1, 180). This contradiction is what enables the question of origins in the first place. It allows the inquiring spirit to stand apart from himself and his time and to look at phenomena as signifying something that is not there – a lost origin, or an invisible principle of development contained in visible seeds. Human beings may contain within their organisms structural aspects of animal (and even plant) biology,[49] but in this inherent contradiction they are unique.

Signifying action is a performance of this contradiction.[50] In so far as Herder has a definition for the human, it is *homo symbolicus*.[51] The natural forces that give rise to humanity as *homo symbolicus* continually reproduce themselves in signifying action, which itself results when the drive to perception encounters an external object. The subject of this encounter is a creature of the species "humanity." That is to say, in Herder's theory, humanity is produced at the intersection of nature's expressive force and the form of objects, but also at the intersection of individual and collective life. Signifying action documents the process of humanity emerging out of nature's expressive force.

Although the scientist sees in the development of individual organisms and individual nations the working of a self-contained system, this did not preclude Herder from believing that it is possible to study the development of humanity as a notional system of systems. In Herder's early writing, he is struggling to push his epistemology in the direction of an organic theory of human development. This applies in equal measure to ontogenesis and phylogenesis. In the *Fourth Critical Grove*, Herder describes the prehistory of humanity as the age when the being we call human (*Mensch*) had only just begun to emerge "from a state of having been merely a thinking and perceiving plant [*Pflanze*] and began to develop into an animal." Its only feeling was the "obscure idea of his ego, so obscure that only a vegetable can feel it" (*HAW* 194, translation modified).[52] This formulation is at first startling, but what Herder intends is quite clear, and thoroughly in keeping with his explanation of development: if it is possible to imagine the moment when humanity distinguishes itself from the rest of organic nature, it has to be on the basis of an organism's ability to respond to its environment, as a plant does, but in humans this response is augmented by ideas that relate to itself as an organism. And the earliest indication of this is already present in the biology of animals.

The privileged forms in which humanity documents nature's formative force are themselves all form-giving, and they include art, technology, politics and, most important, language. Within the grand scheme of nature's development, individuals unfold their inner powers according to nature's plan, as Leibniz had argued. But it was of utmost importance for Herder to find and specify the link between this individual *Bildung* of a monadic individual and the life of the collective. There are two keys that unlock this link. One is the structural homology that makes it possible to speak of the individual organism as unfolding according to the same principles as the collective. The other is language, which is a shared expression of the process of unfolding, an expression that integrates individuals into the collective, and that distinguishes a group from other groups. But it is also language that enables the interaction of groups to form new groups. It is due to language that human aesthetic activity can reproduce nature's force in representation. Language is what defines individuals within nature's plan, and it is what individuals share with each other. For this reason, it is the accession to language that gives individuals their social being. Language is a negotiation between speaking individuals that defines (and constantly redefines) what nature is, and what the collective is. It is through the form-giving acts of language that nature brings individuals into community as a collective; and conversely, in language the collective imagines nature and speaks it into being. This is why Herder's collective has to be grasped empirically, not as a notional or a priori structure. It should also serve to clarify one of the most widespread misconceptions in Herder's writings: What exactly is the collective? The debates around this question have sought to articulate the difference between a people (Herder uses the term *Volk* or *Nation*) and a nation state. Here the consensus has long been to reject attempts to map Herder's "cultural nationalism"[53] onto a monolithic view of national language. But there seems little recognition of just how radical Herder's understanding of the collective is, and how well suited it is to discussions of cultural belonging in the age of globalization, multiculturalism, and hyphenated identities. More recent discussions of Herder's nationalism tend to follow Barnard's insight that a national culture is "the product of a relational process that is embedded in the consciousness of a shared heritage."[54] But even here, this process is seen to establish "internal bonds of a nation's political development as an integral whole."[55] This implies that the collective is a homogeneous language group tending to form homogeneous political unities, such as the nation state. In this vein, it has become common in the scholarship to regard Herder as paying insufficient attention to diversity and heterogeneity within a culture, emphasizing only differences between cultures. Sikka speaks of his "rejection of cultural hybridity within national borders."[56] Spencer, however, convincingly shows the misconception involved here, explaining that Herder "fully accounts for the heterogeneity that exists within cultures."[57] This internal heterogeneity of culture is an unavoidable outcome of Herder's theory of language. Because of the way he articulates the interaction between individuals and collectives, Herder has to problematize the notion of the political group. Even if we think only of language, Herder's model attempts to do justice to multiple affiliations that escape political systematization. Think of the German language at the time he wrote. It was spoken throughout large sections of the Holy Roman Empire, and it enabled a sense of common cause over and above the numerous political entities presided over by princes, dukes, and kings. And yet, these principalities themselves could lay claim to political cohesion on the basis of a shared culture. However, Herder mistrusted such political entities – and for good reason. He understood that, if a political collective could be mapped onto language in this way, it could just as well be confined to a region within a territory, or a town or village. In linguistic terms, the collective is not simply manifest within a language or a dialect, it is also constantly negotiating idiolects – a point Herder returns to constantly with his discussions of idiom. The point is that language immerses the individual at all times in multiple identities, all of which are seeking political expression.

This is another reason why environment has to be considered more carefully in Herder. If identity is established through negotiating multiple linguistic and cultural affiliations, then environment cannot be spoken of as singular or homogeneous. Environment, like linguistic attachment, is at all times multiple and multilayered. Just as language casts the individual into multiple group affiliations, each affiliation presents itself to the individual as a different mediation of nature. As we begin to understand what language does in Herder's conception of nature, the individual, and the collective, we see that – of course – humanity cannot exist without nature, but nature also cannot exist without humanity. Humanity is nature in its self-reflexive, expressive actualization, revealing the principle of its inherent force. And just as it makes no sense to speak of individual organisms outside their place in nature's whole, it makes no sense to conceive of individual humans outside the collective. For this reason, as Herder worked his way through the rapidly growing body of literature on imperialism's expanding world, he did his best to describe the form-giving work of humanity as an activity that expressed the diversity and the unity of the human race, and to do so outside the ideology of imperialism.

This presented him with the problem of how to conceive of the determining force of development as organized, structured, and yet contingent, driven by order and subject to chance. In the passage cited above from the *Fourth Critical Grove* Herder calls the obscure ideas of the self the "vegetal feeling" out of which "all sentiments sprout forth." This process is the same as that whereby "in visible Nature the shoot [*Keim*] carries within it the tree, and every leaf is an image of the whole" (*HAW* 194; translation modified). And the same applies to the growing child, in whose inner being resides "even that which he feels outside him"; his goal is "the internal activity of development," and his essence is "a constant perfection" (*HAW* 194). Herder's constant use of biological and botanical imagery to explain human development around this time is telling, and it begs the question of how he intends to apply biological models of development to explain human history. If all the concepts and ideas of which humanity is capable are contained in the "dark idea" of the self, are they already present in earliest times, preformed but not yet articulated? Do they arise according to an intrinsic developmental plan, or do they require some form of divine guidance? And if the developmental principle that will lead to their emergence is the intrinsic natural plan of the human organism, what role does reflective intelligence play?

The developmental problem in history, as Herder is formulating it, requires an explanation of how cultures blossom and fade while human history as a whole continues on its path. Herder recognized that the idea of a divine plan, steered by a supernatural being, may seem adequate, but, as he states explicitly in *On Lyrical Poetry*, it "does not explain anything; rather, it itself calls for an explanation. It does not explain anything because it merely states that I see effects that I cannot trace to natural causes, therefore they come from God, a conclusion founded upon charity that suspends all further examination" (*HEW* 79). Once he had committed to pushing past the point of charity, Herder had to confront the question of how the diverse and disjoint development of cultures – their blossoming and fading, and their complex cross-fertilizations – relate to the overall development of the human species. As a concept, development "meant that a later stage was not fully contained in its precedent stage. Pre-existent elements and conditions provided the material for a new generation, but the emergence of a new form of life or culture also entailed a new principle of organization."[58] In the history of humanity, it remained to be seen how a new principle of organization can be explained without taking recourse to divine intervention. The most promising scientific discussion of this problem in the 1760s was in biology.

Leibniz's idea of the pre-established harmony between the body and the soul, which he had developed in the *Theodicy* (1710), was intended to explain how natural life can continue to be in accord with the single divine act of creation, even though God is not directly and continuously steering its course. This allowed him "to limit divine intervention to the single moment of Creation, and thus to elaborate Nature conceptually as a system."[59] As Leibniz himself stated, the theory of biological development best suited to this idea was preformationism. During the first half of the eighteenth century, preformationism was the dominant scientific model of biological development, taking the form of germinal preformationism, espoused by notable embryologists such as Albrecht von Haller (1708–77) in Göttingen and Charles Bonnet (1720–93) in Geneva. According to this doctrine, the natural development of organisms consisted of a gradual unfolding of pre-given physiological components present in the ova in microscopic and thus undetectable form. Much of the defence of preformationism revolved around the question of mechanical causes in development, and the visibility of germinal traces of later, mature parts of the organism. Haller, a Newtonian, did not wish to make theoretical claims that relied upon imperceptible evidence.[60] But given the gradual growth of microscopy since the 1660s, it made sense to believe that the problem of evidence was a technological one, and that an adequate theory could look forward to confirmation through technological improvement.[61] This was the position held by Bonnet, who believed that the embryo contains all the parts that will appear in the adult, but that their size and proportion is different, as is their transparency. Development in Bonnet's view is, as Gould puts it, "only apparent; it represents the unfolding of structures preformed at the creation itself. God, the clockwinder, had not only ordained the laws of the universe; he had created all its structures as well: one creation followed by the complete evolution of all preordained structure to the appointed end of time."[62]

By the time Herder began to write in the 1760s, the debates around preformation had acquired a new urgency in academic circles in Germany, having been challenged in France by the Comte de Buffon (1707–88), and in Germany by the physiologist and embryologist Caspar Friedrich Wolff (1733–94). Wolff's dissertation, *Theoria generationis*, published in 1759, reported on how his experiments in embryology had failed to confirm – indeed, in his view, they disproved – the theory of preformationism. Instead, he proposed adopting two existing theories, which he used in tandem – vitalism and epigenesis.[63] Wolff recognized a *vis essentialis* as the organizing force that guides the development of the organism, and epigenesis provided an explanation of development based on a force that was "immanent in the physical world," thereby granting nature "more intrinsic dynamism" than competing theories had.[64]

When Herder studied these debates, he immediately solicited the epigenetic idea of an immanent natural force to oppose the taxonomy of Linnaeus, which he regarded as too rigid, and too intent on the predominance of logic over life. In *Über Thomas Abbts Schriften* (On Thomas Abbt's Writings, 1768) Herder states that philosophy should hold closer to the chaotic multiplicity of life than to the stunting work of categorization: "If our systematic philosophers in the theory of spirit are [like] Linnaeus, in that they idiosyncratically discriminate and classify, it is a good thing to set over against them an unsystematic thinker like Buffon, who [equally] idiosyncratically shakes up their classes and analyses individuals" (*HSW* 2, 258). Herder's originality, Palti notes, lay in

> the application of this concept to history, thus combining a preformism *intra-* with a vitalism *inter-* spirits of the peoples. Upon the idea of *Volksgeist* (of a preformist matrix) Herder superimposed a vitalist concept (of clearly theological connotations), which allowed him to figure out something that up to then seemed inconceivable: the way human history was articulated in order to constitute a meaningful whole. Thus, against epigeneticism, Herder endorsed Bonnet's doctrine that no external reorganization of pre-existent matter (epigenesis) could explain the transformations of the internal spiritual forces which lived inside it (the 'active element which links all [material factors] and transforms them in God's living creature'). But, against preformism, he asserted the creative character of historical evolution, something unthinkable within the frameworks of the preformist concept.[65]

It was now this creative character, this active principle of historical development, that Herder would set out to pursue, and the explanations he would give would set the stage for his further studies in history and language, and ultimately, for a more refined critique of imperialism.

The Politics of Interpretation

I agree with Palti that, ultimately, Herder was not able to provide adequate scientific explanations for the development of humanity as a collective development of individuals and their cultures. But what he did provide was a way of thinking about how our cultural self-understanding itself directs historical outcomes – what might be called the politics of interpretation. The problem of historical development is one of interpretation, whereby interpretation itself becomes both a historical act (since it is embedded in a moment in time and space) and a creative act (since it can affect the further course of history). Interpretation becomes a force of history, in both the passive and active senses.

There are three aspects to this creative force of interpretation that need to be specified: Time, force, and signification. Concerning historical time: In attempting to think of human development as a self-referential process unfolding in time, Herder found himself arguing for a concept of time itself that would provide an alternative to the one that Walter Benjamin would much later call "homogeneous, empty time."[66] This means that the temporality of Being is itself subject to interpretation, and that this interpretation will in turn affect the lives of cultures. In Palti's words, "time became a constitutive dimension in the order of the world; its basic structure was no longer fixed once and for all, but was historically constituted (and did not just 'unfold' over time)."[67] Time itself is culturally mediated and there is no temporal unfolding of humanity which allows one culture to determine the position another culture should or does occupy in the larger history of the species.

Next, the concept of force: The characteristic understanding of force in Herder's early writing arose as an attempt to name that aspect of causality that escapes perception, and in this way to explain how the persistent effects of divine creation can continue into individual acts of creation. Palti believes Herder derived his concept of force from Kant, and his teacher would certainly have provided the immediate reference for his ideas. But Kant himself was referring to an ongoing debate in the eighteenth century. During the 1760s, Kant was in the process of revising his earlier estimation of force as possessing the power to bridge the substantial difference between bodies and souls.[68] In the *Dreams of a Spirit-Seer* (1766), he decisively rejected the idea of naming occult forces as explanatory tools for organic development and using them to avoid the study of empirically verifiable forces.[69]

Like Kant, Herder doubted the usefulness of occult forces as final explanations, but he believed that it was indeed possible to observe the workings of these occult forces directly in empirical phenomena. And furthermore, these forces reveal themselves in the process as mutable. Individual cultures develop their own explanations of force, and these come to be formulated as part of their traditional understanding of what it means to exist in time and space. Force links the spatial and temporal aspects of embodied being. This means that force is not only the persistent working of divine creation, it is also the continual self-examination of its own processes. Poetry is the prime medium of this process. This means that poetic language holds a privileged place in a culture's self-perpetuation, and it gives this self-perpetuation a critical, self-reflexive dimension. In this way, the divine creation of humanity is subject to the constant creative revision of its forms of expression.

Finally, the creative force of interpretation is animated not only by making nature itself the site of mechanical and occult processes, but by making it a collection of signs. Natural processes in this way come to reveal themselves on the surface of phenomena, as it were. Herder's semiotics began to take shape in connection with his theory of human development in the late 1760s, when he considers the legibility of history in myth, and the legibility of organic development in the shape of the organism itself.[70] In his essay "On the Modern Uses of Mythology" (1767), inspired by Lavater's work on physiognomy, Herder began to think of nature in allegorical terms. As Palti observes: "The physiognomic concept allowed Herder to think of how a generative force, despite not being empirically verifiable, made itself manifest in the phenomenal world."[71] Nature becomes a collection of signs, or determining marks, which function allegorically, in that they represent "abstract concepts in terms of the senses" (*HEW* 217). The determining mark in nature thus became a "knot in which matter and idea merged."[72] It represents a force that is occult, but in doing so it renders the force objective. Herder believed that he was correct in describing this process as a representation of force, since it is the way such occult forces as gravity, magnetism, or electricity work. The methodological recognition that emerges with this understanding of the creative force of interpretation is the need for a politics of interpretation appropriate to *homo symbolicus*.

By the time he arrived at this position, Herder was treading on new ground, even though his path can be traced directly from his studies with Kant. On the basis of the epistemological problems he saw formulated in the pre-critical writings, and spurred on by his appraisal of Kant's proposed solutions, Herder developed a holistic view of sensory cognition and logic that grounded thought in the body and located it culturally in history and geography. In order to achieve this, he expanded current debates on aesthetics into a theory of cultural diversity based on the organic unity of the human species. The organic principle of human development governs the historical unfolding of cultures and the development of humanity's languages. An important component of this developmental principle is humanity's essentially self-contradictory nature, expressed psychologically as an inherent restlessness of the human organism, and philosophically as the drive to interpret the world. As a result, the philosopher has a calling to educate and reform, to point out the contradictions in thought that drive a society to false conclusions about itself.

Herder's vision for a populist philosophy, or a politics of interpretation, is set out in 1765 in an unfinished essay which was only published posthumously, and which dealt with the question of how "philosophy can become more universal and useful for the benefit of the people" (*HPW* 3). Zammito reads this essay as a Habermasian outline of the project of Enlightenment, which touches on issues such as "the question of education for women, the problem of a universal history of humankind, and ... political democratization."[73] He also sees in it an attempt to actualize the more radical political implications of Kant's early philosophy. In particular, this applies to Herder's insistence that philosophy can contribute to the "political development [*Bildung*]" of "the people as citizens [*Bürger*]" (*HPW* 25). In consequence, "philosophers are reformers of the state" (*HFA* 1, 103). "The time when philosophers were statesmen" must come again, and it is their duty to attempt to reform the State "from below." This picks up on Rousseau's view of social life as a contract which places distinct obligations on the monarch as well as on the citizen. If the monarch fails to perform his contractual duties, "then the people must force him" (*HPW* 25). Zammito cites this as evidence of "the most radical conjunction between Herder and Kant," since it points to a striking political optimism in Kant's early writings, a belief that philosophy can indeed achieve "moral and political reconstruction," and that this can happen through the education of the people, and not simply the enlightenment of rulers.[74]

Herder uses this idea to push Kant's own insights towards what will later become a biting critique of Kant's metaphysics.[75] The beginnings are clearly evident in this essay, where metaphysics begins to look like the commercial activity he criticized in *On Diligence*. Like the trade in luxury goods, metaphysics "arouses appetites that it cannot fulfil. Taking up this classic theme of Rousseau and locating it precisely in the sphere of metaphysical speculation, Herder writes: 'As soon as our soul extends beyond the limits of need, it becomes insatiable in the desire for superfluities' ([*HFA* 1], 113)."[76] He calls on philosophers to abandon metaphysical speculation and join forces with the people, who themselves apply reason in accordance with the challenges posed by their everyday lives, and in this way remain truer to the human condition, as he had outlined in the *Essay on Being*. If philosophers are party to treasures of human insight, then they need to share these with the people, and if they do not possess such treasures, "if they are themselves useless to the state, then let their caves be destroyed and let the night-owls of Minerva be taught to look at the sun" (*HPW* 7).

This political critique of metaphysics was intended to be read in the spirit of Kantian philosophy, to the point where, Zammito believes, Herder is doing little more than repeating his teacher's position of 1765 on the political obligations of philosophy. But even at that time he was thinking of how he would have to depart from Kant. Indeed, his discontent with Kant seems to have derived from early concerns about both Rousseau's and Kant's inability to explain the historical genesis of what Rousseau saw as humanity's divide from nature.[77] But as a student, Herder looked up to his teacher as a philosopher whose object was the human being, its place in the world, its motivations and obligations, the "unbiased knowledge of nature and ... the moral worth of the human being" (*HSW* 17, 404). In the 1760s, Herder felt that Kant still presented a possible role model for the didactic and populist bent he so desired in philosophy.[78] This faith in Kant's early project probably explains the bitterness of his later attacks on Kant. But for now, Herder is quite clear – academic philosophy is badly in need of reform. It has to stop talking down to its readers (the public), as if it knows something that the public cannot experience themselves, as if they need the authority of logic to tell them what to think. Instead, following Rousseau, Herder admonishes the philosophers to listen to the peasants – the "best observers of nature, who despise the deference paid to tyrants, who do not allow the judgments of others to dominate their own. In short, oh Philosopher, go into the fields and learn the wisdom of the farmers" (*HFA* 1, 127). But Herder is not asking the philosophers to set aside their craft. He is asking them to abandon the rationalist position, to take the "wisdom of the farmers" and conceptualize it – "theorize" it, if you will – to the point where the image becomes an ideal. In this way, philosophy will be able to "overthrow the idol that reveals itself – though not through philosophy – as the ruin of the world" (*HFA* 1, 127).

Philosophy is under an obligation not to determine and control the boundaries of experience, but to analytically expand upon the experience of the senses, enriching it and serving the people who share these experiences.[79] This is why, in the first section of the *Fourth Critical Grove*, Herder so decisively rejects Riedel's claim that common sense is one of the "feelings" enabling an unmediated knowledge of the good, true, and beautiful. What is at stake here is how common sense, being an inherent understanding of a culture's experiences of Being in time and space, is articulated in philosophy. For Herder, the emphasis has to be on the historical determination and the cultural specificity of knowledge,[80] and he asserts that a nation only has *sensus communis* according to its specific cultural and intellectual development in its own environment. This is not simply an assertion of cultural difference based on observed variations in the ideas, myths, and traditions of different peoples. It is a reading of Aristotle's idea (in *De Anima*) that there exists a sensibility that serves to unite the impressions gained by the various senses, a faculty for discerning different kinds of sensory impression and harmonizing them.[81] Since this faculty, in Herder's reading, is intimately related to sensory impressions, it must be understood as a physiological response to environment. Common sense is a shared way of harmonizing the senses. It is a shared cultural horizon for evaluating life, or in Gadamer's words: "It does not mean only that general faculty in all men but the sense that founds community."[82] That is why Herder asks if the common sense of a Hottentot or a Greenlander is the same as "ours," or if that of a scholar is the same as that of a yeoman (*HAW* 198). *Sensus communis* is culturally specific, and it is not possible to judge the judgments of another culture's common sense. It goes against the meaning of the term *sensus communis* to try to explain it on any other basis.

In taking this position, Herder is implicitly criticizing the way his contemporaries removed the political dimension from the idea of community. As soon as *sensus communis* is understood as (in Gadamer's words) "a purely theoretical faculty: theoretical judgment, parallel to moral consciousness (conscience) and taste,"[83] it can be discussed as if the local conditions determining life did not have any political force whatsoever. Kant struggled with this problem, as can be seen in his later attempts to link aesthetic reflection to morality in the *Critique of Judgment*. Herder wanted to retain the plurality of aesthetic experience, and thus he had to emphasize the politics of community over any idea of shared morality. This politicized view of common sense is particularly important for Herder's understanding of the historian's task, as he stated in an unsent letter to the Göttingen *Allgemeine historische Bibliothek* of 1768: "In matters of history in particular, in what measure is the *sensus communis* of judgement consistent among people of different classes and ways of living, among people of varying mixtures of mental powers and above all of varying education and development?"[84] The historian should not attempt to model human development as taking place within a homogeneous society, or as a constant linear progress measurable in terms of the common sense of one particular society. Herder saw this false faith in the progress of homogeneous groups as a direct result of the kind of philosophy from above he had objected to in *Philosophy for the Benefit of the People*. But he also understood that the idea of human progress is more or less inherent in the human condition. The aim of philosophy is not to force the history of humanity into a teleological mould, where the meaning of history is always formulated outside the processes of history and without the input of the participants in historical process.[85] Instead, it is only through looking at history that philosophy's false alliance with the doctrine of progress can be overcome.[86] What Herder wanted was a history based on interpretation – an engagement with cultural self-representation that enabled culturally specific understandings of the past. This would allow the participants in history to take part in the conceptualization of their own place in history.

In terms of his critique of imperialism, there are three important methodological insights that need to be highlighted. First, there is the "leap out of the aporia of philosophy and into aesthetics as a metatheory."[87] This leap is necessitated by Herder's epistemology, with its focus on the temporal and spatial location of Being, and the embodied nature of thought. This is informed by the specific interpretations of location that reveal themselves through a culture's language and traditions, its idioms and grammar, its poetry and mythology. In this tradition of conceptual engagement with location, we find also a cultural negotiation of the forces of nature. As a result, any given culture is engaged in a constant negotiation of its own representation, a politics of interpretation.

Second, in order to enable this politics of interpretation, philosophy needs to stop pretending that it has access to a privileged realm of logical thought that can be radically severed from the experience of cultural location. This means that philosophy needs to retool itself in order to fulfil its anthropological obligations. It needs to grant the concept of Being once again the central position it should have in systems of thought. The result is a historicization of embodied thought, and this historicization is also to be extended to the present day.

Third, it may be possible to use the insights of history and anthropology, as well as those of poetry and myth, to destabilize idealism's claims to truth, but this will only create an impasse between the truth claims of the idealists and their refutation in a different discourse. The idealist position cannot be disproved on the basis of logical possibility (*HMA* 1, 584). The task of a critical philosophy is to demonstrate that the idealist position can only be upheld by refusing engagement with its own non-idealist foundations. If the idealist philosophers are unable to engage constructively with the political discourses in which they operate, then this is the reason. Consequently, a critique of imperialism needs to develop methodologies for unmasking philosophy's complicity with imperialism. This is, once again, a question of the critical analysis of language. The analytic method can point to the aporia in philosophical discourse – the discursive moments where the non-analysability of Being is revealed as the foundation of logic – but it can go even further and demonstrate how these moments are concealed by discursive strategies.

As Karl Menges observes, Herder is pursuing ways of writing against transcendentalism, which "presents itself as the paradigm of the Enlightenment when, in fact, it is only a heteronomous discourse of power."[88] What Herder proposes in its place is a reading and writing strategy that is taking the first steps towards Derrida's project of describing truth as a textual play with presence, and of unmasking the textual strategies upon which truth claims are founded. Like Derrida, Herder attempts to enact the supplementarity of writing, the essential nature of language as a commentary on language, and not as a signification of an external truth.[89] This will allow him to develop an understanding of historiography as (in the words of Michael Mack) a dialectical affirmation of the fact that "the present incorporates the non-presence of the past."[90] Herder consistently rejects "the 'grand narratives' of the Enlightenment which manifest themselves in the 'logocentric bias'" of philosophers such as Descartes and Voltaire.[91] As we will see, Herder takes this critique of logocentrism a step further, linking it, as Spivak proposed, to the project of anti-imperialist writing. In this way, Herder's critique of the metaphysical quest for origins is intimately related to Spivak's early commitment to "the notion that, whether in defense of Derrida or not, a nostalgia for lost origins can be detrimental to the exploration of social realities within the critique of imperialism."[92] Indeed, much can be gained in understanding Herder's problem if we read it in connection with Derrida's observation that (in Spivak's words)

> the project of grammatology is obliged to develop within the discourse of presence. It is not just a critique of presence but an awareness of the itinerary of the discourse of presence in one's own critique, a vigilance precisely against too great a claim for transparency. The word "writing" as the name of the object and model of grammatology is a practice "only within the *historical* closure, that is to say within the limits of science and philosophy" (*OG*, p. 93).[93]

Herder takes this critical project and adds to it a vision of humanity that will become increasingly future-oriented. What emerges is a two-fold task of critical work. The first is semiological, uncovering the traces of original understandings of Being, and showing how they are preserved in the cultural products of humanity. The second is formative – reconstituting the appropriate understanding of Being for the modern age. As Herder refines his understanding of this critical project, his views on imperialism will also become more refined. We will now see how he begins to push this project in the direction of a combined semiology of human development and a pedagogics aimed at intervening in human development. We shall also see how, in certain respects, these two projects begin to work against one another, in ways that are instructive for similar debates today.

3 From Human Restlessness to the Politics of Difference

Two Faces of Cosmopolitanism

On 5 June 1769, Herder, then 24 years old, set sail from Riga in the company of his friend Gustav Berens, a successful Riga merchant, who was bound for France. His intention was to stop in Denmark to visit the poet Klopstock, but he was far from certain what his final destination would be. In fact, his journey was to lead him farther from Riga than he had intended, to the cosmopolitan centre of Europe, to Paris via Nantes. Herder had signed off his last letter from Riga, to J.G. Hamann, with the words: "Today I take ship, tomorrow Venus crosses the sun" (2 June 1769, *HBG* 1, 148). Herder later wrote to Hamann: "I felt the beginnings of a fold in my spirit [*den Anfang einer Falte meines Geistes*], which I was set upon destroying ... I saw that certain years of my life needed to be exploited, and that they would not come again. I saw that I would have to do something unexpected, or else I would simply stay put. I did it" (August 1769, *HBG* 1, 164). Restlessness is the signature of Herder's writings at this time, and it was through restlessness that the challenges of modern life announced themselves to him. As a schoolteacher in Riga, his sphere of activity felt too narrow, while he himself felt "too broad, too strange and too preoccupied for it" (*HJV* 206). He is left with a sense of a "foul and lazy immobility, bordering often on nausea" (*HSW* 4, 345). As a result, he "had to travel" (*HJV* 206). In Germany, this sense of compulsion, of impatience and of confinement was a defining experience for Herder's generation of scholars. It determined the way they thought about their obligations towards their fellow-citizens, and how they imagined the world and their position in it. When he left Riga, Herder's restlessness promised him a cosmopolitan path into what he calls "the big useful world" (*die große nutzbare Welt, HSW* 4, 363). But what is the best way to negotiate the big useful world and to realize the ideals of cosmopolitanism?

Cosmopolitanism was to become a problematic concept in Herder's thought, perhaps even a disturbance, and already in Riga its dimensions were clearly drawn. Looking at Herder's oeuvre, there are two faces of cosmopolitanism. He remained critical towards what F.M. Barnard calls an "empty" or "facile" cosmopolitanism with its disregard for the plurality and specificity of individual nations, their "diversity and color."[1] Later, in 1774, he will satirize this position, identifying it with the dominion of empire:

> How miserable when there were still nations and national character, what reciprocal *hate, aversion* to foreigners, *fixedness* on one's centre of gravity, ancestral *prejudices*, clinging to the *lump of earth* on which we are born and on which we are destined to rot! *Native* manner of thought!, *narrow circle* of ideas – eternal *barbarism*! With us, God be praised!, all *national characters* have been extinguished! We love *all* of us, or rather no one *needs* to love the other. We *socialize with each other*, are completely each other's *like – ethically prosper, polite, blissful*!; indeed have no *fatherland*, no *our-people* for whom we live, but are *friends of humanity* and *citizens of the world*. Already now all of Europe's regents do so, and soon we will *all* speak the French language! And then – bliss! – the Golden Age begins again. (*HPW* 328–9)

This kind of cosmopolitanism can be called empire's cosmopolitanism – it may look like the free exchange between cultures, but in fact it is like the activities of the trading companies. It follows the dictates of European standards of value, the erasure of diversity in the name of a superficial and forced unity.[2] Any hopes for trans-national or trans-local systems based on universal principles alone is, in this view, "a mere abstraction, if not a mirage."[3] It reminds Herder of the imposition of rationalist systems on everyday life. The practical consequence is either to sacrifice one's freedom on a national level or else to force one's own national culture and values on other peoples.[4] Both of these alternatives promote commercial exploitation, corruption, and dependency of one culture on another.

The other face of cosmopolitanism emerged early in Herder's work, where it took the form of a reconceptualization of the public sphere as a place of living communication, not only within a single culture, but across cultures. Dead books must be enlivened with personal relations.

This also led to a fascination with French language and culture. In this view, the highest goal for an intellectual is to be a citizen of the world, because it is this that grants the intellectual the mobility he needs to stitch the experience of diversity into a holistic representation of the world.[5] In an age with a rapidly expanding world horizon, Herder was drawn to the promise of cosmopolitanism as a path into the world, in a similar sense to the Stoic understanding of cosmopolis as a practical relationship to the cosmos.

But it was becoming ever clearer just how problematic the practical relationship with the cosmos was becoming in an age where the unitary world was being explored in the name of knowledge and trade. On the same day in June as Herder set sail from Riga, Captain James Cook was anchored in Matavai Bay on the northern shore of Tahiti, and was belatedly celebrating the king's birthday, having observed the transit of Venus under ideal weather conditions two days earlier, thus fulfilling one of the primary goals of his voyage. Cook had invited several important individuals from the island – "Indian Chiefs," as his first editor John Hawkesworth called them – to take part in the festivities, and to join in drinking His Majesty's health.[6]

Since arriving at the island eight weeks previously, Cook and his party had been busy setting up their instruments, and at the same time taking pains to ensure that relations with the Tahitians were as conducive to their purposes as possible. This meant doing all they could to see that no hostilities broke out, and that the terms of trade were clear. The Europeans had tools, clothing, nails, and beads; the Tahitians had fresh food in abundance, and they knew the value of their produce.[7] The need to retain the value of commodities and to ensure an uninterrupted supply of provisions had a corollary in the exchange of information. Cook is not only thinking about trade, he is also concerned to maintain a steady supply of information with the Tahitians, so as to make his intentions clear to them.[8] Time and again he translates what must for his observers be meaningless or unjustified acts into terms he hopes his hosts will understand. It is important to him that the Tahitians know why he is building an observation station, or why he has shot a Tahitian man for taking a musket. And in exchange he begins to acquire a smattering of knowledge about the geography and customs of the island.[9]

The regime of exchange of commodities and information had a side-effect that was to prove far-reaching in the understanding of European interactions with the inhabitants of the new world. This was the emergence of a discourse of common humanity associated with the exchange

3.1 William Hodges, engraved by W. Watts. *Matavai Bay, The Island of Otahieti*. John Hawkesworth, *An Account of the Voyages undertaken by order of his present Majesty for making Discoveries in the Southern Hemisphere*, plate 4 (London: W. Strahan and T. Cadell, 1773), vol. 2: 80.

of goods and information. As a cardinal rule, Cook had expressly emphasized the need to "endeavour by every fair means, to cultivate a friendship with the natives; and to treat them with all imaginable humanity."[10] The foregrounding of humanity as a precondition to sustained trade would ensure that what Montesquieu had called *doux commerce*, or gentle commerce, would prevail.[11] In his *Spirit of the Laws* (1748), he had written that commerce "cures destructive prejudices, it polishes and softens barbarous mores." Because of this, the "natural effect of commerce is to lead to peace."[12] Not only does commerce presuppose the equal standing of the traders,[13] it also appears to flourish where war is held at bay. In the age of scientific exploration, the regime of gentle commerce had begun to acquire a new necessity in ensuring the success of these expensive voyages, and it was going to set the stage for understanding the common ground that united the newcomers and the natives in acts of exchange.

By the mid-eighteenth century international commerce had long been one of the key issues in deciding whether contact with other cultures was beneficial or detrimental to them. It had become popular to identify it (as Montesquieu had done) as a tool of understanding contributing to the growth of civilization.[14] Commerce was rapidly becoming more viable than conquest as a reason for sending ships from Europe out into the world. In his preface to Cook's journal, Hawkesworth writes: "Your Majesty has, not with a view to the acquisition of treasure, or the extent of dominion, but the improvement of commerce and the increase and diffusion of knowledge, undertaken what has so long been neglected."[15] The distinction between the economics of conquest and of commerce was beginning to change the way Europe saw the rest of the world, and European rulers were beginning to understand that their money was better spent on commerce than on conquest. As a result, the powerful trading nations of Europe were beginning to dominate the world in a different way, through incorporating new and weaker economies into their own, cementing their uneven positions in a new world economy.[16] There is also a growing awareness that the results of these enterprises might not be as immediate as in earlier times. As David Mackay notes, Cook's second voyage was not really a "voyage of discovery – at least in the terms of the expectations of those who sponsored it. Little was discovered in the tempestuous and tropic seas. Exploration and science had undoubtedly been advanced, but the boundaries of empire remained the same." Nevertheless, Cook's voyage was able to serve as a model for interaction, exploration, and exchange, to the point where, "in the 20 years after Cook's death, the navigator's model was employed again and again in traversing the seas which he had found so empty, and the principal aim in each case was to buttress the strategic and commercial foundations of empire."[17] Even as Montesquieu was writing, the dream of a *doux commerce* was yielding to the reality of new forms of imperialism. When Hawkesworth writes of the increase and diffusion of knowledge, when Cook insists on cultivating the Tahitians' friendship and respecting their humanity, they are pointing to the birth of a new anthropology, whose relationship to the needs of the new world economy is far from simple. If knowledge is to be seen as a common good, a component of the common wealth of mankind, it begins to appear that different facts, perhaps even different versions of the truth, can be produced in different places, and that there may be just as much value in the exchange of these facts as there is in the exchange of nails for breadfruit, or axes for hogs.

When Cook makes humanity the founding idea for the commercial restructuring of the world, he begs the question of what this humanity might be. How did it relate to the ideology of domination and exploitation that seemed to be forcing Europe's massive drive for economic and political expansion throughout the globe? Even before he had the opportunity to consider Cook's reports on the inhabitants of the South Seas, Herder was already concerned that the trade in commodities and knowledge may have been intended as a *doux commerce* between free and equal individuals, but in effect had turned out to be just another mechanism for the domination of less powerful peoples by the technologically more advanced nations of Europe.[18] In this respect, he was taking up a long tradition criticizing commercial activity on the grounds that it led to death and enslavement, all for the sake of Europe's indulgence in luxury. From the earliest writings, Herder was prompted to side with this older critique of commerce, drawing, like Montaigne had done before him,[19] on the evidence pointing to the detrimental effects of commerce, and not on the ideals of what commerce might be able to achieve.

One of Herder's early poems is an epigram to Columbus clearly setting down the terms of his discontent:

> Lo, Colon Creator! Lo! thou hast expanded by one-fourth
> Our world with lands, with peoples and with silver treasure,
> With jewels, with adornments –
> And with knowledge!

Alas, Colon Assassin! thou hast as well destroyed
With poison our world and all its beauties,
Its charms, its customs and, alas,
Its life and youthful vigour! (*HSW* 29, 426)[20]

Part of the lasting conviction with which Herder addresses the exploitation of other cultures arises from a feeling that the dual function of trade in commodities and knowledge described in these two verses has not yet been settled. And if it is to be settled, the dispute over knowledge will play a decisive role. For not only is knowledge entering the realm of trade like any other commodity, not only does it provide the framework for understanding the trading process and the trading partners, it has far-reaching social and economic consequences, according to the philosophical allegiances of the knowledge traders. Here again, Herder finds himself opposed to the rationalist faith in logic, and in pursuit of representations that do justice to the diversity of knowledge. In this conception, knowledge promises to reflect upon its own making and to rise above its misuse in the exploitation of other cultures. This struggle for adequate representations is directly related to the problem of gentle commerce. Herder understood that representations of human cultures throughout the world need to be read not simply as objectively accurate, but as bearing traces of the economic interests they embody. This applies to the entirety of European representations, including the written word, paintings, and engravings, as well as maps. Around mid-century, maps depicting European economic interests in other parts of the world began to appear, rendering visible the problematic marriage of scientific objectivity with economic interests (see figure 3.2).

Maps such as these drove home the point that struggles for an adequate conceptualization of the world were at the same time struggles over forms of representation. They show clearly how, as European activity spreads throughout the earth, the anthropological project comes increasingly into conflict with the utilitarian needs of commerce. Following Montesquieu and Rousseau, Herder blamed this on courtly life, with its penchant for unnecessary luxury and its superficial veneer of civility. These attributes of the courtly personality and society were seen to foster greed and the pursuit of personal gain, as opposed to the idea of communal well-being. Herder's critique of aristocratic greed meshes well with his Protestant suspicion of the

3.2 *Vorstellung der Europäischen Handels Plätze in Asien*. Engraving, anon., ca.1770. Photo: AKG Images.

needless excesses, the luxury, vanity, and misery associated with the misuse of power.[21] In his mind, excess and greed at home is beginning to be associated with the structure of exploitation in the expanded world.

In the decades following his departure from Riga, Herder became increasingly interested in how this impacts on the representation of different cultures. Should images of the inhabitants of the New World emphasize their difference from or their similarity to Europeans? Should they be imagined as extensions of Europe's own world, either as an exotic addition to the great family of man or else as living remnants of Europe's own past.[22] This question was raised when Herder saw the illustrations that Cook's artist William Hodges made of Tahiti's inhabitants (see figure 3.3). Hodges renders them strange and exotic, but also domesticated and pastoral, Greek peasants and philosophers in an uncanny landscape, both remote and disturbingly familiar.

Herder concluded that the idea of diversity was best shown not through the idealizing images Hodges brought back from Tahiti,[23] but by collecting "faithful pictures of the differentiation within our species," and laying the foundation to a "speaking natural science and physiognomics of humanity." There can be, he tells us, no application for art that is more philosophical (*HSW* 13, 251). In his major work, *Ideen zur Philosophie der Geschichte der Menschheit* (Ideas for a Philosophy of the History of Humankind, 1784–91),[24] which he commenced some ten years after writing the epigram to Columbus, Herder would emphasize what he saw as the positive side of Cook's project: the great "anthropological wish" of his age (*HSW* 13, 250). In the conclusion to the sixth book of *Ideas*, he speaks of the need to assemble a collective picture of humanity's diversity, and he praises the illustrations from Cook's final voyage for taking the first steps in this direction (*HSW* 13, 251. See figure 3.4).

The "anthropological wish" Herder speaks of was to overcome representations of humankind that promoted practices of domination and exploitation – the development of value systems based on logical possibility, replacing them with images that reflected the alterity of the other. When Cook chose to sit down and celebrate his king's birthday together with the rulers of a distant nation, a nation so many of his contemporaries considered primitive and uncivilized, Herder was convinced he was taking the first steps towards a new understanding of humanity. In this new understanding, humanity would be like a picture gallery, displaying the diversity but also the essential sameness of people everywhere. Herder speaks of his wish "to transform now into pictures all the imprecise verbal descriptions thus far presented, so that I could give to mankind a gallery of his earthly brethren in drawn forms and figures" (*HSW* 13, 250).

3.3 William Hodges, engraved by J.K. Shirwin, *The Landing at Middleburgh*. From James Cook, *A Voyage to the Pacific Ocean*, plate 7 (London: John Stockdale, 1784).

3.4 John Webber, engraved by William Sharp, *Inside of a House in Nootka Sound*, from Cook, *Voyage to the Pacific Ocean*, 2: 317.

The wish expressed here is, as Adler notes, for a new concept of humanity. Herder understands that if the concept *Humanität* (humanity)[25] is to work the way he wants it to within his philosophy, it will have to do so "in terms of function and relationship."[26] As such, the wish for humanity is both anthropological and aesthetic, and in this way Herder hopes to avoid the pitfalls of conceptualization as he finds them in current philosophical discourse. As a relational construct, humanity stands in opposition to the practices of commerce and domination Herder sees when he looks at the history of contact with other cultures. "For centuries we have traversed the earth with swords and crucifixes, with coral beads and brandy barrels; nobody thought to take along peaceful drawing pens" (*HSW* 13, 250). The challenge posed by contact with other cultures is political and moral, but it points to the larger anthropological and aesthetic issues which Herder is intent on introducing into philosophical debates. To conduct a morally and epistemologically defensible philosophy in the expanded world means fashioning an anthropology and an aesthetics capable of resisting the tools of European domination. As he pursues this problem, Herder finds it forcing him to confront some of the fundamental assumptions in currency in philosophy, history, and anthropology. And as he does so, he experiments with new ways of conceptualizing the increasingly diverse picture of human life and human culture. The challenge is how to represent the unity and diversity of humanity outside the models that were preparing it for commercial and political domination and exploitation. In facing this challenge, Herder found himself in pursuit of a new understanding of Humanity. This project would gain nuance as a result of his own experiences of travel.

The Journal of 1769: Imperialism and the Animate World

In France, Herder spent the second half of 1769 working on a journal of his travels, in which he attempted to take stock of the hopes and wishes that had driven him away from Riga.[27] Herder's *Journal meiner Reise im Jahr 1769* (Journal of My Travels in the Year 1769) is a remarkable document, difficult to classify. It was not published in his lifetime, and was only represented in extracts in the first edition of his works (1820–9). It appeared in full in 1846, then in Suphan's *Gesammelte Werke* in 1878. This initial neglect is partly due to its messy form. It is, as Harold Mah observes, "an amalgam of scattered cultural and political observations, introspective inquiry, and outlines of writing and pedagogical projects," marked by "multiple narratives, bursts of self-doubt, and self-exaggeration."[28]

In spite of the general tendency to read the *Journal* as a random set of jottings and notes, I prefer to read it as a literary work – or, better said, as the literary enactment of the impossibility of the scientific work it aspires to be. It is composed so as to bring a number of central themes into dialogue with one another, while leaving the details of their relationship unspecified. In fact, to read it in this way is to understand better the problem that Herder was setting himself in his methodology in general. Just as he had started to do in the *Essay on Being*, he continues here to defer the analytic outcomes of observation to history, anthropology, and aesthetics, without deciding exactly how these articulate with one another. The result is a set of figures of interconnectedness which raise questions rather than positing answers. In this sense, the *Journal* can indeed be read as a program of research, but one in which the object is unclear, and the method less so.

The structure, though carelessly delineated, is easily outlined, and so are the central themes. The *Journal* begins with a short self-study and evaluation (*HJV* 206–14), in which Herder situates his departure from Riga in the context of a perceived dichotomy of living knowledge and dead scholarship. Here he established the inner unrest that will make him a fitting protagonist for the narrative to follow. This unrest is formulated as a quest for experiences suited to his understanding of knowledge as a living thing. There follows a short meditation on the sea, which serves as a counterpoint to the previous section (*HJV* 214–21). Having established the cause and direction of his quest, Herder now looks at his surroundings and meditates on what can and cannot be deduced from observed phenomena.

The following three sections deal with the ship (*HJV* 221–35), the mission in Livonia (*HJV* 235–40), and the challenge of self-formation (*HJV* 240–3). The ship serves as a figure to combine the perspective of the traveller with the modes of perception determined by the sea. It allows Herder to move from the topic of travel to cultures influenced by the sea, then to the alignment of mind and body in the act of reading. The experience of the sea also raises the question of mythology and its relation to rationality, prompting him to propose a fluid boundary between discourses of science and mythology. This causes the ensuing leap to the pedagogical question, the challenge of bringing Enlightenment (though he does not use that word) to Livonia, the wish "to destroy barbarism, to root out ignorance, to spread culture and freedom" (*HJV* 235). Following the pattern he has thus far established, Herder then turns his thoughts inward and asks how he can work at the formation of a nation before he has done the requisite work of self-formation.

There follows a short transition (*HJV* 243–50), in which he again reverses the focus of his attention, and moves from the project of self-formation to the project of a universal history of the world. This time he arrives at this theme via a different path – not the apprehension of a single force at work in the world, directing the movement of fish and of history, but the recognition that the collection of individual notes arising from his own experience will lead directly to a "book for human and Christian development and education [*Bildung*]!" (*HJV* 246; translation modified).

Then come two longer sections, one outlining plans for school reform in Livonia (*HJV* 250–304), and the next setting out a series of "political sea-dreams" (*HJV* 304–64). The former is a practical, matter-of-fact, and thoroughly original exercise in designing a remarkably progressive curriculum aimed at holistic education based on discovery and self-discovery. The latter is a set of speculations on what the European nations would look like without the straightjacket of the state, an attempt to imagine a living history of nations without states.

After this, there is another transition section (*HJV* 364–86), where Herder returns to his voyage, describing the journey from Painboef to Nantes, while at the same time speculating further on the French character and language, and reflecting on how this relates to his own personality. Here he moves once again to his writing projects, conceiving a book on the teaching of Christian doctrine, then sketching a remarkable plan for an aesthetics of touch.[29]

The *Journal* then concludes with a section outlining a project on "the youth and aging of the human soul" (*HJV* 386–409). With this idea, Herder returns to the inner turmoil in which he found himself in Riga, and thinks of his future plans as a remedy for the physical inertia that held him in Riga. The remaining pages of the *Journal* then recapitulate the close relationship between material life and concepts, the notion of embodied thought.

In elaborating these topoi, the *Journal* sets in motion several critical trajectories, which Herder will take on in the following years, in some cases decades. The first of these emerges in the early pages, when he contextualizes his observations as writing-at-sea, under the imperative to "philosophize from nature without books and instruments. Had I had this ability, what a vantage point I would have had, sitting at the foot of a mast on the broad ocean, from which to philosophize on the sky, the sun, the stars, the moon, the air, the wind, the sea, the rain, the currents, the fish and the sea bottom, and to discover the physical laws governing all these from the things themselves" (*HJV* 213–14). Here he is reminding himself of the analytic method he had outlined in the *Essay on Being*, and which he evidently finds so difficult to adhere to, with so much book learning in his way. This difficulty will continue to express itself in Herder's writing as a tension between the Hamannian anti-rationalist critique of the Enlightenment and the extended project of Kant's early analytic philosophy. This tension resides at the core of the *Journal*, in the idea of the primacy of sensation. The primacy of sensation and the need to philosophize from nature will take him to the question of history and historiography via the general change in perspective offered by ship travel and the sea; it will induce meditations on education for life, understood as self-education, the education of children, and political education, and in this way it will introduce the crucial topic of *Bildung*; it will lead to a rethinking of political history; and it will inspire further speculation on embodied thought, and what this means for aesthetics.

All of this is laid out, or at least hinted at in the strikingly original opening sections (Harrison believes that the second half of the eighteenth century "produced few documents more remarkable than the first twenty or so pages of Herder's *Journal*").[30] Presiding over these sections is the awareness that Herder is moving away from familiar territory, that he is floating on a changing seascape, whose visible surface conceals unknown life forms. "Water is a heavier air: waves and currents are its winds, fish its inhabitants; and the sea bottom is a new earth! Who knows this region? What Columbus and Galileo can discover it?" (*HJV* 214–15). The sea appears as the scene of mysterious forces directing the movement of its creatures. Herder speculates on the migration of fish, and he uses the resultant figures of motion to think about the long history of migrating humanity that gave rise to Europe as he knows it. The "shoals of migrating herring" present him a new perspective on human history, driven by a natural urge to motion, by "the nature of men and sea creatures and climates," a restlessness which is also human, and in the shoals of fish he sees "the history of migrating northern peoples" (*HJV* 216). He asks questions about the *vagina hominum*, and isolates two possible "streams" of historical migration:

"One, coming from the East through Greece and Italy, settled gently in southern Europe and has produced a gentle southern religion, a poetry of the imagination, and the music, art, modest manners and science of the South-East. The second stream came from Asia through the North to Europe and there flowed over the first" (*HJV* 216). Since sea travel provides a perspective that includes all nations, it prompts Herder to muse on what he calls the "great theme ... [a] universal history of the formation [*Bildung*] of the world!" (*HJV* 220; translation modified). When we read his later writings on this topic, it is important to remember the image out of which it arose: a natural restlessness in tension with the forces of climate and tradition.

Herder's early work is dominated by the idea that living phenomena represent a continuum of beings within creation. In many senses, the world is alive, and it should be treated as a living being, and yet when it comes to individual objects, beings, or even actions, the distinction between animate and inanimate is not a simple one. Herder's most immediate source for this is Leibniz, for whom life itself is God-given (in that God alone can give rise to entelechy), but the question still remains whether "pre-formed mechanical laws" can give rise "not only to living animals and plants, but also to *animate* clocks and rocks?"[31] In his understanding of the animacy of the world in the sense of a harmonious organization of material bodies, Herder is channelling Leibniz's views on animate matter, and complicating them with the idea of interpretation: that human beings respond to their own particular perspective on their own Being, and on the being of objects.[32] Nature becomes a harmonious whole, composed as a work of art, and organically developing as a living being. This is achieved not only by God's creative force, but by the creative force of language and interpretation. In adopting this view, Herder, like Leibniz, refused to follow the Cartesian dualism of living spirit and dead matter. Instead, he set himself the task of explaining the genesis of the living from the dead, and linking this to the views on *Kraft* as the inexplicable aspect of causality which he had put forward in the *Essay on Being*. In following Leibniz down this path, Herder is using the concept of *force* to sidestep the question of causality, while at the same time seeking the material manifestation of divine creativity. This will lead him to the place we have already described, where his ability to explain the vitality of living things requires a model relating individual development to the harmonious unfolding of the world.

In the *Journal*, Herder will suspend this problem, choosing instead to treat the life of the world as a matter of perspective. There is a certain methodological consistency in this, since – and again, Leibniz also took this position – the "one organization," the "one main force" served by "the eternal rules of wisdom, goodness, and beauty" is only accessible as an analogon, which in turn only expresses one point of view. In fact, this methodological imperative is built into the idea of a single "organization" or organism manifest in countless ways. Not only is the organic principle developmental, in the sense that it is the expression of a unitary internal force, a single organization, it has to be grasped and analysed by way of its countless manifestations. It is this that brings Herder in the *Journal* to extend the opposition between the living and the dead into a polemic on method – a repeated lament on the loss of living experience in dead scholarship, in dead books, and dead libraries. In the following pages I will follow him through the path from the animacy of the world to the question of method, then ask how these impact on his understanding of imperialism.

The fact of the animate world requires a careful conceptual path from the inorganic to the organic, whereby nature's force expresses itself in increasingly complex forms (this is how Herder uses the German term *organisiert*). Herder will explain this in 1784 in the foreword to *Ideas*, where he notes that a philosophy of the history of humanity must begin "in part with a general overview of our dwelling place, in part with a survey of the forms of life [*Organisationen*] which, together with us and beneath us, enjoy the light of our sun" (*HSW* 13, 9). This initial survey and its development from a description of the inorganic to the most complex forms of organic life is a methodological necessity, and amounts to reading from the book of nature:

> No-one will, I hope, consider this pathway too far-fetched or long-winded. Since there is no other path to take when reading the fate of humanity from the book of creation, it cannot be taken too carefully, too studiously. Those who wish simply to engage in metaphysical speculation can take the shorter route. I, however, believe that their separation from experience and analogies of nature are castles in the sky, and seldom reach their goal. God's motions in nature, the thoughts that the eternal one has tangibly placed before us in his works, these are the holy book whose characters I have spelt and will spell – with less skill than an apprentice, but at least with faith and zeal. (*HSW* 13, 9)

With these words, Herder moves quickly from the idea of an increasing complexity in life forms, to acts of interpretation appropriate to this complexity. This same idea is sketched out in the *Journal*, when he discusses the pedagogical project of imparting living knowledge to schoolchildren. He notes that a student "who prates in general terms of arts and handicrafts without having a living perception [*lebendige Anschauung*] of them is still worse than one who knows nothing at all about them" (*HJV* 255). Towards the end of the *Journal*, he recounts how, in Nantes, he became acquainted with a young Swede by the name of Koch, who "had a great deal of taste for what is true, good and really beautiful. I often remarked in him that his eye and his mind were constituted with a stronger sense of what was right than my own; that he had in all things a certain feeling for reality, so that he was not satisfied with hypotheses; that he did not try to learn from books things that depend on experience and practice, but went right into action" (*HJV* 384). Herder, by contrast, feels that his knowledge has been gained "at a distance," that instead of reality, he sees shadows (*HJV* 385). In the early stages of his voyage, this distinction had already been mapped onto the contrast he felt between the motion of the ship and the stagnation of the closed study. On board, Herder is struck by the way the ship, "suspended between sky and sea," gives such "wide scope for thought." He continues: "Everything here gives one's thought wings, motion, and an ample sphere! The fluttering sail, the ever-rolling ship, the rippling waves, the flying clouds, the broad, infinite atmosphere! On land one is chained to a fixed point and restricted to the narrow limits of a situation. Often this point is a student's chair in a musty study, a place at a monotonous boarding-house table, a pulpit, a lecture-desk" (*HJV* 211). As always in the *Journal*, Herder is giving voice to the disconnect between the impressive wealth of knowledge he has gathered from reading voraciously over a relatively short period of time and the deep feelings of dissatisfaction with his lack of worldly experience – a feeling that hurt him all the more for failing to live up to his theory of how true knowledge is to be acquired.

As he develops the association between mobility and living knowledge, and places it in opposition to the stagnation and dormancy of book learning, Herder begins to unfold a theory of how the mobility of the mind aligns with that of the body, giving rise to a living knowledge. The ship becomes an allegorical place where experience is transformed into myth, and myth into knowledge. The mythologization of ship travel is seen as the early dreams issuing from a human urge to travel; and the task of philosophy is not to debunk these dreams, but to understand them for what they are: the mind wandering into new territories, where it experiences new aspects of nature, for which it is struggling to find a language. Mythology is not a primitive precursor to rationalism, something to be overcome and relegated to the prehistory of knowledge. It is, as Herder had already professed in the second *Critical Grove* (which he was considering expanding and revising as he was writing the *Journal*), a poetics of science: "Let us learn from mythology how to give poetic form to the study of nature, instead of learning from science how to banish mythology" (*HSW* 3, 262). The issue at hand is the appropriate forms for representing natural phenomena.

On his voyage to France, the sea is the first place where Herder begins to feel how the immediate experiences of nature can be so powerful that they work against the scientific discourses that try to regulate and confine it. Later, he will remember the effect that sea travel had on his reading of Ossian, which he read while "all at once thrown from the business, tumult and competitive tomfoolery of the bourgeois world, from the armchair of the scholar and from the cushy sofa of the societies … on the open endless sea, in a small state of people … in the middle of the drama of a completely different, living and weaving Nature … Believe me, skalds and bards read differently there than they do in the shadow of the professor's lectern" (*HSW* 5, 168–9).

In Herder's eyes, sedentary life stifles the imagination. It confines the spirit in every possible sense. Herder castigates himself: "The narrowness of your education, the slavery of your native land, the petty, trifling spirit of your century, the uncertain state of your career – all these have limited you, have so debased you that you do not recognize yourself" (*HJV* 237). And yet, it remains unclear just how the dual act of travel and writing will solve this problem. It is by way of the problematic nature of travel description that Herder aligns a set of fundamental philosophical and political issues – the relationship between national specificity and the universality of human experience; between contingent experience and universally valid knowledge; between instrumental and mythological approaches to the world; between the book that confines the spirit to a cage of words and the book that liberates it.

All these relationships are allowed to cluster around the problem of the mobile subject whose identity cannot help but be sedentary, fixed to territory, while at the same time retaining a universality that transcends territory. And since this act of universal transcendence in a sense disqualifies territory, it introduces an essential tension within the idea of mobility. This tension is felt in virtually all philosophical debates of Herder's time, whether they are concerned with personal improvement, natural law, causality, the imagination, or philosophical systems. Personal education and improvement require of the individual an unsettling impulse that sends him away from sedentary life, from book learning and all its narrowness, away from petty nationalisms, out into the world, where humanity is a universal thing, and thus a thing not to be grasped in territorial terms. But Herder emphasizes the danger of using this departure in order to erect a regime of universalism based on logic alone. If one wishes to retain the specificity of human action and experience, while at the same time not losing sight of the fundamental universality of the human condition, it will be necessary to find a form of writing that ties human life to geographical territory and to history.

In Herder's understanding, the traveller's mobile mind in the first instance provides an ongoing account of changing territories, and new experiences of nature. Herder states that he "became a philosopher on the ship – but a philosopher who had as yet learned very imperfectly how to philosophize from nature without books and instruments" (*HJV* 213). But to philosophize from nature without books leads directly to the kind of historical modelling that Herder had encountered every time he tried to explain how truth can issue from an awareness of the inexplicable nature of Being. Now, as he travels by ship, we can see once again how the traveller becomes a philosopher in the moment when he can place the narratives of changing nature on a historical scale of human development, and when he can see with an anthropologist's eye how human development expresses itself in different narratives according to different peoples in different places. As Herder speculates on the secret life beneath the oceans, he finds himself seeing there an analogy to the migrations of peoples, and he starts to think about how to write an alternative history of humanity, one that begins with an awareness of how human life has responded to geography, to the environment in which it develops. The appropriate discourse for this alternative history starts to look ever more like poetic discourse.

Improvement and the Representation of Cultural Difference

It is in this connection that the problems of philosophy propel Herder once again into the field of historiography and the politics of representation. Already in the passage of the second *Critical Grove* cited above, this politics begins to take shape as an imperative to rethink the boundaries between scientific and poetic discourse. He ridicules Klotz's assertion (in the *Epistolae homericae* of 1764)[33] that the discoveries of new lands and the expanding of world horizons provides poetry with a new wealth of embellishments. The expanded world instead forces writers to make fundamental decisions about the most appropriate form of representation for new experiences. The new landscapes are best expressed in painting, not in poetry, while the "new varieties of animals and humans" are better covered by natural history (*HSW* 3, 263). But this is only part of the problem. Herder's growing conviction that different forms of experience require different forms of expression not only forces him to examine the differences between mythological and scientific discourses, it also leads to the question of the cultural diversity of scientific and mythological world views. If the age of discovery has opened the European horizon to new and radically different cultures, and if mythology provides an alternative formulation of experience which is just as valid as the truth claims of science, how are the world views and the mythologies of the world's cultures to be read alongside the mythologies of Herder's own tradition? Here we see the initial signs of a deep divide between the idea of a world populated by diverse cultures with diverse world views and a progressively developing humanity in which some cultures are more advanced than others. Or to put it differently (and this is how the problem presented itself to Herder in the second *Critical Grove*), how does one reconcile the belief that different mythologies are consensual expressions of equally valid world views with the belief that, aesthetically, some mythologies are more valuable, perhaps even more advanced than others. Herder states quite unequivocally that the mythic figures of the Hottentots, the Peruvians, the Hurons and Iroquois can never replace those of the Greeks. It is one thing to think about the diverse forms of cultural expression in anthropological terms, but another to attempt to measure them on a scale of human development. Here, his conclusions are clear: the "Hondatkonsonas of the Iroquois"[34] and the "preposterous stories of African negroes" cannot measure up to the "beautiful genii of the Greeks" or the "noble, poetically rich and beautiful performances of tales of the Homeric gods, their influences on the world, and their deeds among humans" (*HSW* 3, 263–4).

The key word here is beauty, and the way Herder uses it serves to highlight the tension between subjective processes and the quest for objective measurement of value in his early works. Beauty is culturally specific and can only be spoken of in relative terms. And yet, to speak relatively of beauty is to set up value judgments about other cultures, or else to undermine the worth of one's own judgments. Indirectly, this is the problem Kant will set about solving in the Third Critique. For Herder, beauty will continue to provide the flash point for this problem, up to and well beyond the point where it collapses into a mess of irony in his remarkable and widely misunderstood essay published anonymously in the *Gelehrten Beiträgen zu den Rigischen Anzeigen* in 1766: "Ist die Schönheit des Körpers ein Bote von der Schönheit der Seele?" (Is the Beauty of the Body a Herald of the Beauty of the Mind? *HAW* 31–40). Herder opens this essay with the *sine dicendo* that, if the beauty of the body is an indication of the beauty of the mind, then to be given an unfavourable physique is a wretched lot. As he immediately remarks, however, the real problem lies in the fact that the question – Is the beauty of the body a herald of the beauty of the mind? – can only be answered impartially by those who are neither beautiful nor ugly. This joke presides over the entire essay. If you have a beautiful body (and therefore presumably a beautiful mind), your interest in the answer precludes impartiality. The same applies to those with ugly bodies. But the problem is compounded by the fact that the relativity of judgments of beauty renders the idea of impartiality itself meaningless. Beauty and ugliness, being relative and culturally determined judgments, are never in a position to look upon themselves impartially, not even to determine their own impartiality. We can imagine a universal concept of beauty and relate it to the mind, but that leads only to that position of cultural arrogance and intolerance Herder satirizes when he makes the comments that are invariably misread as documenting his lapse into racism – "That Negroes are the brothers of the apes is manifest not only in their lips but also in their bodies as a whole, and even more so in their spirit" (*HAW* 35). To see the irony in this statement one need not read the later denial (in *Ideas*) that "negros" are in any way related to apes – one need only study the structure of Herder's argument. For immediately following this declaration Herder turns to Winckelmann, in order to make the point that the Germans themselves are far removed from their own ideal of beauty and thus not qualified to make judgments of beauty: "If our northern Nature cannot bring the beauty of the body to full perfection, then she cannot also perfect the feeling and refined sense for beauty" (*HAW* 35). From the perspective of the gold standard in beauty, the Greek body, the German body – and hence the German mind – are of inferior nature, and thus scarcely in a position to make universally valid judgments about beauty. In other words: Nothing I have said about beauty so far is reliable, because it is a German speaking. Herder then closes the essay by suggesting that, if the illusion of beauty gives pleasure, why burst the bubble? Sikka completely misses the irony in this essay when she cites it as an example of the dangerous proximity to racism in some of Herder's ideas. This essay does not, as she claims, support "a hierarchical, biologically based typology of the human species."[35] Instead, it plays out in subtle irony the contradictions at the heart of a biological determination of beauty.

What Herder acts out in this essay is how the problem of evaluating cultural difference in anthropological and aesthetic terms as well as in terms of a philosophy of the history of humanity is heightened by the discovery of the new world. In his *Journal*, Herder brings this problem back to Europe. The initial impetus for this is the experience of the sea as a natural field, an anti-territory alien to the territorial divisions that mark the nation states of Europe. This experience causes him to question the idea that political entities like states can express a natural division of humanity. The sea, he observes, is in itself not marked with the national characteristics of the coasts that bound it: "It makes no difference whether these are Courlandish, Prussian, Pomeranian, Danish, Swedish, Norwegian, Dutch, English or French waters; as we navigate today it is just sea everywhere" (*HJV* 235). The objectifying discourses of his day work against the mythological impulses by removing the signs of human life from territory. "In this respect the navigation of the ancients was different: it showed the coasts and different species of human beings [*Menschengattungen*]" (*HJV* 235; translation modified).[36] *Aisthesis* allows Herder to see a world without political division, but the work of aesthetics requires a search for appropriate forms to express the natural order of human cultural diversity. And yet, in the absence of myth, how is he to interpret what he sees without the written word to contain it? As a traveller, he laments the absence of travelogues or other books that might allow him to experience the distant shores he visits in a manner more meaningful than is accorded by the abstract descriptions of views and observations so common in his day. "I wanted to call the travel writers to my aid so that I could meditate about the coasts of each land just as though I could see them; but this too was in vain. I found nothing on the ship but lists of landfalls and saw nothing but distant coasts" (*HJV* 235).

The travelogue Herder has in mind would be the kind that Christoph Friedrich Nicolai was soon to produce, meticulous accounts based on direct experiences of foreign places. But what he finds instead is a continuation of the rationalist idea that new experience can be understood in terms of what is logically possible, and represented in ocular tables. Against this, Herder proposes a series of "political sea-dreams" (*HJV* 304), in which he tries to imagine nations as natural, living entities, expressing the true culture of a people without the straightjackets of nation states.[37] True culture consists "not merely in giving laws, but in the formation of customs and morals [*Sitten bilden*]. What can laws, or imported foreign principles of law, amount to without customs and morals [*Sitten*]?" (*HJV* 308; translation modified). What law and culture have in common is their struggle with self-expression. Law is like the geographical cohesion of the nation – it can express either a foreign imposition of principle or the natural development of a nation. He asks "what seeds lie dormant" in the spirit of the peoples of Europe that will grant to them "a mythology, a poetry, a living culture," and "how, when, and by what agency" this might come about (*HJV* 306). Catholicism is not in a position to impose self-development on the nations. Instead, it seems, the very formulation of this question is to provide the model of living development Herder envisages for these nations. This leads him in pursuit of a scientific historiography, according to which the future of Europe might be deduced from "the conditions of the present-day world and on the analogy of past centuries" (*HJV* 307). This kind of historiography would be able to isolate the "true culture of a people" (*HJV* 308) and describe how it has expressed itself.

As he sketches the bare outlines for such a historiography, Herder finds himself trying to identify the essential spiritual or intellectual influences of the European nations, and once again he touches on some of his favourite themes. Prussia, he explains, has suffered under the Francomania of Frederick the Great. The Hanseatic cities have lost their entrepreneurial spirit, and have become like Riga, a city divided, unable to reconcile its petty political differences and manage its affairs for the good of its citizens. Holland was "a poor, needy, industrious republic" which "raised itself out of its marshes," to become the economic miracle of Europe (*HJV* 320). "Everyone learned from the Dutch; the same spirit spread everywhere: to England with its Navigation Acts, to France, Sweden, Denmark, etc." (*HJV* 320). And yet, Holland too is "on the verge of declining, though naturally only by slow degrees" (*HJV* 320). Herder recognizes the systemic economic problem in the balance of world trade, and forecasts that Holland will become less a trader in goods and more a trader in money, while England will perhaps succumb to its national debt, unable to bear the burden of its American colonies and its competition with other nations. But what concerns him more is that the commercial spirit, upon which Holland as a nation has grown, is itself inherently flawed. It sets structures in place that restrict the innovative and entrepreneurial impulses out of which it emerged. He does not say so here, but we may assume that he is also thinking of his critique of the world market in luxury goods, expressed in *On Diligence*. Herder allows his mind to wander here, and he identifies a similar dynamic of internal decay in the age of Enlightenment. In sermonizing tones, he chides his own age of so-called reason: "Enlightenment is never an end, but always a means; if it becomes the former it is a sign that it has ceased to be the latter" (*HJV* 326). The encyclopedia project of Diderot and D'Allembert is cited as the prime example of this process.

He then turns his attention to France, whose empire and perceived decline interested him more than that of any other European nation. Here, and in letters to friends, he paints a picture of an empire past its prime. When he tells Hamann in August 1769 that the king has just dissolved the East India Company, he mocks the French penchant for putting a positive spin on all royal acts (*HBG* 1,164). On 4 November, commenting on the Russian defeat of the Turkish army in the wake of the Polish civil war, he tells his old friend, the customs officer Begrow, that nothing can resist the Russian fleet, "neither France nor the Turkish sea" (*HBG* 1, 173). In his eyes, France's century, the century of Louis, the age of the French Enlightenment, has come to an end, and "the nation is now living on the ruins" (*HJV* 328). He feels that the French have nothing more to contribute to intellectual and cultural life; their works have become superficial, mannered, and all that is left is a certain code describing what counts as good taste. He speaks of a "chilling of the imagination and feeling" (*HJV* 333), a whittling away of true inspiration in both the arts and politics, until all that is left is an empty sense of "political honour."[38] But what concerns him more than anything else is a conviction that the French language bears an intrinsic penchant for abstraction, thus predisposing it to the kind of rationalism he so despised. "The Frenchman knows nothing of the reality of metaphysics and cannot comprehend that there is anything real in it" (*HJV* 334). The result is a culture of taste, of superficiality. We can see what Herder has in mind. This superficial remove from its own cultural ground is what will prepare the way for French manners to be transported to other European nations, where they can lead a second, hollow life as empty forms into which local cultures are forced. "How can the French manner be imitated in German? It cannot – so much the less since we know little of this monarchy, these courtly conditions, this honneur in literature;

since we cannot have these things and, where we do have them, buy them at a loss" (*HJV* 34). In this way, Herder has taken his political meditations on French political culture back to an aesthetics of culture, and is restating in political terms his earlier stance on rationalism.[39]

But Herder was not only taking a stance on aesthetics, he was attempting to rethink cultural domination itself. As he looked to France, he recognized that some French intellectuals were struggling with the same ideas he was beginning to formulate on the topic of cultural, political, and economic domination. There is good reason to believe that when Herder arrived in France in July 1769, Diderot was just in the process of commencing his collaboration with the Abbé Raynal on the latter's monumental *Histoire des deux Indes* (History of the Two Indias),[40] in which he (Diderot) develops a subtle perspective on European imperialism, one that would prove highly influential on subsequent writers.[41] In his thinking about imperialism and colonialism, Diderot appears to prefigure the position that Kant will later develop in his discussion of *jus cosmopoliticum* (*Weltbürgerrecht*) in paragraph 62 of the first part of the *Metaphysik der Moral* (Metaphysics of Morals, 1797).[42] In a way, this is a continuation of the *doux commerce* idea, and Herder found it attractive to a certain extent – particularly when he thought about cultural exchange. In the first collection of *Fragments* he observes that "the literature of foreign peoples and languages has often been introduced to other nations like a foreign colony. It was unavoidable that this mixing of ideas, customs, ways of seeing and thinking, of languages and sciences would all take on a different form, and that if we follow literature through the ages and the peoples and the languages it appears as a true Proteus" (*HSW* 2, 19). The new structure of the world economy and the rapid distribution of news in print media ensured that European activity in the New World would from now on always be closely aligned with what was happening in Europe.[43] But as literary and other writings began to spread, the consequences became ever more unpredictable.

Herder's early writings are marked by a fascination with the endless possibilities for cultural improvement, for uplifting the lives of the less fortunate inhabitants of underdeveloped regions of Europe, which for him meant first and foremost Livonia. In this respect, his faith in modernization, typical for an Enlightenment intellectual, remains unshaken. And yet, the idea of colonization based on a respectful interaction of cultures stands in such a sharp contrast to the historical reality he sees when he begins to study world imperialism, that it points to a serious problem in this approach. The problem is the same one he formulated in his critique of rationalism. How can we be sure the rational principles that guarantee the possibility of a just and beneficial colonialism are not the same ones that violently impose an abstract system on a foreign situation? This problem took Herder back to the obligations of the public intellectual.

When Herder left Riga, he intended to return, triumphant, fitted out with all the necessary learning, wisdom, and cosmopolitan flair he would need to fulfil his mission as an enlightened theologian, teacher, and civilizing missionary in the German colony there. In his mind, his intellectual identity was framed by the space between the town where he worked and the wide world. Herder was beginning to see himself as a public intellectual, whose responsibility was to foster the progress of his culture and thus of humanity. This implied a hope that the destructive forces of imperialist expansionism could be countered with what might be called the colonialism of improvement – a dissemination of cultural values that are in themselves opposed to economic and political exploitation. This optimistic faith in his own profession as a teacher, preacher, and a cultural emissary is important for Herder's understanding of colonialism. This is how he speaks of the difference between exploitation and improvement: "Livonia is a province, given over to foreigners! And many foreigners have enjoyed it in the past, but only in the merchants' way, in order to get rich from it; to me, also a foreigner, it is given for a higher purpose, that I may form [*bilden*] it! Let it be the purpose of my clerical office to make it the colony of a perfected evangelical religion: not by writing, by pen-warfare, but through practical work, through education [*Bildung*]" (*HJV* 237).

When Herder confronts his own aspirations as a public intellectual, but also his position as a stranger in a colony that has not yet become home, he begins to understand European activity in the expanding world as facing a fundamental choice between imperialist exploitation and cultural exchange. In this regard, as the above sentences indicate, modernization itself places a burden of moral responsibility on the individual. Self-enrichment and exploitation versus generosity of spirit, self-improvement, and the improvement of others (*Bildung* in its widest sense) – this is the choice facing the Enlightenment intellectual, and it will determine Herder's views on colonialism throughout his life. Even at this early stage in his life, he realizes that this choice impacts directly on cultural work. For Herder, the key to a responsible colonialism lies in cultural dissemination; the intellectual should become a public intellectual, working to ensure that trade and colonization are conducted for the sake of freedom, improvement, and modernization, not barbarism and exploitation. This strong sense of moral obligation is already clearly evident in the *Journal*.[44] One of its by-products is national and historical consciousness, but the consciousness of how the cross-fertilization of cultures can benefit humanity. Herder calls this a "theory of fable, a philosophical history of daydreams in the making, a genetic explanation of the wonderful and the romantic based on human nature, a logic of the powers of poetry; and – extended over all ages, all peoples, all types of legend from the Chinese to the Jews, from the Jews to the Egyptians, Greeks, Normans – how great, how useful a work!" (*HJV* 232). In his aspiring to such a philosophy, we see signs of interference from his own cultural horizon. The book he dreams of writing is *"a book for human and Christian education*!" (*HJV* 246). This book will contain a program of national education and improvement aimed at distilling what is best in the universal human spirit and disseminating it in German territory. The knowledge of the expanded world revitalizes the philosophical spirit, inspiring astonishment in the face of the world: "With what amazement I myself boarded the ship! Did I not at first glance find everything more wonderful, larger, more amazing, more fearful than afterwards, when everything was familiar to me ...?" (*HJV* 229). But astonishment alone is not sufficient. The journey into the world makes truth itself unstable, and creates – as if in a tautological and recuperating gesture – the need for the philosophical journey as a return to narration. And in the return to narration, wonder itself begins to destabilize the distinction between objective observation and poetic vision.

> Now take together this desire to see wonders and this disposition of the eye to find them at the first encounter: what becomes of true narratives? How everything becomes poetic! Without being able to or wishing to tell a lie, Herodotus becomes a poet [*Ohne daß man lügen kann und will, wird Herodot ein Dichter*]; and in how fresh a way he and Orphaeus and Homer and Pindar and the tragic poets can be read from this point of view. (*HJV* 229-30; translation modified)

Herder had been thinking about this organic determination of vision as a mediator between specific and universal qualities the previous year when he wrote in an unsent letter to the *Allgemeine historische Bibliothek* in Göttingen that "every human eye has always had its own point of view: every one throws forth the object before it in a projection, in its own way."[45] For this reason, he reads a historian like Herodotus as offering great insight into the views of his contemporaries.[46] But as he contemplates rereading the classics at sea, Herder has the idea that it might be possible to draw on the poetic vision of the classical authors as a way of crystallizing the common ground of perception out of the contingency of their historical vision. Travel complicates the semiotic process of reading the classics, but here lies its productive potential. As one's experience of the world expands, historical discourse reveals itself not simply as a distant moment of a dead culture. It begins to take on the qualities of a poetics of wonder, and this process is grounded in the physiological nature of seeing, as it is common to all human beings through the ages and in all places. The eye itself begins to function as the organ of restlessness, the means of testing knowledge of the world by pursuing not facts but wonder and desire.

This is also felt as a new way of thinking about action. Action, like vision, seems to require the poetic instinct in order to give it qualities that transcended the contingent. It becomes easier to draw on the imaginary scope of the entire world and to imagine intellectuals everywhere being forced to make the same kind of choices concerning the local and translocal dimensions of action. In Europe, these choices were complicated by the need to evaluate and act on the stories that were coming from her increasingly far-flung sphere of influence. The resultant emphasis on perspective led to a revitalization and reconceptualization of the idea that thought depends on embodied sensibility. Situated experience began to take on forms that had to be thought of in terms of the opposition between the local sphere of the writer's activity and the imaginary world outside. This rethinking of spatiality and action left indelible marks on Herder's thought, not least in the realm of historiography. In opposition to a general abstract historiography, an idealist imposition of pre-existing categories, Herder felt that the key to understanding local history was to allow the imagination to build upon lived experience, pointing the way to a general theory of humanity.[47] It is this that makes the link between travel and historiography – a link Herder had already begun to explore three years earlier in his essay *On the Change in Taste*. Here he notes that "the spirit of changes is the kernel of history, and whoever does not make it his main focus to separate out this spirit, so to speak, to put together in imagination the taste and the character of each age, and to travel through the various periods of the world events with the penetrating look of a traveller hungry to learn, he, like that blind man, sees human beings as trees, and consumes in history a dish of husks without a kernel, in order to ruin his stomach" (*HPW* 254).

This new way of thinking about lived experience and the geography of action spoke directly to the growing sense of cosmopolitanism that characterized intellectual life in Herder's day. As a concept, cosmopolitanism embodied Herder's persistent hope that there is a way for the intellectual to access the universal quality of humanity without losing sight of its diversity and plurality. Cosmopolitanism is also a model for thinking about communication. It promises a striving towards an ideal form of communication that is at the same time deeply rooted in the practicalities and contingencies of everyday life. The cosmopolitan intellectual, in Herder's conception, becomes the driving force in promoting unity-in-diversity, and countering the false claims of cultural imperialism, which is the enactment, through travel, of preconceived universal values, irrespective of the way local circumstances refuse to fit with these values. What is at stake in this distinction is the same problem he had faced when thinking about the forms of experience most appropriate to avoiding the rationalist preconception of experience. Herder responded according to the latest trends in philosophy which sought to remedy the abstractions of the book with experience and experimentation (identified with Newton), as well as with a new popular tone in philosophical discourse (identified with Rousseau). What Herder added to this was a somatics of thought that started to question the distinction between rationalism and empiricism itself. Just as one would aid a troubled digestive system through work and movement, so the modern reader's damaged soul might be healed through a changed mode of reading – through recognizing "the necessity of giving up my constant reading, or more precisely of being able to stroll while reading [*lesend schlendern*]" (*HJV* 408; translation modified). To read in this manner aligns the movements of the body with the movements of the mind. The problem is that you can run from your books, but not from your own body. Herder writes from Nantes: "Is it the sea or the change in air, I don't know what has become of my humours. They rot in my body and because of my body. I can't just await the end, and so tomorrow I shall cast myself into the postal coach for Paris" (to J.F. Hartknoch, October 1769, *HBG* 1, 169). In speaking of flight, Herder begins to speak the language of psychosomatics. Later, in his *Ideas* he will speak of the need to study "the semiotics of the soul" alongside "the semiotics of the body" (*HSW* 13, 187).

Herder's departure from Riga looked to him like an excursion away from the sedentary world of books in pursuit of a restless and unsettled experience of the world and of himself. In his *Journal* he wrote of what life might have been without book learning: "I would have avoided situations which confined my spirit, restricting it to a false, *intensive* knowledge of human nature, whereas it should rather have learned to know the world, men, societies, women and pleasure extensively – with the noble fiery curiosity of a youth, who enters the world and runs quickly and tirelessly from one experience to another" (*HJV* 209). Because of his understanding of the somatics of thought, the flight from books is also a return to books. Herder ends the journal with a short statement on books and reading, linking them directly to questions of mobility. In the closing paragraphs – part summary, part question mark, part wishful thinking – he introspectively dwells on the kind of reading that preserves the freshness of experience, and with it the vitality of youth, converting the hermeneutic act to practice, almost as if the books he was reading were not there. The remedy for his age's excessive reading practices is "reading little, reflecting a great deal and with a certain vigor and conciseness, and finally, practicing and applying what one has thought" (*HJV* 408). Such a dedicated reading requires a special pact between the writer and the reader, allowing the writer to preserve the immediacy of experience, while the reader must be capable of an act of concentration that will distil this immediacy for his own imagination. Herder laments the plight of those excessive readers (*den Vielbelesnen und Zuviellesenden*), who lack the vitality to read "as though they themselves saw, felt, experienced and applied what they were reading," or who inundate themselves with reading to the point where they become weakened or distracted and ultimately sacrifice their own selves (*HJV* 407).

In conclusion, he wonders if perhaps the purpose of his travels might not be a therapeutic remedy for false reading. In Herder's *Journal* there is a strong sense that reading is a life-defining activity, but one that must disappear behind the imperatives of other, more essential activities. Reading is a momentary inflammation of the imagination that comes from a carefully cultivated mobility of the body together with an opening up of shared pathways of thought, of shared contemplative walks (*Gedankenspaziergänge*). To read and to stroll, to travel in search of a cure for inappropriate acts of reading, to depart and return – these life-defining activities bring with them the obligations of the teacher. For Herder, the politically aware critic is not simply the servant of a pre-constituted public; his relationship to books is itself constitutive of the public. The closing sentences of the existing manuscript of the *Journal* are an exclamation of Herder's desire to be able to read books with a definitive certainty. "Then, when I take up a book, it will be only with full enjoyment and avidity – in such a way that I shall finally reach the point of being able to read a book *once* and know it entirely and *forever* – know it in my inmost soul, however I may be called upon to apply it and whatever form the application may take. Such reading must become conversation, half inspiration, or it will be nothing!" (*HJV* 409). To be a reader is to enter into dialogue with an imaginary community of other readers. It is the same activity as writing, which addresses the great German-speaking public. And the only way to negotiate these two worlds is through personal mobility. This is the direction Herder attempts to take his meditations on *Bildung* in the *Journal*, and it is also apparent in his letters. He writes to Hartknoch in August 1769: "You cannot imagine how many new things you see when you find your way out of a specific situation. That is the point outside the world that Archimedes sought in order to move the whole world, and for the situations that have prevailed in my life, that is my journey. My first task will be to attain legitimacy for prior experiences by a new and complete revision of my writings" (*HBG* 1, 156). In working on this Archimedean point, Herder was imagining a new community of readers.[48]

We have seen how Herder uses the concept of *Bildung* to speak of the organic development of the world through history (the universal history of the *Bildung* of the world), and to link his own intellectual development to the development of others. This was heightened by his dual function as a pastor and teacher in Riga, and in the *Journal* it will lead him to extensive plans concerning the curriculum. At all times, the general understanding of *Bildung* as organic development will work in concert with his epistemology, relating learning to the direct sensate experience on which knowledge is founded. This is important for his understanding of the act of reading as a task aimed at reclaiming experience and making it useful. In reading, the physicality of the reader and of the book itself appear in tension with the abstract ideas contained in the book, and one of the tasks of reading is to relate the two experiential spheres to one another. In highlighting the difference between sense impressions of the new and the body of knowledge that exists about new places and new experiences, mobility brings the interpretation of texts into dialogue with the analysis of sensory experience. In this way, it appears to provide the key to unlocking the abstractions of knowledge, revealing its experiential core. Mobility promises Herder an Archimedean point for critically examining his own world view, and in doing so, it provides him with a unique dialectic of temporality and spatiality. Mobility allows him to think of himself as a critical intellectual (and for Herder this will increasingly mean the critique of imperialism). It does this by showing how spatial and temporal displacement provide a critical perspective on the present, shifting the circumstances under examination into the realm of representation. What Herder begins to understand is that this displacement is more than just a shifted perspective enabled by mobility. The spatial and temporal displacement is the way representation works. To get at the heart of the present is to engage with the presenting strategies of representation.

France: The Politics of Representation

In the *Journal*, the engagement with strategies of representation takes many forms, perhaps the most important of which is historical representation. In his strikingly modern suggestions for school reform, Herder proposes leading his students from questions of geography to history via a deepening understanding of representation. "The natural history of various realms leads to geography, which is the most difficult at the very beginning. How can I use my visible position on earth as a point of departure? How is the natural appearance of an island, a peninsula, a land mass, etc. reproduced on a map?" (*HJV* 261). From questions like these, the student is to be led from the representation of geographical diversity to the knowledge of nature's unity, so he can discover "that each land has its own men and its own creatures; I learn to know them thoroughly, to set each in its place and to see the whole setting in which they all belong, the entire body of the earth" (*HJV* 262). This discovery of natural diversity and unity in geography is then repeated in the discovery of human diversity and unity:

> But a still larger field comes next – history. This must become even at this stage a history of peoples, and how can this be done? By remaining true to the pattern of the geography course, by telling only of the principal changes and revolutions through which the spirit of culture, knowledge, religion, the sciences, manners, the arts and inventions has passed between one [age of the] world and another; how much sank from view and was lost, while new things arose and propagated themselves; how one taste

> replaced another and maintained itself, and how the stream of time has always rolled on until it has reached our own age, the point at which we now stand. It can be seen that this history is nothing but a series of pictures in many categories; but in no category must a single dead, abstract idea be taught, or everything is lost. (*HJV* 264).

This history, derived from geography, is an empirical natural history of the diverse forms of humanity, but its aim is a representation of humanity unified. Herder is still not sure how this is to be verified, but when it comes to the curriculum, it can be achieved by assembling a chorus of histories of the nations that have been written by outstanding historians. Herder notes that "they can all profitably be used," even though "none of them can be used as it stands" (*HJV* 265). Instead, he declares that he "will not rest" until he has "a complete small compilation of the best in each kind," out of which he has made himself "a history of the human race" (*HJV* 267). But for his own purposes, the principle of common humanity is less clear, and it becomes less so as he expands on what he sees as the natural characteristics that have given the individual nations their diverse histories.

In the *Journal*, the test case of this view of historical representation is France, whose relationship to Germany is clearly understood as cultural imperialism. In the *Fragments*, Herder had been concerned to show that the kind of cultural transfer that was taking place from France to Germany, most notably in the theatre, was not only groundless when it came to actual experiences of Being, but detrimental to German cultural development. France had already lived through the age of maturity which Germany was, as Herder saw it, now entering. And even if it were seen to be on the same developmental stage, it was a plant growing on different ground from Germany, to use Herder's own metaphor, and the result was the false forms of expression he identified with the German imitation of French culture.[49]

The French empire may have been in ruins, but the German nations still needed to define their own culture through writing against the imitation of all things French.[50] This crucial difference also has a political correlate, expressed in the very different development of the French political system, whereby a centralized monarchy promoted a courtly culture of imitation and demonstrative social standing. In the *Journal*, he calls this "gallantry," "taste," and "manner," and he sees it as fundamentally opposed to the natural genius of a people. It is not concerned with portraying "tenderness and truthfulness of feeling but only its attractive side, preoccupied with its own mode of expression, its power of making conquests – thus did the gallantry of the French novel and the coquetry of French style develop" (*HJV* 350). Herder saw this language-thought-politics system as suppressing the natural development of the individual by curbing the inner spirit. "But because of this spirit of decorum the French have almost entirely lost their inner feeling [*innre Gefühl*]. Just as the regularity of their language is constantly distorted on this account, so that they never express themselves truthfully and bluntly, so in general decorum erects barriers for the mind [*Barrierre für den Geist*]. Their *vive le roi* is words – a mere expression, which they feel, as they feel everything, frivolously, without thinking, superficially, without any real basis; and they are happy in this – they praise him, serve him, do everything *pour le roi*" (*HJV* 360–1; translation modified). In these comments we see a partial explanation for Herder's later support·for the Revolution.

But the revolution will raise an issue that is potentially disruptive to his understanding of the language-thought-politics system in his early works. If it is possible to describe this system in the blanket terms he adopts in the *Journal* and elsewhere, how will he explain the forces which led to the Revolution? Where will he locate the impetus for the radical reversal of the political system, if not in some inner vitality of French thought? Did he fail to recognize this potential for revolutionary overthrow of an outmoded political system? For now, these questions seem not to have occurred to Herder, but they raise a consideration which should have troubled him, even in 1769. If the French language determines the shape of French philosophy, Herder seems to be condemning some of his favourite philosophers to a mannered, unnecessarily abstract, and ultimately an atrophied picture of life. He reads the *Encyclopédie* – "this very book, which the French regard as their triumph" – as "the principal sign of their decline. They have nothing to write, and so make *abrégés, dictionnaires, histoires, vocabulaires, esprits*, encyclopedias, etc. Original works are not produced" (*HJV* 327). Harrison takes this up when he observes that Herder fails to do justice to the complexity of French intellectual reactions to their nation's own history, and in particular to their own sense that the seventeenth century had been the age of French cultural glory and was now past.[51] If Herder had looked more carefully, he would have seen that the *Encyclopédie* is "the product of [a] society whose whole scheme of values is moving away from Louis XIV and toward bourgeois republicanism in politics, emancipation from tradition and authority in criticism and science, and emphasis on originality and sentiment in art: in short, toward the idea of a secular middle-class culture."[52]

It may seem that Herder is disregarding his own insights on historical method and basing his comments on an idealist scheme of historical development, instead of analysing observed phenomena. Herder is indeed running the risk of this kind of simplification of historical processes. This is because he believes history can be written as the history of cultural forms, even if these are tied up in a system that includes political structures and organizations. The reason he places his focus on the history of culture is that he is convinced that the most important interactions between nations takes place through the exchange and the cross-fertilization of cultural forms. Whenever Herder considers the development of humanity, he takes recourse to this idea. In the *Journal*, for example, he describes Montesquieu as "the man of all Frenchmen who has learned most from his friends the Romans and Orientals." And he goes on to note to himself the need to read more widely in order to gain an understanding of how the European tradition of borrowing from other cultures sheds light on cultural difference. "In this connection I will reread Saint-Foix's *Lettres Turques* and see how this delicate mind handles Orientalism! ... Then a glance at the Turkish spies, the Chinese, Jewish, Iroquois and barbarian letters, at the French heroic writings of oriental extraction, at the oriental tales in the English weekly papers, in Wieland, Sonnenfels, Bodmer in order to observe from all this the difference in the genius of languages" (*HJV* 356–7). Cultural difference is couched in the genius of different languages, and in their different stages of development. And as the different cultures interact and borrow from one another, cultural practice finds itself placed under a dual imperative. The genius of individual cultures needs to be respected, but cultural exchange is part of the development of universal humanity. This is felt by the individual writer as a tension between the need to write as a member of a linguistic group while at the same time writing outside this group in the name of humanity.

In his engagement with French culture, we see Herder taking a decisive step beyond existing ideas on what universality means for culture in the representation of human life, and this brings him to the topic of Greek art. When Hamann observed that things French were "as universal in our times as things Greek" had once been,[53] he was repeating the commonplace notion that Greek culture is the measuring rod for universality. But Herder, in his article on Shakespeare, which appeared in *On German Style and Art* in 1773, chides his contemporaries for believing it possible to reproduce Greek drama in a modern age, and states that it is hardly possible to think of a more perfect example of the futile attempts to emulate Greek theatre than those in present-day France. Having rejected Hamann's views on the poetic age as the pinnacle of history, Herder also finds himself objecting to his views on the universality of the Greeks. As we saw in his response to Hodges's paintings of the Tahitians, it is one thing to acknowledge the perfection of Greek culture, but another to use Greek representational form to render other cultures intelligible to contemporary Europe. This also coloured his reception of Johann Joachim Winckelmann, the influential archaeologist and art historian, who had been murdered in Trieste the year before Herder left Riga.[54] As Zammito notes, it is in his study of Winckelmann's revival of Greek aesthetics that "Herder set down his earliest methodological views on historical interpretation"[55] – what amounted to a rejection of any attempts to establish timeless a priori guidelines in favour of an empirical and pragmatic historiography.[56] In the 42nd *Letter on the Advancement of Humanity*, Herder asks: "We Germans wish to compare ourselves with the Greeks? And what would be the exact, unfalsified measure? And who would be the impartial judge?" (*HFA* 7, 225).

Writing on Winckelmann's *Gedanken über die Nachahmung der Griechischen Werke in der Malerei und Bildhauerkunst* (Reflections on the Imitation of Greek Works in Painting and Sculpture, 1756), Herder criticized what he saw as Winckelmann's tendency to play down the historicity of Greek art – its emergence from the art of the Egyptians, and its decline and appropriation by the Romans. Winckelmann presents Greek art as if it had invented itself, whereas Herder wants to take account of the historical ties out of which it emerged. This means understanding that the Greek depiction of the body was itself influenced by Egyptian forms. In spite of his great achievements, Winckelmann had failed to recognize the imperative to historicize artistic production. If art history and artistic production are to do justice to Winckelmann's insights, they will have to ask not how to reproduce the forms of Greek art, but how to realize its ideals in today's world (as Winckelmann did, for example, in his own drawings: see figure 3.5).

Herder wanted the artist and the art historian to acknowledge the distance between his own times and times past. In his Shakespeare essay, Herder puts it like this: "As everything in the world changes, so Nature, the true creator of Greek drama, was bound to change also.

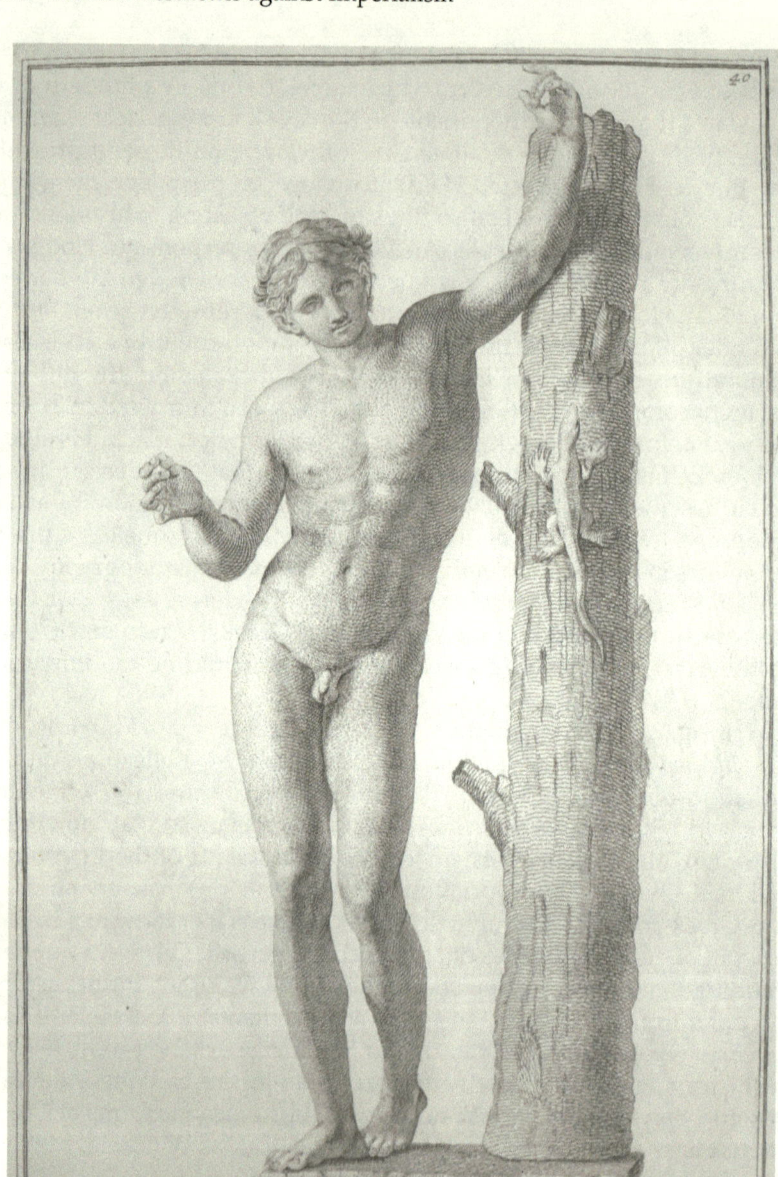

3.5 Giovanni Battista Casanova, *Apolito Sauroktonos*. From Winckelmann, *Monumenti antichi inediti*, ed. Pietro Paolo Montagnani-Mirabili (Rome: A spese dell'autore, 1821).[57]

The Greek worldview, manners, the state of the republics, the tradition of the heroic age, religion, even *music, expression,* and *the degrees of* [theatrical] *illusion* changed" (*HAW* 294). The problem with cultural imitation is that it remains abstract and superficial in its adoption of classical forms. By contrast, the classical achievements in literature and philosophy can only be replicated by way of analogy, which is to say by developing organic forms of expression appropriate to modernity. Classicism, on the other hand, becomes an empty set of rules, or as Herder observed in his "Ausweg zu den Liedern fremder Völker" (Access to the Songs of Foreign Peoples, 1778), the Greeks have to be seen "with healthy eyes for the people they were," and not for "rules pinned to the wall, idealistic caricatures of the world and posterity" (*HFA* 3, 64). The correlate in Herder's own time to this idealization of Greek art was the spread of French cultural imperialism through the cultural politics of the nobility. Whereas the French suppressed the remnants of their own living culture in their emulation of the Greeks, modern European nations run the risk of suppressing the living cultures of the new world by subjecting them to alien systems of value, instead of understanding them in their essence, "as human beings, who possess language, souls, and sensitivity" (*HFA* 3, 59). Commenting on this passage, Menges states that only "if we change our perspective and take this inside approach, while discarding the 'babble' of 'European fools,' will we do justice to their sensuous, 'uncivilized' songs, which will lead us back not only to *their* identity but to our own as well. For the overarching connection between the savages and us is our common humanity."[58] This is a critical imperative placed on the reading of historical and geographical difference.

In the analysis of historical and geographical difference, the critical intellectual's task becomes both semiological and formative. The semiological work is to uncover the traces of an original way of relating to Being. The formative work is to develop these traces into a general principle which can be translated for the context in which the critic is writing. The work of writing is closely allied to historical insight, and its guarantee lies in the nature of human language.[59] The course of Herder's *Journal* traces this process – it is an act of language, embracing a departure from the confines of sedentary life, out into a world enriched by the imagination, returning to a sense of community strengthened by the knowledge of universal humanity – an identity based on history and territory. The universality of certain fundamentals in human experience allows the author to set out from the dry confines of an inadequate library, to experience a world stretched out between mythological and scientific books, and to return to a mode of writing where books exist for genuine improvement, for promoting a dialectic of world culture and local identity.

The understanding of cultural specificity and cross-cultural communication resulting from his first-hand encounters with French culture had a lasting and decisive effect on Herder's thought.[60] What finally emerged was the concept of humanity, which was to become so important in his later writings, culminating in the *Letters on the Advancement of Humanity*, written in the 1790s. Here, and in all of Herder's later works humanity will become the central concept for thinking about the world's cultures in terms of their unity and their diversity. Humanity would later be called on to explain the balance of forces that both unify and diversify human life. Herder is already taking the first steps in that direction when he touches in the *Journal* on the manifestation of human restlessness, the urge for mobility that, in his opinion, makes human beings human, and when he tries to bring that into accord with the urge to settle and form communities.[61] Restlessness is the human face of the same natural force that causes the migration of fish, and it raises the question of humanity, because it holds the potential for cross-cultural communication. It is essential for Herder that this common H umanity be developed out of experiences of difference, not the kind of abstract rationalism he criticizes. The key is the way language inscribes the historical and geographical dimensions of human life into the individual psyche, but also into the group psyches of cultures. Doing justice to this involves what John Zammito calls "a rigorous, genetic-psychological examination of the 'history of human understanding' starting from the physiology of the human senses."[62] With this realization, Herder has now set himself firmly on the path to a philosophy of language and history in which the critique of imperialism will come to hold a pivotal position.

4 From the Location of Language to the Multiplicity of Reason

The Wild Peoples and the Origin of Language

By December 1769, Herder was ready to leave France. He was increasingly disillusioned in Paris, where he had trouble with the language, was running out of money, had no friends, and was disappointed to find that the reputation he enjoyed in the German-speaking world had not preceded him. Initially, he had intended to leave Paris and visit Italy, England, and Holland, but as his money dwindled he realized that his travels would have to be curtailed. He found his way to the Netherlands, then to Hamburg, where he met Lessing, and finally to Kiel, where, in April 1770, he was offered a position accompanying the Prince of Holstein-Eutin, the melancholic son of the Prince-Bishop of Lübeck on his *Bildungsreise* through Europe. Herder set out with his charge for Hamburg via Brussels and Amsterdam. According to design, he was to embark for Italy together with the prince, serving as a personal educator and mentor for the young man as he followed in the footsteps of so many other young members of the European nobility intent on rounding out their personalities and obtaining an education in art, culture, and history. The planned route to Italy took Herder to Darmstadt, where he met Caroline Flachsland, his future wife, then to Karlsruhe, where he discussed plans for an Institute of the Arts and Sciences with the Margrave Carl Friedrich of Baden-Durlach. But Herder never left Germany, since a long-standing eye ailment took him to Strasbourg, where he underwent surgery. The treatment, which proved to be much more complicated and more painful than anticipated, kept Herder in Strasbourg long enough to attract a number of visitors and admirers. One of these was the young poet and student of law Johann Wolfgang Goethe.

The two soon became friends, and, on Herder's advice, Goethe began to collect folk songs from the Alsace region, wandering the villages and noting text and melody as they were sung to him by the local inhabitants. In 1771 he wrote Herder from Frankfurt, telling him, "I've brought along from the Alsace twelve more songs which I captured on my sorties straight from the throats of the oldest mothers" (*GWA* 4/2, 2). And the way Goethe thought about his own poetry began to be strongly influenced by Herder's belief that folk songs were best read as a cultural documentation of how, since the beginnings of time, humanity had interacted rationally and deliberately with the natural environment. Like an ethnographer, Herder was adopting a practical approach to culture and beginning to explore cultural practice as a matter for empirical research into local peculiarities. Goethe's interest in Herder's theory of *Volksdichtung* familiarized him with the idea that the clarity of natural expression lost by the refined nations was still vibrant in the songs of cultures still untouched by modernity (Herder calls them *die Wilden* – the savages or, literally, *the wild ones*). In contrast to the refined world's "artificial, scientific way of thinking, speaking and writing,"[1] the *Volkslied* represented the life of the wild ones, who always visualize what they want to say "sensuously, clearly, and dynamically" (*HSW* 5, 181). Herder's view on these cultures already included the inhabitants of the New World, such as "the *Five Nations in North America*" (*HSW* 5, 166). Herder's lesson from the German *Volkslied* was not one of primitivism, but of cultural diversity and world community:

> You laugh at my enthusiasm for savages almost like Voltaire laughed at Rousseau for saying he took such pleasure in walking on all fours; don't believe I therefore despise our ethical and cultivated merits, whatever they may be. Humankind is destined to undergo a progression of scenes, of forms, of mores: woe betide the person who dislikes the scene in which he is to appear, act, and live out his life! But woe betide also the philosopher of humanity and mores whose own scene is the only one, and who also always mistakes the first one for the worst. If all belong together to the whole of the advancing play, in each one a new, quite remarkable side of humanity is manifest. (*HSW* 5, 168)

The reference to Voltaire is a sideswipe at a view of history that Herder has found to be unsustainable: what John Zammito calls a "complacent Eurocentric presentism, the beginning of what we know as 'Whig history,' practiced in significant measure as well by Montesquieu and even Hume."[2] From his earliest writings, the best way Herder knew to unsettle this presentism was to shift perspective to what was known about the inhabitants of the New World. Already in April 1769, as he was preparing to leave Riga, Herder had written to Moses Mendelssohn, spelling out his discontent with any attempts to rank the apparent achievements of European science and philosophy above those of the wild peoples:

> For this world everything is perfected; but for the future, nothing, nothing in the world is perfected. First of all the utterly diverse people! O! For the enjoyment of this world they may all be good in their way, *Laplander* and *Hottentot*, *Newton* and the *orang-utan*, but for development towards a future one? For the development of the soul's powers out towards it? Not a one! That's why Newton achieved as little as Franke,[3] and Franke as Voltaire, and Voltaire as the Patagonians. The view opening outwards *towards local configurations* offers up *a novel of eternity*, which everyone must *compose* differently. (*HBG* 1, 141)

It seems that, at the very moment when Herder was displacing the problems of epistemology onto the philosophy of history, he began to understand that history will present him with an entirely new set of problems that were different from but related to those he had uncovered in his encounter with Kant, Wolff, and Baumgarten. Herder is emphasizing the chasm between ideals of the future and the potential in present-day societies to meet those ideals. As soon as the philosopher begins to recognize that future ideals are indeed ideals, then the fact of present-day diversity makes it impossible to state what exactly it is about life in the present – not only among the wild peoples, but in civilized society – that might unfold into the future he dreams of. This is a remarkable early statement of the need to conserve diversity and what we would today call multiculturalism. Since we do not know what benefits humanity will derive from any one culture, we need to do everything we can to preserve its diversity, while developing a correct understanding of the forces that create unity in diversity. But it is also a statement about how the past can be used to address the present. Herder is well aware of the problems arising out of the discrepancy between the past as it reveals itself to the historian and the conceptualization of the continuum that binds the past and the present.[4]

Already in his earliest writings, Herder understood language to be the medium of this continuum. Starting with his earliest works, he sees language as the force that gives human life its totality and diversity. This conception of language is sketched out in his *Treatise on the Origin of Language*, written in Strasbourg in the closing months of 1770, then submitted to the Königlich Preussische Academie der Wissenschaften in response to the prize question for 1769: "Supposing men abandoned to their natural faculties, are they in a position to invent language? And by what means do they come to this invention?" This question had been occupying many European scholars in one form or another over the past two decades, resulting in a number of important publications, which Herder knew well. These included the writings of Locke and Adam Smith in England, Condillac and Rousseau in France, and Hamann, Michaelis, and Moses Mendelssohn in Germany. Discussions touched on diverse topics, such as the relationship between speech and sign systems, vowels and consonants, physiological and cognitive dimensions of language, animal and human forms of expression, and divinity and language.[5] The most important dimensions of this debate for Herder were the linguistic mediation between sensory perception and abstraction, the physiology of speech, and the idea of an origin and development of language as it stands in relationship to the historical development of humanity. In June 1771, the academy awarded him its academic prize for the year 1770. When the essay was published in 1772, it was Herder's first work published under his own name.

The prize of the Prussian Academy was intended to elicit decisive positions on the role that language played in the development of the mind and of rational thought. Most immediately, the academy wanted a stance on the positions taken by Pierre-Louis Moreau de Maupertuis (whom Frederick the Great had appointed president of the academy in 1746) and the pastor and demographer Johann Peter Süssmilch. Maupertuis, following Condillac and Locke, believed it was possible to describe the process by which language was invented out of natural human faculties.[6] Süssmilch, by contrast, believed that logic disallowed this conclusion, leaving divine intervention as the only possible explanation.[7] Through his previous work on the genesis of language, Herder found himself almost automatically writing against Süssmilch – or at least the position he decided to ascribe to Süssmilch.[8] First of all, his commitment to analytic method convinced him that Süssmilch's argument could not stand. Instead of approaching language through Wolffian logic, Herder wanted to identify the principle of emergence of language through a careful analysis of the empirical evidence on language. In keeping with his studies so far, this evidence was taken to be biological, anthropological, and historical.

Early on in the *Treatise on the Origin of Language* Herder begins to list the ethnographic evidence against the idea of a single divine origin of language, casting his reference points as widely as "the foot of the *Cordilleras* or in the snow of the *Iroquois*, in *Brazil* or on the *Caribbean Islands*," (*HPW* 69) but also taking account of the remaining indigenous peoples of Europe. Herder understands his investigations into the history of specific cultures as encounters with the divine force that makes the history of humanity, but this force is given substance in human activity itself. This is why he refuses to allow historical specificity to disappear behind the universality of human history, no matter how this universality might be conceived. Humanity exists in balance between thought and action, divine creation and human recreation, between a common purpose and its diverse manifestations. For this reason, it makes no sense to conceive of divine intervention as the cause of language.

In rejecting Süssmilch's position, Herder found himself inheriting a problem that had characterized theories of the natural invention of language for some time already: the belief that communities speaking natural languages were somehow suspended on a lower level of cognitive development than those more civilized speakers of French, English, and German. Locke had argued just such a position, comparing "children, idiots, savages, and the grossly illiterate," all of whose thought lacks universal principles. "Their notions are few and narrow, borrowed only from those objects they have had most to do with, and which have made upon their senses the frequentest and strongest impressions. A child knows his nurse and his cradle, and by degrees the play-things of a little more advanced age: And a young savage has, perhaps, his head filled with love and hunting, according to the fashion of his tribe. But he that from a child untaught, or a wild inhabitant of the woods, will expect these abstract maxims and reputed principles of science, will, I fear, find himself mistaken. Such kind of general propositions are seldom mentioned in the huts of Indians, much less are they to be found in the thoughts of children, or any impressions of them on the minds of naturals."[9]

It may seem to follow from Herder's commitment to analytic method that language itself had developed analytically, in just the manner described by Locke: from initial encounters with sensory perceptions or images, and initial actions in the world of objects, language had progressed from a purely descriptive and instrumental function to become increasingly abstract. But, as we shall see, Herder's understanding of what it means to engage in abstraction is different from Locke's, and the language of the wild peoples provides the pivotal point of difference. Locke's progression from a primitive sensualism to a civilized capacity for abstraction was very much in vogue at the time, and it seemed to be confirmed by studying the languages of those who appeared more primitive. This speculative ethnolinguistic study of "primitive" peoples was a favourite topic in the eighteenth century.[10] It promoted a view of the languages that supported the increasingly popular image of natural man.[11] As Anthony Pagden has pointed out, speculative ethnolinguistics coupled to theories of the origin of language played an important role in fashioning the figure of Adario[12] as a man who was both wise and innocent at the same time.[13] The position that emerged from the Lockean theories of language would have the noble savage closer to the truth, since he responded directly to sensory information, and yet at the same time further from the truth, since this very spontaneity of expression prevented him from abstraction and hence from universal knowledge.[14]

The Multiplicity of Reason and the Nature of Community

It is precisely at this point that Herder proposes an alternative view on language acquisition, culture, and the origin of language. By employing what Gaier calls a "system of theories" (*HFA* 1, 1284), he will demonstrate the perceived weaknesses in current debates around the origins of language, and at the same time propose a truly original alternative. His starting point is the grounds that make it possible to speak of human language as if it were related to animal language. This ground is given by physiological impulses to respond to sensations with direct expressions, an impulse which humans and animals have in common. This provides the famous starting point of Herder's essay: "Schon als Tier, hat der Mensch Sprache" (Already as an animal, the human being has language; *HFA* 1, 697, *HPW* 65). The "schon" (already) in this sentence can be interpreted either analytically (if we speak of human responses in their physiological dimension, we are already speaking of the animal nature of human life); or genetically (humanity arose out of a condition of animality, and in its origins, the human animal was already human). While the former is foregrounded in the essay, the genetic and historical interpretation is always present, if only in the background. To speak about origins is to project the analysis of language acquisition onto historical speculations about the development of humanity. This would seem at first to confirm the position held by the followers of Locke. But Herder departs from Locke, Condillac, and Maupertuis in important ways. To start with, he sees language acquisition as a physiological process driven by passion, not by need. The impulse of passion is one of communication, which means that, in the physiological drive to language, nature no more created us "as isolated rocks" than as "egoistic monads" (*HPW* 65). Instead, he speculates on the possibility of demonstrating psychological processes neurologically, and concludes that, if this were possible, it would demonstrate that stimulation produces communication.[15] Physiologically, or neurologically, the animal cries of passion are directed at "other creatures. The struck string performs its natural duty: it sounds!, it calls to a similarly feeling Echo – even when noone is there, even when it does not hope or expect to be answered by one" (*HPW* 66).

But if this communicative nature of language is indeed shared with animals, that is, if it is physiologically immanent in expressive organisms, then it remains to discover what distinguishes human communication. Here, both Condillac and Rousseau failed to understand the wide chasm that language cuts between humans and animals. Condillac speaks of animals as if they were human, while Rousseau speaks of humans as if they were animals (*HPW* 77). Herder's response is that, where animals react instinctively to stimuli, the "whole disposition" of human nature is "awareness," or what he calls *Besonnenheit*. This term is introduced "in order to escape the confusions with specific forces of reason, etc." (*HEW* 84). *Besonnenheit* is usually translated as "reflection," which is slightly misleading, since that could imply the forces of reason Herder wishes to unsettle. Michael Mack's "mindfulness" is probably better.[16] *Besonnenheit* means awareness of the sensual world, reflective awareness, consciousness, "the mind's dependence on the senses."[17] It is "the reflective capacity that enables us to put into words, and thus bring to the level of explicit awareness, the impressions of a living being embedded in a reality first registered through senses and affects";[18] that is to say, it includes the Socratic moment of *thaumazeín*, of speechless wonder, and of speaking about wonder. Taken literally, *Besonnenheit* names the condition of having thought about stimuli.[19] This is an innate condition of the human organism, and it sets it apart from the animal organism. The condition of having thought about stimuli is, as Jürgen Trabant puts it, "a cognitive need," and as such it is "totally different from the animal need to communicate." It follows that "language originates as specifically human only out of the semantico-cognitive relationship to the world, and hence – and this is what is decisive and radically new in Herder – thought is the word."[20] To this may be added that thought is embodied thought, and that it is thus always located thought.

Language may arise from a direct perception of objects, but a careful reconstruction of the psychological and somatic processes this involves would demonstrate that this process is not prior to reason and abstraction. The reconstruction Herder famously proposes involves the image of a lamb as it presents itself to the eye. The inquisitive human observer is not distracted by any instinctive impulse that binds the lamb to it. This is left to the "hungry, scenting wolf," the "blood-licking lion," or the "aroused ram" (*HPW* 88). Human desire is a desire for knowledge, and it seeks instead a "mark" or a sensual quality (*Merkmal*) that can distinguish the lamb and hold it as a form in memory: "His soul, operating with awareness [*seine besonnen sich übende Seele*], seeks a characteristic mark [*Merkmal*] – *the sheep bleats*! – his soul has found a characteristic mark" (*HPW* 88). In Herder's example, this quality is not visual, it is auditory. It distances the listener from the object in a contemplative manner, and it internalizes the sign of its presence. As a result, it serves to present the sheep in its absence. Thus internalized, the distinguishing mark of the sheep becomes a word and a sign (*ein innerliches Merkwort*). "The human being recognized the sheep by its bleating; this was a *grasped sign* on the occasion of *which the soul distinctly recalled to awareness* [*besann*] *an idea*. What else is that but a word? And what is the *whole of human language* but a *collection of such words*?" (*HPW* 89).

In commenting on this paragraph, Jürgen Trabant underscores the "sequence of key expressions" that lead from the initial perception via sound to the emergence of language itself: "mark, inner mark, name of the sheep, sign, word, human language."[21] By way of *Besonnenheit*, language is directed by and directs reason and abstraction. The emergence of language in the act of naming binds sensory perception to the concept of the object without the interest accompanying instinctual drives. What this means is that a certain cognitive distance, a disinterest, which is the first step to abstraction, is a component of the earliest stages of language acquisition. At the same time, this proposes a binding of the freedom of thought with sense perception in a way that anticipates the problems addressed in Kant's third critique, and proposes an answer that remains implicit and unexamined there – the idea of commonality.[22] The thought/language system combines the cognitive structuring of sense perception with freedom of thought. It does this in a single capacity, which Herder opposes to instinct and names freedom (*HPW* 82). This predisposition to language/thought is so deeply embedded in the human organism that it makes no sense to speak of the human condition without it. "If, that is to say, reason is no compartmentalized, separately effective force but an orientation of all forces that is distinctive to his species, *then the human being must have it in the first condition in which he is a human being*. This awareness must reveal itself in the first thought of the child, just as in the case of the insect [it had to be evident] that it was an insect" (*HPW* 85). The human child does not grow into the condition of thinking about stimuli, it is born with a biological drive to activate this condition, and to tie it to expressive communication in language. It is born mute but possessing hidden powers of language in the place of instinct. And, as Herder will note in a sideswipe at Rousseau, it makes no sense to speak of reason as a potential that may or may not be actualized.[23] It is a potential that can be abstractly distinguished from its actualization, but this distinction has no bearing on the life of the organism. "It is sophistry that the use can transform an ability into force, something merely possible into something actual; if force is not already present, then of course it cannot be used and applied" (*HPW* 86). Herder draws on his analysis in the *Essay on Being*, and identifies the cause of language acquisition as an unnamed force giving rise to logical thought in the moment of sensory perception (*HMA* 1, 582). Potential and actualization are part of the same power or force. This is the move that Herder has to make, as he had done in the *Essay on Being*, to counter the rationalist argument that pre-structures thought before experience. Instead, Herder proposes what Menges calls a "simple and yet revolutionary" idea: Because cognition is based on language, "every identification is linked to a process of differential signification that sets it apart from others. That setting apart, however, is essential for it to become identical with itself. For just as presence arrives only through absence, so does identity define itself only through difference from others."[24]

Herder finds himself arguing that reason and its cause become one and the same thing in the moment of sensory perception, where Being is apprehended. At the same time, he insists that the form of language itself (i.e., the grammar and lexica of the individual languages) is not innate. But how can this be? If the potentiality of language is innate (and it is called *Besonnenheit*), and if the capacity for reason cannot be distinguished in practice from its actualization, then why are the rationalists wrong when they argue for an a priori, internal structure of language? And, for the immediate purposes of his prize essay, how could he then argue against Süssmilch's hypothesis of the divine origin of language? This apparent contradiction will force Herder to return to the problem of linguistic multiplicity, which, it will be recalled, he had already addressed in *On Diligence*. There, he had argued that the different languages emerge through different environmental and historical influences at different times and in different places. This same idea is now revisited as a way of demonstrating that the condition of humanity, which is the potential for language, takes on many forms depending on environment and history. Herder's point is that the analytic distinction between the capacity for language and language itself is not wrong; it is simply misleading, in that it separates in logic what cannot be separated in practice. It gives the impression that there is an aspect of thought which is different from language. But this is not the case: "Without language the human being has no reason, and without reason no language" (*HPW* 91). What is more, as he had shown in *On Diligence*, language formalizes reason in relation to environment and tradition. And reason is only ever accessible as linguistically formalized reason.

As the prize essay unfolds, the full significance of Herder's understanding of reason becomes clear. The diverse language communities of humanity are not simply actualizing a fundamentally uniform, single kind of reason in different ways; the speakers of the world's languages, through linguistic practice, are enacting the same drive to knowledge/language, but in doing so, they are producing different yet equally valid forms of reason. This idea struggles for recognition in Herder's essay. It threatens to be submerged beneath the argument that there is a natural life somehow closer to the invention of language, less sophisticated than European civilization, and thus lower down on the developmental scale. The diversity of human development he sees throughout the world leads him to draw conclusions about the beginnings of language. He asks: "But do we not, then, already know human beings in such various ages, regions, and levels of development [*Bildung*] that this so transformed great drama would teach us to infer with greater sureness back to its first scene?" (*HPW* 137; translation modified). Here the meaning of *Bildung* as organic coming-to-form struggles with its other meaning: refinement, progress, education. Speaking as if there is indeed a single universal reason, he asks: "Do we not, then, know that precisely in the corners of the earth where reason is still least cast into the fine, societal, many-sided, scholarly form, sensuality and primitive cleverness and cunning and courageous efficacy and passion and spirit of invention – the whole undivided human soul – still operates in the most lively way? Still operates in the most lively way – because, not yet brought to any long-winded rules, this soul still ever lives whole in a circle of needs, of dangers, of pressing demands, and hence ever feels new and whole. There, only there, does the soul reveal forces to form [*bilden*] language for itself and to develop it [*fortzubilden*]!" (*HPW* 137–8; translation modified). The condition of wildness here described could be read as a more primitive precursor to civilization, or as an alternative moment of language-acquisition and therefore an alternative moment of reason. One of the underlying and unspoken obstacles Herder struggles with in this essay is untangling these two possible meanings of wildness. This cannot be done without a clearer picture of how nature's force relates to the historical and geographical unfolding of the human condition.

In the *Treatise*, this problem takes the form of distinguishing what is known about wild peoples and their languages from what can be said about the state of nature. Already in the opening pages of Herder's essay, the cries of the wild peoples are described as closer to nature, more like the expressions of animals, more the result of passion and less of reason. In this way, they seem to be "closer to the origin," and can thus provide insight into the childhood of humanity in a way that is not accessible to the "child of reason and society," who is so "refined, civilized and humanized" (*HPW* 68). Herder draws extensively on ethnographic, anthropological, and travel writing to support his claim that the "dances of war and religion, the songs of mourning and happiness, of all savages" is animated by the same natural impulses that brought to being the elegies, psalms, poems, and songs of "the oldest Eastern languages" (*HPW* 69). As we have seen, his points of reference are the languages of those who dwell in the New World. This serves as a good argument against Süßmilch's claim that "*the sounds of all languages known to us can be reduced to some twenty letters*," which in turn is taken as proof of the "divine order" of language (*HPW* 69). Herder counters this with the point that the natural sounds are sounds of passion. They have arisen "not from letters in God's grammar but from wild sounds [*aus wilden Tönen*] belonging to free organs" (*HPW* 72; translation modified). And he relates this form of expression directly to that of the animals.

Most of the first section of part 1 of the *Treatise* can easily be read in this vein. But then Herder switches tack and begins to argue that what he has been calling a "language of nature" persists in "civilized" people as a neurological substratum, a somatic system comprising the "internal nerve structure" (*HPW* 73) of the body and the organs of speech. He concludes that it is wrong to see in this system the origins of language. The sympathetic cries (speech is saying too much) aroused in the nervous system are no more than "*the natural law of a sensitive machine*" (*HPW* 74), and have little or nothing to do with the moment of language acquisition, which he will go on to describe in the next section. The neurological system already evokes a certain sociability in the expressive individual, since expression assumes the resonance of another *sympathetic* being (intended in a purely biological sense). But this is the sociability of the organism, not of the reasoning human. Herder leaves it open at this stage whether this implies that his previous analogy of the sounds of animals, children, and savages (as well as women, people of delicate constitution, invalids, the lonely, and the depressed, *HPW* 74) is evidence that the world's cultures are developing along different scales. Instead of pursuing this theory of uneven development, he will reiterate his position that the birth of human language has nothing to do with the expressive cries of the animals – and he will take both Condillac and Rousseau to task for refusing to see this.

In particular, in his critique of Rousseau, we can see the problem that is beginning to take shape. In using the idea of an expressive machine to differentiate his own theory of language, Herder is taking aim at Rousseau's idea that language emerges when the animal nature of man is supplemented with the workings of free thought. This idea, which Herder calls the "phantom" of "natural man," assumes that reason acquires a sense of self through reflecting upon the animal nature of man. The perfectibility of human life becomes a "distinctive character trait," a potential to be realized intellectually, through the self-awareness of the enlightened, speaking animal. In this view, the path of self-realization is measured by the intellectual distance from the state of nature (*HPW* 94). Implicit in this is the idea that human nature is unchangeable, and is only improved upon with increasing self-awareness. This "belief in the immutability of human nature" was, as Barnard observes, dominant at the time.[25]

In rejecting this commonplace, Herder will have to find an alternative explanation for the developmental principle that appears to drive history, and also for the different manifestations of human culture in different parts of the world. This is answered in the second part of the *Treatise*, whose intimate connection to the much more frequently commented-upon first part is often overlooked.[26] In fact, what we have is an essential component of the theory, where the structural explanation of linguistic origin is expanded and tested for its historical and anthropological consequences. Here, language is the key to understanding nature's force in the development of humanity in all its diversity. Herder attempts to demonstrate how the national languages have developed individually as a result of the specific geographical, environmental, and social conditions of individual cultures. As a result, it becomes impossible to seek origin in either divine intervention or a naive and unreflecting state of nature. Language is part of the condition of being human; it developed together with humanity, with humanity's societies and its cultural environments: that is, within the natural environment, but also within the environments that have been created through social activity and through the interpretation of nature. Language is the essential expression of humanity's self-realization, its *Bildung*. Here *Bildung* expresses the socialization, the education of the individual, but it also expresses the self-realization of the individual's inner potential.

The fact that part 2 is a quest for the immanent principle of this development may be seen in the way Herder structures his argument of the linguistic development of humanity around four natural laws (*Naturgesetze*). These are the laws of nature that cause humanity to develop on an individual, social, and historical level. They state that (1) the human being is characterized by freedom of thought and by his active nature, and this predisposes him to self-development and to language; (2) he is a social being, and therefore language is natural and a necessity to him; (3) diversity lies in the nature of social life, but also in the nature of language itself; and (4) "in all probability," this social and linguistic diversity is developing according to a single principle which binds humanity and unites the diverse languages into a single "chain of formation and development [*die ganze Kette der* Bildung]" (*HPW* 154; translation modified). Implicit here is the quest for a single developmental principle that is organic and conceptual, social and linguistic at the same time. Trabant notes the proximity to the Bible of the four stages in this process, but Herder wants more.[27] The biblical story of human development may provide a broad framework for thinking about the development of humanity, but it says little about the imminent natural principle that guides it. After all, if the process of human development were completely covered by the story of divinity on earth, then what would be the point of refuting Süßkind? In the same way that human language was born not out of divine intervention, nor out of the animal nature of humans, but out of the interaction of reason and sensation, so human history must be propelled by the workings of *Besonnenheit* as it confronts the sensory world. For now, Herder is content to put off the quest for the principle and describe the process.

He begins by reiterating that human beings are born with an inner drive to language, and that this drive is of intense organic vitality. The development of language is "*as much an inner imperative* as is the impulse of the embryo to be born at the moment when it reaches maturity. The whole of nature storms at the human being in order to develop his senses until he is a human being" (*HPW* 129). If there is a constancy in human nature, it lies in its drive to development, to the realization of the natural laws that distinguish it from the rest of creation. But because the natural force that pushes the human being towards language at the same time pushes him towards reason, the condition of having reflected upon sensation (*Besonnenheit*), the human condition, is marked by a strange incompleteness. Reason knows itself and confirms the humanity of the thinker only after the fact. This is where nature's force in the human organism exceeds the purely organic, so that development becomes both a physiological and an intellectual process. "The essential feature of our life is never enjoyment but always progression, and we have never been human beings until we have lived out our lives. By contrast, the bee was a bee when it built its first cell" (*HPW* 131). The time of the human is the strange temporality introduced by the preservation of the non-present in language, creating within reason the illusion that it is always responding to an object.

But how can Herder maintain this position while having claimed earlier that the human being possesses the powers of reason "*in the first condition in which he is a human being*" (*HPW* 85)? This apparent contradiction is the key to understanding what reason means to Herder. As a force of nature, it marks human beings as human from the very first "thought of the child" (*HPW* 85). Seen in this light, the human capacity for reason is unremarkable; it is merely the performance of a natural drive for organizing other biological drives in the organism. It is like Spinoza's *intellectus*, reason residing unconsciously in nature. But to this is added *cogitatio*, the capacity to reflect consciously on unconscious processes.[28] One of the most important distinctions Herder is trying to make in his *Treatise* is between the instinctive alignment of forces in nature and their reflection in conscious acts of reason. In doing so, he retains Spinoza's central emphasis on the mind as bodily process.[29] Since the natural organizing drive of reason is determined biologically in the neurological structure of the human body, unconscious thought is a bodily process. But consciousness, the capacity for reflection, is no less physiological. It is characterized by the delay between organic process and its apperception. What has not been adequately understood – and Herder himself did not follow up on this – is that his theory of *Besonnenheit* implies a radical rethinking of the nature of time, and with it, history.

What reason does is open up this temporal gap in human life. Into this gap enters the sociability which language implies and which is inherent in human development. And because sociability is enabled by temporality, it is inherently historical in nature. The drive to language is not only psychological, conditioned by the workings of the intellect in confronting sensory perception, but is also a biological component of the development of the individual as a member of a group ("a creature of the herd," *HPW* 139) – and a group that is characterized by historical development. Because the drive to development is a drive to language, it is also a drive to sociability, and sociability involves the development of communication. This is the purport of the second natural law. And it is the biological necessity of language in human development that gives to *Bildung* its extended meaning of education. The underdeveloped human being enters the world in need of nurturing by its immediate and extended society, and this involves fostering communicative skills, and with them, intellectual growth (*HPW* 140–1).

The development of the individual is a systemic process, and it combines psychological, intellectual, biological, and social processes, none of which can be seen in isolation from the others. Rousseau and Süssmilch fail to understand the origins of language because they do not do sufficient justice to this fact. Herder then introduces the anthropological and ethnographic dimensions of Süssmilch's argument to show that, here too, a language and its culture functions as a system within a system. When he turns to the wild peoples, Herder claims, Süssmilch sees Lucretius's dumb and ugly beasts (*mutum et turpe pecus*, *HPW* 146), and this provides him with additional proof that only divine intervention could provoke these inherently mute and lazy creatures to speak. Herder corrects Süssmilch both on his misrepresentation of fact (there is no evidence that the wild peoples were ever without language, nor that their languages have not been subject to the same process of development as our own), and on the conclusion he draws regarding the intervention of divinity. Herder states clearly that even the "most barbarous human nation" has language, and that to be human is to dwell in "the philosophers' abstractions" and that language, regardless of who speaks it, is involved in the process of *Bildung* (*HPW* 146).

Out of this fundamental systemic unity in the acquisition and development of language there emerges a diversity of languages and cultures, and this process is also inherent in the biology-psychology-language system. Seen in one way, language is a fundamental shared human trait, but seen in another way, language breaks down into a multiplicity of languages, dialects, sociolects, idiolects. "As little as there can be two human beings who share exactly the same form and facial traits, just as little can there be two languages in the mouths of two human beings which would in fact still be only one language, even merely *in terms of pronunciation*" (*HPW* 148). Furthermore, it is in the nature of language to change, and change happens on a micro as well as a macro level. This quality of language has necessarily led to a wide divergence in grammars, lexica, intonation, and all the other components of language, and this in itself is taken as evidence of the fact that humanity is biologically predetermined to inhabit all the earth (*HPW* 150). This is why the diversity of languages is the third natural law.

Taking a sideswipe at Voltaire, referred to as one of the "new, fashionable philosophers" (*HPW* 150), Herder then discounts those arguments that use diversity as evidence for polygenesis, presenting instead what is probably his strongest early defence of monogenesis. He argues that the physiological differences in the appearances of inhabitants of different climes are easily misused as evidence of a fundamental difference in genetic origin. (He uses as examples the "Laplanders" and the "Negroes," rejecting the possibility that they may have emerged separately, from "a human-animal original to Lapland," or that the negro is "a natural brother of the apes of the same clime," *HPW* 150.) Human diversity is indeed physiological. In fact, as he spells it out in 1776, it is also neurological (*HFA* 1, 154). But this diversity is not pre-cast, it is a system of interaction between environment and organism, and it is subject to what could be called feedback loops from reason, tradition, and culture, all of which are embedded in language. This is why, while monogenesis might provide the overall model of human development, the evidence available to the researcher of history points not to paths of influence leading back to Adam, but to a shared cultural understanding of human life.[30] It is important to recognize the complexity of Herder's systemic model of cultural evidence. This model requires a biological foundation out of which language can emerge, but also an understanding of how biological determinants are modified or set aside by the other aspects at work in language formation. Where Voltaire continues to see biological forces at work in language, Herder uses sociological explanation. Herder's speaking being is not like Rousseau's man of the woods, since he has language, but he is also not like Hobbes's wolf, since he has a familial language (*HPW* 151). The only way to explain the diversity of languages, even in close proximity, is through social affiliations, what Herder calls "*reciprocal familial and national hatred*" (*HPW*, 151), and he uses the story of Babel to illustrate this.

As Trabant notes, "Herder would not be Herder if he did not celebrate this diversity with enthusiasm," but, equally characteristically, he only does so within a larger framework of fundamental human unity – his concept of humanity.[31] This is the intention of the fourth natural law, which states that "just as in all probability the human species [*Geschlecht*] constitutes a single progressive whole with a single origin in a single great household-economy, likewise all languages too, and with them the whole chain of civilization [*Bildung*]" (*HPW* 154). The challenge Herder faced in the *Treatise on the Origin of Language* was to demonstrate the falsity of Süssmilch's hypothesis of the divine origin of language, but to do so in a way that does not set up a simplistic progressive history of humanity based on levels of linguistic abstraction among various language groups. The prospect of doing this had already been building up in Herder's work for the past several years, as is evident in *On Diligence,* as well as the first *Critical Grove.* In the *Fragments,* Herder had clearly situated language as the key to the development of thought as an action that is both individual and shared (see chapter 1). Thinking has been learned in concert with language acquisition by humanity's diverse peoples. It is this dialectic of thought and expression that accounts for divine force. The divine manifests itself in humanity through the dual creative acts of thought and language, not through a single act of divine creation.

Having described how the development of thought/language in the individual proceeds alongside the emergence and consolidation of language communities, Herder then devotes his final section on the natural laws of language to demonstrating the need to think of how this dual process must be conceived in unitary terms, as a process that all humanity shares, and that is propelling humanity on its own common course of development. In this final natural law, Herder is combining his work on language with his epistemology, his anthropology, and his history, and the result is what he calls a "plan," a threefold determination of human life that directly affects the life of the individual, of the linguistic group, and of humanity as a whole. Here, "plan" is another word for *Kraft*, for the workings of a natural force shaping life. In the unfolding of the plan, the analytic movement from sensory perception to abstract concepts is harmonized with the development of language. The plan for the individual is described as the habitual alignment of that which the soul perceives in the present with what it has perceived in the past. Through *Besonnenheit*, individual sensory perception is tied to memory, resulting in "a progressive unity of all conditions of life," and thus the "further formation [*Fortbildung*] of language" (*HPW* 155). The plan for any one community of individuals involves the active development of the younger generation by their elders, what Herder calls the "chain of instruction" (*HPW* 15). Within this plan, the development and perfection of language is effected through the collection and dissemination of the group's wisdom, as it is passed on from one generation to the next. In this way, the individual's development is secured as a component part of the group's development.

The fourth natural law expands on this development of the community as a cohesive group, bound by kinship, language, and education, extending it to the entirety of humanity. Herder is not clear about the mechanism at work here, but he is certain about the work itself. He states: "Just as I can perform no action, think no thought, that does not have a natural effect on the whole immeasurable sphere of *my* existence, likewise neither I nor any creature of my kind [*Gattung*] can do so without also having an effect with each [action or thought] for *the whole kind* and for the continuing totality of the whole kind" (*HPW* 155). The reason why Herder can state this collective dimension of the natural plan with such certainty is linked to his monogenetic theory of human development. Since the post-Babylonian diversity of the languages and cultures points to a lost unity, and since it is in the nature of individuals, communities, and languages to grow and to develop, diversity itself must be understood as a distinct moment in the collective development and self-formation of humanity as a whole. At this stage in his argument Herder again makes reference to the false conclusions he sees in Voltaire's polygenetic philosophy of history, including the misplaced belief that nations are somehow natural formations. "If human beings were national animals so that each such animal had invented its own language for itself quite independently and separately from others, then this language would certainly have to display '*a difference in type*,' such as the inhabitants of Saturn and of the earth may perhaps have vis-à-vis each other. And yet it is obvious that with us *everything develops on a single basis*" (*HPW* 158).

The unity of humanity is not only conceptual, it is a natural law, and Herder now has to propose a mechanism of unification, whereby the natural tendency to form language communities is counteracted with an equal, or perhaps even stronger, natural drive to communicate across linguistic barriers. "Here nature has linked a new chain: tradition from people to people! '*In this way arts, science, culture, and language have refined themselves in a great progression over the course of nations'* – the finest *bond of further formation that nature has chosen*" (*HPW* 160). This is the same idea we saw him developing in *On Diligence*, and in his musings on restlessness. Nature has created an individual drive to restlessness which wants to exceed the sphere of tradition defined by the mother tongue, and surpass its limitations. This drive is not mentioned in the *Treatise*, but it is clearly evident in the way Herder describes the effect it has had on the culture of Germany: "We Germans would still, like the Americans, live quietly in our forests, or rather still roughly wage war and be heroes in them, if the chain of foreign cultures had not pressed so near to us and compelled us with the force of whole centuries to participate in it" (*HPW* 160–1).

This natural force promoting communication across the cultures and between the languages works towards the collective advancement of humanity. But it does not lead to homogeneity.[32] Herder's commitment both to the natural principle that unites humanity and to the forces that lead to a parallel development of individuals and cultures allows him to take apparently contradictory stances on the development of nations and of humanity. He seems to take it for granted that some nations are more backward than others, or at least less "refined," as he likes to put it. However, even this uneven development among the world's cultures is taken as evidence for a collective force of development, built upon and driven not by divine intervention, but by human invention: "Human invention has everything speaking for it and nothing at all against it: *essence of the human soul* and *element of language; analogy of the human species* and *analogy of the advances of language – the great example of all peoples, times, and parts of the world*!" (*HPW* 163). But the problem remains: if humanity's development is the story of monogenetic origins, dispersal, and diversity, how can we speak of a common humanity, without imposing this commonality artificially from above, as it were, as a logical concept that is prior to the analysis of the human condition? In what way do the disparate understandings of life that are embedded in the world's languages provide evidence for a common principle that binds them together, and that is inherent in their natures?

Once such a principle is identified, how is it possible to tell the story of common humanity without overriding the tales, concepts, and world views that allow individual cultures to understand their place in the world? And further, once a common humanity is assumed, how is it possible to conceive of disparate development without introducing the idea of historical hierarchy, the Lockean idea that historical development of individual cultures follows the same or similar paths, and that some cultures are more advanced than others?[33]

Herder's answer is equally original and ingenious: the claim for a common plan, a common *Bildung* for all of humanity is developed alongside his claims for the universality of linguistic structures. But this universality is not understood as a common deep structure, which must be derived analytically; rather it is a systemic universality, in which the performance of language itself contributes to the individual and regional development of *a* language, but also to the common growth of *the* human language. "Each human being has, to be sure, all the abilities that his whole species has, and each nation the abilities that all nations have. However, it is nevertheless true that *a society invents more than a human being*, and *the whole human species invents more than a single people* – and this indeed not merely *as a result of the quantity of heads* but *as a result of the manifold and intensive increase of relational circumstances*" (*HPW* 159). In order to make this claim, Herder has to understand language development as a realization of inherent possibilities in the human propensity to reflect upon and abstract from experience, much in the same way Leibniz had understood entelechy. And here we must recall the argument in his *Essay on Being*, that logical possibility is in no way prior to Being, but is at all times a conceptual expansion upon real possibility, itself dependent on Being. What Herder has now added to this is the idea that human development is biological and neurological, the expression of a natural law of the species, and this law manifests itself in language, out of which is born the delay mechanisms of reason.

Beginning with the opening sentence, Herder develops a dialectical argument on nature, thought, and expression that will much later emerge as one of the seminal statements of modern philosophies of language. Language enables humans to reach consensus on the nature of the world, or, to put it differently, it is through language that humans invent the world – and in doing so they invent themselves. This dual invention is possible because language emerges as that which no animal has, as an articulated thought system whose coherence depends on its symbolic self-referentiality and its foundation in bodily experience.

And language involves a play with reflection, temporality, and presence, whose name is reason. This is why all philosophy must be a philosophy of language. Herder will insist on this understanding of philosophy throughout his life, up to the point where, in his later years, it will provide the foundation for his rejection of Kant's critical philosophy (above all in his *Metakritik zur Kritik der reinen Vernunft* [Metacritique of the Critique of Pure Reason, 1799]).[34] Philosophy cannot be in pursuit of the universality of thought; instead, it must always hover on the verge of history and anthropology, on the articulation of the specificity of human expression. This specificity is personal and defines the individual, in the sense that "every human being can and must think in his language alone" (*HSW* 21, 32n1). But at the same time, human expression is a shared project and one that different societies develop in different ways, depending on their own specific environment and their place in history. Each individual must think in his language, but language is not only an individual's possession. Language founds culture. This is what makes the cultures of humanity both unitary and plural. Any claim for universality in language must be founded on the potential for development within specific language/thought systems. This potential governs human life, and it is to be understood only by examining the myriad ways in which this system has in fact developed. Out of this historical and anthropological enterprise, the unity of humanity emerges as an incomplete unity, a systemic striving towards a goal that is itself defined in the act of striving. This will serve as the guiding idea for his next major work, the essay on the philosophy of history, *Auch eine Philosophie der Geschichte zur Bildung der Menschheit*, published in 1774.

Prejudice and the Limits of Thought

In April 1771, Herder left Strasbourg for the town of Bückeburg near Hanover, where the liberal-minded Count Wilhelm von Schaumburg-Lippe had offered him the position of Counsellor of the Consistory and Court Chaplain. Choosing Herder was highly controversial, since he had already established a reputation as a free thinker, a non-conforming individualist, and an eccentric interpreter of scripture. Herder held this position in Bückeburg for five years, regarding it at best as a period of transition during which he attempted to find something he felt was more in line with his calling. The most important publication of these years was the essay to which he gave the ironic title *Auch eine Philosophie der Geschichte zur Bildung der Menschheit* (This Too a Philosophy of History for the Formation of Humanity, sometimes translated as Another Philosophy of History). Already in the *Journal* of 1769, it is clear what significance Herder attached to the philosophical study of history, the philosophy of history, history-as-philosophy. Now we can see him starting to experiment in the appropriate method for writing history as a genealogical investigation into the diversity of world views, but also as a speculative pursuit of humanity's destiny, that future time when "the genius of illumination" will have "permeated the whole earth!" (*HJV* 220). Herder uses the word *Erleuchtung* (illumination) to describe the telos of humanity. This sets it apart from *Aufklärung*, while retaining the metaphor of Enlightenment. Humanity will not find its destiny in the rationalism of Enlightenment, but in what can only be called a collective *Besonnenheit*. It is this understanding of humanity's common fate that ties the empirical work of historiography to what Zammito calls Herder's "speculative" philosophy of history.[35] What Herder calls (in the *Journal*) a "universal history of world culture" will be universal in the temporal sense: it collects stories of the past with the aim of finding the force that realizes the common destiny towards illumination. The possibility of speculating on the future rests with the historian's philosophical work, which amounts to uncovering natural principles that drive humanity towards a collective future.[36] This is what Herder has in mind when he asks in the *Journal* if it is not possible to "make conjectures" about how "the habits of thought of the various nations," but also their religion and technologies will cause the nations of Europe to develop in consort, just as the Greeks had done before them. The historian speculates on the future "from the condition of the present-day world and on the analogy of past centuries" (*HJV* 307). He goes on to show that this is an interdisciplinary task, held together by the discourses of natural science and philosophy. And because it is a collective intellectual pursuit, it should also be able to help determine future events.[37]

The deciphering of analogy that makes historical pursuits philosophical is not only temporal, it also renders history universal in a spatial sense. The universality of human history must speak of humanity's common future geographically, in a way that takes account of human diversity. As we have seen, this is the concern of the second part of the *Treatise on the Origin of Language*. In the *Journal* Herder made it clear that history as a discipline follows directly upon geography, in that it is founded in the study of geographical diversity. History is "a history of peoples," an understanding of humanity's diversity and unity on a spatial and temporal scale. Universal history shows "the seeds of all theories and all histories ... in so far as they can be seen swimming past in the stream of time" (*HJV* 265). The challenge faced by the historian is to understand unity from the point of view of diversity, and vice versa. This is also what makes the disciplines of history and geography holistic and democratic (*HJV* 270–4). But Herder's position on Being could not remain satisfied with explanations that seemed to make the relationship between unity and diversity a matter of the observer's correct perspective. He would also have to try to explain diversity as the manifestation of unity, as a natural force; and unity as a collective performance of diversity, also a natural force. The process of explanation itself, however, is caught in the very temporality and spatiality that defines the human condition – the play of reason that is structured by absence and delay. This realization provides the peculiar theological dimension of *This Too a Philosophy of History*, which Herder succinctly states in the first section when he observes that "every *general image*, every *general concept*, is only an *abstraction* – it is only the Creator who *thinks* the whole *unity of one, of all*, nations in all their *manifoldness* without having the *unity* thereby fade for him" (*HPW* 293). As Michael Mack puts it, "from the omniscient perspective of God, unity is diversity," but the philosopher will never be able to fully apprehend unity in diversity or diversity in unity.[38] The philosophy of history is conducted in the shadow of this double realization.

This forms the ground on which *This Too a Philosophy of History* unfolds. Initially, Herder had intended the essay to address the question "What sorts of virtues or unvirtues have governed human beings at all times, and has the tendency of human beings been improved or worsened with time, or always remained the same?" Later he modified this question to read: "Have human beings' inclinations changed from time to time, and what are the virtues and vices that have governed them here and there, more or less?" (*HPW* 268). If this is to be the point of departure, then everything depends on the understanding of the collective. On what basis can the philosopher speak of a nation, a people, or of all of humanity, when he realizes that the apprehension of unity is beyond him? Or to put it differently, what criteria allow the philosopher to view history as a collection of diverse cultures, each with its own set of values, traditions, its own language, its own past and stories about itself, when he realizes that viewing diversity is a way of creating artificial unities? How does one describe the general development of humanity in the face of the great diversity of cultures and languages without doing violence to nature? Much of *This Too a Philosophy of History* addresses the methodological consequences arising out of the fundamental realization that history embodies a double enigma: as history it must be thought as a natural system of development that is concealed from human inquiry, that is only accessible by analogy; and as historiography it involves intervening in the sequence of stories by which cultures make sense of the past and speculate on the future. The consequence Herder draws is to see both the science of analogy and the writing of history as models of historical unity, while presenting themselves as nothing more than models. This is the appropriate form of rationality with which to inquire into history, and it raises the task of the historian to the level of science.

Herder develops his ideas on historical method by dismissing some of the most common errors he sees in historiography. Discussing Egypt, he speaks of the "stupidity" that causes historians "to tear a *single Egyptian virtue* out of the land, the time, and the boyhood of the human spirit and to measure it with the *criterion of another time*!" Against this tendency to measure the past on a single temporal scale, he proposes a geographical positioning that involves seeing the Egyptian "merely *in his place*." Failing this, "one sees, especially looking hither from Europe, the most distorted caricature" (*HPW* 282). As we saw in the *Journal*, geography renders history democratic (*HJV* 270–4), not through a historical relativism of different cultures in different places, but by understanding location as the key that can unlock what the historian's home culture shares with the culture under investigation, while at the same time highlighting that which separates them.[39]

If the past is mediated through language and through texts, then the building blocks of language re-enact this very problem. The shared structures of human language are what makes the past accessible. However, words alone are nothing but "worn-out, incomplete silhouettes" (*HMA* 1, 612). There is an important point where the relativists and historicists are right, and that is their attempt to counter the projection of historical values onto earlier times. But what are the correct methodological tools of this countering? Herder believes that the most obvious path to understanding another culture is through sympathy, by moving as close as possible to the cognitive universe out of which cultural products arose. In this way, the texts of distant cultures are brought to life. They begin to appear within a self-contained system accessible first and foremost through sympathetic interpretation. The challenge facing the historian is that the "whole living painting of mode of life, habits, needs, peculiarities of land and climate, would have to *be added* or to have *preceded*" the act of interpretation. And this of course implies a sympathetic identification with the entirety of the culture: "One would have first to *sympathize* with the nation in order to feel a *single one* of its *inclinations* or *actions all together*, one would have to *find* a single word, to *imagine* everything in its fullness – or one reads – *a word*!" (*HPW* 292).

This is precisely the historian's dilemma. The gulf between the present and the past, or between the European interpreter of geographically distant cultures and their own cognitive world can, it would seem, be bridged by the shared human nature that drives cultural production. Herder had, after all, begun his initial draft of this essay with a clear statement that "the human heart has always remained the same in inclinations, just as the mind has in abilities, and, whatever sort of angelic or devilish forms people have sometimes wished to imagine in it, has always been only human" (*HPW* 268). But does this shared human nature authorize the sympathetic acts of identification on which interpretation is based? At first glance the answer would seem to be yes: "We all believe that we still now have *paternal* and *household* and *human drives* as the Oriental had them; that we can have *faithfulness* and *diligence in art* as the Egyptian possessed them; *Phoenician activeness, Greek love of freedom, Roman strength of soul* – who does not think that he feels a *disposition* for all that[?]" (*HPW* 292).

But here lies the problem. In order to be able to activate the inner potential that binds the historian with the Greek, the Roman, the Phoenician, the historian would have to become that which he is not, thereby negating the entire historical project. "*The whole nature* of the soul, which *rules* through everything, which *models* all other inclinations and forces of the soul *in accordance with itself*, and in addition *colors* even the most indifferent actions – in order to share in feeling this, answer not on the basis of the word but go into the age, into the clime, the whole history, feel yourself into everything – only now are you on the way to understanding the word. But also only now will you lose the thought 'as though you too are all that taken individually or collectively.' You all taken collectively? *Quintessence of all times and peoples*? That really shows stupidity!"(*HPW* 292).

The stupidity of historical sympathy lies in its inability to negotiate the paradoxes of difference and unity in human nature and human expression. If the historian is to straddle the gulf that divides the past and the distant from the here and now, he will have to do so by incorporating the limits of his own cognition in the act of interpretation. This is what Herder calls prejudice (*Vorurteil*), and it is why he can claim that people are "ennobled through fair *prejudices*" (*HPW* 296). Prejudice, he implies, is the domain of poetry, and the strength of poetic discourse lies in the way it circumscribes its own prejudice – its own horizon of meaning. It is only when the discourses are mixed, when "the poet is a historian, a philosopher, as most of them pretend to be, and these model all centuries after the one form of their time" (*HPW* 296), that prejudice becomes a perversion of truth.

This is another way of saying that prejudice marks the moments where thought finds itself confined by the boundaries of its location and its tradition, where the limits of culture are revealed.[40] But these limits are for Herder not only cultural or national limits, they mark the limits of thought itself. Beyond the limits staked out by prejudice, the prejudices of other cultures become the unthought of one's own culture. In this way, prejudice allows thought to persist as if it were confronting truth, whereas in fact it is only confronting the cultural dimension of truth. Otherwise, happiness would not be possible. Thanks to prejudice, "each nation has its *center* of happiness *in itself*, like every sphere its center of gravity!" (*HPW* 297).[41] Happiness has a historical and a geographical dimension (see *HPW* 296), tying it closely to prejudice. In this way, prejudices are, as Karl Menges notes, "part of a pre-rational, mythopoetic tradition in that they unite people and make them happy on the basis of collective sentiment rather than critical reflection."[42] Herder describes this as a natural survival mechanism of nature, one that allows the cultural diversity of humanity to speak in concert. "The good mother has taken care well here too. She put dispositions to *manifoldness* into the heart, but made each of them in itself so little *pressing* that if only a few get satisfied the soul quickly forms *a concert* for itself from these awakened notes and does not feel the unawakened ones except insofar as they *silently* and obscurely *support* the sounding song. She put dispositions of *manifoldness* into the heart, and then *a part* of the manifoldness in a circle about us, available to us; then she reigned in the human view so that after a small period of habituation the circle became *horizon* for him" (*HPW* 297). In this way, prejudice not only guarantees happiness, it also enables knowledge in a world where only God can survey the whole. Taking up the question of his original draft, he explains that virtue is not something that could be grasped by "one form of humanity and one region of the earth"; and so "it got distributed into a thousand forms, it roams forth – an eternal

Proteus! – through all parts of the world and all centuries" (*HPW* 298). Prejudice alerts us to the existence of other models of thought, while hiding them from view. But it also alerts us to the limits of our own models. "Precisely the *limitedness* of my point on the earth, the *blinding* of my looks, the failure of my purposes, the *riddle* of my inclinations and desires, the *worsting* of my forces only serving the whole *of a day, of a year, of a nation, of a century* – precisely this is a guarantee for me that *I* am nothing but the *whole* is *everything*" (*HPW* 357). Another way of saying this is that the discrepancy between the apprehension of diversity and the knowledge of unity is of the same order as that between Being and its conception.[43] In this sense, the historian could be said to be engaged in a critique of prejudice, an examination of the limits of his own world view, a critique of located reason.

The critique of prejudice is aimed at the blindness and arrogance of the philosopher who mistakes prejudice for truth. And the most egregious example of this is the philosopher of progress, about whom Herder states that he

> is most an *animal* when he would wish to be most reliably *a God* – thus also in the confident calculation of the *perfection* of the world. Of course, if only it were true that everything proceeded prettily *in a straight line* and every *succeeding human being* and *every succeeding race* got *perfected* according to *his* ideal in a *beautiful progression* for which he alone knew to give the *exponent* of virtue and happiness! Then in that case it always came to him *last of all* – he the last, highest member with which everything *concludes*. "Behold, the world has risen to such enlightenment, virtue, happiness! I, high on the swing-bar! *the golden pointer* of the world-scales – *behold* me!" (*HPW* 334)

This is the Enlightenment historian at his worst – an arrogant rationalist forcing his own plan for humanity onto the rest of the world. Although Herder doesn't say so right here, he is thinking of Voltaire. The name of the famous French Enlightenment philosopher, both admired and criticized by Herder, appears in the essay whenever he wishes to show historiography gone wrong. As he stated in the opening pages of his essay, Voltaire's historiography judges the early history of humanity as "mere *ruins of worldly history*" accessible only "by the hastiest rationalizing" (*HPW* 275).[44]

Herder recognized that the ability to write a philosophy of history was dependent on the way the historian approaches the problem of progress.[45] In his initial draft introduction, he calls this the "single problem whose solution would perhaps also take precedence over all the preceding ones." This question is stated as follows: "Is there, historically and physically, a certain progress in the inclinations of the human species? Can one observe in the bond between the diverse periods, connections, and revolutions of the peoples of this earthly sphere a thread and plan of formation [*Bildung*] for developing in the human heart little by little certain inclinations and forces for which people previously and on another path saw no clear trace? And which, then, would be the inclinations on this path which were developed at this point and that, of which people did not yet find any trace in advance or in a neighboring region, which had to arise, ferment up, decline, and bring forth others in turn precisely thus and now? In short, if there exists in the hand of fate the thread of the development of human forces through all the centuries and revolutions, and if a human heart can observe it – which is it?" (*HPW* 269). Herder raises these questions in order to oppose, as Menges puts it, "the rationalistic generalizations inherent in any 'Universalgeschichte'" with "the plurality of histories emanating from the singularity of nature."[46] This position also assumes a very different idea of perfection, one drawn (as Michael Mack argues) from Spinoza and formulated "not in terms of teleology, but in terms of sustainability on both an individual and a social scale."[47] To oppose the progressivist philosophy of history is also to reject Kant's later understanding of morality as requiring the idea of a progressive advancement of reason in human history.

As the essay draws to a close, the criticism of false aims in historiography merges with the criticism of Voltaire and the ideals of the French Enlightenment as Herder saw them. Here he returns to the themes that had guided his critique of French cultural imperialism a few years earlier. The French philosophers of history, with their smug and superficial faith in the values of their own age and their own nation, are like Machiavelli, yet worse. They mask oppression behind discourses of universality. "The universal dress of *philosophy* and *love of humankind* can hide *oppressions, attacks* on true, *personal freedom of human beings* and *lands, citizens* and *peoples*, of just the sort that *Cesare Borgia* would wish for. All that *in accordance with* the *accepted first principles* of the *century*, with a *decent appearance of virtue, wisdom, love of humankind*, and *care for* peoples" (*HPW* 351). As Sonia Sikka observes, Herder's position is that beneath the rhetoric of universal brotherhood lies "imperialism – economic, political, and cultural."[48]

In Herder's view, Voltaire is just such a disguised Machiavellian. Herder will later speak of the "author *of a hundred years* who without quarrel or contradiction has had an effect on his century *like a monarch* – read, learned, admired, and (what is still more) *followed* from *Lisbon* to *Kamchatka*, from *Novaya Zemlya* as far as the *colonies of India*." Voltaire has won admiration throughout the world with "his *language*, with his hundredfold tolerance for *wording*, with his *lightness*, with his *bold abundance of flowery ideas* [*Schwunge von Ideen auf lauter Blumen*]." And Herder acknowledges, albeit in a backhanded manner, the great benefits Voltaire has brought to the century of Enlightenment: "*Light* spread abroad, so-called *philosophy* of *humanity, tolerance, facility* in *independent thought, gleam of virtue* in a hundred amiable *shapes, thinned* and *sweetened little human inclinations – as an author without doubt on the greatest height* of the century!" These words of apparent praise are then carefully qualified. Voltaire's achievements are bought at the price of "miserable *recklessness, weakness, uncertainty* and *coldness*!" together with "*shallowness, planlessness, scepticism* about *virtue, happiness*, and *merit*!" Together with this comes a crass inability to see his own privilege. Voltaire's "mischievous hand" dissolves the "gentle, pleasant, and necessary bonds" of ordinary life, "without giving us, who do not all reside at the Chateau de Fernay, the least thing in their place." The Enlightenment philosopher aids oppression by situating his ideas in a vacuum where there is no self-aware grounding in culture, and no recognition of divine force – what Herder calls "all this philosophy and aestheticism in manner of thought without morality or firm human sensation" (*HPW* 355–6; translation modified). The pursuit of universality in human life, which Voltaire has adopted from Descartes, has caused him to see the Enlightenment project as liberating humanity from the specificity of cultural grounding – a pointless and impossible task in Herder's eyes.[49] The pointlessness of this issues from the fundamental misunderstanding of what it means to talk about humanity in universal terms. The human mind cannot measure universal development, because it cannot grasp perfection. As Michael Mack observes, humanity does not persist "because of its supposed linear progression toward ethical perfection. On the contrary, human history moves through different stages that mutually oppose each other in order to make up for their intrinsic lack; for their various points of strength which are at the same time insufficiencies."[50] Because of this, any resolution of the divide between cultural particularity and historical universals requires a shift in perspective towards the cosmological or the theological.[51]

This is why, in the end, it is Voltaire's nihilistic denial of religion that Herder finds most offensive. Authors who dress oppression in the clothing of universality are writing "philosophically, wittily, French, and of course – without religion" (*HPW* 351). This last point is vital. Religion for Herder is the capacity of thought to glimpse its own horizon of prejudice. And in this sense, theology is to a large extent always liberation theology, a doctrine of divine order that compels struggle against domination and exploitation. For to recognize the horizon of one's own thought and to see it as culturally determined, is to see the bonds that tie it to the regime of oppression that issues from one's own privileged position in the world. The promise of religion is its shift in perspective beyond the cultural horizon of one's own life, towards a unity which cannot be grasped, only pointed to by representational strategies derived from poetry. Voltaire's biggest mistake is his reduction of history to a single progressive development culminating in his own present, his own Europe, his own language.[52]

In the critique of prejudice, the central point of Herder's essay emerges. Herder saw it as an irrefutable fact that there is a plan uniting human diversity into one single developmental being he called humanity. He called this his "great theme": the fact that "a plan of developmental striving becomes visible" (*HMA* 1, 619).[53] And it is the fact of prejudice that warns us against naming that plan in terms developed within our own horizon of understanding. This idea is so important that he ends the essay by restating it:

> And if one day we found a *standpoint* to take an overview of the whole merely of our species! – whither the chain between peoples and regions of the earth which initially advanced *so slowly*, then wound its way through nations *with so much clashing*, and finally, with a gentler but *stricter drawing-together*, was destined to *bind*, and – whither? – to *lead*, these nations – whither this chain reaches – we received the *ripe harvest* of the *seeds* which, strewn among the peoples *out of a blind sieve*, we saw sprout so *peculiarly*, bloom *so variously*, yield such *ambiguous* hopes of fruit – we will ourselves be in a position to savor what sort of *good taste* the *leaven* that fermented so long, so cloudily, and with such bad taste in the end produced for the *universal formation of humanity*." (*HPW* 358)

This process is one presided over by divinity, which also presides over the limited capacity of any individual to perceive the plan that drives nature. The whole world, which Herder earlier called "the vision of

God *at one moment*," is described as "a great work *without a name* and everywhere *full of names*" (*HPW* 336). Conducted correctly, historiography is a branch of theology, and its theological dimension aligns it with poetry – but again, not for the Hamannian reason that poetry always brings us closer to the lost Golden Age. Historiography is related to poetry and to theology by their shared preoccupation with presenting the unpresentable.

As always, when Herder approaches the vision of the plan for humanity, his language becomes poetic, his orthography points to the limits of language, and his metaphors beg the question of the appropriate model for human development. It is in this limitation of language, in the distinction between the vision of the plan and the naming of the plan, that he begins to develop his characteristic philosophy of history. Because the plan can be apprehended but not named, his philosophy of history is directed against the popular Enlightenment notion that history represents a constant march of progress, where the betterment of humanity can more or less be taken for granted. His views of modernity are far too critical to allow him to take this stance. Instead, he sees history presenting humanity with ever-changing sets of choices which must be formulated and decided on in different ways by each particular culture according to their specific history and environment. As Pross has shown, the philosopher finds in history "the Protean forms of appearance of that which is human. In the stream of time, these forms condense into fixed phenomena, then they decay again, and – as long as the basic foundation of matter is not exhausted – they realign in new foundations" (*HMA* 1, 852). This view of a continually changing store of matter and energy forces Herder's philosophy of history away from Voltaire's notion of progress. It is a contradiction in terms to see historical development as a constant improvement, when in fact it is in the essence of things, embedded in the biology of the organism, that matter remains the same, while the forms of matter – the actors in history – grow and decay.[54]

Progress and Human Diversity

Because of his convictions concerning the unification of diverse cultures into a single humanity, Herder's historiography was bound to erupt in this essay into an unequivocal critique of imperialism. European modernity has no grounds for assuming that it is the most perfect form of expression nature has developed. The essay expresses what Zammito refers to as Herder's "outrage with smug presentism, with European despotism and imperialism cloaked in glorious 'philosophical' rationalizations."[55] In its critique of Enlightenment philosophies of history, *This Too a Philosophy of History* was beginning to work through the contradictions in the way the expanding world economy shapes Europe's interactions with other cultures. Herder sees contemporary Europe as holding "all peoples and parts of the world under our shade, so to speak, and when a storm shakes two small twigs in Europe how the whole world quakes and bleeds! When has the whole earth ever so universally converged together *on so few united threads* as now? When have more *power* and *mechanism* been possessed for shaking whole nations to the core with one *press*, with one *movement of a finger*?" (*HPW* 325). This recognition of Europe's power and its position in the world brings with it a bitingly ironic critique of the exploitation associated with progressive theories of history. Together with Europe's expansion of power comes its expansion of "wisdom" and Enlightenment. After all, he tells us, "already almost the *whole earth* shines with *Voltaire's clarity*!" (*HPW*, 325). In words of deep irony, he goes on to state:

> And how this seems to advance further and further! Whither do European colonies not *reach*, and whither *will* they not reach! Everywhere the savages, the more they become fond of our brandy and luxury, become *ripe* for our *conversion* too! Everywhere approach, especially through brandy and luxury, *our culture*. Will soon, God help us!, all be human beings like us! – *good, strong, happy human beings*! *Trade* and *papacy*, how much you have already contributed to this great business! *Spaniards, Jesuits*, and *Dutchmen* – you human-friendly, unselfish, noble, and virtuous nations! – how much has not the *civilization* [*Bildung*] of *humanity* to be grateful to you for already in all parts of the world! (*HPW* 325)

Herder's understanding of the connection between the kind of universal history Voltaire wanted to write and the European exploitation of the world is probably what led him from the original question about the universality of morals directly to the problem of progress. The idea of progress not only skews the Enlightenment philosopher's view of history, it translates directly into the structural relationship that sees Europe dominating the rest of the world and that determines the social life of his contemporaries. Herder calls this relationship "our system of trade" and he argues that the supposed spread of wisdom and tolerance throughout the world is only a foil for the predominance of economic utilitarianism and the exploitation it brings with it. Even the abolition of slavery is based on such utilitarianism:

> "Our system of trade!" Can one imagine anything superior to the *subtlety* of this *all-embracing science*? What miserable *Spartans* they were who used their *Helots* for agriculture, and what barbaric *Romans* who shut up their slaves in prisons of the earth! In Europe slavery has been abolished because it has been calculated how much more these slaves would cost and how much less they would bring in than free people. (*HPW* 328)

And where Europe claims to have abolished slavery and exported its tolerant views, Herder sees a hypocritical outsourcing of slavery to other parts of the world:

> Only one thing we have still permitted ourselves: *to use as slaves*, to *trade*, to *exile* into silver mines and sugar mills, *three parts of the world* – but those are not *Europeans*, not *Christians*, and in return we receive silver and gemstones, spices, sugar, and – secret disease; thus for the sake of trade and for the *reciprocal brotherly help* and *community* of the lands. (*HPW* 328)

He then goes on to observe that, because Europe's economic well-being depends on the unjust structure of the world economy, everyone is implicated:

> Who is there who is not constrained to participate in the great *tornado* that is sucking Europe dry, who is not constrained to press his way into it, and, if he cannot do this to other children, to drain out his own children, as the greatest *man of trade*? The old title "shepherd of the people" has been turned into "monopolist" – and when, now, the whole tornado breaks loose with a hundred storm winds – great god Mammon – whom we *all now serve* – help us! (*HPW* 328)

In spite of this bitter critique of Europe's stake in the world economy, Herder sustains his faith in the non-exploitative interaction of the world's peoples. This is the vision that dominates in the third section: "through *one sort of education, philosophy, irreligion, enlightenment, vice*, and finally, as a bonus, through *oppression, bloodthirstiness*, and *insatiable avarice* ... we are all becoming brothers" (*HPW* 350). It is already apparent in this formulation that Herder's theological perspective on the development of the world is sooner or later going to get in the way of his critique of imperialism. It is also going to prove problematic when it comes to the search for a natural model for development. If imperialism is but another step on the path to the perfection of humanity, why exactly should it be opposed? This point is closely related to the problems Herder had seen when contemplating the pedagogue's obligations in the *Journal*. There, his critique of commercial exploitation assumed a dialectic of improvement where action became comprehensible by staking humanity's claims on the lives, thoughts, and possessions of the inhabitants of the provinces. Clearly, this is a risky position to take, and it would have required of Herder a serious commitment to defining the difference between exploitation and improvement – between a world system dominated by imperialism, and one aimed at rights and equality. He never takes that step. Instead, he finds himself moving back and forth between theological universalism, in which even injustice is a part of the divine plan, and liberation theology, which sees European exploitation leading directly to insurrection: "The more we Europeans invent *means* and *tools* to subjugate, to deceive, and to plunder you other parts of the world … Perhaps it will one day be precisely your turn to *triumph*! We affix chains with which *you* will pull *us*; the *inverted pyramids* of our constitutions will turn *upright* on your ground." But even with this vision of a time when the empire will seek vengeance for injustice, instead of asking what might bring on this resistance or revolution, Herder interrupts himself with another vision of wholeness, where "we are approaching a new act [of the play], even if admittedly only through decay!"(*HPW* 352). Instead of pinning his hopes on a consciously driven political process, Herder retains faith in organic processes which will link the individual's response to injustice to the organic development of world history, the unfolding of the divine plan.

The problem lies with consciousness itself. In attempting to pin down the moral obligations of Europeans towards other cultures, Herder wants the public intellectual to take on the task of improvement as if the contradictions in the modern world were playing themselves out in his own body. This is one of the major themes that runs through *This Too a Philosophy of History*, and it is yet another indicator of how closely Herder identified historiography with philosophy. The pursuit of a model for the underlying forces at work in the history of humanity is at the same time an attempt to model how the force of nature works in the body of the individual.[56] If nature can resolve the contradictions of history through the ages, and if the thinking, feeling, and acting individual is the agent through which this resolution is attained, then the forces that drive historical process must announce themselves as forces at work in the body. On a certain level, this becomes Herder's problem in his essay: how to speak of the forces that pull the individual towards the perfection of the species, but that also ground him and locate him in an environment and a tradition.

In order to accomplish this, Herder tries out various possible models for the unity of human development. As was common in historical writing at the time, he seems to take it for granted that history is humanity's lifetime, that prehistory is its childhood, and that the present is the time of maturity, perhaps even old age. Herder also adopts – seemingly uncritically – the common assumption that the childhood of humanity is also the state of nature lived out by the wild peoples in far-flung places. "If you say, human being, that this revelation [of the oldest times of human childhood] is *too old* for you in your overly clever, old-man's years – look around you! – the greatest part of the nations of the earth is still in *childhood*, all still speak *that* language, have *those* ethics, provide the paradigms of *that* level of development [*Bildung*]" (*HPW* 341). This points to a central tension in Herder's thought. His opposition to Voltaire's presentism and progressive Eurocentric history should have warned him against this simplistic assumption that the inhabitants of the New World are somehow comparable in their manners and traditions to the prehistoric Europeans. But more than this, the equation of the wild peoples with humanity's childhood goes against his central Leibnizian thesis of the diversity of human life giving rise to the diversity of human thought, and this multi-vocal diversity providing the unity of human life. Herder has arrived at the point where his geography of human diversity is beginning to stand at odds with his historical pursuit of unified humanity.

From his earliest writings, there seems to be little doubt that Herder saw the physiological diversity of the world's peoples in intimate connection with the diverse wealth of conceptual models for understanding life. In his sketch *Von der Veränderung des Geschmacks* (On the Change of Taste, most probably written in 1776), which bears the subheading "On the diversity of taste and of manner of thought among human beings" (*HPW* 247), Herder outlines the "great diversities in relation to the structure of the human body: in size and shape, in color and lineaments, in the proportion and the varying firmness of the parts" (*HPW* 250). Drawing heavily on Buffon, he mentions the appearances of the inhabitants of Africa, North America, and Lapland as examples of extreme physiological diversity. He then assures us, however, that he does not want to talk about "this formation of the body in general, but only insofar as it has an influence on the manner of thought, and here I am talking about the *senses*, which, after all, are so to speak the door for all our concepts, or the *optical medium* through which the idea comes in like a ray of sunlight. Now if these instruments are constituted in a special way, then the manner of thought arising therefrom must be formed in a special way as well. And this can therefore be the first source of the diversity in *concepts* and in *sensation*" (*HPW* 250).

How then is this diversity of concepts to be squared with the idea that the cultures of the New World are but Europeans in their childhood? Is the history of humanity the story of a single lifetime, or is it the endlessly varied collection of lifetimes, each developing in different ways? Is human development tracked along a single timeline, on which human diversity unfolds in time and space, giving rise to a single mosaic of diverse cultures? Or will there be one culture which reaches perfection before the others, who remain frozen in time, living examples of uneven development? When we read Herder's rapturous prose on the divine plan for humanity, he clearly imagines a great chorus of human cultures singing together, or a mosaic of individual appearances. But when he seeks a model for the organic force driving the *Bildung* of humanity, he is less certain. Could this be because every time he approaches the idea that diversity in physiology is accompanied by a diversity in concepts, he must face the relativist problem that radically different views of the world might be equally true? That his model for the multiple nature of truth unsettles the very discourse in which he is attempting to grasp diversity? This radical challenge to his ideas on the lifetime of humanity is clearly visible in *On the Change of Taste*. He begins the essay with a short introduction, then moves straight into the central question: "Are human beings diverse in relation to the judgments of the senses?" (*HPW* 249). He works through this question to the point where he confronts the way individuals conceptualize their own upbringing and their own gender, calling into question the natural determination of their development. At this point the essay is interrupted. He then starts it again with the image of the chain of generations linked together in a single "spirit of changes" which forms the "kernel of history" (*HPW* 254). And yet, the spirit of changes affects the fundamental judgments of life – "taste and manner of thought" (*HPW* 256), to the point where the empirical evidence would indicate that "truth, fairness, moral goodness" are not necessarily "the same at all times" (*HPW* 256). Here again, Herder's text breaks off, but not before he writes: "This skepticism should almost put us off trusting our own taste and sensation" (*HPW* 256).

The interrupted encounter with the diversity of concepts reflects one of the central problems in *This Too a Philosophy of History*. Here, instead of taking the Kantian route of proving the necessity of a universal constancy of truth, fairness, and moral goodness, the method of choice is to seek an organic model to explain how diversity in human life and thought can still yield a single composite truth of humanity. In this essay, *Bildung* is starting to emerge as the umbrella concept that collects possible models of organic development, models for explaining the form of nature's force at work in history (the developmental ages of humanity), in geography (those distant places where developmental differences become visible, preserved in time), in nature, and in art. But again, the closer he looks at his models, the more problematic they become. Throughout the essay, he plays with possible models for relating the lives of individuals to the progress of humanity. Picking up on an image that was important in earlier works,[57] he explains that as soon as we inquire as to purpose in history, the sequence of historical events is like a chain whose ends are hidden from view: "The chain of the almighty, all-wise goodness is entwined one part *into* and *through* the other thousandfold – but each member in the chain is in its place a *member* – hangs on the chain and does not see *where in the end the chain hangs*. Each in its delusion feels itself to be the *central point*, in its delusion feels *everything around itself only to the extent* that it pours rays or waves on this point – beautiful delusion!" (*HPW* 335). Because of this delusion of historical cause and purpose, the historian acts as a philosopher, one could almost say as a critic of ideology. The ability to see historical phenomena as links in a chain whose ends are obscure, but whose links are not, is what makes historiography philosophical. Seen philosophically, every historical event in the world

> has its grounds and causes which, so to speak, produced its nature; it also has consequences of its nature – and what else is a description of this but a historical doctrinal structure? Finally, every occurrence is merely a link in a chain, it is woven into the connection with others, it is defective in the coming together of worldly things through attraction and repulsion – and a plan of this connection, of this world-system of effects, is this not a historical doctrinal structure? Is a historian of this scope not a philosopher? Not a pragmatic systematizer?" (*Older Critical Grove*, *HPW* 258)

The philosopher/historian looks at historical events as part of a world system whose purpose is obscure, but whose rules of development can be investigated and modelled through scientific inquiry.

One of the most important models for investigating the organic growth of humanity in his essay is the development of a tree.[58] Again and again, he presents us with the image of humanity developing from a single trunk or stem (*Stamm* is the word for trunk and stem, but also tribe), branching out into an ever more complex diversity. Speaking of the need to see continuity "*progress* toward a *greater whole*," he states: "From the Orient to Rome it was *tribal stem* [*Stamm*]; now *branches* and *twigs* came forth from the tribal stem – none of them in itself *firm like the stem* but *more extensive, airier, higher*!" (*HPW* 310). In the Middle Ages, the tribal stem appears as a crown: "precisely the aspect of *non-unity*, the aspect of *confusion*, the rich *excess of branches and twigs* – this constitutes this spirit's nature! There hang the blooms of *the spirit of chivalry*; there at some future time, when the storm blows off the leaves, will hang the more beautiful *fruits*"(*HPW* 311). And his own age is the time when the individual branches and twigs have become so fine, so delicate, so lofty, that they threaten to lose sight of their connection to the stem, the trunk, the tribe: "We are the *thin, airy twigs* up there, freely shaking and *whispering* with every wind [...] Do people not see that we lack all the *vices* and *virtues* of times past because we – altogether lack their *firm footing, forces* and *sap, space* and *element*?" (*HPW* 332).

The model acquires a strong presence and power of explanation in the course of the essay. At the same time, it raises the question of the single natural force driving development. By the time Herder has come to the third and final section, he can speak of humanity as the "*Great creature of God*! Work of *three parts of the world* and almost *six millennia*! The delicate, sap-filled *root*; the slender, blossoming *shoot*; the mighty *stem*; the strongly striving, entwined *branches*; the airy, wide-spread *twigs* – how everything rests on each other, has grown from each other. – *Great creature of God*! But *for what? For what purpose*?" (*HPW* 331). The arboreal model allows him to pose once again the fundamental question of his inquiry, that is, how should the present think of the purpose (or at least the purposiveness, to use Kant's term) of history. And it has taken him to the place where he can criticize not only the mechanistic, superficial, materialistic bent of his century, but also its inability to see its connections to its own past, and the damage it does in its imperialistic ventures in other parts of the world (much of his critique of imperialism in this essay takes the form of interjections in his elaboration of the growing tree of humanity).

But here the model begins to unravel. If humanity is a growing tree, how exactly does its historical development relate to its geographical expansion? Are the peoples and nations of the world destined to languish in the shade of the crown which is Europe's Middle Ages, its Reformation and Age of Enlightenment, as he implies repeatedly?[59] And is the tree a German tree, in which the twigs exist "*beside* each other, *wove, tangled* together, each with its own *sap*," but as "*brother nations*" that are "all of one *German family* [*Geschlecht*], all in accordance with *one ideal* of *constitution*, all in *faith in one religion*?" (*HPW* 311; translation modified). Then what does that make humanity – a forest? Herder has arrived at the same problem that caused him to break off the inquiry into the change of taste – the model that sees a single humanity growing through time is unsettled by the fact of geographical, physiological, and cultural difference. He attempts to counter this by using the same model to explain the geographical expansion of humanity throughout the world,[60] but all this does is point to the discrepancy between the arboreal model's historical and its geographical application. If human history has grown and branched out like a tree, then the geography of diversity cannot be taken as evidence of a consort of diverse cultures collectively constituting humanity. For in Herder's own conception of culture, each culture would have to see itself as environmentally rooted, as heir to its own history and traditions, its own peculiar interactions with other cultures. In fact, one of the shortcomings of the philosopher of progress is that he fails to see the true nature of what Herder calls "this hidden *double creature*": that the human being "can be modified a thousandfold, and, given the structure of our earth, almost must be – that there is a creation of clime, of circumstances of an age ... That there can and must be all this but that inside beneath the manyfold transformed husk the same kernel of the essential nature and of capacity for happiness can still be preserved, and according to all human expectation almost will be so" (*HPW* 335–6). In the history of the single force of nature acting for human development, humanity is a tree. But in the geography of diversity, each culture is a tree, and humanity is a forest.

There is another way of saying this. In order to make the organic model work on a macro-historical level, Herder has to disregard its foundations in the environment and the body – but this is where his evidence lies, this is what brought him to the model in the first place.

When he speaks of a common project for the betterment of humanity, individual deeds appear as the seeds and sprouts of a plant – what he calls the "the noblest plant of humanity, civilization [*Bildung*], education, strengthening of nature in its most imperfect [*bedürftigsten*] nerves, love of human beings, sympathy, and brotherly bliss." In striving for a unity of humankind, these formative deeds nurture the soul as the seat of human life, and do not dwell on what he calls "*merely bodily* and *political purposes*" (*HPW* 353). And yet, it is clear from his earliest writings that Herder regarded bodily and political purposes as vital components in the nurturing of humanity in its wholeness. The purpose of the bodily and the political in an individual's life are best grasped in terms of "a physics of history, psychology [*Seelenlehre*], and politics," and they must be thought of as part of the same purpose that leads to the betterment of humanity (*HPW* 269; translation modified). In fact, as he noted in his essay *Über Thomas Abbts Schriften* (On Thomas Abbt's Writings, 1768), the author himself embodies historical force, and in this way he too becomes arboreal: "He is held by the bonds of his age, and he offers his book as a gift to his age. He stands in his own century like a tree in the ground, taking root and drawing sap from it, with which he provides for the proportions of his development" (*HFA* 2, 579). This function of the roots that hold one's body grounded in tradition is necessary for growth, but it is the philosopher's obligation to always take note of the existence and dimensions of these roots, thereby linking the body to its ground.

The discrepancies in these models highlight the contradictions in the positions Herder is trying to take. Seen in one way – and he himself acknowledges this – his models are little more than analogies, whereby nature becomes "God's speaking exemplary model in all works!" (*HPW* 299). This follows Thomas Aquinas's understanding of analogy as a way of approaching God's unfathomable reason via inadequate human thought. Here, analogy is possible because human life follows the same rules as the rest of nature, and thus the principles driving the natural growth of trees, for example, must apply in some way to the lives of human beings. History in this way becomes the testing ground for analogy.[61] Extending this, the fact of analogy – the capacity of human thought to grasp (if not to fully comprehend) the rules and to hear the speech of God's exemplary nature – is itself proof that human thought does not stand opposite divine reason, but partakes in it.[62] But seen in another way, analogy separates thought from the divine. Analogy is a linguistic sign, and it partakes in the splitting of signification. It signifies by virtue of not being what it means. Analogical thought has arisen from the human capacity not only to read nature, but to create meaning. And in the semiotic creation of meaning, human thought is partaking in the divine processes these signs seek to decipher, but it is also acting independently. Analogy is at once a way of distancing thought from divinity and of merging the two.

These contrasting understandings of analogy will remain unresolved in Herder. As Kant will later (1783) point out, analogy is useful not in determining the object of reason (in this case the force and purpose of growth in nature and in history), but in establishing the rule that links reason with its objects.[63] This view of analogy will later develop into the Kantian problem of purposiveness without purpose and of the application of teleological judgment to natural processes. By separating discourses on the rules of nature from those of purpose in the *Critique of Judgment*, Kant is able to retain the mechanistic understanding of natural processes (explained in the *Critique of Pure Reason*) without sacrificing the guiding principle of higher purposes (as set out in *Critique of Practical Reason*).

Herder is not prepared to go along with this. His historiography is not intended to analyse the past and the present *as if* the course of human history took part in a natural process of growth, driven by divine purpose and aimed at a transcendent goal. Historical knowledge, since it is a form of cognition, is itself a process of life.[64] It is a semiotic act, and this means it is an essential component of model formation in the sciences.[65] In historiography, analogical thought reflects upon history, bringing forth meaning in accordance with the very purpose scientific inquiry seeks to discover. In this sense historical knowledge gives access to what Herder was, at the same time he was writing *This Too a Philosophy of History*, calling the "hieroglyphics of creation" (*HSW* 6, 289). As Menges observes, "Nature, being as much history as creation, constitutes the visible and legible text of creation, and that text is God's poetry."[66] It is the wager of *This Too a Philosophy of History* that the structural patterns, if not the actual meaning of this text can be deciphered. What will emerge, Herder hopes, is a schematic representation of the divine plan actualized in history, psychology, and politics.

The philosopher's gift is his ability to recognize the large scheme of development within the variety of organic life cycles that constitute nature and human nature. In this way, historical inquiry merges divine prescience with the human capacity for having reflected on the senses (*Besonnenheit*). And as we have seen, *Besonnenheit* locates thought in language and ties it to environment and tradition.[67] From the point of view of the divine plan, the individual's reason appears a part of the world's life processes. But seen from the point of view of the individual's capacity to grasp these life processes, they begin to appear as blind fate. This leads Herder to state

> concerning the excessively high renown of the *human understanding* that, if I may put the matter so, *it* had less and less effect in this *universal alteration of the world* than a *blind fate* that cast and guided things. Either they were such great, so to speak, *cast-forth* events which went beyond all human *forces* and *prospects*, which human beings usually *resisted*, where no one [even] dreamed of the *consequences* as a *considered plan*, or they were small *accidental happenings*, more *finds* than *interventions*, applications of a thing that one had *had for a long time* and not seen, not used – or nothing at all but a *simple mechanism*, new *knack*, *manual skill*, that changed the world. Philosophers of the eighteenth century, if that is so, then where does that leave your *idolatry* towards the *human spirit*? (*HPW* 313)

With this question we can see how Herder's understanding of reason will prevent him from taking the Kantian path, separating those judgments which address the mechanisms of nature from those which address purpose, freedom, and the possibility of a divine plan. Herder sees the divine plan so deeply inscribed in phenomena themselves, but also in the capacity of thought to understand phenomena, that he rejects any mechanistic model of nature as hopelessly inadequate to grasping the true nature of phenomena and thought, while at the same time discussing mechanistic models of thought as themselves related to divine reason (see *HPW* 317–18). As he considers what his contribution to the philosophy of history will be, his biggest challenge is to find the model that will explain this process. It will have to describe diversity in a way that sheds light on the universal plan guiding humanity's development according to principles that are both divine and natural. And it will have to leave room for individual cognition and aesthetic production within this plan. This set of challenges will drive Herder's next major project.

Reason in Philosophy and Government

When, in the early 1780s *This Too a Philosophy of History* was out of print, Herder took it upon himself to revise it and expand it according to plans he had already been considering for many years. The result was his *Ideas concerning the Philosophy of the History of Humanity*, begun in 1782.

In the meantime, he had left Bückeburg to take on the position of general superintendent and chief pastor of the parish church in Weimar, where he arrived on 1 October 1776, just a year after Goethe. Weimar was to remain his home for the rest of his life.

Herder's first decade in Weimar was to see a sustained dialogue with his friend on matters of history, science, art, politics, and education. Ever since parting in Strasbourg, Goethe and Herder had remained in contact, exchanging letters, and apparently remaining on the best of terms. Now, with Herder in Weimar, the old association was re-established, and their intense intellectual interaction began anew. They discussed current literary and scientific projects, mulled over Germany's intellectual life, and generally encouraged one another in their respective endeavours. In his letters to friends, Goethe repeatedly expressed his enthusiasm over Herder's presence in Weimar – and he began to allude to an underlying conflict he hoped might have come to an end.[68] In December 1780 Herder would write to Hamann complaining that the high salary offered to Friedrich Carl Ludwig von Moser by the Duchy of Cassel was paid using ill-gotten funds obtained through the sale of mercenaries to fight in the American War of Independence, and implying that Goethe and Carl August were indirectly involved in the appointment (*HBG* 4, 148). From the very moment he set foot in Weimar, Herder's reliance on Goethe and Carl August were bound to come into conflict with his investigations into the way European history was propelled by the world economy he had criticized in *This Too a Philosophy of History*. This led to a set of problems that lay at the heart of the relationship between philosophy and government, and how the two dealt with the question of morality. The Thirty Years' War had shown the political disaster that resulted from the theological claim to absolute morality in the realm of politics, and the most successful Enlightenment sovereigns had tried their best to free the political decision-making process from the moral rule of the churches. By doing their best to exclude morality from politics, they were not so much concerned with the way morality operated in everyday life, but the way theology claimed exclusive dominion when it spoke morality to politicians. And in this, they were in agreement with the dominant trend in Enlightenment philosophy.

On one level, Herder remained conservative in his conviction that theology was the discourse in which morality had to be discussed, at least to the extent that theology provided a language for speaking about the divine plan for humanity, and this served him as the ultimate measure of action.[69] It is true, he gave this conservatism an important twist with his belief that the political structure of a society is forced to negotiate in one way or another the plan for the unfolding of human life on earth. What this means for theology is that its effect on politics is not to be tempered by removing universal discourses on human action from the practice of politics, but in redefining how philosophers and politicians alike speak about practice. This meant rethinking the relationship between theory and practice, but also between public and private reason in government. Here Herder was deeply suspicious of pietist leanings towards political quietism. Religion could not serve its true purpose if it remained confined to private life, announcing its presence through conscience, or creed. Instead, it would have to become integral with philosophical discourses of truth, and with political practices of government. This conservative argument about the dominion of theology blends seamlessly with a political radicalism that argues for a full accountability of government in terms of public morality.

Starting at an early age, Herder began to ask what Spinoza's ideas on God and politics meant for his own time. In the opening paragraphs of his unfinished *Tractatus Theologico-Politicus*, Spinoza argues that the philosopher and the statesman are both caught up in the same impasse of theory and practice. The philosopher (Herder would have to qualify this as the idealist philosopher) can only see human beings in terms of their ideals, not their true selves, with their passions, their prejudices, and their messy corporeal lives. The statesman, being so used to calculating the moves of power according to this latter aspect of human life, finds himself at odds with the philosopher. What theology can offer is a guiding discourse that will overcome the philosopher's naive faith in reason (which, Spinoza insists in paragraph 5, is like a dream of the poetic golden age or of a stage play) and take account of human passions, while at the same time steering the reason of state towards a mode of government that takes account of the true nature of human life.

Herder had absorbed these and similar ideas at an early age through his reading of the *Tractatus*, which according to Michael N. Forster influenced him strongly in the Riga years.[70] The *Tractatus* inspired a fundamental rethinking of Herder's politics. In the years leading up to *This Too a Philosophy of History*, he absorbs the Spinozist position to the point where he has undergone what Forster calls a complete reversal, abandoning his previous praise of Catherine the Great's enlightened absolutism and presenting himself as "a harsh critic of modern monarchy, and by contrast an enthusiast for democratic republicanism and freedom."[71] Herder will never turn his back on this political position.

In the eighth *Letter on the Advancement of Humanity*, he will quote Friedrich II lamenting in 1742 that "deception, guile, duplicity, disloyalty are unfortunately the dominant character of most people who stand at the forefront of nations." If they were to reveal their true natures in public, Friedrich observes, "they would only reap the indignation of the public" (*HSW* 17, 39). Herder mentions this to press home his conviction that the task of humanity is to secure the public sphere so as to ensure that the contradictory demands of the various domains of reason not be concealed, but negotiated for the betterment of all. This is after all one of the most important inflections that the term *Bildung* had acquired by the time Herder wrote. And if the philosopher has any meaningful role to play at all, it is to coordinate this process in a manner that can be called theological (since it uses thought in a manner consistent with divine force) and scientific (since it develops consistent models to explain how human nature partakes of divine force). Herder is beginning to explore the territory that will later be opened up by Marx in the *German Ideology* (1845–6), where political life is not defined in separating the realms of reason, but in coordinating their effects.[72]

These ideas on government and reason were becoming increasingly important to Herder as he made the move from Riga, where he experienced a vibrant form of republican government, to Bückeburg, whose conservative, absolutist government was typical for the post-Westphalian principalities, then to Weimar, a glowing example of enlightened absolutism.[73] Increasingly, the public use of reason, the relationship between theory and practice, and the blending of scientific method with a theological world view would steer the course of inquiry in Herder's philosophy of history. And since he was pursuing his studies once again in close proximity to Goethe, Herder's ideas also started to be defined, at least in part, in relationship to those of his protégé. In spite of sustained variances in their understandings of political life, Goethe and Herder continued a productive exchange of ideas throughout the 1780s.[74]

The most important dimension of the dialogue that was established between Herder and Goethe in Weimar was the cross-fertilization of Herder's work on the philosophy of history and Goethe's studies in natural history. If it is possible to formulate a common question that brought the two together at the time, it would have to be the pursuit of a model capable of explaining how human thought and aesthetic production take part in the natural processes of life. For both of them, this seemed attainable as an empirical interrogation of the boundary between human life and the forces of nature. This empirical work seemed to confirm that the closer they looked at this boundary, the more they realized that it is not a found boundary, but that the distinction between objective nature and human nature is drawn in the act of observing, interpreting, and giving expression to natural phenomena. Later in life, Goethe would on a number of instances openly acknowledge the importance of his friend's influence on his general intellectual pursuits at that time. For example, in the foreword to *Zur Morphologie* (published in 1817), he writes:

> My arduous, agonizing research was made easier, in fact sweetened, when Herder began to write down the *Ideas on the History of Humanity*. Our daily conversations concerned the primal origins of the waters – Earth, and the organic creatures which have forever been developing upon it. The primal beginning and its unceasing further development were constantly discussed and our scientific holdings were daily refined and enriched through reciprocal communication and opposition. (*GHA* 13, 63)

This process of distillation began to look like a common project for securing what Friedrich Schlegel later called a "new mythology"[75] – a struggle for a formal negotiation of the boundaries of human life. These boundaries were, seen from one side, performed in language, and seen from another side, perpetuated in political systems. A new mythology promised a way of thinking about the unity of life, a question heightened by Herder's dislike for Kantian dualism. Life cannot be lived as if it were split down the middle and played out in two different worlds, and this is what Herder thought Kant was advocating.

The Parallelism of Heaven and Earth

But matters were not that simple. If Herder wants to understand the natural drives governing life as a unity, he still has to find a way to speak of their different aspects. Unconscious reason has to be approached differently from conscious reason; and the same applies to the distinction between public and private reason, between individual life and the life of the species, between culture and humanity. Herder grasped this problem as central to his work, and he understood it as the problem of divinity at work in human life. He addresses it in *Vom Geist der Ebräischen Poesie* (The Spirit of Hebrew Poetry), which occupied him in the early 1780s, and which he published in two volumes (1782 and 1783). Herder had made it clear on a number of occasions that he regarded his history of Hebrew poetry as a continuation of his larger project on the history of humanity. He gave the work the subtitle "A Guide for Connoisseurs thereof and of the Oldest History of the Human Spirit," pointing to his growing interest in the collective history of ideas. In the outline presented at the beginning of the book, he addresses himself to all those "who cherish a liberal curiosity respecting the progress of knowledge, divine, and human, as connected with the earlier history of our race,"[76] explaining that his larger aim is to investigate "the phenomenon and the effect of these writings [*das Phänomen und das Resultat dieser Schriften*] and of their spirit in the whole history of culture [*Kultur*], and of transformations of the world [*Weltveränderungen*], so far as known to us."[77]

If he was to solve the problem of how the individual manifestations of the human spirit relate to the idea of humanity as a whole, Herder would have to discover the mechanism that allows him to understand the divergence of the world's many cultures as representing a kaleidoscopic display of humanity's single life. The mechanism Herder speaks of in *The Spirit of Hebrew Poetry* is the "parallelism of heaven and earth." This parallelism of heaven and earth is the force that introduces "unity and order into the chaos of world creation" (*HSW* 11, 255). Herder had been working on the idea of the parallelism of heaven and earth for a long time, and he restates it again and again throughout his work. It is so important to him that it can in some respects be seen as the theological foundation upon which his entire work is built – from the theory of human language, through the centrality of humanity in the world, to the rejection of Kant's critical theory. The formulation he chooses in 1782 in *The Spirit of Hebrew Poetry* is telling: "When, through the concept of One creator, the world became One World (χοσμος), the spirit [*Gemüth*] of humanity, the world's splendid reflection [*Abglanz*], supplemented it [*machte sich dazu*] and learned wisdom, order, and beauty" (*HSW* 11, 255).

In this statement, everything is up for grabs. Everything depends on the self-supporting interplay between human language and humanity's conceptualization of itself, its world, its creator. Nothing abstract is given – not God, not the world, not humanity; everything is conceptualized and formed in language. God did not create the world, this world became one world through the concept of one creator. And in the process, humanity decides what is to be experienced as a real and powerful component of human life. Humanity decides – that is what is important. And it decides in different ways according to the circumstances of its social and environmental conditions. My translation is awkward, but I have tried to retain the difficult yet powerful function of agency in Herder's meticulously formulated German sentence. Agency works here through a dual act of human imagination and conceptualization: through the concept of a single creator, humanity allowed itself to imagine the world as we know it, as χοσμος, cosmos; and by recognizing and thinking about its own act of imagination, humanity's spirit brings itself into being alongside the cosmos and the creator. In this way, thought reproduces divine creation, and it continues to operate parallel to the forces of God.

God may have created the force of human spirit, but the only definitive statement that can be made about both the human spirit and the creator is that the former is a concept out of which arose the cosmos, and that humanity arose alongside the cosmos and the concept. The formulation *machte sich dazu*, which literally means *additionally brought itself into being* or *made itself alongside*, contains the idea of humanity's parallel life alongside the world and the creator, but it also underlines the creative agency exercised by humanity in this process. This multiple parallelism expresses Herder's idea of the active role played by human creativity and critique in the ongoing process of creation. This process gives humanity a collective shape and it unfolds parallel to the organic development of individuals and societies. Creative and cognitive activity always partakes of both the collective development of humanity and the organic development of individuals and groups. The collective shape of human society has to do with how different cultures negotiate their divergent interpretations of the world. This is how Herder understands diversity in unity.

To say this, however, is merely to point to the problem Herder was attempting to resolve – if the evidence of cultural diversity points to an endless variety in world views and mythologies, how will it be possible to discover a model that does justice to the singular development of humanity throughout history? Are there natural principles uniting human life in its infinite variety? Are there fundamental principles of organic growth that apply to an individual's life in the same way they do to an entire culture, and to all of humanity – indeed to all of creation? If so, what practices of representation and interpretation allow access to these principles? The only way to address these questions, in Herder's project, is through aesthetic acts – provided the aesthetic is understood as an act of imagination mediating reason and the senses, as the conceptualization of one creator and the "making itself" of the world's reflection. In this sense, *Ideas* can be read (as Gaier reads it) as the practical implementation of Herder's epistemology and his poetics.[78]

Herder's philosophy of history aimed at a narrative of the development not only of human history, but of the natural world. This begins with an inquiry into the place of the human in the world, including the specific qualities of humanity's home, and humanity's formal adaptation to its home.[79] This meant also discovering the forms of expression through which different peoples reflect upon the nature of their home and on the forms of intercultural communication that cause cultures to change (as he had discussed in the fourth natural law in the *Treatise*). It was not possible to ignore the way European expansionism factored into this problem. As we saw, when Herder considered inter-cultural communication, he thought immediately of the cultures of the New World, and his evidence was all coming to him within the context of European expansionism. The moves from analysis of this evidence to the theses about common humanity was given added impetus by a strong moralizing discourse about imperialism that was rapidly gaining ground in Europe.

In April 1782, the Abbé Raynal visited Weimar. Raynal, who was at that time living in exile from France, was already an iconic opponent of the imperial exploitation and domination of the world outside Europe. Looking back in 1791, Christian Friedrich Daniel Schubart put it like this: "With his History of the Two Indies he inspired the nation with enthusiasm for freedom and human dignity; he painted the despotic horror, the moral compulsion, and the spirit of persecution in incendiary colors; in short, he was heard and admired by all of Europe as a preacher of political liberty and of freedom of conscience."[80] Raynal placed his critique of European injustice in the context of nascent globalization, in which "new connexions were formed by the inhabitants of the most distant regions, for the supply of wants they had never before experienced [... and] a general intercourse of opinions, laws and customs, diseases and remedies, virtues and vices, was established among men."[81]

Following Raynal's visit, Goethe founded a reading group that met thrice weekly to work its way systematically through the *History of the Two Indies*, comparing his observations to maps of the relevant regions.[82] Herder was less impressed by Raynal's visit. He too made sure that he had the latest edition of the *History of the Two Indies*, and that he was prepared to enter into dialogue with Raynal. However, he made slow progress in the reading because, as he wrote to Hamann, "I don't see

4.1 Frontispiece to Guillaume Thomas François Raynal, *Histoire philosophique et politique des établissements et du commerce des européens dans les deux Indes* (Geneva: Jean-Léonard Pellet, 1781).

anything useful in it for myself" (28 April 1782, *HBG* 4, 217). In the person of Raynal he found, as he complained to Johannes Müller, "the worst windbag I have encountered, in all respects the blossom of this century" (1 June 1782, *HBG* 4, 221).[83] But this masks the debt Herder owed to Raynal. The original formulation of *This Too a Philosophy of History* had begun in pursuit of constancy in moral values throughout history and of a general principle of *Bildung* for describing how moral principles may have developed over the ages (*HMA* 1, 685). Constancy of moral principles was one of Raynal's main concerns, and their relationship to the development of human inclinations with time had been derived in that earlier work, as Pross observes, from Herder's reading of *History of the Two Indias.* This applies in particular to book 19, "in which, for the first time, a coherent and future-oriented law of history is postulated as an alternative to Rousseau's negative views on development and Voltaire's skeptical perspective on history" (*HMA* 1, 862–3). Herder may not have been impressed by Raynal's conversation, but the political and moral importance of a philosophy of history that did not rely on Eurocentric progressivism remained with Herder.

More important still was that Herder recognized in Raynal's writing a necessary response to what Koselleck describes as the crisis in the relation between the European bourgeoisie and the two pillars of power and moral authority, the church and the state.[84] In the letter to Johannes Müller cited above, Herder names the only thing he finds worthy of great respect in the book, Raynal's "*jargon philosophique et politique.*" Koselleck argues that Raynal's philosophy of history took part in the general Enlightenment repositioning of the bourgeoisie as the critical moral voice of historical progress.[85] This voice seized on the theological idea of a final moral reckoning with unjust sovereigns, but recast it as a secular philosophy of history in which the present has an obligation to write against and act against injustice. Just two years before his visit to Weimar, Raynal had written that "when society and the laws take revenge for the crimes of individuals, the good man hopes that the punishment of the guilty can prevent further crimes."[86]

This is not necessarily a political program in the sense we would understand it today. As Arnd Bohm observes, the German word *Politik* "was used to designate the tactics of governing, somewhere between today's 'policy' and 'political science.'"[87] What politics does promise is to align the question of morality with that of government. Herder would later put it like this: "For politics, the human being is a *means*; for ethics he is an *end.*"[88] When, in the fifty-eighth *Letter on Humanity*,

Herder argues for a reappraisal of Machiavelli, this is his point of reference. In the course of the eighteenth century, Machiavelli had increasingly become the object of intense criticism by German intellectuals, culminating in the *Anti-Machiavel* of Frederick the Great, published in 1740, and written just before his assuming the throne.[89] With this book, written under the influence of Voltaire (in whose name it was initially published),[90] Frederick had sought to set out the political program of an enlightened monarchy. He constructs a moral argument on the grounds of the necessary character and insight of the monarch. To do this, he refutes point by point the arguments of Machiavelli. Herder questions the foundation of this criticism, and he concludes that it has to do with "the relationship of politics and morality" (*HFA* 7, 340). The problem facing contemporary politics and morals is "that the two had become visibly and completely separated" (*HFA* 7, 340). And this had important ramifications for religion. Now that religion has become "completely sequestered from morality," it itself becomes politics. The primary law of politics is "the reason of state (la agione del stato); its guiding principle is the capacity to use things, each in its own time and according to its maturity (conocer las cosas en sa piato, en sa sazon, y saber las lograr)" (*HFA* 7, 341). Machiavelli saw this development and wrote a handbook for its correct implementation. Herder argues that to criticize the morality of this book is to miss the point. It has to be read historically, otherwise the reader will mistake a historically contingent analysis of morality for a statement on morals in general. This is not to condone Machiavelli. On the contrary, Herder wants to reject his instrumental reason of state not on the basis of universal morality, but because of what it says about the public exercise of reason and international law at that moment in history. By reading him in this way, Herder attempts to place Machiavelli's instrumental doctrine in the context of a larger historical trend that condemns it to failure, because its historical unsustainability is the same thing as its failed morality. Here, history embodies the principle of its own development, and reveals this principle as a moral one.

As Koselleck shows, the Enlightenment attempts to see history as itself containing the principle of morality pushes the philosophy of history into a central position, where it becomes the quintessential bourgeois act of self-affirmation. The philosophy of history defines the political role of the bourgeoisie as the voice of freedom that resists blind submission to church and state. But in doing so, the philosophy of history defines the terms in which the current crisis can be resolved – as

Diderot wrote, in slavery or in liberty.[91] By seeking to define the terms of future resolution and thereby to influence the course of history, or, to put it differently, by becoming both the prophet and the agent of historical teleology, the historian becomes aligned with the theologian.

Herder recognized this, and drew two important consequences, both of them developed in his reading of Raynal: first, that the critical interpretation of the present and the prognosis for a positive outcome in the future requires a theological understanding of the processes of history; and second, that the fact of European imperialism is the testing ground for this view of history. Regarding the second point, Raynal and Diderot had both understood the challenges that European imperialism presented for the claims to a monopoly on morality on the part of the European state.[92] If the exercise of corrupt power was understood as a cynical union of politics and an equally corrupt morality, then the critical force of the Enlightenment public intellectual lay in an appeal to moral innocence of the kind that was increasingly identified with the New World. In this way, the geographical dispersal of cultures is solicited in the service of the philosophy of history. "The natural and innocent realm of trans-oceanic wilderness, up to now the great reservoir of an indirect critic of despotism, now takes on the historical role of the new society." By narrating the "economic and colonial history of the European states overseas," Raynal is showing how world history reveals itself to the critical mind as the scene of a world court of justice.[93]

By constructing his views on world history around European expansionism, Raynal was also asking, at least by implication, what a philosophy of geographical difference might look like. This same question is raised more explicitly in one of the most influential German travelogues of the time, the report of James Cook's second voyage by Georg Forster. Forster was ten years younger than Herder and a child prodigy who, in 1767, at the tender age of twelve, had already been commended by the London Society of Antiquaries for his translation of Mikhail Lomonosov's *Short History of Russia* into English. The young Forster had learned Russian while accompanying his father, Johann Reinhold Forster, to Russia, where he had been commissioned in 1765 to study the conditions of settlers in the newly established German colonies on the Volga River. The elder Forster was appointed naturalist to accompany James Cook on his second voyage to the South Seas (1772–5) by the admiralty, replacing Sir Joseph Banks, and he took Georg with him, who was then seventeen years old.

Like Herder, Forster is intent on introducing representation as a problem in philosophical systems, and his suspicion of systematic philosophy caused him to give the travelogue priority. Forster recognizes here the problem of empiricism: how observed facts and subjective perception can be systematized to yield knowledge – the problem that prompted Kant's polemic against Hume in the *Critique of Pure Reason*. Forster is not willing to sacrifice the abstract in the name of experience, but he is also not prepared to defer to what, in an essay on James Cook, he calls "armchair philosophy" (*die Philosophie im Lehnstuhl*).[94] The problem with armchair philosophy is that its demonstrable inability to account for the wealth of experience opened up in voyages of discovery to the New World has led to an equally damaging proliferation of scientific studies that do nothing but collect disparate facts. In *A Voyage round the World*, Forster puts it like this:

> The learned, at last grown tired of being deceived by the powers of rhetoric, and by sophistical arguments, raised a general cry after a simple collection of facts. They had their wish; facts were collected in all parts of the world, and yet knowledge was not increased. They received a confused heap of disjointed limbs, which no art could reunite into a whole; and the rage of hunting after facts soon rendered them incapable of forming and resolving a single proposition; like those minute enquirers, whose life is wholly spent in the anatomical dissection of flies, from whence they never draw a single conclusion for the use of mankind, or even of brutes.[95]

Forster, like Herder, is intent upon distilling an essence of universal validity from experience. And for Forster, the path to universality is a similar one to that of Herder. It is analytical, and relies upon collecting a diversity of observations into a system that possesses narrative coherence as well as philosophical cogency. For Forster, as for Herder, travel relies not on an a priori system of knowledge that the transcendent and authoritative European subject bears with him, but on the empirical interactions with other people in other places, the linguistic and imaginative negotiation of diverse world views.[96] Like Herder, Forster uses the challenge of the expanding world to put forward an understanding of fact based on analysis of experience, and a consensus on representation negotiated through the medium of print. In this respect, even before the *Critique of Pure Reason*, Forster is inflecting Kant's problem with the moral challenges raised by imperialism.

Herder understood that Forster was working in parallel with his own writings. When the third part of Herder's *Ideas* appeared in 1787, Herder wrote to Hartknoch asking him to send Forster a copy (*HBG* 5, 226). This volume contains the crucial pages in which Herder explains his understanding of the concept of humanity. We know from Forster's letters to Herder that he was an ardent admirer of the *Ideas*.[97] And when, in the 116th *Letter on Humanity*, Herder discusses the work of the travelogue, he makes specific reference to Forster. The travelogue, he claims, has a special position in promoting the sense of humanity's unity; in fact, when it comes to recognizing the "humanity in humans," he considers "faithful travelogues" to be much more reliable than "systems." Herder sounds remarkably like Forster when he spells out what he expects of faithful travelogues. "A classification of travel descriptions, not, as might be entertained, only according to noteworthy features of natural history, but also according to the inner content *of the travel describers themselves*, to what extent they had a pure eye and in their breast *universal natural* and *human sensitivity* – such a work would be very useful for the distracted flock of readers who do not know right from left" (*HPW* 397). But here the problem of universality re-emerges. How can Herder be sure that what he sees as natural, human sensitivity is indeed universal? How are they different from the claims to universality he so abhorred in the rationalists? The answer lies in the word sensitivity. Herder is not talking about an abstract capacity for appreciating the finer things seen in travelling. He is talking about the shared human way of being in the world – as creatures of the senses. It is this which makes the common ground on which different interpretations of the world can be negotiated. And a good travelogue is a guide to this process.

Herder is advocating what he calls a *Hodopaedia* – a descriptive practice, but also a guideline for practical interactions with the forms of life encountered by the traveller. He speaks of "principles for how humans and animals are to be regarded and treated." This representational practice is, he believes, capable of countering what he sees as imperialism and globalization – the "divisum toto orbe Britannum" and the practices of the "monarchic merchant," who need not have a "fatherland" at all. This is an important move. It starts to speak of systematic thought as a kind of tyranny; and it sets a precedent opposing this perceived tyranny with dialogue based on shared representations. The dialogues leading to negotiation are seen as a response to the trauma of European domination and exploitation of other cultures – a kind of truth and reconciliation process for the scientific community. "Travel descriptions of such a sort – of which (let us be thankful to humanity!) we have many [and here he names Forster] – expand our horizon and multiply our sensitivity for every situation of our brothers. Without losing a word about this, they preach sympathy, tolerance, forgiveness, praise, pity, many-sided culture of the mind, satisfaction, wisdom" (*HPW* 397).

Herder followed Forster's work sporadically for a number of years. When the latter visited Weimar in October 1785, Herder expressed concern that the young man's health had been harmed through having travelled "too early to the South Pole" (to Hamann, October 1785, *HBG* 5: 139). And when Forster learned that same year that he was to go on a four-year voyage to the South Seas, sponsored by Russian research money, Herder was eager to provide him with a compendium of questions to take with him (and he encouraged Goethe to do the same). In fact, in the exchange between Herder and Forster, it becomes clear that both are concerned not only to frame the right questions, but to present them in the appropriate form to the scientific and lay public. This meant taking account of the dictates of fashion and the expectations of empire – particularly in light of the fact that the sponsors are a world power with imperialist ambitions.

When Forster died in 1794, Herder wrote (in the 106th *Letter on Humanity*) of how much had been lost with his death, and he lamented the fact that, unlike Forster, contemporary writers and critics are so seldom able to familiarize the German reading public with "the most treasured products of other countries." He then muses that "an evil genius must be at work, in that he tries … to sever the thread that ties us to the thoughts of other nations!" (*HSW* 18: 132). Seen in this light, the parallelism of heaven and earth requires the mediation of the critical intellectual to decipher the signs of divine force as they appear in nature. This involves a politics of historical development, but also of geographical difference. By the time he was working on *Ideas*, Herder understood his philosophy as pointing towards a methodology of parallelism.

5 From Human Diversity to the Politics of Natural Development

Bildung and Diversity

As Herder set about collecting the wealth of information about other cultures that would form the backbone of *Ideas*, it became increasingly apparent that one of the main tasks would be to specify what it is that enables intercultural communication, the thread that leads to the thoughts of other nations, and that might allow such communication to bypass the interests of imperialism. This alternative communication must be grounded in a more authentic representation of nature than what imperialism offers. But how will this be possible, if the pursuit of this project depends on the backing of imperialist nations? This problem would lead him back to the workings of natural forces in the unfolding of world history, since individual cultures express a fundamental natural force in keeping with their own languages, environments, and traditions. We have already seen how important the concept of force was when it came to linking cognition and history. In the 1780s Herder was thinking more carefully about what this study of the history of forces in the world would have to look like. In a set of notes which Pross publishes under the heading "Wie bringt eine Kraft die andre hervor?" (How Does One Force Give Rise to Another? *HMA* 3/1, 1107–12), and which he dates to 1778–80, Herder begins to think about the manifestations of the world's driving forces in the same way he will later explore world history – as a play of inner and outer forces whose interaction is indeterminate and open to exploration (Suphan gave these notes the title "Versuch über die Kräfte [Essay on Forces]: Nach Hume, Leibniz, Spinoza," *HSW* 14, 605–8). In this very sketchy outline, Herder tries to formulate the questions that need to be asked if natural force is to be investigated. In his conception, the natural forces of life are both internally and externally determined, each requiring appropriate methods of understanding and description. The external operation of force is associated with analogies of similar kinds of force, such as physical motion or thought. By this, presumably, he means that the senses perceive external motion or evidence of the thoughts of another person, and act in analogy to what is perceived, motivated by the passions. This gives rise to art, to artifice, rhetoric, and the strategies of education. The internal operation of force is identified with Spinoza's use of the concept *conatus* (which literally means impulse, striving, drive) to mean the "drive to self-maintenance and coherence," which is "a universal feature both of any person's mind and of his body."[1] This drive is for Spinoza a drive to self-preservation, and it is one of the pillars of his entire philosophy.[2] Because self-preservation is a concern not only for the individual but for the species, it complicates the distinction between the drives to individuation and to socialization. And because it is a natural drive, it works both internally and externally. Herder is attempting to describe a matrix of natural force, where human life plays out between internal and external forces, forces of individuation and of socialization, forces seeking unification and those seeking diversification. This is why Michael Mack understands Herder's concept of culture as a unique development of Spinoza's *conatus*, which Herder extends "from the sphere of nature to the social realm of history and aesthetics."[3]

Herder was not alone in this. The drive to self-preservation had acquired a political inflection by the early eighteenth century. As Jonathan Lamb has shown, there was a strong case being made in the opening decades of the century by writers such as Mandeville (who was not important to Herder) and Shaftesbury (who was) that what Mandeville called "the Business of Self-Preservation" was intimately related to all that is positive in the social relations of individuals.[4] In this way, "Mandeville demonstrated that the paradoxes of self-preservation conform to the primordial logic of the human organism, which at its farthest sociable extent is never out of reach of the senses."[5] Shaftesbury emphasized the positive effects of the drive to self-preservation, thereby cementing the idea that morality is not something that civilization brings to nature. Herder took this not only as an argument in favour of the continuum between the natural and civilized forms of life, but as reinforcing his belief that art and aesthetic activity should be seen as part of the natural drive to self-preservation, and not as a late addition to and unsettling of natural life.

The tendency to see natural forces as driving the positive and moral sides of social life also affected the understanding of the formative drive in nature – *Bildung*. In the second half of the century, scientific research into the development of organisms was giving *Bildung* an important formal-biological meaning. By the time Herder wrote, this was starting to coalesce with other, more literal understandings of the term, such as the form-giving education that was desirable in the creation of the whole person – *l'éducation* in the sense of Rousseau or *paideia* (παιδεία) in the sense of Plato and Aristotle.[6] Or the form-giving act of aesthetic production (this latter understanding would move to the centre of the philosophy of the Romantics, and Schelling).[7] Wherever the term *Bildung* took Herder, it always led him back to a critique of European expansionism and imperialism. And this, in turn, as we saw in the discussion of the *Treatise on the Origin of Language*, presented him with a fundamental uncertainty about how to conceptualize the development of other cultures in relation to his own, and to his understanding of world history. The problem he encountered there – how to think of diverse world views in the unfolding of human history – started to look like it might be solved by linking *Bildung* to the idea of force he had been developing from Spinoza and Leibniz.

As Herder followed the various manifestations of these forces, they began to take on encyclopaedic proportions. Under headings that moved from cosmology and geology through natural history to anthropology and history, he began to collect documents from a wide range of sources.[8] In the course of his lifetime, *Bildung* developed as an interdisciplinary concept, and became the specifically German formulation of the Enlightenment concern with natural organic development in all its social, psychological, and political manifestations. *Bildung* served as a constellation of ideas, providing a model for scientists and historians, theorists of culture, and poets. In Herder's reading, it promised to retain the idea that natural phenomena contained inherent developmental principles that tended towards a harmonious unity of phenomena, an idea which Leibniz had adopted from the Aristotelian understanding of entelechy.[9] Gradually, during the latter half of the eighteenth century, *Bildung* came to serve as one of the central concepts for articulating the connections between natural and social principles. In this, it offered an explanation for how the life of the individual might be both a single organism and a part of a larger organism, and for how the forces at work in organisms express themselves in many different ways. One of the most important statements of the concept came from the writings of the physiologist, physician, and anthropologist Johann Friedrich Blumenbach, who was eight years younger than Herder and held the position of professor of medicine at the University of Göttingen from 1776 until his death at the age of eighty-eight in 1840. Herder and Goethe both read Blumenbach.[10] Like Herder, Blumenbach understood humanity as a single species, but unlike Herder he proposed (in his doctoral dissertation of 1775) a fivefold division of humanity according to race.[11] In 1780–1, Blumenbach authored a treatise on the principle of natural development, published in two parts in the *Göttingisches Magazin der Wissenschaft und Litteratur* (Göttingen Magazine for Science and Literature),[12] then in 1781 as a single volume entitled *Über den Bildungstrieb und das Zeugungsgeschäft* (On the Formative Drive and Procreation).[13] This was an attempted revision of the evolutionist views held by many of his contemporaries, most notably Albrecht von Haller (1708–77), in whose view the natural development of organisms consisted of a gradual unfolding of pre-given physiological components already present structurally at birth in microscopic and thus often undetectable form.[14] Siding with the theorists of epigenesis, Blumenbach argued that the lives of organisms are governed by a formative principle of generation and regeneration that acts as a force of life. But by concentrating on the formal aspects of this force he hoped to avoid some of the pitfalls of epigenesis. He was convinced that "in all animated creatures from the human to the maggot and from the cedar down to mould, there is a specific, innate drive that is active for as long as life persists – first a drive to assume a particular form, then to maintain it, and if it is damaged, to repair it as far as possible. A drive (or tendency or striving, however one wants to call it) … which I shall here, in order to avoid all misinterpretation and distinguish it from other forces of nature, call the formative drive (*nisus formativus*)."[15]

Blumenbach's understanding of the drive to *Bildung* had a profound influence on scientists and writers of the time, who used it to think through a number of related issues in different discourses, encompassing scientific, cultural, and aesthetic dimensions, to the point where it began to look like a truly interdisciplinary concept. Blumenbach himself attached a pronounced historical and geographical dimension to his understanding of the concept. The historical dimension arose almost by necessity when Blumenbach attempted to think through the consequences of his theory in terms that extended beyond the life of the individual organism. Thus, he took issue with "a very celebrated naturalist of Geneva" who had put forward the hypothesis "*first*, that we are all much older than what we suppose ourselves to be, *secondly*, that all mankind are exactly the same age, the great grandfather not a second older than the youngest of his great grand children, *thirdly*, that this respectable age, which we all share, may be about six thousand years."[16]

The historical problems posed by this "extravagant and romantic" hypothesis, as Blumenbach called it, are the very ones Herder needed to solve: given the theological framework of monogenesis that dominated attempts to think humanity's common origin, and given the scientific fact of diversity, how is the development of the individual to be thought alongside the development of the human species? In the 1780 version of *On the Formative Drive*, Blumenbach briefly laid out what the consequences of his theory might mean in these terms. Here he speaks of the "genesis of forms and varieties among organic bodies,"[17] the hereditary modifications of the *Bildungstrieb*[18] caused possibly by environmental factors or temperament, and resulting in diverse national or family characteristics; Blumenbach also refers to the varieties that arise when "negroes and whites" procreate to produce "mulattos and mixes."[19] Blumenbach discusses at length examples he draws from various travelogues and scientific studies, citing them as evidence of the cultural modification of the *Bildungstrieb*. Thus, for example, he cites Hippocrates' claim that the Colchians of the southern Black Sea area bind their infants' heads for cosmetic purposes, and that, over many generations, this has resulted in hereditary elongation of the skull among this population. Similarly, Blumenbach claims, among the civilized nations the habit of binding babies ears to their head with tightly fitting caps has resulted in a hereditary differentiation between them and wild peoples, whose ears are closer to those of animals (and whose hearing is correspondingly better than that of their civilized cousins). If, however, European parents were to cease placing caps over their babies' ears, then after several generations their descendants would most probably have "ears and hearing like savages."[20] Another example is the beardless men native to North and South America, whose condition has arisen out of practices of removing facial hair. Finally, he cites instances of baby boys in the Orient who are born circumcised.

These examples, with their varying degrees of credibility, are all derived from the reports Blumenbach is reading about the inhabitants of the earth's far-flung regions. In citing them, he is concerned to make it clear to his readers that his theory of *Bildung* has to be read in the context of the extreme cultural and geographical diversity of world populations. This was important enough to him that the year after his book appeared he published an article in the *Göttingisches Magazin der Wissenschaften und Litteratur* entitled "Einige zerstreute Bemerkungen über die Fähigkeiten und Sitten der Wilden" (Miscellaneous Remarks on the Abilities and Customs of the Wild Peoples).[21] This article aims to relativize the variations in cultural and geographical expression of nature's *Bildungstrieb*, emphasizing diversity as an expression of natural variety, rather than as a sign of the superiority or inferiority of individual groups.

Blumenbach's *Bildungstrieb* explained *Bildung* in the same way Herder understood it. As an organic drive, it is, in Richards's words, "a force, deriving from an unknown cause, that can only be characterized by its conspicuous effects."[22] It is a natural force that is form-giving and reveals itself in its forms (one could say it is aesthetic in nature), and it is innate, but can be expressed in a variety of ways. This looked remarkably similar to what Herder was trying to formulate in his work on natural forces. But Herder wanted to be careful how he conceptualized the organic nature of this drive, adding the critical influence of agency. In Blumenbach's conception, epigenesis became what Richards calls a "perceptible effect" of the *Bildungstrieb*.[23] Herder followed him in this respect, to the extent that Menges speaks of a "substantial shift" in Herder's ideas on biology in the *Ideas*.[24] But it is important to realize that Herder wanted to retain the active formative aspect – its aesthetic component – and to use it as an alternative to the conflict of epigenesis and preformationism. By combining Spinoza's ideas on nature with Leibniz's formative forces, *Bildung* suggested a way of bypassing the opposition of preformationism and epigenesis.[25] The interdisciplinary nature of the concept, if not simply its broad semantic field, allowed Herder to think of the forces at work on and in the organism as more than just biological. Herder gave book 5 of *Ideas* (1784) the title "No Force of Nature Is without an Organ; but the Organ Is Never the Force Itself, Which Only Has Effect through the Organ" (*HMA* 3/1, 158). The study of *Bildung* is the study not of biological force itself, but of the way force aligns form and process within the organism. Furthermore, as Palti notes, this alignment of form and process allows Herder to conceptualize "immanent organic finality," a teleology that goes well beyond what Kant thought could be said about immanent processes in organisms.[26] Herder goes on to note in this chapter that "no eye has seen the preformed germs [*Keime*] which have lain dormant since the beginning of creation. What can be seen from the first moment that a creature comes into being are effective *organic forces*" (*HMA* 3/1, 159). These organic forces are "the finger of the divine" (160). They cannot be grasped, only followed by way of analogy. For this reason, Herder believes that it is "disingenuous" to speak of "germs that merely unfold, or of an epigenesis, according to which limbs have grown through external forces. It is *Bildung* (genesis), an effect of internal forces, for which nature has prepared the matter which forms by way of a drive to become visible" (*HMA* 3/1, 159–60). Neither preformationism nor epigenesis proper do justice to the vitality of the formative force of nature.

This continues to be the guiding idea for talking about natural force in *Ideas*. Around the same time that Blumenbach's article appeared, Herder was becoming interested in the findings of the physiologist and founder of modern embryology Caspar Friedrich Wolff, published in *Theoria generationis* (1759), which, as Herder mentions in a letter to Knebel of 5 January 1785, he intended to give to Goethe, "since I have found many of his favourite ideas in the raw substance of this book" (*HBG* 5, 101). Wolff's genetic theory, like Blumenbach's doctrine of the *Bildungstrieb*, opposed the position of preformation taken by Haller. Making direct reference to Wolff, Herder would write in these years, as a subheading in the seventh book of the *Ideas*, that "the Genetic Power is the Mother of all the Forms upon Earth, Climate acting merely as an Auxiliary or Antagonist" (*HRP* 20).[27]

If nature's force, the force of *Bildung*, is a unitary process with diverse manifestations, then it makes sense to take the next step and to add the additional dimension of a world-project, aimed at furthering the cause of a unitary humanity. Indeed, Herder takes this step. In *This Too a Philosophy of History* he speaks of a common project for the betterment of humanity, in which individual deeds appear as the seeds and sprouts of a plant – what he calls "the noblest plant of humanity, civilization [*Bildung*], education, strengthening of nature in its most imperfect [*bedürftigsten*] nerves, love of human beings, sympathy, and brotherly bliss." In striving for a unity of humankind, these formative deeds nurture the soul as the seat of human life, and do not dwell on what he calls "*merely bodily* and *political purposes*" (*HPW* 353). With this, he is dismissing the instrumental view of purpose, while attempting to retain the central importance of the physiological and the political in the development of humanity in its wholeness.

And yet, the problem he brought with him to Weimar remained: if the development of humanity in its wholeness has both a physiological and a political dimension, how do those two dimensions articulate with one another? How is it possible to bring the politics of personal life into critical discourse? What is the appropriate language or register for this undertaking? How does it relate to scientific languages that themselves bear traces of the imperialist ventures out of which they arose? In his next major work, Herder would approach these questions via a route now familiar to him: the scientific articulation of environment, tradition, and representation, and the coordination of these in the idea of human development.

Natural History and Colonization

Herder began work on the revision and expansion of his philosophy of history in the fall of 1782, intending to write two volumes. In the end he published four parts, appearing in 1784, 1785, 1787 and 1791 respectively. These took him from the earliest conceivable moment in creation, through the history of the planet and its cultures, more or less up until the European middle ages. From the outset, Herder understands the philosophy of human history as part of a larger narrative on the becoming of the world, and he is careful to frame the beginning in a theological context while explaining development in non-theological terms. The reason for this is clear. Looking back to the origin of the cosmos is like looking at Being. All that can be seen are the signs of nature that point to an act of creation which cannot in itself be explained. But that moment bears absolute certainty. Unexplainable and certain, there is nothing to say about it. And Herder doesn't try. Instead, under the title "Our Earth Is a Star among Stars," the first book begins with these sentences:

> It is from the heavens that our philosophy of the history of the human race must begin, if it is to be in some measure deserving of this name. Our place of dwelling, the earth, is nothing in itself, but its constitution and form, its ability to organize and sustain all creatures is received from heavenly forces that extend through our entire universe. Thus, it must be observed first and foremost not alone and in solitude, but in the choir of worlds in which it has been placed. (*HSW* 13, 13)

Herder divides the first book into seven chapters, with the titles

- Our Earth Is a Star among Stars,
- Our Earth Is One of the Middle Planets,
- Our Earth Went through Many Revolutions before It Became What It Has Become,

- Our Earth Is a Sphere Which Rotates about Its Axis and Circles the Sun in a Skewed Direction,
- Our Earth Is Enveloped in Mists and Is in Conflict with Several Heavenly Stars,
- The Planet on Which We Dwell Is a Range of Earth Mountains Rising above the Surface of the Waters, and
- Through the Stretches of Mountain Ranges Our Two Hemispheres Became a Showcase of the Most Remarkable Differences and Diversity.

As the chapter titles indicate, the general direction of this book follows in the broadest terms the model of human development already adopted in *This Too a Philosophy of History*, moving from the descriptions of origins through increasing diversification to the point where human culture can be celebrated as the manifestation of difference and diversity on earth. And in the same way, Herder is begging the question of the driving force that allows him to think about human development as a part of the world's natural development.

The problem of a natural history of humanity had of necessity emerged from Herder's interest in general questions of the origins, evolution, and genetics of humanity as an organic unity but also as a collection of diverse nations. Already in early sketches he had expressed interest in how different cultures relate to their own origins, not only as receptors and propagators of myth, but in quasi-scientific acts of revision and retelling of their own traditions. Writing on the tradition of ancient national songs in 1764, he had put it like this: "Every people thus had the idea of knowing a *cosmogony*, an *anthropogenesis*, a *philosophy* about the evil and good of the world, particularly of its own region, a *genealogy* and *history* of its forefathers, ethics and customs: to have what are called *Origines, original records*" (*HSW* 32, 149). With these words he outlines the problem that he will set himself in the *Ideas*: how to explain what might be called the dialectic of natural history in the development of human culture. This dialectic must take account first of all of the complex interactions of historical and environmental factors (what he calls the "Opposition between Genesis and Climate," *HRP* 28); but it must overlay this with a narrative of how individual cultures struggle to explain their diversity, their specificity, and their becoming in terms of their own particular environmental conditions, their traditions, their mythologies.

This complex interaction of organic determinations or drives, environmental factors, language, and cultural tradition determines the nature of the human being. Herder returns time and again to the description of this system of human nature. He introduces it in the fifth book of part 1, where he argues that the genesis of earth and its life forms is characterized by a "sequence of ascending and advancing forms and forces [*eine Reihe aufsteigender Formen und Kräfte*]" (*HMA* 3/1, 154). These culminate in the human being, whose "blood and all his components, however we might call them, are a compendium of the world: calcium and earth, salt and acids, oil and water, forces of vegetation, stimuli, sensations are all organically combined and interwoven within him" (*HMA* 3/1, 155). The force of nature is subject to infinite variety and modification, but it is also subject to a principle of conservation of matter and energy.[28] Once we accept Herder's model of a single natural force, with both its Spinozist and Leibnizian elements, it makes sense to follow him to the point where the distinction between mind and body, between nature and freedom, and between reason and unreason becomes difficult to specify. The human mind or psyche (*Seele*) has advanced so far beyond the capacity of the lower organisms that "it not only rules over a thousand organic forces within my body with a kind of omnipresence and omnipotence, like a queen; but it also (wonder of wonders!) has the capacity to look within itself and to rule over itself." The human mind becomes a mediating instance between the organic forces at work in the body and the force of divinity within which the history of creation unfolds. "In all that he thinks, the human being breathes according to the organizing aspect of divinity, and in all he does and wills, he breathes according to the creative aspect; no matter how unreasonable his thoughts may be. The similarity lies in the matter itself, it is embedded in the nature of his mind [*Seele*]" (*HMA* 3/1, 157–8).

Because of this, the mind's models for interpreting life are themselves part of the creative and organizing processes at work in organic nature. With its capacity to look within, the mind becomes an interpreter not only of nature, but of its place within nature – and even of its own interpretations. In short, a project aimed at imagining the diversity of humanity in the world must do so by studying not only their material circumstances but also the models they have developed for interpreting these circumstances. In the note on national songs cited earlier, Herder describes this in the following terms:

> When a human soul is nourished over the course of its whole youth by strong, unrefined, sensuous concepts, and all of its thought is formed according to them: it is still processing these materials, even when it wants

> to be thinking freely. Such that no people could think about the causes and origin of the objects named by its language, except through the materials and premises of its previous condition. The uppermost, formless, coarse skin it was able to remove; but could it likewise transform the entire body formed according to such a mythology? (*HSW* 32: 149)

In asking this question, Herder is setting the stage for the discussions of natural history that will continue to be refined through the work of Marx and Adorno.[29] Herder never delves very deeply into the problem of how, in their expressive and interpretive actions, individuals and societies actualize their own nature and history. But he begins to formulate a powerful model for how language is used to negotiate the dividing line between what is given and what is mutable in the representation of both nature and history. He is also pointing the way to the profound dilemma of the intellectual as a political agent. If one reads Herder's rules of natural history carefully, he is returning to the same problem of diversity and unity he had faced in earlier writings. His attempts to elevate the descriptions of the world's cultures to the level of scientific investigation leads him to speak against prejudice and political interest on the part of the scientist. For how else would objective description be possible? But at the same time, he is cautioning against any descriptive writing that forgets the act of cultural invention in which it necessarily partakes when it walks the fine line between nature and history. He states this in his *Letters on the Advancement of Humanity*: "All separatings-off and dissections through which the character of our species gets destroyed yield semi-concepts or delusive ones, speculations" (*HFA* 7, 700–1). And a history that uses these illusory and arbitrary divisions to write superficial descriptions of customs and manners is little more than "a charnel house, a storage place for the equipment and clothes of different peoples" (*HFA* 7, 700). This superficiality brings with it the danger of writing natural history from the perspective of some "favourite tribe" or "favoured people": "If, in the extreme case, the beloved people were merely a collective name (Celts, Semites, Cushites, etc.) that has perhaps nowhere existed, whose origins and perpetuation cannot be proved, then one would have written at sheer wild random" (*HFA* 7, 698). This realization extends to Herder's own culture: European culture cannot possibly serve as the measure of humanity's general well-being and value. European culture itself is "an abstracted concept [*ein abgezogener Begriff*], a name. Where does it exist entirely? With which people? In which times?" (*HFA* 7, 700). Instead of imagining humanity's divisions along the lines of superiority and inferiority, the natural historian of humanity writes on the understanding that "the genius of human natural history lives with and in each people as though this people were the only one on earth" (*HFA* 7, 700).

The invention of specific human natures and human histories lends itself to preferential perspectives. On the basis of this simple observation, Herder explores the close association of politics, law, and commercial advantage, and he shows how this association is given substance when unexamined acts of imaginary grouping lead to violent exploitation. What should be a natural history of humanity becomes an ideology of exploitation. The example he uses is Pope Nicholas V, who, in 1455 had "given away the unknown world; he pontifically gave permission to the white and nobler human beings to turn all unbelievers into slaves" (*HFA* 7, 698). The problem lies not simply in the act of exploitation itself, but in the fact that the practical implementation of this imaginary division of humanity remains unreflected on and unnegotiated, a perversion of how the story of humanity could and should be told:

> Kakistocracy [i.e., government under the control of a nation's least qualified citizens] asserts its rights in practice without us having to authorize it to do so theoretically and therefore having to invert the history of humanity. Should, for example, someone express the opinion that "if it *can* be demonstrated that no coffee, sugar, rice, or tobacco plantations *can* survive without negroes, then the *legitimacy* of the trade in negroes is simultaneously proved, in that this trade benefits more than harms the whole human species, that is, the white, *nobler* human beings"; in this way one such principle would immediately destroy the whole history of humanity. (*HFA* 7, 698–9)[30]

Herder's engagement with the interface between ideas of justice and natural history had, from an early age, provided him with a model for thinking about the unity and diversity of humanity. It also more or less forced him to confront the injustices of those ideologies that would seek to reframe diversity for the sake of the exploitation of the world's less powerful citizens. Now, with the investigations into natural history in *Ideas*, Herder has arrived at the place Kant had foreseen, where it appears impossible to base political action on the freedom of thought. But Herder has an alternative in mind. This has to do with the relationship between the drive to restlessness, the imagination, and the capacity for interpretation. By bringing these form-giving and form-defining actions into line with biological processes, he hopes to find a way out of the Kantian dilemma. How does he propose this be done? The answer will lie in Herder's belief that there is something about the structure of the mind which aligns free thought with the natural force that drives human history.

As Herder continues his investigations, he becomes increasingly aware that the writing of human history is a component of natural history. Towards the end of his *Letters on the Advancement of Humanity*, Herder addresses the question of what he calls a "*natural history of humanity* written in a purely human spirit" (*HFA* 7, 700). The "dream of such a history" which he unfolds in the 116th letter sets out a subtle position on how to write humanity's diversity as both a natural and a historical fact, but also as a fact that is called forth in the act of writing. To start with, he spells out a number of rules: the writer of natural history should be impartial ("*unbiased* like the genius of humanity itself" *HFA* 7, 698); he should avoid any disparaging perspective by which uneven power relations or relations of exploitation might be justified ("let no one put into the hands of any people on earth the sceptre over other peoples on grounds of '*innate superiority*' – much less the sword and the slave whip," *HFA* 7, 699). The recognition of how power/knowledge works in the expanding world places the natural historian of humanity under an obligation to promote equality. But, since there is no necessary reason why the recognition of political interests should promote equality, Herder needs to explain what it is about the desire of the historian-philosopher that promotes progressive tendencies in history. Implicit in his philosophy of history is the idea that the critical intellectual is motivated by a desire for historical progress, and that human desire itself links the individual's psychology to the forces of nature, and ultimately to the divine plan for humanity.[31] But what are the mechanisms for this desire, and how do they relate to the freedom of thought?

In book 8/2 of *Ideas*, Herder outlines a cultural theory of imagination that points towards a political theory of desire. The title of this chapter is "Human Imagination Is Everywhere Organic and Climatic, but It Is Also Always Guided by Tradition." His starting point is the observation that our ability to conceptualize the world is determined by our environment. "The story of a king of Siam, who considered ice and snow as nonentities, is in a thousand instances our own history [*unsre eigne Geschichte*]" (*HRP* 41; translation modified). It is the role of the imagination to break through this narrowly conceptualized world into the wider world of humanity: "Happy the chosen few, who proceed, as far as possible in our limited sphere, from fantasies to the essence [*von Phantasieen zum Wesen*], that is from infancy to manhood, and who, with a clear spirit [*mit reinem Geist*], go through the history of their brethren with this end in view" (*HRP* 49; translation modified). The freedom to criticize existing political structures and practices is derived analytically from observed political and social conditions, then modified in the imagination. Freedom is the application of the imagination in conceptualizing alternatives. This is evident in Herder's unpublished notes to book 9 (which Suphan also omitted from his edition of *Ideas*). Here he states that the many examples of bad government can be explained, but, he asks, can they be justified? Can it be shown to be "the order of God derived from unchanging laws of human nature according to this activity, and to that land and climate? If this does not appal reason, I do not know what might appal it. Philosophy and history contradict such claims, no matter how much they support and embellish themselves with philosophy and history" (*HMA* 3/2, 516). The reason philosophy is able to contradict the ideological self-justification of bad government is because of its opposition to homogeneous, a priori models of truth. In its diversity, humanity is constantly resisting single dominant ideologies, and it is up to philosophy and historiography to show how this takes place. But more than that, the structure of the mind forces it to confront the multiplicity of truth. If freedom of thought is the temporality opened up in the condition of having reflected on stimuli, then the challenge facing political thought is to use this delay to recognize how specific stimuli relate to universal patterns of thought. This is the work of the imagination.

The imagination steers the mind out of the predestination of history and the confines of geography, and in doing so it paves the way for individuals to leave their familiar conceptual ground and discover the richness of other perspectives on the world, of other imaginations and fantasies. "The soul nobly expands when it is able to emerge from the narrow circle which climate and education have drawn round it, and from other nations at least learn of what one might do without" (*HRP* 49; translation modified). Physical need is the initial impulse that links human life to climate or the environment, and imagination is the first self-conceptualization of this link; but the imagination sets the mind and the body in motion to a point where it becomes possible to conceptualize a political economy of humanity, not simply of one group in a given environment. This restless desire is ambivalent because it is both the foundational activity of a poetical philosophy and also the desire that sets the stage for the economic exploitation of the world.

Here too, the epistemological frame is easily mapped onto territoriality. To be sedentary, content, satisfied is in many respects the opposite of the desire for knowledge that characterizes the human condition. Herder describes the scientific and artistic drives as restless urges that work against contentedness and happiness, indicating that this is a problem of modernity. It is not that science, art, and artifice take us away from Rousseau's natural idyll and thus must be rejected, but that free thought must decide where these essential human qualities are beneficial and where they are harmful. All societies in all parts of the world have to make this decision in accordance with their own particular environments, their government, and their traditions. And for Herder it is clear that imperialism is one of the testing grounds where this question must be decided. Imperialism is the activity where the positive restlessness of the enquiring spirit, with its beneficial effects and its mutual help, collides with the exploitation and violence issuing from the European desire for travel and wonder, for commerce and profit, and the acquisition of new territory. But imperialism is not only a moral challenge, a challenge for the freedom of thought – it is also an aesthetic one. In the realm of representation, it tests the limits of narrative as a link between the restless body and the restless spirit. As restlessness became increasingly politicized under European expansionism, this link became more than simply figurative or metaphorical. Restlessness named a constellation of political, representational, and communicative practices, none of which would have made sense without the others. This constellation becomes visible, perhaps for the first time in its full significance, with the advent and gradual intensification of European imperialism.

With this in mind, Herder continued his meditations on the place of Europeans in the world, using the ambivalence of commerce to deepen his critique of imperialism. And as in his earlier works, the reason why Herder is prepared to speak out so decisively against imperialist and commercial exploitation is because of his faith in forms of cultural exchange that promote peace and understanding. He has many examples of this: the Arabs, the Chinese, Ancient Greece, the Slavs. Speaking of the "happy and peaceful nations" who dwell "at the foot of the Mountains of the Moon," he states that "Europe is not worthy of witnessing" their happiness. Somewhat bizarrely, given the history of slavery, he claims that "the peacefully trading Arabs move through the land

and have founded colonies far and wide" (*HSW* 13, 233). Arab colonialism serves here as a positive counterpart to European exploitation. Similarly, he claims that "Chinese foreign trade takes place without any enslavement," while Europeans "roam through the whole world as merchants or robbers" (*HSW* 14, 37). If we look back into Europe's history, we see that Europe itself would be barbaric if it weren't for cultural exchange. If the inhabitants of the Mediterranean had not felt the colonizing urge, the "northern Europeans would still be barbarians." In this context, colonialism looks to Herder like the "benevolent breath of fate" that wafts "the spiritual blossoms" of the more cultured nations out into the world's wilder places (*HSW* 14, 298). Taken in the positive sense, colonization, together with climatic and human diversity, contributes to the betterment of humanity (*HSW* 13, 347). Ancient Greece established colonies in Asia Minor, which blossomed into a higher culture (*HSW* 14, 96), just as the Slavs took over land that had been abandoned by other peoples, "cultivating and utilizing it as colonists, shepherds, and agriculturalists" (*HSW* 14, 278). History shows that "no peoples in Europe have acquired the status of culture by themselves" (*HSW* 14, 289). "The history of the world shows incontestably that, wherever a country has raised itself to an exceptional level of culture, it has had an effect on its neighbours" (*HSW* 14, 16). The result is what he calls a "noble expansion of the soul" (*HSW* 13, 315).

Colonization is the manifestation of a natural drive to intercultural communication that acts to improve humanity. Herder sees the nature of colonial projects as an indicator of the positive and negative consequences of restlessness. But what causes restlessness to have either a positive or a negative outcome, and how can a critical historian intervene in this process? In the age of imperialism, this question addresses the politics of freedom. In the *Journal*, where colonialism still bears a largely positive valence, it tends to be equated with the transfer of culture. Greece is his favourite example: it was a culture established as a colony of seafarers, and it lived on in a kind of mobile cultural expression. "It was seafarers who brought the Greeks their first religion, all of Greece was a colony on the sea – it therefore could not have a mythology like that of the Egyptians and Arabs on the other side of their sandy deserts, but had instead a religion of the beyond, of the sea and of the groves – it must therefore also be read at sea" (*HSW* 4, 357). Cultures must be interpreted according to their own mode of being, so mobile cultures require a similar mobility of reception. By interpreting the documents of history, the historian is facilitating the connection between individual groups and the common human destiny in which they take part. This is another example of reason operating collectively as human reason, but at the same time as located and culturally specific. Cultural location and politics make reason an incomplete expression of what it could be; and the notion that it could be more – reason's restlessness – relativizes its operations. In the unpublished notes, he observes that

> everywhere, human beings are created so as to help themselves make their way through the world [*sich selbst durch die Welt zu helfen*], and where they need help, to be supported voluntarily, or in a reasoned manner. Other forms of healthy reason are bound to no other climate, no other part of the world, than this one; and they are bound in such plainly evident matters. In this matter, the wildest peoples often have more good judgment and more powerful will than the cultivated, i.e., the enervated peoples. But everywhere the most cautiously formed government is misused and people mishandled, in Africa as in Europe, in the name of Aristocracy, or Monarchy, or Despotism. But the name doesn't matter, only the fact, for all forms of government are imperfect and are only justified by convention and necessity. (*HMA* 3/1, 516)

This means that every government, including those that strike us as ideal, is only as good as could be produced at that particular moment in history, and at that particular place.

In book 13 of *Ideas* (1787), Herder repeats and expands the idea that Greece was geographically privileged to be the seat of culture at that particular moment in world history. But the strength and lasting influence of Greece is due to the fact that it was a culture of mobility: "There is scarcely a nation of Greece, that has not migrated, and many more than once. Every thing here has been in motion from the oldest times" (*HRP* 169). But Greece itself is the product of cultural mobility. "Asia Minor is the mother of Greece, not only in its settlement and propagation [*Anpflanzung*] but also in the main features of its earliest development [*Bildung*]; in return it sent colonies back to the coasts of its motherland and lived through a second, more glorious culture in them" (*HSW* 14, 96). Cultural mobility in this understanding also distinguishes *doux commerce* from exploitation, domination, and violence. "The conqueror conquers for himself; the trading nations serve themselves and other nations" (*HSW* 14, 71). Herder hoped that "voyages of conquest will become voyages of trade, founded upon mutual justice and protection, a continual competition in industrious and excellent manufacture; in short, upon humanity and its eternal laws" (*HSW* 14, 217). The Phoenicians, he believed, explored the world "not as conquerors, but as traders and colonists. Through commerce, language, and goods they unified nations that had been divided by the sea, and their inventions cleverly served this commerce" (*HSW* 14, 71). Trade, even colonization, has the potential to serve nature's plan for humanity by furthering the peaceful interaction of the world's cultures. As he puts it, "The barbarian dominates, while the educated, well-formed conqueror educates and forms others [*Der Barbar beherrscht, der gebildete Überwinder bildet*]" (*HSW* 14, 289). He condemns Carthage because it was "not interested in spreading humanity, but in collecting treasures" (*HSW* 14, 73), thereby denying the common project of humanity, mutual aid and communal improvement.

But Herder realizes how tenuous this vision of trade as a medium of cultural exchange really is. The more he looks around him, the more he sees that commerce builds not on humanist principles but on the exploitation of weaker economies. One of the reasons for the failure of *doux commerce* and the predominance of violent conquest has to do with the way desire is perverted and works against free thought. The science and technology of conquest speaks to a perverse identification with the conquering nation. In their quest for unnatural pleasures and luxury, these conquerors destabilize the world. The opulence of European society has caused us (Herder uses the first-person plural) to "unsettle and rob entire regions of the world." Then he asks (repeating a theme from *This Too a Philosophy of History*): "What is the purpose? New and hot spices for a numbed tongue." And he adds: "Nature can hardly have given us our tongues so that a few warts on it become the goal of our onerous lives or the despair of other unfortunate ones" (*HSW* 13, 295). If desire clouds judgment in this way, it also opens the door to racist doctrines of cultural superiority. These are ineffective because of a fundamental misunderstanding of agency:

> The pride of many a European rabble, when it imagines itself superior to all three continents in everything having to do with Enlightenment, art and science, and thinks all the inventions of Europe its own, is as vain as that madman in the harbour who imagines all the ships there to belong to himself for no other reason than that he happened to be born at the point of confluence of these inventions and traditions. Poor fellow, did you invent any of these arts? Do you reflect at all on how you have absorbed all your traditions? That you learned to use them is the work of

> a machine; that you suck up the juice of science is the accomplishment of a sponge that just happened to be growing on this dank spot. When you steer a ship towards the Tahitians or fire off a cannon at the Hebrideans, you are in truth no smarter nor more skilled than the Hebrideans or the Tahitians, who artfully steer the boats they built for themselves with their own hands. (*HSW* 13, 371)

Individual perverse desire leads not only to the illusion of racial and cultural superiority. It also promotes an unhealthy centralization of ownership and power. This is part of a vicious circle, whereby greed drives warring groups into foreign territories; they conquer and subdue, and divide the spoils among themselves according to their hierarchies of ownership and privilege. This, Herder claims, is how Germany was settled, and how the systems of liege and chattel slavery emerged. It also characterized the imperial expansion of Rome, Greece, and the Alexandrine Orient. "Violent conquest took the place of justice ... Descendents and heirs received, the father of the tribe took; and it goes without saying that those who already had, received even more, so that they could enjoy plenty; this is the natural sequence of the original ownership of land and people described above" (*HSW* 13, 378–9).

In this way, greed profits from conquest, and it paves the way for further conquest. This interrelation of individual greed and organized conquest implicates commerce, making it an accessory to the structured violation of human rights. A telling example of this was the crusades, where the real winners were the "transporters, financial agents, and suppliers." Herder speaks of "shameful theft on the part of merchants" (*HSW* 14, 470). Because communal acts of exploitation are expressions of individual greed, of "unchecked affluence," or of "misguided reason" (*HSW* 13, 394), the balance of trade must be appreciated and evaluated not in terms of profit, increased flow of knowledge and information, nor the accessibility of exotic products; but of the damage done to the human cause. As long as humanity was divided into more or less distinct economies, it was not open in the same degree to the detrimental effects of perverse desire. But now the economy is a world economy, and it brings with it a heightened disparity in wealth and in justice.

> From ancient times the East Indian trade was a rich one; the industrious, modest people served other nations at sea and overland generously with many of its continent's treasures and remained on account of its remove in a relatively peaceful state – until finally Europeans, for whom nothing

> is too far away, came and bestowed upon themselves kingdoms there. All the news and goods which they send us from there are no compensation for the evil they visit upon a people who committed nothing against them. (*HSW* 14, 32)

Time and again Herder reminds us that the spirit of conquest violates the natural community of humanity. Societies that are artificially united in this manner are monstrous, perverse. The imperial acts of conquest that create these societies are doomed to failure, because they violate the principles of nature. Herder insists that the detrimental effects of these perverse acts impact on the colonizer and colonized alike. In his discussion of the interactions of environment and development in book 7 of *Ideas,* he states that any attempt to violently interfere with other cultures and other environments will be harmful to the "colonizers and the colonized alike; for nature is everywhere a living whole, and it wants to be gently followed and improved, but not violently dominated" (*HSW* 13, 288). The language Herder chooses here (he speaks of the cultivators – *Kultivatoren* – and the cultivated – *Kultivierten*) allows violation of human rights to appear as violations of natural principles.

In Herder's eyes, domination and slavery count among the basest of human activities. They destroy the natural character of the dominated, reducing them to the "conniving, brutal indolence of the servant" (*HSW* 14, 279); they prevent the technologically advanced nations of Europe from sharing their scientific knowledge in a manner that would otherwise contribute to the advancement of humanity; and they violate the natural rights of the oppressed to their own land. Herder's choice of words is telling when he addresses the conquerors, asking, "What right did you monsters have even to approach the land of these unfortunates, let alone to tear it away from them through thievery, deception, and brutality?" (*HSW* 13, 263).

For all these reasons, Herder has a great deal of sympathy for those who seek to violently overthrow the exploitative Europeans and thereby regain their dignity, their culture, and their land. And yet, he sees in this process a historical dialectic that is deeply ambivalent. In the history of displacement and resettlement that has produced the current configuration of human cultures, conflicts over proper place necessarily lead to ethical questions regarding the legitimate and illegitimate expansion of cultures. As a natural reaction to the barbarism of exploitation, resistance and rebellion become barbaric: what Europeans sees as barbaric customs are often a socially determined response to oppression and domination.

> With extreme cruelty, the savages wage their wars for their country and for its children, their brethren, who have been torn from it, degraded and oppressed. Hence, for instance, the lasting hatred of the natives of America towards Europeans, even when they treat them tolerably: they cannot suppress the feeling: "This land is ours; you have no business here." Hence the treachery of all savages, as they are called, even when they appeared altogether pacified by the courtesy of European visitors. The moment their hereditary national feelings awoke, the flame they had, with difficulty, long smothered broke out, raged with violence, and frequently was not appeased, till the flesh of the strangers had been torn by the teeth of the natives. To us this seems horrible; and it is so, no doubt: yet the Europeans first forced them to this misdeed: for why did they visit their country? (*HMA* 3/1, 236–7)

Herder's question – why did the Europeans come to the lands of the New World? – must be regarded as more than simply rhetorical. For it is this question that forces the historian to take a position on European expansionism, evaluating individual acts as moments in the history of cultural exchange or of exploitation. On the one hand we have a natural expression of human diversity, on the other a disregard for nature's boundaries that can only lead to destruction, conquest, exploitation, and degeneration (*HSW* 13, 285). Humanity must protect itself from social forms that express the unnatural urge for unevenness and exploitation; it is in these forms that individual perverse desire finds collective expression.

This is why, in the words of Isaiah Berlin, Herder "believed in kinship, social solidarity, *Volkstum*, nationhood, but to the end of his life he detested and denounced every form of centralization, coercion and conquest, which were embodied and symbolized both for him, and for his teacher Hamann, in the accursed state. Nature creates nations, not states."[32] In the state, Herder sees an oppressive organization, in which "hundreds go hungry so that one might feast and luxuriate; tens of thousands are oppressed and harried to death so one crowned fool or wise man might live out their fantasies; ... millions all over the planet live without states" (*HSW* 13, 341). The critique of the state is never far removed from a critique of "the unnatural expansion of states, the random mixing of humanity's types and nations under *one* sceptre" (*HSW*

13, 384). The term *unnatural* is decisive here. Against the state, Herder seeks to mobilize what he sees as the force of nature.

> It was therefore merciful of Providence to prefer the easier happiness of individuals to the artificial ends of great societies, and spare generations these costly machines of state as much as possible. It has wonderfully separated nations, not only by woods and mountains, seas and deserts, rivers and climates, but more particularly by languages, inclinations, and characters; that the work of subjugating despotism might be rendered more difficult, that all the four quarters of the Globe might not be crammed into the belly of a wooden horse. (*HRP* 77–8)

Through climate and various other diversifying means, nature has ensured that exploitative forms of state unification, domination, and imperialism are regressive tendencies. Humanity's task is to guarantee that nature's force (God's will) finds adequate expression – indeed, that it will come into being through human language. Within this creative act, philosophy has to recognize these regressive tendencies and clarify their relationship to natural right and human rights. This is the political work of free thought, and it is done by acts of interpretation.

Monogenesis and the Problem of Race

For Herder, the notion of cultural interdependence and intercommunication was the solution to the old theological problem of how to think the common Adamic origin of humanity together with the empirical evidence of humanity's geographical dispersion. Medieval scholars had looked at the geography of the world and seen it divided into regions separated by insurmountable ocean, and they speculated on the possibility and type of human habitation these regions might support.[33] The reasonable conclusion seemed to be that put forward by Augustine in the *City of God*, that "it is too absurd to say that some men might have set sail from this side and, traversing the immense expanse of ocean, have propagated there a race of human beings descended from that one first man."[34] But for Herder, writing in the face of European expansion throughout the globe, this paradox was hardly worth taking seriously. History and geography both demonstrated the possibility of a monogenetic peopling of the earth, by way of cultural exchange and colonization.

The defence of monogenesis was to become increasingly important in the context of nineteenth-century colonialism,[35] and the reasons are already clear in debates in the late eighteenth century. For Herder, monogenesis is the model of human diversity and unity that is theologically, empirically, and ethically defensible. It is, in his opinion, "only the ignorance of previous times that creates autochthons" (*HSW* 13, 406).

Herder had no time for those who thought physiological and cultural diversity could be taken as evidence of a polygenetic division of humanity into various sub-humanities.[36] He was also sharply opposed to those of his contemporaries who took the customs of other cultures as signs of their backwardness or moral inferiority. In a footnote he observes that "some European professors of international law" are unable to comprehend the lack of gratitude and manners on the part of conquered peoples. He also alludes critically to "a famous philosopher," who "couldn't help but assume a double origin of the human race, which gave rise to both the sociable and the hostile nations" (*HSW* 13, 264n1a).[37] Herder's faith in positive cultural interaction stems from his theologically grounded adherence to the doctrine of monogenesis – but a monogenesis augmented by his theory of climate, his Spinozist position on the way force works in nature, and a passionate defence of unity in diversity. He had opened *This Too a Philosophy of History* with the claim that, as studies in ancient history progressed, it became increasingly probable that humanity had its origins in a single race (*HPW* 272). His constant recourse to monogenetic arguments is partly theological. For example in *Ideas*, book 7, chapter 2, he states: "The ancient allegorical tradition says, that Adam was formed out of the dust of all the four quarters of the Globe, and animated by the powers and spirits of the whole Earth. Wherever his children have bent their course, and fixed their abode, in the lapse of ages, there they have taken root as trees, and produced leaves and fruit adapted to the climate" (*HRP* 10), and in book 10, chapter 2: "'God created man,' says the peoples' oldest written tradition, 'in his image; he created in him a semblance of God, a man and a woman, after creating an infinity of things, he created the smallest number; then he rested and made nothing more'" (*HMA* 3/1, 353). But more important than this is his belief that good science, the impartial assessment of evidence, shows the common foundation of humanity. Diversity in physiology and social organization can be explained by diverse environmental factors, while diversity in culture results from different interpretations of environment, but these forms of diversity only cement the unity of the human species.

In the eighteenth century, the doctrine of monogenesis needed to explain the empirical evidence of diversity within the single human species. This gave rise to a great deal of debate around the concept of race. Herder remained adamant that there is only one human race. In the *Ideas* he moves swiftly and elegantly from the theological doctrine of monogenesis to a climatic theory of culture, then to a rejection of racial theories of humanity in favour of a picture of common purpose and mutual cooperation. This association of ideas leads Herder to a complex picture on race which, as Sikka observes, does indeed leave room for "biologically distinct human types about which some limited judgements of higher and lower can be made." But "the individuals belonging to these types are all fully human, and deserving of the moral consideration due to every member of this species."[38] What this means is that the question of physiological diversity is for him a simple matter of environment and genetics, though the genetic process itself remains obscure. The "negro's" physiology, he writes in the seventh book of the *Ideas*, can be perpetuated and changed only through genetics. If we were to bring a black man to Europe, Herder writes, he would remain what he is. If, however, he were to have children with a white woman, "a single generation will effect a change, which the skin-lightening climate [*das bleichende Klima*] could not have produced in ages. It is the same with the formations [*Bildungen*] of all nations: the environment [*Weltgegend*] alters them very slowly; but by intermixture with foreigners, in a few generations every Mongolian [*Mongolischen*], Chinese, or American feature vanishes" (*HRP* 24–5; translation modified). He titles the chapter in which this idea is elaborated: "Notwithstanding the Varieties of the Human Form, There Is but One and the Same Species of Man throughout the Whole of Our Earth" (*HRP* 3). Humanity is not preformed, and human diversity is not the expression of diversity in the original form of the human organism. Herder objects to this idea for scientific reasons, because he sees no evidence for polygenetics, but also for ideological reasons, because he does not want to accept the political consequences. The scientist must recognize the common bond that unites all peoples, rejecting the concept of race and racial classification, and the political consequence is an abolition of slavery and exploitation based on race. To this is added the Leibnizian idea of infinitesimal differences:

> Lastly, I ask that the distinctions, which a laudable zeal for schematic science has forced on the human species, not be carried beyond due bounds.

> Some for instance have dared to employ the term of *races* for four or five divisions, originally made in consequence of country or even color: but I see no reason for this appellation. Race refers to a difference of origin, which in this case either does not exist, or in each of these countries, and among people of each of these colours, comprises the most different races. For every people is a people, having its own national form just as it has its own language: the climate, it is true, stamps on each its mark, or spreads over it a slight veil, but not sufficient to destroy the original national character. This originality of character extends even to families, and its transitions are as variable as imperceptible. In short, there are neither four or five races, nor exclusive varieties, on this Earth. Colours run into each other: forms serve the genetic character: and upon the whole, all are at last shades of the same great picture, extending through all ages, and over all parts of the Earth. They belong not, therefore, so properly to systematic natural history, as to the physico-geographical history of humanity. (*HMA* 3/1, 231)

In the 116th *Letter on the Advancement of Humanity* (1797) Herder underlines the importance of this position for an egalitarian stance on human history and on the politics of the world economy. Here he reiterates that natural diversity should be conceived as the actualization of the infinite potential that lies within nature and that is expressed as nature's force:

> In that period when everything was taking form, nature developed the form of the *human type* as manifoldly as her workshop required and allowed. She developed in form, not various *germs* [*Keime*] (a word which is empty and which contradicts the formation of humankind), but various *forces* in various proportions, as many of them as lay in her type and as the various climes of the earth could develop in form. (*HPW* 396; translation modified)

The political consequences are clear. To see the cultures of indigenous Americans or Africans, for example, as the less developed forms of our own culture (a position implicit in all forms of historical progressivism, including those of Voltaire and Kant) would have indefensible consequences for a politics of humanity. It would justify any kind of interference that purports to shape another culture in the forms of the more dominant culture, ultimately providing the perfect ideological justification for military force and domination. Instead of this, Herder wants us to see cultural diversity as an expression of nature's force at work in different environments. He even goes on to claim that, if Europeans call black people "a beast" or "a black animal," then the negro has just as much right "to consider the white man a degenerate, a born cockroach" (*HPW* 394–5). Humanity can only be meaningful if all the letters in its diverse alphabet are allowed equal force of expression. This means that the geographical dispersal of humanity expresses the infinite potential within humanity. In this sense, climate is not humanity's fate, its curtailment, but its actualization.

Herder's geographical materialism (to borrow an expression from Heinz Stolpe),[39] is augmented with an innovative theory of culture, which, together with language, becomes the key to understanding how human diversity evolves out of climatic and geographical differences. Not race, but culture is the key concept in understanding the interrelationships of diverse peoples. In *Ideas* he takes care to couple this understanding of human diversity with an impassioned commitment to human equality and human rights: "For each genus Nature has done enough, and to each has given its proper progeny. The ape she has divided into as many species and varieties as possible, and extended these as far as she could: but thou, O man, honour thyself: neither the *pongo* nor the *longimanus* is thy brother: the American and the Negro are; these therefore thou shouldst not oppress, nor murder, nor steal; for they are men, like thee: with the ape thou canst not enter into fraternity" (*HRP* 6–7).[40]

The reference to apes pointed to an ongoing public debate on race.[41] The central figures in this debate were Henry Home (Lord Kames), Buffon, Sömmering, and Kant. Herder's polemic was directed primarily against the latter and was occasioned by the appearance in 1777 of Kant's "Von den verschiedenen Rassen der Menschen" (On the Different Races of Humankind).[42] In it and in subsequent articles published in the 1780s, Kant attempted to delineate race as the conceptual tool that explains the diversity of peoples.[43]

Herder was too aware of the cultural and political consequences of such a position to be able to accept it without the greatest discontent. In his responses to the race debate, he ensures that the notion of common humanity remains the main driving force behind his argument, and for this reason he was particularly unsettled by Kant's attempts to argue for distinct racial groups on the basis of biological difference. Instead, he uses empirical evidence to argue that the manifestations of physical difference are too subtle and too gradual ("colours fading into one another") to allow even the very concept of race ("on the whole, everything becomes shadings of one and the same great picture," *HMA* 3/1, 231). Again, his reasoning is Leibnizian: because the human condition is given innumerable situations in which its potential can be actualized, human diversity is nothing more than the many faces of the same creature, the many realizations of the natural force that is human life. And because the human condition falls short of divinity, there is no human position from which to comment on the relative worth of these diverse expressions of human life. Nor is it possible to imagine what the potential might look like independent of its actualizations.

In 1786, Georg Forster sided publicly with Herder, insisting that diversity testifies to climatic influence, not to the existence of distinct racial groups. Responding to Kant's essay, Forster asks: "Who would not prefer the few observations of a solitary yet perceptive and reliable empiricist to the many embroidered ones of a biased systematist?"[44] The reliable empiricists he has in mind are "recent travellers," including Buffon, Carteret, Bougainville, Dampier, and Cook, whose observations, he claims, have provided valuable evidence on the endless variety of humans populating the world.[45] Like Herder, Forster uses an epistemological argument to shore up his conviction that the very concept of race will inevitably lead to exploitation and injustice. While remaining agnostic on the question of mono- versus polygenesis,[46] Forster is adamant about the need to further the human dignity of black and white alike. He insists that "by ascribing the Negro to an originally distinct branch and separating him from the white person, are we not severing the last thread that tied this abused people to ourselves, and which provided it with some protection and some grace in the face of European cruelty?"[47]

The subtleties in the eighteenth-century debates on race all point to the central problem of the status of empirical knowledge in understanding human diversity – and in trying to find both biological and philosophical models for thinking about the principles that unite diverse expressions of humanity.[48] The readers of Herder, Forster, and others understood that the observations of European travellers presented a challenge not simply to the scattered anecdotes on the primitive nature and inferiority of other races and cultures, but to the very concept of race as a marker of difference, and – at least in Herder's opinion – to the philosophy of race with its arrogant claims to know other cultures without even understanding their languages or exploring their world views.

Klima: The Politics of Environment

Herder's understanding of natural history gives language a creative function (the self-determination of humanity), which is at the same time a political function (negotiating the concepts out of which human identity arises). Environment is both a natural force in shaping humanity in its diversity and an expression of human interactions with nature. It is the material effect of geography on human life, but it is also a concept for formulating the limits of a culture's geographical determination. As we have seen, the concept which, in the course of Herder's life, became increasingly important in expressing this idea was *Klima*. However, it is really only in *Ideas* that it begins to assume central importance in his work. Citing *De Aëre, Aquis, Locis*, Herder states that for him Hippocrates is "the main writer on climate" (*HSW* 13, 269n). In Hippocrates he praises the analytic method of studying environment, which begins by specifying "individual regions on the basis of climate and then slowly, slowly derives general conclusions" (*HSW* 13, 269). In addition, Zammito mentions "the quite substantial" influence of Buffon, with his belief that the diversity of species requires a bio-geographical model.[49] His most immediate reference however is Montesquieu, who had situated climate among the determining factors of human society. While adopting this fundamental recognition of the importance of environment, Herder criticized Montesquieu's lack of a world perspective – the fact that, in attempting to develop an empirical method, he had too narrow a knowledge of various social and political systems to be able to make meaningful generalizations (see *HSW* 13, 465–6).[50]

Climate is a useful concept for thinking about how nature impacts on humanity, but it makes no sense to speak of it as if it were more than a concept. Or, as Herder puts it: "Of course, we are clay, formable in the hands of climate; but its fingers form in such diverse ways, and the laws that work against it are so many, that perhaps only the genius of the human race is capable of presenting all these forces in a single equation" (*HSW* 13, 268). Climate for Herder is much more than just a physiological force that works by directly influencing the nerves and muscles of the organism. It is a topological force shaping the entire complex system in which the organism develops, including the conceptual system that makes sense of the environment.

In this way, Herder manages to bypass the rather quaint physiological determinism of the first three chapters in book 14 of Montesquieu's *L'esprit des lois* (The Spirit of the Laws, 1748), in which he sketches a theory of climatic determinism. Montesquieu believes that in hot countries, "where the tissue of the skin is relaxed, the ends of the nerves are open and exposed to the weakest action of the slightest objects. In cold countries, the tissue of the skin is contracted and the papillae compressed. The little bunches are in a way paralyzed; sensation hardly passes to the brain except when it is extremely strong and is of the entire nerve together. But imagination, taste, sensitivity, and vivacity depend on an infinite number of small sensations."[51] He then goes on to base laws, customs, and manners on this physiological determination of climate.

Herder borrows from Montesquieu the conviction that nature organizes societies in groups according to climatic and territorial determinations. But he avoids the physiological explanations that caused Montesquieu to base different social and moral regimes on neurological and physiological responses to heat and cold. Nor is he about to adopt Montesquieu's rather wide-eyed approach to the travellers' tales that had been flooding European circles since the seventeenth century. Herder has a much more self-conscious approach when it comes to observing strange and distant cultures through the filter of European morality and law, and the consequence for his theory of climate is a much more complex view of human culture. Society, as a rational response to environment, can develop in ways that deviate from the simple physiological expression of nature posited by Montesquieu. But this does not make them any less natural.[52]

Montesquieu's view of climate led him to adopt a highly territorialized view of human diversity. World geography becomes intelligible for him in terms of the climatic features of different territories and the resultant physiological, moral, and social forms in human life. Herder problematizes the relationship between nations and geographical territory by historicizing the influence of environment on humanity. The natural expression of human diversity is constantly changing. There are indeed strong territorial components to the national cohesion of individual cultures, both historical and geographical, but Herder makes it clear that cultures are in constant flux, in terms both of historical development and geographical interaction and of cross-fertilization with other cultures. This introduces an important and innovative nuance into Herder's philosophy: his understanding of how environmental factors call forth rational responses in the form of *Besonnenheit*. Not only are humans constantly adapting to their environment, they have, since the beginning of human life, pursued the representation of environment most appropriate to them; and they have been reflecting critically on the suitability of their adaptive and representational strategies. Barnard puts it well when he describes Herder's theory of *Klima* as aimed at "the *process* of fusion between the 'merely objective' and the 'merely subjective,' the continuous emergence of a continuum between man and his environment."[53] But it is wrong, I believe to fault him, as Barnard does, for "the excessively comprehensive sense in which he employs the term 'climate.'"[54] The whole point of the climate discussion is that nature is never nature-without-humans, it is always mediated nature, and culture is the expression of this ongoing negotiation with nature. Culture gives form to both historical and geographical change, as it is experienced, conceptualized, and articulated by a particular society at a particular moment in a specific environment. This is the extended work of *Besonnenheit* on a collective scale, and it is the political expression of freedom of thought. Cultures are not something distinct from nature; they are caught up in the gradual unfolding of nature over the ages. This means that the philosopher of history must make active choices in deciding to what extent a culture is passively responding to its environment, and to what extent it is actively determining, selecting, and modifying its environment. It also places a certain onus on him to make ethical choices regarding the appropriate expression of each and every individual culture in the way it imagines its natural environment.

There are two directions Herder can take in this regard, and, in the course of his writings, he hints at both, without ever really specifying what they mean for his philosophical position. Repeatedly, he seems to believe that there is indeed a set of values to which he has access which allow him to make judgments about the cultures he studies. This is strongest where he believes that his concept of humanity provides a universal measure of the development of other cultures. As he prepares the way for his discussion of advancements in contemporary European science, and as he approaches the close of *Ideas*, Herder announces that Europe is to take shape as the seat of "humanity and reason," and that these "are to encompass the globe" (*HMA* 3/1, 824). But even when proposing the universal validity of humanity, it is unclear just how committed he is to the idea that humanity is a European concept that can be applied in understanding other cultures.[55] In my opinion, the strong reading of Herder's theory of humanity is that he never intended it to be a concept enabling a priori judgments about cultures outside Europe, similar, say, to Kant's categorical imperative. This would contradict his entire epistemology. It's true, the idea of humanity does threaten to undo his anti-Kantian position, revealing its most fundamental problems. But if we read deeper into Herder's work, *humanity* begins to look less and less like a concept, and more like an aesthetic process, a code for interpreting and representing cultural specificity. *Humanity* does not reveal what to think about the actions, laws, mores, and cultural products of any nation, nor does it provide a moral scale against which they can be measured. Instead, it is a heuristic notion that enables processes for representing diverse cultures collectively.

This is evident in Herder's discussion of environment in *Ideas*. He spells out the implications for imagining natural environment in the "Concluding Remarks on the Conflict between Genesis and Climate" at the close of the seventh book of *Ideas*, written in the early 1780s in Weimar.[56] Here he also puts the task of the philosopher of nature and history in a new perspective informed by European expansionism and questions of race; and in the process, he sketches out a theory of environmental protection in the context of the world economy. On the way to this theory, he needs first to specify the conceptual apparatus whereby science can grasp the collective negotiation and interpretation of environment. The key disciplines at work here are geography (the science of climate) and history (the science of genesis); and it is not by chance that the testing ground for the ability of these sciences to explain the development of humanity is colonialism. When Herder speaks of the need to overcome the opposition between history and geography, his prime example is the way the movement of peoples, primarily in the development of colonies, creates macro-historical trends. The task of the geohistorian is to collect observations of historians and travellers to derive a general model of how culture mediates history and geography, and of how they interact through mobility and cultural cross-fertilization. "We should never overlook the climate from which a people came, the mode of life it brought with it, the country that lay before it, the nations with which it intermingled, and the revolutions it has undergone in its new seat" (*HRP* 29). Herder calls this study a "physical-geographical history of the origins [*Abstammung*] and dispersion [*Verartung*] of our race [*Geschlecht*] according to climates and epochs" (*HRP* 29; translation modified). And the lesson he derives for contemporary expansionist movements is one of gentle, productive interaction, respect for other cultures and environmental conservatism. Gentle, productive interaction is after all the way of nature: "Too sudden, too drastic [*rasch*] transitions to an opposite hemisphere and climate are seldom salutary to a nation; for Nature has not established her boundaries between remote lands in vain" (*HRP* 29; translation modified).

And for this reason, any expansionist movement that attempts a sudden, violent domination of other cultures and the appropriation of their land cannot help but be detrimental to both colonizers and colonized. Herder looks at the "history of conquests, as well as of the trading companies [*Handelsgesellschaften*], and especially that of missions" and sees "a melancholy, and in some respects a laughable picture" (*HRP* 29–30; translation modified). Arrogant, indulgent Europeans degenerate in a foreign climate, and their failure to adapt spells their downfall. A part of this failure is the destruction of environments. Herder is remarkably prescient when he writes: "*Let it not be imagined that human art can with blusterous capriciousness* [mit stürmender Willkür] *convert at once a foreign region into another Europe*, by cutting down its forests, and cultivating its soil: for all of living creation coheres in a nexus which responds only to careful modification [*die ganze lebendige Schöpfung ist im Zusammenahnge und dieser will nur mit Vorsicht geändert werden*]" (*HRP* 31; translation modified).

In taking this proto-environmentalist turn, Herder was particularly impressed by the writings of Peter Kalm, the Swedish professor of economics (*Haushaltungskunst*) and student of Linnaeus who had visited North America in 1748–9, and whose observations appeared in translation in the *Göttingische Sammlung neuer und merkwürdiger Reisen zu Wasser und zu Lande* (Göttingen Collection of New and Remarkable Journeys by Water and Land) in 1754 and 1757.[57] Kalm's report contains repeated references to the effects of immigration, colonization, and commerce on the natural environment not only of the New World, but of Europe. Repeatedly, Kalm provides warning examples of the failure of humans to adapt to their environment. He criticizes the short-sightedness of the citizens of Philadelphia who roof their houses with cedar shingles: "Now, however, these trees have nearly all been cut down, and not the least action has yet been taken to raise new ones."[58] Similarly, the growing scarcity of firewood there results from the growing population and industry, together with the lack of adequate forestry management.[59] He also notes the bad management of pasture by the settlers, who clear the land completely, depleting its nutrients and allowing it to gradually decline in quality: "The exceedingly rich garden soil which the first European farmers discovered, and which had probably never been ploughed or broken up, was the original occasion of this agricultural negligence – and it is still being perpetuated by many."[60]

The environmental degradation resulting from settler colonization described in Kalm's report was of great interest to Herder, not least because alongside his warnings, Kalm presents examples of positive cultural interaction. For example, he discusses how the Europeans learned to grow squash from the native Americans, while the latter obtained peas from the Europeans.[61] But this cultural cooperation needs to be carefully fostered in the face of the environmental damage that can be done by settlement and trade. Kalm provides many examples of how local pests have been transported across the globe through immigration and trade. For example, cockroaches have been brought to New York from the "American Islands" (West Indies), and he recounts an episode in which he himself almost transports the larvae of *Bruchus americae septentrionalis*, which had devastated the pea harvest there, back to Sweden.[62]

Above all, Herder was interested in Kalm's description of the irreparable damage resulting from the lack of respect that displaced Europeans showed for their new environment. He cites Kalm's warning against the disastrous effects that the "speedy destruction of the woods and cultivation of the land" had in North America. It led not only to a drastic reduction in "edible birds, which were found in innumerable multitudes in the forests and on the waters, and of fishes with which the brooks and rivers swarmed, and diminished the lakes, streams, rivulets, springs, rains, thick long grass of the woods, etc.; but this extinction [*diese Ausrottung*] seemed to affect the health and longevity of the inhabitants, and influence the seasons." The point is that "Nature loves not too speedy, too violent a change, even in the best work, that man can perform, the cultivation of a country" (*HRP* 31; translation modified).[63]

This lesson extends to the behaviour of traders and colonizers, who are equally subject to nature's law of gradual change. He calls the arrogant agents of European exploitation the "sons of Daedalus" and the "driving force of fate on earth [*Kreisel des Schicksals auf der Erde*]." He chides his fellows for squandering their potential for spreading prosperity "in a humane and conserving manner." Instead, "a proud and defiant greed for profit" has led them astray. And yet, the force of nature is powerful enough that it will exact revenge: "And does not Nature avenge every crime committed against her? What happened to the conquests of former times, their showplaces, their invasions, after the heterogeneous nation went into a distant, foreign land in order to plunder or devastate it? The still breath of the climate dissipated or consumed them, and it was not difficult for the natives to give the finishing stroke to the rootless tree" (*HMA* 3/1, 258).

The alternative to this cultural, economic, and environmental violence is acclimatization, which involves the respect for foreign environments, not as raw material for exploitation, but as expressions of nature's – and by extension, humanity's – diversity. "The quiet plant, on the other hand, that has accommodated itself to the laws of Nature, has not only preserved its own existence, but has also beneficially diffused the seeds of culture [*Cultur*] through a new land" (*HRP* 33; translation modified). This image of gentle development, mutual aid, and acclimatization provides the model for cultural and economic interaction, and it forms the basis of Herder's understanding of the inherent rationality of natural development. At the core of his understanding of nature's rationality is the firm belief that it is not the same thing as the technical advancement of Western society. Indeed, the rationality he speaks of is more easily attributed to indigenous societies than to European colonizers. "All newcomers from foreign lands who were wise enough to naturalize themselves with the inhabitants have not only enjoyed their love and friendship, but have ultimately found that their climatic way of life was not altogether unsuitable; but how few such have been! how seldom has a European deserved to hear from the native of any country the praise: 'He is a rational man like us!'" (*HMA* 3/1, 258).

The choice facing humanity is to express this rationality through social interaction, or to disregard it – and face the consequences. This is why the rule of gradual change applies not only to natural and historical development, but to the conceptual evaluation of nature and history. The philosopher of natural history needs to adopt a perspective of macro development if he is to do justice to the workings of nature. The theological plan for nature and humanity, viewed with a secular eye, sees the power of human concepts in regulating society's relationship to the environment, but it needs to take the long historical view, not only of the past, but of the future. "The next millennium [*das folgende Jahrtausend*] may decide, what benefit, or injury, our genius has conferred on other climates, and other climates on our genius" (*HRP* 33; translation modified). Human history can be seen in this light as an unfolding of nature's laws, its self-expression. In this progressivist mode (whose optimism has a lot to do with Protestant theology) he sees the semiotic work of humanity in negotiating natural laws, expressing them, and interpreting them for the good of humanity. But the more he looks around him, the harder it is to uphold this optimism. The result is a tension throughout Herder's work between his adherence to the idea that human development is advancing towards a goal that can only be specified in the vaguest of terms, and his condemnation of how European greed and exploitation are harming humanity and impeding this development. Sometimes he attempts to reconcile the two positions by arguing that the exploitative and violent regimes doom themselves to demise (as above); sometimes he argues that even these regimes have called forth positive reactions among other peoples. Thus, he claims that even Roman imperialism, which in his mind compared highly unfavourably to the kind of colonialism that characterized Ancient Greece, ultimately had a positive effect on the advancement of humanity.[64] He even goes as far as to suggest that conquest, exploitation, and slavery might in fact not be such a bad thing after all, since it ensures the most productive use of all parts of the earth (*HSW* 13, 381). This last point is at first confusing, but Herder needs to believe it if he is to take the position he takes on the deeper significance of history for human development: "If there is indeed a God in nature, then he is also in history; human beings too are a part of creation and even in their wildest excesses and passions they must follow laws that are not less beautiful and admirable than those that govern the movements of all heavenly and earthly bodies" (*HMA* 3/1, 580). As he has explained in the lead-up to this statement, cultures rise and fall, blossom and disappear, giving the impression of an inherent futility in human life. But this must be viewed against the background of the divine principle at work in nature and history. This idea is a necessary consequence of Herder's rejection of a simplistic historical teleology based on the perspective of one culture alone, attempting instead to think of human history as a kaleidoscope of histories. "Natural history has reaped no advantages from the philosophy of final causes, the proponents of which have been inclined to satisfy themselves with probable illusions rather than investigation: how much less the history of humankind, with its thousands of interrelated purposes!" (*HMA* 3/1, 575).

Cultural exchange is part of the process driving this intertwined history of humanity. "The history of the world shows incontestably that, wherever a country has raised itself to an exceptional level of culture, it has had an effect on its neighbours" (*HSW* 14, 16). The result is what he calls a "noble expansion of the soul" (*HSW* 13, 309). In this sense, climatic diversity, and with it human diversity, contributes to the betterment of humanity (*HSW* 13, 347). Herder tries his best to retain a sense of cultural relativism in determining which cultures are the bearers and which the recipients of advancement. He never tires of reminding his reader that even those peoples commonly referred to as savage or barbaric are the manifestations of humanity, morals, and culture, and that Enlightenment as a concept cannot simply be restricted to Europe in the seventeenth and eighteenth centuries.[65] Conversely, European cultural and technological privilege is due to the cultural work of others in the past. "We northern Europeans would still be barbarians if a well-meaning wind of fate had not at least carried blossoms of these peoples' spirit over to us, so that by the implantation of beautiful branches among wild stems [*Stämme*], ours too would be ennobled over time" (*HSW* 13, 228). Later he declares that "no peoples in Europe have acquired the status of culture by themselves" (*HSW* 14, 289). Cultural progress always happens through cultural transfer. And just as Herder's own Europe was enriched by cultures that were more developed, it is under the obligation to pass its own riches on to those less-developed cultures in other parts of the world. This obligation is natural in the sense that it is in the nature of the global environment to have made humanity cohabiting and neighbourly. The global environment has caused humankind to have "mutually given one another its plagues, illnesses, and climatic encumbrances," but it has also "transmitted climatic warmth and other benefits" (*HSW* 13, 271). But of course in this reading, everything turns on the understanding of development. If development means that some cultures are farther on the path to perfection than others, then Voltaire must be right, and Europe is the pinnacle of history. If development is always only measured in relative terms, it is ultimately nonsensical to speak of a development of humanity. This is where Herder makes the innovative move of linking historical development to aesthetics. Aesthetic processes become the expression of development in relative terms, but they are also the common ground on which individual development can be measured. Aesthetics enables a dialogue between the relative development of cultures and the vision of humanity's shared development. In the realm of the aesthetic, the diverse appearances of cultures become signs of a shared relationship to nature's force, and the theology and the teleology of this force is open to interpretation.

The Aesthetics of Cultural Difference

Climate has created humanity as a unity of diverse manifestations, and because of this, humanity as a concept appears as a collection of signs that must be correctly interpreted if individuals and nations are to fulfil their obligations to one another. This is expressed in book 7 of *Ideas*:

> Thus, I think, Physiognomy would return to her old natural way, to which her name points; and in which she would be neither Ethognomy nor Technognomy, but the expositor of the *living nature* of a man, the interpreter as it were of his genius rendered visible. As within these bounds she remains true to the analogy of the whole, which is likewise best articulated in the face, Pathognomy must become her sister, Physiology and Semiotics her friends and assistants: for the external figure of man is but the shell of his internal mechanism, a consistent whole in which every letter indeed belongs to the word, but only the whole word has a meaning. (*HMA* 3/1, 251)

What Herder is trying to highlight in this compounding of neologisms is the need for a scientific study of the body-environment system as an aesthetic pursuit. The repeated use of the suffix *-gnomy* indicates that Herder, in a move similar to the one outlined in the *Essay on Being*, is shifting the grounds of judgment (*gnosis*) towards recognition of the forms in which life is expressed. Physiognomy is the study of structures within systems.[66] In *Ideas* and related writings he speaks of the physiognomy of the faces of animals (*HMA* 3/1, 86), of the national languages (*HMA* 3/1, 1135), of a people's discourse (*HMA* 3/1, 322). Understanding the whole means reading and interpreting the signs that reveal the essence of its manifestations. The *Ideas* were intended as just this kind of interpretation. Zammito calls this "Herder's grand project in the *Ideen*," namely, "to discover how man as a creature of nature figured in man as an artifice of culture, to read these two dimensions in continuity."[67]

The crucial point is that the appearance of the diverse nations is part of nature's language, and humans have to learn how to read it. This involves a composite science of nature's signs, a physiognomy in the true sense of the word. The scientist in pursuit of this true physiognomy of human life interprets "a person's living nature" in the dual sense of exegesis, laying out meaning – *auslegen*, and of translating – *dolmetschen*. This semiotics of human appearance is the opposite of the racializing gaze – it apprehends the form of individual appearance as diverse actualizations of the same potentiality, as "clothing the inner drives, a harmonious whole, in which the word requires each letter, but only the word yields meaning" (*HSW* 13, 280). Because of this understanding of diversity in humanity, the interpreter of nature's appearances is called upon to recognize the "endless hues" in the "painting of the nations," which change with time and space. Just as a painting has to be viewed from the correct position, human diversity requires the

5.1 Eberhard Zimmermann, *Tabula mundi geographico zoologica* (1760). Staatsbibliothek zu Berlin Preußischer Kulturbesitz – Kartenabteilung.

correct conceptual perspective. "If our founding concept is European culture, we will only find it in Europe." Instead of this conceptual violence, the interpreter of nature should contemplate that which nature has "placed before our eyes in the form of human life and development [*menschliche Bildung*]" (*HSW* 13, 348–9).

Herder thought hard about the aesthetics of this process, the forms best suited to the presentation of human diversity and unity. At one point he proposes a scientific map of nature's diversity and the unity of humankind: "an anthropological map of earth, like the zoological one attempted by *Zimmermann*, on which nothing need be indicated but the diversity of humanity, but in all its manifestations and in every respect: such a map would ennoble our philanthropic work" (*HWS* 13: 251).[68] (See figure 5.1.)

What is it about a map that can enlighten the viewer as to the process of human development, and what specifically did Herder find in Zimmermann's map? In the preceding chapters, Herder has provided a quick run-through of what he calls the "organization" of the peoples of the world – and by this he means, as we have seen, their organic structural features, what would later be called their physical anthropology. As he progresses with this, he has to realize that his gross generalizations present him with a problem, particularly considering his Leibniz-influenced take on race. Generalizations about peoples should be offered "as seldom as possible," he concludes. "Whoever claims that America is warm, healthy, damp, low-lying, fertile is correct. Another person who claims the opposite is also correct, but in regard to different seasons and places. The same applies to the nations, for the peoples of one hemisphere are found in all zones" (*HMA* 3/1, 223). And yet, Herder continues to offer just the kind of generalizations he warns against. This, he realizes, is an inherent problem with anthropological description, one that he will tackle in the seventh book, which he entitles "The Human Race Appears in So Many Different Forms upon Earth, but It Is Still Everywhere One and the Same Human Species" (*HMA* 3/1, 227). The challenge facing scientific description is to show diversity without breaching the bounds of human unity, and this is a problem which is built into the language of description – in fact, it is built into language itself.

In the conclusion to book 6, Herder stresses the need to look upon human diversity with a scientific eye. He laments the shortcomings of verbal description, and expresses the wish "that I could now use a magic wand to transform into paintings all the vague verbal descriptions I have given thus far and present people with a gallery of graphic representations showing the forms and shapes of their brothers on earth" (*HMA* 3/1, 225). What Herder is looking for is a disinterested eye, a scientific eye. As Pross observes, Herder is intent on showing how existing representations of "exotic" cultures are skewed according to the interests that led to the production of the images. Those ideological representations seemed to demonstrate that the inhabitants of the New World were less than human and thus deserving of the enslavement that the conquerors saw as their fate (*HMA* 3/2, 395). Herder sees his "anthropological wish" impeded by the fact that "for centuries, we have traversed the earth with sword and cross, with corals and kegs of brandy." This instrumental and exploitative approach to other cultures, together with an undue emphasis on the power of verbal description, has blinded Herder's own culture to the fact that "no form can be drawn with words, least of all the most subtle and diverse of all forms, and that which is always deviating in all forms" (*HMA* 3/1, 225).

If the human figure is to be shown as a biologically specific member of the species, then the mode of representation will have to be cleansed of commercial and political interest, in the same way a zoologist hopes to represent an animal impartially. The same should be aspired to in the representation of the human form (this is the point at which, in a footnote, Herder mentions Forster's criticism of Hodges's idealization of the Tahitians). Art, he tells us, can scarcely become more philosophical than when it achieves this kind of description (*HMA* 3/1, 226).

The art of Zimmermann's map lies first of all in the panorama it provides of diversity among animals, and their distribution according to regions, emphasizing the climatic and geographical determination of diversity. At the same time, it makes visible the discrepancy between verbal description and geographical determination. The details show the species to be found in different locations (see figure 5.2). The viewer knows there will be other species there too, but that the representational convention does not allow all of them to be listed. And similarly, the viewer sees that the words on the map cannot give any precise geographical location for the animals it names. If the words name the locations of a species, where are the boundaries beyond which that species will not be found? And what other species live there where there was no room to name them? Anyone who takes this map seriously sees immediately the limitations of its representational conventions. An ethnographic map would, presumably, provoke the same kind of ironic interrogation of its representational limits.[69] Reading (in the broadest sense), analysis, interpretation: these are the foundations of aesthetic work, and they have, Herder hopes, the capacity not only to improve the understanding of human nature, but to contribute to the betterment of humanity. But what exactly does this mean? What is betterment, and what is humanity? How is it possible for the philosopher of history to use observations on the infinite varieties of human nature and culture in order to deduce underlying forces and principles that cannot be verified or themselves described? And how can this lead to a vision of the future that is capable of playing a regulatory function when making judgments about the present? Doesn't this go against everything philosophy stands for? These are the difficult questions Kant asked of Herder when he reviewed the first two parts of Herder's *Ideas* in 1785.

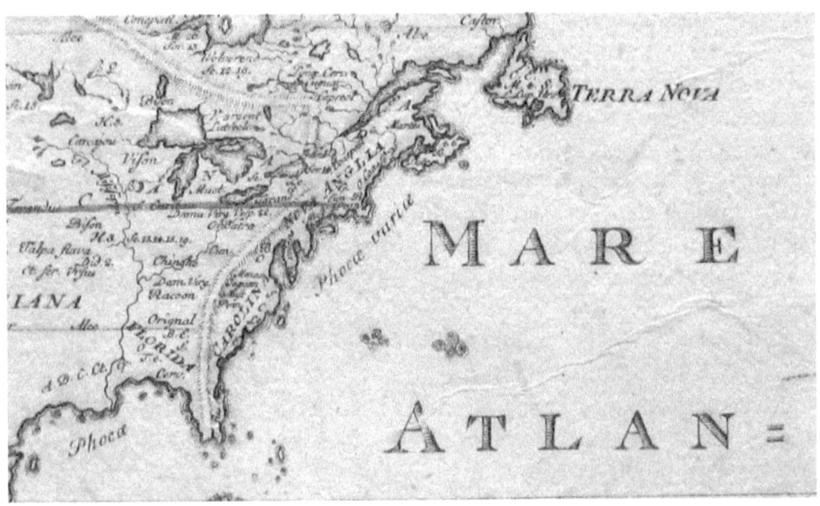

5.2 Zimmermann, *Tabula mundi* (detail).

When the first volume of Herder's *Ideas* appeared in 1784, Christian Gottfried Schütz, professor of philology and philosophy in Jena, asked Kant to write a review for his *Jenaische Allegmeine Literaturzeitung*. Reading Herder, Kant would have recognized some similarities to his own position, primarily the idea that there is a learning process at work in human history and that this process has to do with improved social relations and the exercise of freedom.[70] But when Kant's anonymous review appeared, it zeroed in on what he saw as some of Herder's unsustainable claims. He objects to Herder's particular vision of a progressive refinement and development of the force of nature through history (the betterment of humanity). In what strikes me as an uncharacteristically careless reading, Kant thought Herder was arguing for a radical transformation of the human organism. He accused his student of harbouring a vision that could only lead to the conclusion that the human species itself will have to evolve into something higher, that "*somewhere else*, perhaps on another planet, there might in turn be creatures representing the next higher stage of organic life beyond humanity [*die nächst höhere Stufe der Organisation über den Menschen*], but not that *the same individual* will progress to it" (*KPW* 208; translation modified). Since individuals cannot themselves evolve beyond themselves through palingenesis, in the same way flies might emerge from maggots, there is nothing in the lives of humans to warrant the assumption of a higher stage, not on another planet, not after death. He objects on similar grounds to the monogenetic view of natural history. The fact of natural variety cannot be disputed, but the claim of kinship [*Verwandtschaft*] among them "whereby one genus arose out of the other and all of them out of a single original genus, or alternatively, whereby all of them emerged from a single procreative womb, would lead to *ideas* so monstrous that reason recoils from them" (*KPW* 210). What exactly these ideas are, Kant doesn't say, but we can guess: it's not just that humanity is the product of incest (as Judaeo-Christian mythology must have it), but that the species themselves have interbred.

More serious than this is Herder's insistence that nature and human life are both determined by invisible forces. In the preface to his work, Herder had noted that for many readers, the writings of his age had led to the term "Nature" becoming "meaningless and base," and proposed that instead of thinking about nature, one consider "that all-powerful force, goodness and wisdom, and name in one's soul the invisible being that no earthly language is able to name" (*HMA* 3/1, 15). This is developed throughout *Ideas*, where Herder argues that (as in his title for chapter 4 of book 7) "Genetic Force Is the Mother of All Formations [*Bildungen*] on Earth, and Environment [*Klima*] Only Acts upon It, either in a Hospitable or a Hostile Manner" (*HMA* 3/1, 245). Taking up the revolutionary ideas of Caspar Friedrich Wolff, he goes on to explain how anyone viewing any exemplar of organic nature would have to conclude not only that a "*living, organic force*" is at work there, but that "the invisible force is not forming at random, but that it is only *revealing* itself in accordance with its inner nature. It becomes visible within that measure appropriate to it, and must bear the *typus* of its appearance within itself, no matter where it is and where it comes from. The new creature is nothing but an idea of creative nature (which always only thinks actively) that has become reality" (*HMA* 3/1, 246).

For Kant the idea of an occult force determining the formations of nature is nothing but mysticism, and he criticizes the doctrine of invisible forces on epistemological grounds, but also as a false use of analogy.[71] Kant had gone to great trouble to determine the limits of reason in its ability to grasp what makes phenomena in the natural world behave the way they do; it is certainly possible to grasp the laws of mechanical cause and effect (in fact, it is a precondition of experience); but it is not possible to name their hidden cause. Because of this, it is necessary to draw a boundary between mechanical phenomena, where the laws of causality are clear and constant, and organic nature, where they are not. In his attempt to place hidden organic forces at the foundation of all phenomena, organic and mechanic, Herder has disregarded this – with the result that "mechanical forces themselves appear as a form of organic force."[72] Furthermore, the laws of nature that the understanding employs in order to enable experience are at all times to be distinguished sharply from the laws that govern the freedom of thought. One of the testing grounds for this distinction is given by those cases where scientific inquiry attempts to recognize fundamental unities in the diversity of natural phenomena. Correct scientific method involves recognizing those cases where the laws governing phenomena are similar, justifying a conceptual unity of phenomena. Herder, in Kant's opinion, uses analogy to impose his own preconceived ideas of similarity on all phenomena, reducing them to the same type, and falling prey to the very same metaphysical determination of experience a priori that he so vehemently rejects.

Kant's main point of contention in his reading of *Ideas* concerns the correct method for philosophical inquiry and Herder's failure to engage a truly philosophical discourse, in the sense of a critical and systematic development of concepts. To Kant, this appears as an irrational deference to feeling and a dogmatic faith in the powers of irrational argument. This is most clearly in evidence in Herder's use of analogy and poetic language. What Herder calls a philosophy of history is not in fact

> a logical precision in the determination of concepts or careful distinctions and consistence in the use of principles, but rather a cursory and comprehensive vision and a ready facility for discovering analogies, together with a bold imagination in putting these analogies to use. This is combined with an aptitude for awakening sympathy for his subject – which is always kept at a dark distance – by means of feelings and sentiments; and these in turn, as the product of weighty thoughts or as highly significant pointers, lead us to expect more of them than cool assessment would ever be likely to discover. (*KPW* 201)

It is important to highlight this use of analogy, since Kant believes that one of the fundamental intentions of *Ideas* is to "demonstrate that the human psyche is mental in nature [*geistige Natur der menschlichen Seele*]" as well as its "enduring quality and increasing perfection." This is to be accomplished "by analogy with the natural forms of matter, particularly in their organic structures [*Organisation*], without the help of any metaphysical investigations" (*KPW* 208; translation modified). While I believe he is misrepresenting Herder's intentions regarding the enduring quality and perfection of the soul (or at least he is placing undue emphasis on this idea), he has put his finger on the central methodological problem in Herder's project. Kant read this as a predominance of the "poetic spirit," which substitutes "synonyms for explanations, and allegories for truths" (*KPW* 215). Kant certainly had room in his system for a philosophy of history as a rendering intelligible of historical processes, but he saw no chance of doing this using Herder's method:

> But what are we to think of the whole hypothesis of invisible forces determining organic structures [*Organisation*], and hence of the author's attempt to explain *what is not understood* in terms of *what is understood even less*? In the former case we can at least possibly discover its laws through experience, although the causes underlying them remain unknown; but in the latter case, we are denied even the possibility of experiencing it, and what can the philosopher then adduce in support of his assertion except despair of ever finding the answer in any knowledge of nature, and an enforced decision to look for this answer in the fertile field of the poetic imagination. (*KPW* 209; translation modified)

In this view, historical processes are not natural processes. They have to do with human freedom of choice, and they are a matter of how the categorical imperative is understood and acted upon in different times and places. History, Kant argues, provides tangible evidence of this process.

Seen in this light, the kind of philosophy of history Herder is engaged in had to look to Kant like a confused mix of poetic language, irrationalism, and speculative philosophy, by way of which observed natural phenomena are linked randomly to the idea of a hidden force of development. The worst example of this Kant finds in Herder's explanation of how physiological development led to the emergence of reason. We already know this argument in terms of the acquisition of language, but in *Ideas*, Herder extends this to the upright posture of humans. He does this by arguing in chapter 6 of book 3 that the upright posture of early humans had a direct effect on the development of the brain, which in turn gave rise to the capacity for reason. Kant has no time for this, believing it is futile "to try to determine which organic structures

[*Organisierung*] of the head, both in its external shape and in the internal configuration of the brain within it, are necessarily associated with the aptitude [*Anlage*] to walk – let alone to try to determine how an organic process [*Organisation*] directed solely to this end [walking upright] can contain the basis of that rational faculty which the human animal thereby acquires" (*KPW* 210; translation modified). To claim that reason developed out of an unexplained accident of physiological development is pure speculation: it is "obviously beyond the scope of human reason" (*KPW* 210). Kant is so deeply invested in this point because for him reason has to take priority in explaining the genesis of reason. To philosophize otherwise is to speculate or to fall into superstition. Herder's error lies in believing that (and here he cites Herder) "it was not our rational mind [*vernünftige Seele*] which formed the body, but the finger of the deity, i.e. organic force" (*HMA* 3/1, 160, cited in *KPW* 206). If there is change in history, it has to happen on the basis of reason. And to look to the historical limits of reason, to the birth of intelligence, is to examine that which escapes knowledge and forces the writer into analogy and poetic devices.

To some of the simpler objections Herder would have had answers. Kant patently misrepresents his theory of development, which was aimed neither at extraterrestrials nor at life after death, nor at the growth of the soul. Nor was it to be grasped via a progressive historical optimism on the part of the European Enlightenment. The measure of historical progress lies in the conceptualization of collective humanity. This could be seen as teleological in the Kantian sense, in that it is a necessary understanding of the goals of historical progress as seen from the point of view of the present – but Herder insisted that this conforms to a natural principle, and he attempted to model and to represent this principle. He was, in this respect, not looking for occult forces of the kind Kant had in mind, but for the underlying principle that reveals itself in the development of humanity, just as it does in the development of the organism.[73] Here, Herder has uncovered a conceptual dilemma in Kant's argument, as Menges notes: "While Kant's dismissive treatment of the analogical concept illustrates the epistemological difference to critical philosophy, it implicitly legitimizes Herder's approach as an alternative discourse that deserves recognition, not the least due to its solid foundation in the history of science."[74] Kant's criticism of Herder was only possible because he disregarded the larger context of contemporary research which was increasingly making it plausible to speak of hidden formal forces.[75] And, as the theory of evolution has shown, monogenesis is not to be seen as reductively as Kant understands it. To see in it nothing but the biblical story is to go against his own principles and attempt to gaze into an origin which, as he explained, cannot be seen. And even if there were something traumatic to be found along the way, there should be nothing monstrous enough to warrant reason shutting it out of its field of inquiry, as the Kantian philosopher Karl Leonhard Reinhold pointed out in his reply to the review (which also appeared anonymously).[76]

But other of Kant's criticisms cut deeper. There is, for example, Herder's attempt to understand mind and body as part of the same organic process. If the mind is of the same nature as the body, Kant will ask, why treat it as something special? On the other hand, even if it is nothing more than an effect of organic processes – if it reveals itself as mind, i.e., as a process capable of reflecting on itself as process – doesn't this mean that it has to be dealt with as something separate from the body? Kant asks why Herder "did not transfer the thinking principle in man, which is of a purely mental nature [*geistige Natur*]" directly to the "invisible realm of active and autonomous forces." Why does Herder want to first raise this principle "up out of chaos through the edifice of organic structures [*das Bauwerk der Organisation*]?" After all, Herder believes (Kant thinks) "that he could reliably deduce the existence of such a realm from organic creation." And if he is not prepared to equate the mind with the realm of invisible forces at work in creation, he should recognize that they are "something altogether different from the human soul or psyche [*Seele*]." The consequence of this second position would be to regard the psyche "not as a particular substance, but merely as the effect of an invisible universal nature which acts on matter and gives it life" (*KPW* 209; translation modified).

In refusing to decide whether the mind is a part of organic nature or a separate effect of organic nature, Kant felt, Herder was trying to have it both ways. In fact, Herder's views on this point are always fuzzy, and they reveal a central problem, not only in his attempts to link mind and body, but with his theory of critical thinking, and how it relates to the betterment of humanity. Where Kant wants critical thinking to reflect the freedom of thought, thereby enabling political interventions, Herder remains uncertain whether his own political interventions, and by implication those of all others, are authorized by the greater plan for humanity – which paradoxically makes them more or less irrelevant, since humanity's plan is inherent and inevitable – or if a critical intervention is a special capacity of some minds, a creative proximity to divine thought, a spark of genius in the critical process. This is a problem which will haunt critical theory ever after.

Then there is the problem of deriving a unitary theory of human development from the wide range of ethnographic evidence and other documents Herder consulted. Kant feels that if this is the methodology to which Herder is committed, it would have been necessary for a "historical and critical mind" to have studied "the boundless mass of ethnographical descriptions and travelogues," concentrating on those instances that did not support a theory of unitary human development, but that focus on those which are contradictory. Instead, he accuses Herder of selectively choosing his evidence.

> But as it is, one may prove, if one wishes, from numerous descriptions of various countries, that [Native] Americans, Tibetans, and other genuine Mongolian peoples are beardless – but also, if one prefers, that they are all naturally bearded and merely pluck their hair out. Or one may prove that [Native] Americans and Negros are races which have sunk below the level of other members of the species in terms of intellectual abilities – or alternatively, on the evidence of no less plausible accounts, that they should be regarded as equal in natural ability to all the other inhabitants of the world. Thus, the philosopher is at liberty to choose whether he wishes to assume natural differences or to judge everything by the principle *tout comme chez nous*, with the result that all the systems he constructs on such unstable foundations must take on the appearance of ramshackle hypotheses (*KPW* 217).

This is intimately related to the previous criticism. If the task of critical analysis is to read the appearances of human culture as evidence of environmental regularities in order to arrive at more fundamental unities, then this is where the philosopher will concentrate his efforts. But in doing so, how can he be sure that he is not falsifying evidence. And more important, if the mind is an expression of the same force that created the evidence in the first place, where does the freedom of thought lie?

Herder recognized the unsuitability of Kant's critical philosophy in addressing what he saw as the central task in the study of nature and of history, the description of natural principles that are occult yet effective, whose true nature cannot be known, only modelled in scientific discourses or represented in aesthetic production. Kant was interested in judgment and freedom, not in modelling organic processes. Where Kant accused Herder of falling into the very same metaphysical traps he claims to dismiss (*KPW* 209), Herder felt that the philosophy of history requires a different method from metaphysics. Herder was clear in his praise of metaphysics as a philosophical method, but he recognized that it is not appropriate for the study of organic processes. Concealed in this praise is a far-reaching criticism of metaphysics, since in his view organic processes lie at the foundation of conceptualization itself. Metaphysics "has no place in a philosophy of history, which does not represent 'developments a priori,' but a 'philosophy about facta.'"[77] In other words, the philosophy of history is something different from metaphysics, since it starts with an analysis of facts. This, as we have seen, involves an aesthetics of the organic. The prime function of the aesthetic is to bring to philosophy a vision of unity; and the underlying assumption that necessitates this method is that unity cannot be grasped in a discourse that develops its concepts as if truth were not accessed through sensory perception. As early as 1773, in his praise of Shakespeare in *On German Style and Art*, Herder had claimed that "only the poet" is capable of grasping the unity of various "peoples, classes and souls, all of them the most diverse and in their actions divided machines" (*HSW* 5, 219–20). Kant, on the contrary, feels that poetic knowledge needs to be carefully distinguished from philosophy, "which is more concerned with pruning luxuriant growths than with propagating them" (*KPW* 211). And yet, Herder was perceptive in seeing that the analysis of history is a matter for aesthetics: we cannot take human actions themselves as historical evidence, since in the analysis of history, we only have access to representations of actions. And furthermore (following Hamann), Herder understood that these representations are always built on a ruse of authority which extends to Kant's metaphysics itself.

State Power and Nature: Aesthetics against Imperialism

Together with this rejection of Herder's attempts to release philosophy from the idealist system, Kant objects to his refusal to see the state as a domesticating instance to which the individual's acts of reason must be subordinated if collective life is to function for the good of all. Because of this (as Sonia Sikka has shown), the question of happiness comes to assume a defining position in their different views of historical progress.[78] Like Aristotle, Herder saw happiness not only as a central index of the quality of life, but as the aim of human action.[79] This makes it not only a measure of success in realizing the human condition, but also a central aspect of the struggle for improved living conditions. It also militates against any universalist take on government. But more important still in the context of my argument is the fact that the specific understanding of happiness found in any context (whether this be individual or cultural) depends on how it is represented to those pursuing it.[80] For Kant, if progress in history is to be evaluated and understood by the tenets of reason, happiness cannot be a measure of historical progress. Progress means developing the appropriate form of government if the individual is to attain that degree of happiness possible under given historical circumstances – and this is always a limited and curtailed happiness, a renunciation of the self-serving side of desire. This implies a Hobbesian understanding of human nature, which Herder rejects: "It may be a simple tenet for the philosophy of human history, but it is an evil one to claim that man is an animal who needs a master, from whom, or in relationship to whom he expects to receive the happiness of his final destiny" (*HMA* 3/1, 336–7). Herder equates state power with this kind of artificial attempt to channel individual happiness for the purposes of a specific regime of power. And again, his evidence is ethnological and historical. He finds it incomprehensible "that man should have been created for the state, that his first and true happiness should necessarily sprout from its institutions, for how many peoples on earth know nothing of the state, and yet are happier than many crucified benefactors" (*HMA* 3/1, 304). Herder goes on to praise providence (and Kant cites him here) for making the "artificial final goals of great societies" dependent not on what he calls the "costly machine of the state" (*kostbaren Staatsmaschinen*), but on "the more feasible happiness of single individuals" (*HMA* 3/1, 305).

Kant takes this opportunity to point to his own philosophy of history, which of necessity culminates in the state. This is a direct consequence of his postulate that the state of nature is one in which individuals express their self-serving nature by fighting all others for their own advantage.[81] If human nature leads of necessity to a general state of lawlessness, as Hobbes had proclaimed, and as Kant repeats in this section, then the state is an essential institution, and an expression of a legal obligation residing within humanity itself. The state became one of the central objects of dispute between Kant and Herder, not only because it highlighted their different views on nature and reason, but because it served to illustrate how far apart their views on morality were. With the principle of *exeundum e statu naturali* (the state of nature is to be left behind), Kant takes what Kersting calls the unprecedented step of arguing the necessity of the state not on pragmatic grounds, but on the basis of theoretical reason.[82] But from Herder's point of view, if human nature is indeed *nature*, it is nonsense to assume it can in any way be left behind or exited. The state for Herder tends to be viewed as an immoral institution, since its raison d'être lies in a denial of nature, whereas for Kant it is the prime institution of morality, to the degree that one's stance on the state is a measure of one's morality.[83] Government should not be in the hands of individual rulers; it should not be inherited, nor should it be imposed on a people from without. In order to safeguard it from tyranny, government should be for and by the people, that is, it should be controlled by the state.[84]

However, Kant argues, this must be seen within the processes of historical development, whereby happiness goes through stages corresponding to the growth of the individual and of society: "First comes the happiness of the animal, then that of the child, then that of the youth, and finally that of the man" (*KPW* 219). We can disregard for the moment the contradiction Kant embroils himself in by using this kind of metaphor for historical processes, and by implying that there is indeed an organic development from the condition of the animal to that of the mature human, and that this process is the same as that presiding over history – thereby committing the same methodological error he accuses Herder of. What is important is that, in this view, historical development necessarily progresses towards the formation of the state. If there is a purpose towards which providence is directed, this must lie in "a political constitution based on concepts of human right." This is the work not of organic processes, but of human design, and the happiness of individuals is only important to the extent that it remains a shadow of what it could be, causing individuals to contribute to the "continuing and growing activity and culture" (*KPW* 219).[85]

Kant had already explained this position in his essay "What Is Enlightenment?," which had appeared the previous year, and which had sketched the idea of historical progress in the context of his moral philosophy. From the point of view of morality and the freedom of thought, history has to be thought of as teleological. Progress in history is required by the idea of freedom, since freedom always considers the past critically from the point of view of the moral law, and seeks to act accordingly. In doing so, the moral law expresses a hope for the future, while at the same time enabling political action in the present. As long as individual humans or human societies have not attained the celebrated maturity – *Mündigkeit* – that Enlightenment promises them, the state is there primarily to enable and protect freedom of thought, to educate, perhaps even to force its citizens into maturity. This is why Kant claims that this age of enlightenment in which he lives could also be called "the century of Frederick [the Great]" (*KPW* 58). Frederick has set an example for how the condition of freedom need not in any way stand in opposition to "public concord and the unity of the commonwealth" (*KPW* 59). An enlightened head of state, such as Frederick has shown himself to be, understands that "there is no danger even to his *legislation* if he allows his subjects to make *public* use of their own reason and to put before the public their thoughts on better ways of drawing up laws, even if this entails forthright criticism of the current legislation" (*KPW* 59). Kant understands the paradoxes involved in claiming that historical progress involves the emancipation of reason, but that its pinnacle has been the kind of enlightened despotism he finds under Frederick the Great. However, he is prepared to take this in stride, given the alternatives – either despotism (the suppression of any impulses towards human progress) or stagnation (the lack of such impulses).

The situation of stagnation is described in the review of *Ideas*, and here it becomes apparent that Herder was right in setting imperialism as the testing ground for European views on natural development, historical progress, and morality. To make his point, Kant draws his evidence from the South Seas: "Does the author really mean that, if the happy inhabitants of Tahiti, never visited by more civilized nations, were destined to live in their peaceful indolence for thousands of centuries, it would be possible to give a satisfactory answer to the question of why they should exist at all, and of whether it would not have been just as good if this island had been occupied by happy sheep and cattle as by happy human beings who merely enjoy themselves" (*KPW* 220). This sentence always asks to be reread to find out whether Kant is really saying what he seems to be saying.[86] And indeed, he is. From the point of view of his historical teleology, the inhabitants of the New World can only be thought to be worthy of living to the extent that they are capable of improvement, seen from the perspective of European enlightenment. As Sikka puts it, "Kant finds it hard to see how the imagined life of these simple people could have any purpose, unless it were eventually 'improved' by contact with nations whose inhabitants are simultaneously more disciplined and more energetic, since he does not consider happiness to be an end in itself. What matters to Kant, in the final analysis, is the industrious unfolding of practical reason within the world."[87] Herder foresaw this conceptual trap. The paradoxical pairing of enlightenment with the state – and here we have to qualify Kant's Prussia as an example of the expansionist European state – even in Herder's day revealed itself as an apology for imperialism, perhaps even genocide. Of course, Kant would not agree to this, but his example of Tahiti together with the fact of imperialism serves to direct Herder's attention towards the practical (in Kant's own sense) weaknesses in Kant's philosophy of history, and perhaps even in the foundation of his philosophy itself.[88] The European philosopher should not use his own understanding of happiness to make judgments about another culture's conception and practice of happiness. Instead, Herder wanted to show that happiness is, in Wolfgang Pross' words, "the product of a cultural struggle; this becomes evident where humanity has extended to the climatic border zones" (*HMA* 3/2, 542).

Herder's understanding of reason is grounded in a completely different view of human nature to that of Kant, and he believed that ethnographic evidence supported him. The true measure of this evidence lay not in preconceived views of morality, but in the happiness of a society's citizens. Herder observes that many societies who know nothing of the state nevertheless promote individual happiness. Happiness is always relative, conditioned, and enabled by the historical circumstances and the horizon of expectations in which an individual finds himself.[89] But this does not mean that it is a curtailment of naturally destructive desire. Desire itself, as a natural impulse, seeks fulfilment in happiness, and in the process it becomes named within the context in which it unfolds. Herder uses this view of happiness as a cultural struggle, and not a question of state power, when he launches on his criticism of the state. Reversing the Hobbesian claim that humans are animals in need of a master, he argues that a human in need of a master is but an animal (*HMA* 3/1, 337). And again, the fact of imperialism informs this view. The critique of the state is never far removed from a critique of "the unnatural expansion of states, the savage mixing of humanity's types and nations under *one* sceptre" (*HSW* 13, 384). And this is fed by injustice at home. "In the great states, hundreds starve so that one might feast and luxuriate. Tens of thousands are persecuted and sent to their deaths so a crowned fool or wise man can live out his fantasies." The lesson to be learned from observing societies in the New World is not that imperialism and the civilizing mission are necessary curtailments of natural desires, but that the question of happiness needs to be dissociated from the power of the state. "Does not each and every one of us have to begin where the savages begin, that he obtains and preserves his health and spiritual power, the good fortune of his house and hearth, not from the state but from himself" (*HSW* 13, 340–1).[90]

In claiming that the state is needed to contain and enable human happiness, and in dismissing the happiness of the Tahitians, Kant is demonstrating that it is not possible to take his own advice and judge history by the actions of individuals, without at the same time admitting that the measure of these judgments is itself historically conditioned. Or to put it differently, we have in our own rationality no basis for the kind of judgment Kant makes about the Tahitians, since reason is too closely tied to our own culture. This is the true challenge that the fact of imperialism causes Herder to raise for Kant's philosophy.

Kant's review perceptively highlights some of the major weakness of Herder's project, but it fails to address what was probably the single most important challenge to his own system: the imperialist dramatization of how judgments are culturally determined, and how they enter into collusion with specific regimes of power. When Kant accused Herder of being unphilosophical because he allows his own perceptions and not the principles of rationality to form the basis of historical investigation, he was pointing to a central problem within his own philosophy. There is no way of knowing how the individual's perspective relates to that of others, except by way of culturally and linguistically specific representations. Kant's philosophy stands or falls on this point, and Herder was early in recognizing this. He opens his essay *On the Change of Taste* (1766) with the observation that, as soon as I find something true or beautiful, "nothing is more natural than the expectation that every human being will have the same feeling, the same opinion, with me. Otherwise, of course, there would be no basic rule of truth and no firm basis for taste. As soon as it is shown that what I on the basis of reasons take to be true, beautiful, good, pleasant can likewise on the basis of reasons be regarded by another as false, ugly, bad, unpleasant, then truth, beauty, and moral value is a phantom that appears to each person in another way, in another shape" (*HPW* 247). Kant would try to solve this problem in the *Critique of Judgment*, but what remains unanswered is how aesthetic judgment relates to the cultural specificity of representations, and how uneven power relations play out in this relationship. On the matter of how aesthetics relates to imperialism, Kant has no answers.

Herder understood the bind in which the Kantian philosophy places the historian. If he attempts to understand historical change from the point of view of an unchanging moral law, it can only be deciphered as change within the parameters laid down by that law, as interpreted by the historian. This applies even to a law as simple and apparently universal as Kant's categorical imperative. And if he attempts to understand history as the unfolding of a natural teleology, the framework for evaluating any one moment in history is given by the historian's own position. History advances simply because it has to in order for the present conception of freedom to be viable. As an alternative to this bind, Herder proposed a natural principle of development that is not the same as progress towards Enlightenment. This is coupled to a principle of legibility that makes natural development accessible but obscure, representable but not understandable. Inherent in the natural principle of development is the fact of cultural and linguistic diversity, and this is accompanied by diversity in the interpretation of natural principles. Collectively, these interpretations and other cultural practices make up what Herder calls Humanity, and in the ideal form they collectively and retrospectively agree on the incomprehensible.

Herder was not prepared to see freedom as set aside from nature through reason's ability to recognize nature's voice as the voice of blind instinct, and in this act to raise itself triumphantly above the dictates of nature. Nor did he place the imagination in conflict with reason. In his view, it makes no sense to distinguish between the innate qualities that raise reason above nature and the qualities of the imagination that dream of a raw condition of nature prior to the advent of reason. Herder could not have acceded to the distinction Kant draws between the "history of *nature*" as the "*work of God*" and the "history of *freedom*" as the "work of *humans* [*Menschenwerk*]" (*KPW* 227; translation modified). Nature does not stand opposite humanity as the world of things, to be entered via one path only – the path of reason, while imagination and instinct are dead ends leading to the unexamined life. Nature exists and is realized in human life as the work of the imagination and of language, but also as that which expresses itself in concerted acts of imagination and reason. Nature is God's work, and it is the work of human reason, imagination, and expression. In this sense, the distinction between *aisthesis* and *aesthesis* begins to blur, and the aesthetic becomes the realm where difference can be negotiated, revealing the underlying unity of its principles. The aesthetic acts that name nature's force are the same acts that distinguish the rational aspect of nature's force from its blindness. This view of freedom as part of the expression of nature is central to Herder's understanding of humanity as unity in diversity, and it is the key that he believes will take him beyond the impasses Kant thought he had identified in *Ideas.*

6 The Aesthetics of Revolution and the Critique of Imperialism

Common Sense: A Political Aesthetics

Herder had always been deeply troubled by public criticism of his works. We only need cast our minds back to the unfortunate affair surrounding his attack on Klotz and the anonymous publication of the *Critical Groves* while he was in Riga. Although Kant's review of *Ideas* appeared anonymously, there is good reason to believe that Herder realized that it was his ex-teacher who was mounting such a sharp criticism of this, his most important work to date.[1] And anyway, he knew from Kant's own essay on progress in history, *Idee zu einer allgemeinen Geschichte in weltbürgerlicher Absicht* (Idea for a Universal History with a Cosmopolitan Purpose), published in the previous year, that his teacher's view of history was diametrically opposed to his own. He responded in two ways, first by carefully reviewing his ideas on the progress of human society and the importance of the state, and second by refining his position on the poetics of human life. This dual response to Kant's criticism found immediate expression in a flurry of writing in the year 1787. Wulf Koepke considers these writings to be of decisive importance, so much so that he speaks of a "turning point," at which Herder's thought begins to take a different direction.[2]

While I don't wish to argue Koepke's case for a "turning point," I agree that Herder was engaged in a kind of stocktaking at this time, and I would argue that it was Kant's criticism that initiated this. The seminal writings of this year can be read as attempts to revise and restate his fundamental thinking in matters of politics and religion, and to commit once again to an aesthetics of human life – to the idea that the study of human life is best conducted using the tools of aesthetics. In *Idea for a Universal History*, Kant's intention had been to demonstrate how philosophy could contribute to human freedom by creating the conditions for a real progress of humanity towards Enlightenment. Kant had no hesitation in basing his study of history on the reasoned assumption that it is unfolding according to a natural plan. After all, history is driven by human actions, making it a collective expression of free will, and the manifestation of free will is "determined in accordance with natural laws, as is every other natural event" (*KPW* 41). So, even if that plan remains in essence unknowable, it should still be possible to discover in history "a regular progression among freely willed actions" (*KPW* 41). Here lies the crucial difference between Herder and Kant. In the ninth thesis Kant states that "a philosophical attempt to work out a universal history of the world in accordance with a plan of nature aimed at a perfect civil union of humankind [*Menschengattung*], must be regarded as possible and even as capable of furthering the purpose of nature itself" (*KPW* 51, translation modified). But human thought is "too short-sighted" to apprehend the "hidden mechanisms" that drive the plan of nature's unfolding – and that includes the operations of human freedom. Nevertheless, if reason dictates the necessity of such an unfolding, philosophy must be able to see itself striving to further it. It is not actual events that reason will be capable of predicting, as Newtonian physics can accomplish in the case of mechanical phenomena, but large trends and the overall direction of human history.

The *Idea for a Universal History* pre-empted the other central contention in the review of Herder, the belief in universal progression towards the state.[3] In the unfolding of history, nature compels the human species to attain the highest purpose of nature. We may not be able to know what this purpose is, but we can know the social form ideally suited to attaining it, namely, "a society which has not only the greatest freedom, and therefore a continual antagonism among its members, but also the most precise specification and preservation of the limits of this freedom in order that it can co-exist with the freedom of others" (*KPW* 45). This society is, as we have seen, a civil society promoting a "law-given civil constitution among individual men" (*KPW* 47). Taken to the level of international relations, humanity strives towards a commonwealth of states, whose carefully regulated freedom is the same as that of the individual citizen within the individual state.

Kant agrees with Herder that history is progressing according to natural laws. After all – and Kant himself begins his essay with this observation – Newton and Kepler have discovered laws of nature to explain the orbits of planets "in terms of a universal natural cause" (*KPW* 42). But Herder believes science is capable of modelling and describing these laws. In his *Gespräche über die Seelenwanderung* (Conversations on the Transmigration of Souls, 1782) he had stated: "In Nature everything is connected, morality and physics, like the spirit and the body. Morality is merely a higher physics of the spirit" (*HSW* 15, 275). And taking this one step further, he hints that the progressive development of the spirit can be described in the same terms Newton had developed to explain the physical relationship of cosmic bodies. But the model will have to differ from that of Newtonian physics in three important ways: it will describe not only mechanical nature, but the forces underlying both organic and mechanical nature; it will be a model that works by analogy, and thus retains something of the poetic (what Gaier calls Herder's "epistemologically founded decision to use metaphors");[4] and its universality cannot be grasped in the same terms as the universality of mechanical laws. This means that the laws of nature assume a much more comprehensive status than Kant is prepared to ascribe them. And in doing so, they necessarily lose their representational transparency. They become a matter for interpretation. Finally, Kant's conviction that the state is the most perfect society in which nature can fulfil its plan is by no means binding. What then are the alternatives, and is it even possible to specify the most perfect social order?

The essay that attempts to address this question was *Idee zum ersten patriotischen Institut für den Allgemeingeist Deutschlands* (Idea for the First Patriotic Institute for the Common Spirit of Germany), which Herder began in 1785 and completed in 1787. The idea for this institute had originated with Carl Friedrich of Baden, whose plan it was to design and build a number of what he referred to as "patriotic" institutions to foster political and economic unity in the German principalities. In political terms, the envisaged assembly of academics across European borders would act as a proxy parliament, "an alternative to the one the Holy Roman Empire never convened. The territorial divisions and boundaries would be subject to the authority of a general assembly."[5] In this essay, Herder implicitly weighs his political position against that of Kant, whom he does not mention. He begins by repeating, almost verbatim, Kant's sixth proposition in *Ideas for a Universal History*, that the establishment of a just society is the most difficult, but the greatest, achievement at which human history aims. Like Kant, he speaks of this process as governed by natural principles. "Since unity and diversity are the perfections that characterize all lasting works of nature and its imitator, art, there is no doubt that the highest, most difficult and useful human art, the establishment of a nation that exists for the general welfare, must strive, and indeed strives unnoticed towards these qualities" (*HSW* 16, 600). With this opening sentence, it is clear that he is speaking to Kant. But he is modifying Kant's philosophy of history in a direction we have come to expect. It is not a progressive refinement of universal reason that propels history, but the collective self-expression, the universal actualization of reason in all its diversity. This principle motivates acts of reason, in so far as human artifice is an exercise of freedom. And the principle of antagonism driving history, which Kant adopted from Hobbes, is recast here as the natural principle of unity and diversity. Ever since reading Kant's *Metaphysics of Morals*, Herder had been realizing that Kant's theory of the state was anathema to his own position. In February 1785 he wrote to Hamann that he had "no use" for Kant's "childish plan according to which the human being is created for the species and the most perfect state-machine at the end of time" (*HBG* 5, 106).[6] This is why he speaks of the nation, presumably because a nation can take on any number of political forms.

Nevertheless, when it comes to Germany, Herder concedes that Kant was right in his description of the state. From an enlightened point of view ("the more light enters this monstrous forest of human endeavour"), the "single great final purpose, national welfare" is achieved when, domestically, the state maximizes its "cohesiveness, order, and legally entrenched freedom while exercising increased 'power, dignity, and wisdom' in its external affairs" (*HSW* 16, 601). In Germany, this amounts to a process of consolidation and unification, and its goal does indeed seem to be the state and a civil constitution. But this has not been arrived at through reason opposing the chaos of nature with a priori principles, but has been derived analytically from the organic structures of nature through a process of political struggle. The relationship reason holds to the nature it has helped structure can only be determined in retrospect.

In spite of his apparent initial agreement with Kant, Herder is striking out again on his own path. Even the word constitution, as Herder uses it, refers to the organic cohesion of the body politic, and not to a legally binding document of state.[7] In order to cement this point, he then turns his attention to the promotion of the German language. It is in the linguistic development of the nation that a correct balance of unity and diversity will be found. This is another way of putting forward the idea of an organic development of the state.[8] As we shall see, the notion of the organic state will be decisive for the further course of Herder's political thought, and particularly his appraisal of the French Revolution, but also his implicit defence of violence in the overthrow of imperialist regimes.

The apparent concessions to Kant that frame this essay are only intended to underline what Herder sees as the true approach to history. In his other writings of 1787, this approach appears as a heightened awareness of human history as an expression of natural principles. This brings with it the need to develop a language capable of dramatizing the limits of conceptual thought in the understanding of history, and of identifying patterns that might allow the future to be predicted. If Herder's non-conceptual language achieves this end, then it can still claim to be a scientific study of history, even if it is no longer philosophy in the Kantian sense.

This was the purpose of the essay *Über Bild, Dichtung und Fabel,* (On Image, Poetic Production and Fables, 1787) which Gaier calls "Herder's epistemological answer to Kant."[9] This appeared in his *Zerstreute Blätter* (Scattered Notes), which he had been publishing since 1785, and which consisted of (in Clark's words) "short essays, some of them among the best in the German language, of translations from the manifold literatures known to Herder, of dialogues on philosophical subjects, and of works in a new genre developed by Herder, the *Nachdichtung*."[10] The form of the *Scattered Notes* was intended to address the public culture of Enlightenment in a form that would be at once entertaining and instructive. It is telling that Herder chooses to explain his aesthetic and epistemological statement of purpose in this context, since it shows his understanding of the didactic role of the public intellectual. And the lesson is of vital importance to Herder – that "our whole life ... is to a certain extent *poetics*" (*HAW* 358).[11] Why should this be? Herder explains that "all the objects of our senses become ours only to the extent that we become aware of them; that is, we designate them, in a more or less clear and vivid fashion, with the stamp of our consciousness" (*HAW* 358). We know this from the *Treatise on the Origin of Language* – the process Herder is describing is the emergence of objects and concepts in language. In *On Image* he explains once again, as he had already done in the *Treatise* and the *Essay on Being*, that the conceptualization of the world begins with the senses. Sight and hearing, touch, taste, and smell bring objects forth from the "sea of impressions" on which one floats. And this takes place in concert, so that the "largely obscure sensations" given to the senses work together secretly to affect "the sum of his whole condition at all times." That is to say (and this is the statement that opens Herder's essay): "Human beings are such compound, artificial beings that despite every effort they can never achieve a wholly simple state" (*HAW* 357, translation modified). Instead, the nature of human life is a constant process of balancing the information given to the senses, in order to derive concepts of the world.

There are two important features of this process of balancing sensory impressions to derive concepts. The first is that "every sensation, like every object of the same, possesses its own rules of perfection" (*HAW* 357). The structuring elements of time, space, and force are not categories that relate the understanding to the senses, they are rules of perfection that are inherent in the senses as they interact with the world. As Norton observes, Herder did not conceive of the concepts of time, space, and force "only as a priori forms of intuition, as Kant would later describe them, but as the actual structuring principles of reality and thus as part of physical experience itself."[12] Because of this (and this is the second feature), philosophy merges with aesthetics, not in terms of "the *philosophy of the beautiful*," but as "a *philosophy of sensuous feelings*" (*HAW* 357). Aesthetics describes precisely the objects of philosophy, as well as "the subject of their effect" (*HAW* 358). The aesthetic organization of the world in philosophy is just that – it is an organization in the sense Herder likes to use the word: a derivation and recognition of inherent organic structures. At the most fundamental stage of human cognition, Herder departs from Kant. "General mechanical laws are of no help here, for, as I have said, what we see in external objects does not lie merely in the things themselves but is primarily dependent on the organ that perceives them, and the inner sense that becomes conscious of them" (*HAW* 360). When Herder states that general mechanical laws are of no help here, he means that they will not take us any further in understanding the principles that structure human life. This then is Herder's initial answer to Kant: "Our mind, our psyche [*Seele*], like our language, allegorizes constantly" (*HAW* 359). Allegorization is philosophical to the extent that it allows thought to participate in the poetics of life. What this means is that thought is a part of that natural force that seeks constantly to create unified structures out of diversity (which is itself a product of the natural force of diversification). The result could be either concepts (philosophical images) or allegories (poetic images), but either way, the process is the same.[13]

Allegorization is, as Koepke notes, not intended here to mean the realization of an abstract concept in the form of an image, but the production of a signifying image from sensory impressions.[14] This point is vital in understanding why Herder's aesthetics is fundamental not only to his epistemology, but to his political theory. Signifying images or concepts are mental images that emerge from the manifold of sensory perception. They are translations of translations, and they are only possible because the mind harmonizes and balances the impressions of the various senses. Reason itself requires this "communicability among our several senses and the harmony prevailing between them, whereupon this communication rests – only this constitutes the inner form or so-called perfectibility of man" (*HAW* 359). Perfectibility is the process whereby the natural principle of unification, consolidation, and communication is realized in the life of the individual.

But this process does not only happen within the individual in isolation. It is the same process as the acquisition of language, and it becomes a shared horizon of meaning within any one linguistic group. Herder had developed this idea in his *Fourth Critical Grove*, where he addressed the dual meaning of *sensus communis* as both the harmonization of the senses and the culturally specific "common sense" that results from this. The senses themselves respond to environmental factors, and so does the harmonizing faculty of *sensus communis*. The shared political life of a people thus depends on the kind of shared processes of translation from sensory perception to concepts described above. Another way of saying this is that what we call philosophy is intimately related to every mythology that has emerged throughout history and throughout the world. "The oldest mythology and poetics is therefore a *philosophy about the laws of Nature*, an attempt to explain the vicissitudes of the universe in its becoming, persistence, and destruction" (*HAW* 365). Common sense, and with it the fundamental consensus on judgment that Kant seemed to take for granted, is culturally and environmentally determined. And consequently, there is no hierarchy of knowledge among different cultures, there is only a collection of mythologies. Europeans "know no more about the inner forces of Nature than does a tribe of Negroes" (*HAW* 363).

The task of the philosopher-aesthetician-historian-poet is thus first of all to recognize that the body of thought issuing from any one culture is nothing more than that culture's mythology, no matter what claims it might make on universal reason and truth. And then, in consequence, the task is to analyse this mythology as that culture's interpretation of the laws of nature. Finally, these endlessly diverse mythologies are themselves to be understood as diverse expressions of the same law of nature, diverse interpretations of nature's force. In this way, the developmental law of nature can be shown to reside in history, and aesthetics is the appropriate methodology for showing this. This is a far cry from Kant's position that, if we want to think of a developmental law at work in human history, there is no other way to conceive of it except as the progressive realization of freedom. But Herder takes it a step further. Not only is aesthetics the methodology proper to the study of humanity as the collective expression of nature's force, aesthetic activity itself becomes the distinguishing feature of humanity.

The natural forces that give rise to humanity, to *homo symbolicus*, continually reproduce themselves in signifying action, which itself is the result of the encounter between the drive to perception and an external object. The subject of this encounter is a creature of the species "humanity." That is to say, in Herder's theory, humanity is produced at the intersection of nature's expressive force and the form of objects, but also at the intersection of individual and collective life. Signifying action documents the process of humanity emerging out of nature's expressive force. As he puts it in 1795 in the opening sentences of the sixth collection of the *Letters on the Advancement of Humanity*, "When nature, which reveals itself alive and dwelling in all that it brings forth, ascended to the greatest heights of its efficacy, it invented the creature called human" (*HSW* 17, 343). Notice how, while making clear reference to the Old Testament story of creation, Herder is careful to remove any reference to the Old Testament God from his explanation of causality. The result is a Spinozist vision of humanity holding a mirror to nature, enabling its self-recognition. All of nature, he notes in this letter, recognizes itself in the human being, "as in a living mirror; it sees through his eye, thinks behind his brow, feels in his breast, and acts and creates with his hands." This is why Herder calls humanity the "most *aesthetic* creature on earth [das höchst-*ästhetische* Geschöpf der Erde]," and why the human being had to become "an emulating, ordering, representing – a *poetic* and a *political* being." The privileged forms in which humanity documents nature's force are aesthetic – humanity is form-giving in the realm of material objects, language, and sound (poetic), but also in the form of social and cultural collectives (political). Herder sees human nature as "the highest art of nature-at-large, which in human nature strives for its most effective force." And since nature's force works in a creative-formative manner, human nature must in essence be aesthetic. "The shaper [*Bildner*] of our thoughts, our manners, our constitution is an artist. Should not then art, which is the essence and purpose of our nature, and which concerns itself representationally with the image of the human being and all its inherent forces, be of great value to humanity?" (*HSW* 17, 343–4).

The privileged forms in which humanity realizes nature's formative force are themselves all form-giving, and they include art, technology, politics, and, most important, language. Within the grand scheme of nature's development, individuals unfold their inner powers according to nature's plan, as Leibniz had described. But it was of utmost importance for Herder to find and specify the link between this individual *Bildung* of a monadic individual and the life of the collective. The key to this link is language. It is due to language that human aesthetic activity can reproduce nature's force in representation. Language is what defines human beings within nature's plan, and (as we have seen) its bond to cognition is fundamental to human biology. For this reason, it is the accession to language that brings individuals into being as members of the collective, and as individuals. Language is a negotiation between speaking individuals that defines (and constantly redefines) what nature is, and what the collective is. It is through the form-giving acts of language that nature brings individuals into community as a collective; and conversely, in language the collective imagines nature and speaks it into being. This is why Herder's collective has to be grasped empirically, not as a notional or a priori structure. And this is why politics and aesthetics are part of the same process.

As we begin to understand what language does in Herder's conception of nature, the individual, and the collective, we see that just as humanity cannot exist without nature, nature also cannot exist without humanity. Humanity is nature in its self-reflexive, expressive actualization, revealing the principle of its inherent force. And just as it makes no sense to speak of individual organisms outside their place in nature's whole, it makes no sense to conceive of individual humans outside the collective. For this reason, as Herder worked his way through the rapidly expanding body of literature on imperialism's expanding world, he did his best to describe the form-giving work of humanity as providing real alternatives, as a way of expressing the diversity and the unity of the human race. Herder understands his investigations into the history of specific cultures as encounters with the divine force that makes the history of humanity, but this force is given substance in human activity itself. This is why he refuses to allow historical specificity to disappear behind the universality of human history – no matter how this universality might be conceived. Humanity exists in balance between thought and action, divine creation and human recreation, between a common purpose and its diverse manifestations.

Spinoza: Desire and the Politics of Interpretation

Throughout the 1780s, Herder had been in pursuit of a philosophical language capable of expressing this delicate balance. During these years, he was revisiting the philosopher he thought came closest to providing him with a model for how nature and God are manifest in human life: Spinoza. During this time, Spinoza was a name on everyone's lips. In September 1784 the well-known philosopher and writer Friedrich Heinrich Jacobi visited Weimar. A rumour was doing the rounds at the time that Lessing, who had died in 1781, had been a Spinozist, and Jacobi had written a series of letters to Lessing's friend Moses Mendelssohn to try to convince him of the errors of Lessing's ways. These developed into an anti-Spinozist treatise, and Jacobi sent the as yet unpublished manuscript *Über die Lehre des Spinoza* (On the Spinozist Doctrine) to Herder (who also gave it to Goethe to read). This work, which would be published in 1785,[15] was intended as a pronounced rejection of Spinoza's purported pantheism, which Jacobi saw as arising directly out of rationalist metaphysics. Jacobi believed that Spinoza's God was cast in a mould dictated by the needs of reason, and thus incompatible with the idea of a personal God of faith.[16] It may be possible to describe nature by reasoned argument, but ultimately nature conceals God. For human beings, the path to God is not via rational thought, but faith. Jacobi rejects the radical Cartesian doubt which leads, he believes, to a progressive hollowing-out and degradation of Being, leaving only the thinking mind intact. And he cannot accept Kant's argument that God is a regulative idea of reason.[17] But it is Spinoza whom Jacobi takes as the object of attack, since his philosophy represents for Jacobi the most consistent development of the rationalist proof of God. And what Jacobi concludes is that the rational demonstration of the existence of God leads to pantheism, and to atheism, which amounts to the same thing.[18] Spinoza's proof of the existence of God is exemplary in its attempt to measure that which cannot be measured using the deficient means of human intellect.[19]

Much of Jacobi's argument appealed to Herder, since it found real weaknesses in the rationalist discussions around the proof of God's existence. But Jacobi's belief that a proof of God's existence was out of the range of philosophy made just as little sense to Herder as the rationalist approach to God. Herder regarded God as self-affirming, and nature as the place of self-affirmation. But he took the matter further than that, regarding human cognition as equally the place of God's self-affirmation. In this view, Jacobi's attempt to draw a sharp distinction between the rational exposition of nature and the faith-based understanding of a personal God made no sense and met with a sharp rebuttal on the part of Herder, and Goethe too.[20] The philosophical authority who was asked to stand surety for their position was Spinoza. For Herder, it was absurd to speak of a nature in which God might be revealed or concealed, distinguishing it from a realm of human *Empfindung* (sensibility, feeling) in which God could be approached by a faithful humanity. God's revelation is the same thing as God's Being, and this is the same thing as nature.[21] In its dynamic principles of development and in its revelation, nature merges with the forms of humanity's interaction with nature.

Herder was highly critical of Jacobi's belief that God is accessible first and foremost through faith, not human reason, and that Spinoza's views on nature and God should be rejected on these grounds. Herder understood Spinoza's views on nature as a justification of scientific methodology and of a metaphysics that follows the same path Herder had outlined in the *Essay on Being*. Herder must have realized how far Spinoza's methodology was from his own, but this did not stop him from understanding their aim as shared. Increasingly, he was convinced that the study of humanity must immerse itself in the unity of the human sphere and resist all temptations to force the human condition into any duality that went farther than his linguistic theory of parallelism. In Herder's reading, Spinoza showed that the relationship between an individual and God cannot be adequately described using the duality of rationalism and faith.

As Herder saw it, Jacobi was "brooding over Spinoza. Mendelssohn is, as he writes, strongly encouraging him, and it seems the latter is merely using the occasion to help him [Jacobi] become an Anti-Spinoza. For me this disceptation is grist to my mill, since I am anyway coming to hate all metaphysics more with each passing day; it leaves the book of nature sealed, or even closes it itself, while painting its characters on the cover" (to Hamann, 23 April 1785; *HBG* 5, 121). When Herder speaks out so strongly against metaphysics, he is objecting to Jacobi's attempt to remove nature from the sphere in which humanity expresses its divine origins and the concomitant persistence of God's force. To turn away from God's working in nature is to condemn humanity to a homogeneous pursuit of a single God, rather than sifting through the diversity with which humanity has arranged its place in the order of things. In 1774, he had expressed it like this:

> "*God's course through the nations! Spirit of the laws, ages, ethics,* and *arts* – how they have *followed!, prepared, developed,* and *displaced!* one another." If only we had such a *mirror of the human species* in all its faithfulness, fullness, and feeling of *God's revelation*. Enough preliminary works, but everything in husk and disorder! We have crept and rummaged through our *present epoch* of almost all nations and similarly the *history* of almost all earlier times almost without ourselves knowing *why* we have rummaged through them. Historical facts and investigations, discoveries and travel descriptions, lie there – who will separate and sift them? (*HPW*, 340)[22]

The task of thought is not to mark its own failings every time it bumps up against the incomprehensibility of God, nor to deny its affiliation with nature's diversity. Thought speaks itself into being, and in doing so it gives form to nature's diversity, aligns itself with the force of God that brought forth diversity, and allows diversity to persist. Humanity confirms its place in creation not by turning its back on the world, but by speaking it into being, by inventing the world. Herder's life-long love-hate relationship with metaphysics derives from his recognition that this process can legitimately claim to be metaphysical, but that it must also be understood as integral to natural processes, as part of physics.

Herder responded to Jacobi in 1787 by publishing *Gott. Einige Gespräche* (God, Some Conversations). This was a dialogue between two fictional friends, working through what Herder saw as the important challenges posed by Spinoza in his own time. Put in the broadest terms, Spinoza presented Herder with the conceptual apparatus for imagining the development of the world as an expression of divine force, and for undertaking a scientific investigation into the place which human creativity and the attendant drive to representation occupy in this process.[23] There is a great deal of debate in the literature regarding the extent to which Herder's position is true to Spinoza and how well he understood the obscure theses of the *Tractatus* and the *Ethics*.[24] I will not attempt to untangle the complicated web of positions around Spinoza in the 1780s. In its manifestations of this decade, Herder's own Spinozism is tempered by the deist position of Shaftesbury, with its rejection of the idea of a personal God and of miracles and revelation, as well as the

Leibnizian concept of force. Herder had originally planned to give his book the title *Spinoza, Shaftesburi, Leibniz* (*HMA* 2, 735). What Spinoza promises Herder is an alternative to Jacobi's condemnation of rationalism in matters of the divine. Herder realized that he was taking not only a philosophical position, but a political one. A discourse that does justice to the workings of God in the world as Herder understood it was not only a poetics of nature, or of human history. It was also a politics of human expression. This is in part because of the way Herder derives from Spinoza's pantheism a confirmation of his own conviction that tolerance is a key to humanity's progress. But more importantly, he sees Spinoza confirming his understanding of how expressive acts reflect the world. For Herder, Spinoza was a key to understanding how aesthetics has to be grasped as political. This is, as we have seen, because aesthetics contributes to human perfection. But how does it do this?

At the same time that Herder was writing *On Image*, he was incorporating the theory of human perfectibility as the natural law residing in history into *Ideas*. Where Koepke calls the former essay Herder's aesthetic credo, he refers to book 15 of *Ideas* as the credo on the meaning of human history.[25] In this book, Herder argues that "if there is a God in nature, he is also in history" (*HMA* 3/1, 580). God in history is the principle that drives humanity towards perfection, and that aligns this drive with the natural laws of diversification and unification. Everything in history falls apart and disappears, but the natural law of history is driving humanity towards perfection. As the heading to chapter 1 of this book states, "Humanity is the purpose of human nature, and with this purpose God placed his own fate in our hands" (*HMA* 3/1, 580). This strange statement points to all that is problematic in Herder's understanding of the perfection of humanity, a process described by Koepke as "the coming-unto-itself of humankind, which is at the same time the harmonious integration into divine nature."[26] But if Herder is correct in asserting that the natural laws governing the genesis of thought out of sensory experience also reside in history, in what way is humanity not already self-fulfilled? Herder attempts to answer this by conceiving of humanity's development and perfection as a balance of the essential forces of nature – an endless striving towards the unification and diversification of all phenomena. In a certain sense, this balance is constantly enacted and re-enacted in individual cognition, since analytic reason performs the unifying work of nature, while both tolerance and (paradoxically) prejudice make up its diversifying side.[27] Similarly, humanity has to be conceived as already having attained this balance, even if historical consciousness has not yet seen it. Either humanity will never reach perfection, but always be striving for it; or else humanity is always already in a state of fulfilment.

Herder does not draw this logical conclusion from his idea of humanity, but the problem remains with him in the form of the conflicting tendencies of human desire and government. To be more precise: desire will have to be the deciding factor in balancing analytic reason with the capacity for prejudice and tolerance, and in harmonizing self-preservation with the good of the community. Government is the formalization of this balance. But how are we to tell if government is what Kant asked it to be, a strict delineation of the limits of personal freedom and therefore beneficial to the commonwealth, or if it is a harmful restriction of human growth? And if it is the latter, then how is a political response to injustice and despotism possible, when every form of government is a manifestation of human potential, of human diversity? If human beings, both individually and collectively, are agents of the fate that God has placed in our hands, does this make us gods, or does it make us impotent instruments of fate?

These questions cannot but trouble Herder's ideas on the politics of interpretation. If politics is by nature a politics of interpretation, how is the historian to overcome the radical doubt that must preside over the act of interpretation? If the historian is possessed by the desire to interpret history correctly, and if the forces propelling humanity towards its final goal are the same as those inspiring interpretation, how can he be certain that his desire – and therefore his interpretations – are correct? Is there not something inherent in human nature that positions itself contrary to the forces of history? And is this contrariness not essential to human self-consciousness?

Human Nature and the Problem of Government

Herder seemed not to be troubled by these vexing questions about desire, which were by necessity also challenges to his Spinozist philosophy of mind. His need to see humanity as nature's self-expression of its own drive to perfection caused him to gloss over some of the most problematic aspects of psychology and how it relates to politics. These were to become increasingly visible as the 1780s drew to a close, and German intellectuals watched the unfolding of political events in France. The revolutionary turn of events was forcing them to take a stance on the true nature of human desire, which started to look like an element of the dark side of nature itself. This discontent, fostered by the aftermath of the revolution, revealed itself at that moment in intellectual history when the question "What is the Human?" will not tolerate either a biological or a social answer alone, but instead expresses the inner contradictions in the growing discursive divisions of knowledge. The life of the body always bumps up against social life, and vice versa. This negativity at the heart of the human lurks in the background of any attempt to negotiate the boundary separating humanity from the rest of nature, thereby threatening to undo the vision of humanity Herder worked so hard to sustain.

Herder's response was to problematize the distinction between human nature and society. The chapter on government in the *Ideas*, which was causing him so much difficulty in the late 1780s, opens with a clear statement of this thought: "The state of nature for a human is the state of society; for it is herein that he is born and raised, it is hither that he is guided by the awaking impulse of his fair youth, and the sweetest names of humanity, father, child, brother, sister, beloved, friend, provider, are bonds of natural law which occur in the state of every primitive human society" (*HSW* 13, 375).

By this time Herder apparently takes it for granted that Goethe is his superego in matters of government. The chapters on government in the *Ideas* are, as he writes to Hamann in April 1785, costing him "terrible effort" (*entsetzliche Mühe*). In particular, he is concerned about the "caput mortuum of government, upon which depends the entire sorry story which Mr. Immanuel and the public demand of universal history" (*HBG* 5, 121). Herder had already asked Goethe to go through the chapter on government with a critical eye to its suitability for publication. He was hoping that the experienced statesman would be able to help him ascertain just how seriously he needed to take his own suspicion that what he was writing was dangerous. As Herder then related to Hamann, Goethe informed him that not a single word could remain. Goethe saw clearly that Herder's position on government would appear little less than incendiary in the context of Weimar's enlightened absolutism. The growing concerns in government circles regarding the dangers of free speech had, during the 1780s, led to increasing censorship of books and articles. In 1788, the Prussian minister J.C. Wöllner had drafted an edict sharpening censorship and aimed at minimizing the free expression of any ideas that appeared incendiary or blasphemous. Herder would have known that, in the years before the tumultuous revolution in France, his draft on revolutions, just like his chapter on government, would scarcely have been able to stand unaltered. He complained to Knebel that "having to pay deference to the governments is plaguing me in an unheard of way; I do not want to and cannot lie; hence all my twisting and turning."[28] Even after having of his own volition removed much of the more radical material on the revolution, Herder continued to worry that his book would meet with strong opposition in Weimar, and he decided to publish it outside Carl August's dominion.[29] Herder concludes his April 1785 letter to Hamann: "That's what happens when the stomach is full of foul political humours; the *repraesentatio mundi pro positu corporis nostri* [world represented according to the constitution of our bodies] is a true doctrine" (*HBG* 5, 121). What he had observed in his sketches of the Riga years begins to look like it will not cease to haunt him: the interpretation of the world involves a semiotics founded on the self-perception of the body. The world of which philosophy would speak is conjured though bodily acts of production, foremost among these being language. To produce language is to produce the world, not as an inanimate thing, but as an extension of one's own body.

Through the "terrible effort" of formulating his thoughts on government, Herder arrived at a constellation of ideas that brought together his anti-imperialism, his conviction that God works in nature, his faith in human happiness, and his belief that humanity is a creative being whose form-giving activities are essentially one with the formative forces of nature. As a result, the linguistic endeavours of humanity are played out at the forefront of nature's struggle for self-realization, and it is in these linguistic endeavours that nature's self-realization is pitted against the inhibiting, crippling, and deforming tendencies of imperialism.

When he initially set his ideas on government to paper, Herder found himself building upon the arbitrariness of nature's self-expression, and the fact that humanity is constantly negotiating the role of language in this process. As a result, the gist of his critique is aimed at the arbitrariness of individual forms of government. He begins the chapter under the heading: "The Forms of Government Are Mere Earthly Phenomena, and Neither the Climate Nor the Way of Life of a Nation Necessarily Determines Their Design in an Immutable Way" (*HSW* 13, 448). In a subsequent draft, he states that governments are "artificial machines" (*Kunstmachinen*, *HSW* 13, 452) of humanity based upon tradition. Herder recognizes and does his best to develop the radical critique of government itself that is implicit in this position: "That some abstract word such as fear, honour, or love of the fatherland should be indissolubly fixed to certain lines of latitude and longitude, or even to arbitrary forms of government which owe their existence to sheer accident or to the cruellest barbarism, I do not, to the comfort of humanity, believe – and I find the opposite manifest through all periods and in the generational succession of every nation" (*HSW* 13, 451).

Because human social arrangements lack the naturally determined, goal-oriented behaviour found, for example, in the social lives of ants and bees, it is wrong to imagine a single, natural human social order. Herder expresses astonishment that "so many worthy men could have had the idea of constructing, from the history of humanity of all continents and nations, beehives and anthills according to immutable rules of nature" (*HSW* 13, 449).

Herder is directing his critique of government against ideologies that seek to legitimate exploitative or unjust regimes on the basis of a purported natural order of domination: "But that one free human being, one mother's child would by nature's laws have a right or power above any other one: this cannot be explained any other way than by the fist of the one or by the good-hearted stupidity of the other, if we are to give an account according to original natural laws" (*HSW* 13, 449n1). In this respect at least, Herder understands his task in terms of the critique of ideology. Ideological claims to the natural determination of unjust government are "contradicted by philosophy and history," in spite of the fact that these claims "are nonetheless adorned and embellished by philosophy and history" (*HSW* 13, 450). As a philosopher and a historian, Herder saw himself obliged to enlighten his readers as to the ideological misuse of his disciplines. After all, "beneath the most frigid as well as the most torrid skies there are freer peoples than at the lauded centre of all culture and wisdom" (*HSW* 13, 451). This makes these disciplines into oppositional discourses aimed at decentring Europe's ideological claims to superiority. In this respect, European science still has "much to do, first of all with the help of geography and history, to invalidate the false universal propositions which have been rashly made about everything of this sort; only then can we hope for a true philosophy of the history of humanity, with a view also to the good or evil of its forms of government" (*HSW* 13, 451).

An adequate description of the principle of government is only possible by way of "the philosophical, living representation of bourgeois history, in which, as monotonous as it seems, the same scene is never played twice" (*HSW* 13, 387). This observation is in conflict with the fact that this descriptive process unfolds within the context of imperfect societies, which leads to such contradictory moments as when he asserts, "[That] the husband should have authority over his wife, that the father should have power over his children, is the law of nature" (*HSW* 13, 449).

Herder's mistrust of government is closely related to his critique of imperialism. Wilful acts of government, like imperialism, attempt to take control of bodies, wrenching them from nature, and misusing them in acts of despotism. This runs contrary to nature's cohesive force, with its tendencies towards both diversification and unification. False government unites through violence what nature has created as diverse. He concludes the eighth book of *Ideas* with a clear statement of this natural force of diversity, and it is easy to see here why this force is at the same time a force of anti-imperialism. Here, the state appears as an imperialist machine that seeks to control all peoples, and in doing so to work against their happiness. Against this, Herder develops the view that the state is not a universal phenomenon, nor is it the necessary pinnacle of historical development. On the contrary, every state is in itself "a machine, and no machine has reason, regardless of how reason-like it may be built to look" (*HSW* 13, 453). Against the workings of the state he posits individual happiness, which he identifies with savagery or wildness. There is a force at work in nature – Herder calls it *Vorsehung* (providence) here; elsewhere he will call it *Gott* – which privileges the happiness of individuals over the "artificial final purposes of great societies," and which tends to "deal sparingly throughout the ages with these costly state-machines." The subjects of the "artificial state" must acquire the savage knowledge that happiness is given not by the state, but must be acquired and sustained by the individual. "Millions on the planet live without States." And although the state can give us "artificial tools," it can deprive us of "something far more essential, our very selves" (*HSW* 13, 341).

This vision of individual happiness beyond the reach of the state is not intended as a praise of Rousseau's savagery,[30] though it does derive from it. In his *Briefwechsel über Ossian* (Letters on Ossian, 1773), he had observed that his "enthusiasm for wild peoples" should not be confused with Rousseau's (*HSW* 5, 168). For Herder, the fact of wildness is intended to render visible the intertwining of human society with the forces of nature. In Herder's view, Europe has been united for centuries in its single-minded pursuit of world domination, and he appeals to the peoples of the world to recognize that world history is neither intended nor destined to end this way. In dividing humanity into distinct peoples, nature created linguistic diversity as the most essential tool of humanity's self-production. Herder did not view language as an expression of the limitations of reason in the face of divine force, nor did he see it as negotiating the divide between reason and the senses, or as negotiating what could not be decided a priori (hence his opposition to Kant). For him it is the force out of which humanity creates the world, and in doing so, emerges as humanity. As he states in an essay of 1795, "It is only through common language that people become humanized."[31]

Diversity is the natural form of this humanization, and the presence of infinitely diverse forms of human life demonstrates the fact that political domination and the hegemony of universal history are profoundly opposed to nature. But it also highlights the fact that a science of form is required if nature's manifestations in human life are to be understood. He concludes the eighth book of *Ideas* with a clear statement of this natural force of diversity:

> If happiness is to be met with upon Earth, then it is in every feeling being; it must be in every one by Nature, and art too must assist with enjoyment and become nature in each. Every person has the measure of his happiness within him; he bears the form in itself to which he has been shaped [*er trägt die Form an sich, zu der er gebildet worden*], and in the pure delineation of which alone he can become happy. This is exactly the purpose for which Nature exhausted all the varieties of human form on Earth, that she might also find for each, in its time and place, an enjoyment with which to delude the mortal from one end of his life to the other. (*HMA* 3/1, 305)

The experience of happiness is a *telos* of nature, but it is an illusion for humans. Since all humans possess *Besonnenheit*, their experience of happiness is also one of lack. This recognition works against the idea of complacency which Kant had attributed to the happy, superfluous Tahitians.

This commitment to formal diversity is intended to pave the way for a critique of monolithic, homogeneous government in the following chapter. Here, at the moment in his history of humanity where he approaches the question of contemporary world government, Herder finds himself face to face with the French Revolution and its aftermath. He will discover that his responses to the revolution are intimately related to his views on European imperialism. The task of aesthetics in the wake of the French Revolution must be worked out in the same way he had been working on an anti-imperialist aesthetic.

The Politics of Interpretation and the Nature of Revolution

By the end of the 1780s, Herder had successfully brought the discussion in the *Ideas* more or less to the point where he could begin to talk about contemporary politics. The fourth and final part, which was published in 1791, was intended to explain the emergence of the contemporary political situation in Europe. It begins with an ethnography of the European peoples and ends with an outline of the political, cultural, and economic factors that define Herder's own present. The final chapter (20) draws this present along a timeline from when Europe was beginning to be restructured by the crusades and the growth of world trade, following through to the age of reason and discovery and the effects it had on Europe and the rest of the world. And all this was to be read against the backdrop of the revolution.

The fifth book of *Ideas* was never published, but Herder's drafts and notes reveal his intention to engage the topic of revolution directly, concluding then with a section on the perfection of humankind (see *HSW* 14, 648–51). By the time the fourth book of *Ideas* had appeared in October 1791, the French constitution with its preamble on the rights of man had been formally, if reluctantly, adopted by Louis XVI, and the legislative assembly had begun to meet. Together with the Holy Roman Emperor Leopold II, Friedrich II had issued the Declaration of Pilnitz, proclaiming solidarity with the French king and threatening retribution should his authority be damaged. Germany was fast being swept up in the events in France, and Herder's closest friends would be implicated. In August 1792, Goethe himself would join the Prussian troops as they marched against revolutionary France, joining in what Herder would later call "the most disastrous of wars" (*HFA* 7, 717). Together with Carl August, Goethe took part in the siege of Mainz, where Georg Forster was an active member of the revolutionary government. At this time, Herder was on medical leave in Aachen, 200 kilometres further down the Rhine, a city that had already experienced social unrest in sympathy with the revolution, and it was here that he began to conceive of the continuation of the *Ideas* in slightly different terms. Out of the breakdown of his own discourse on government was to emerge the *Letters on Humanity*. As he wrote, he heard of the September massacres in Paris, followed by the battle of Valmy, where the revolutionary army defeated an all-too-confident alliance between the Prussians, Austrians, and a significant number of émigrés hoping to defeat the forces that had driven them out of France. His letters of the time indicate an intense interest in the political situation of the day; late in 1792, he writes to the clergyman and poet Johann Ludwig Gleim: "The times will not permit us to remain silent; they force our mouths open" (12 November 1792; *HBG* 6, 292).

Herder's views on the revolution were relatively well known in Weimar. He had long been a staunch defender of the free determination of peoples, and a believer in the rights associated with a republic.[32] After *This Too a Philosophy of History*, he never lets go of the idea that government owes its people free development. By 1780, he was explicitly promoting freedom of speech (the German word is *Gedankenfreiheit*, literally *freedom of thought*) as one of the obligations governments have in encouraging the advancement of learning and the development of the sciences.[33] And he was linking this directly to the observation that the regimes of human knowledge change with the fates of governments: "Every state has its *period of becoming*, *of subsisting*, and *of decaying*, and its sciences and arts adapt accordingly."[34] This is accompanied by a deep-seated and lasting conviction that the nobility has somehow failed in this task, and if enlightened governments have been successful in the way Kant had hoped, it is more by chance than by design. As his friend Georg Müller would later observe, Herder was "terribly averse to the nobility, because it is opposed to human equality and all the principles of Christianity while also being a monument to human stupidity."[35] We can get a sense of just how much Herder sympathized with the revolution if we look at some of the verses he was writing at the time.

(Auf den 14. Juli 1790.)

Rings um den hohen Altar siehst du die Franken zu Brüdern
    Und zu Menschen sich weihn; Göttliches, heiliges Fest!
Wie spricht Jehovah zum Volk? Spricht er in Donner und Blitzen?
    Milder kommt er hinab; Wasser des Himmels entsühnt
Weihend die Menge zum neuen Geschlecht mit der Taufe der Menschheit.
    Vierzehnter Julius, dich sehn unsre Enkel einmal! (*HSW* 29, 659–60)

(Upon the 14th of July, 1790.)

All about the high altar you see the Franks anointing themselves
As brothers and human beings; divine, holy festival!
How does Jehovah speak to the people? Does he speak in thunder and lightning?
He comes more mildly; water from heaven absolves

And consecrates the crowd as a new race with the baptism of humanity.
Fourteenth of July, our grandchildren will see you one day!

And a year later, he writes:

Flieg herüber zu uns, Du zarter fränkischer Vogel,
Ueber den Thüringer Wald steure den fröhlichen Flug
Glücklich; und ruh' dann aus in Deinen Jenischen Auen,
Ehe die Blüthe noch, die Dich erwartete, sinkt. (*HSW* 29, 674)

Fly over to us, you gentle Frankish bird,
Across the Thuringian Forest turn your joyful flight
Successfully; and then relax in your meadows at Jena,
Before the blossom, which has been awaiting you, wilts.

Herder's main concern at this time seems to have been to investigate the gradual and beneficial aspect of revolution, and to differentiate it from the kind of revolution that involves massive destruction and reorganization of phenomena – such as "in the creation of the earth" or "when a room is swept out, piles of rubble." But he understood that the order of nature is not always gentle and gradual. Revolution can just as well be violent and sudden. Here he lists the origins of the solar system, the creation of earth and moon, and the original appearance of organic life on earth. When it comes to organic life, the distinction between gentle and sudden change becomes more difficult. Here he speaks of such diverse phenomena as the revolution of the planetary bodies, the recurrence of the seasons, the gentle and gradual transitions that mark the changing of the time of life, and so on. Nature "knows no rest." The waves of the sea, the swinging of a rope, the oscillations of a musical instrument's strings, the vibrations of electricity and magnetism – these are all evidence of nature's restlessness and its predilection for repetitive, recurrent change (*HSW* 14, 648–9). Restlessness, which, as we have seen, is also the natural drive to communication between cultures, has now been identified as inherent in the natural laws of change, and it has become a driving force for revolution. Herder is probably assuming that the reader still has the beginning of *Ideas* in mind, where he spells out what it means to live on a planet that has (as he puts it in the title to the third chapter in book 1) "gone through all sorts of revolutions before becoming what it is now" (*HSW* 13, 21). The trajectory of this short chapter had moved from natural revolution through the emergence of diversity and ends with a reference to constant change as a determining feature of human history. The creation of the earth as we now know it has come about through intense and violent natural revolutions: "Water overflowed and formed strata, mountains, valleys; fire raged, ruptured the crust, raised mountains, and poured out the molten viscera from deep within; air, captured within the earth, created caves and encouraged the eruption of those powerful elements; winds blustered on the surface, and a cause yet more powerful even changed the geographical zones" (*HSW* 13, 21).

The proximity of this idea to the central notion of diversity in unity is plain to see. Without these constant natural revolutions, the diversity of the world would not have come into being. Whether benevolent or violent, revolutions are the phenomena whereby "Nature has preserved the greatest diversity from an infinitely progressing simplicity" (*HSW* 13, 22). In the draft version of his *Letters*, he expressed the belief that "in the great progression of nature something new will emerge out of the old, as long as there is to be found in the old anything of use" (*HFA* 7, 777). This is the question. Revolutions have had the effect of division of environmental zones, and an accompanying specialization of the creatures that occupy them: "the manifold kinds of soil, of rocks, of crystallizations, indeed of organization into mussels, plants, animals, finally into humans – how many decompositions and revolutions of the one into the other do they presuppose!" (*HSW* 13, 23).

Herder tells this story as a kind of biological recoding of Genesis, whereby nature is differentiated to the point where humanity can emerge as the crown of creation: "Many plants had to have emerged and died before an animal organization could arise; and when it did, insects, birds, aquatic and nocturnal animals preceded the more complex terrestrial and diurnal animals, until finally after all of them, the crown of organization on our earth, the human, made his entrance: microcosm. He, the son of all elements and beings, their purest essence and at once the blossom of earthen creation, could not help but be the last child of Nature's womb, whose formation and reception had to be prepared by numerous developments and revolutions" (*HSW* 13, 23).

Out of nature's chaos emerges the diversity of humanity; but in humanity nature's force expresses the singularity of its purpose. If humanity is the expression of nature's diversity in unity, revolution is one of nature's tools for holding diversity and unity in balance, thereby fostering the *Bildung* of humanity. The task of the historian is to describe this natural phenomenon in human development, and to distinguish it from the artificial, forced changes that become entrenched in political systems whenever government is founded on a priori principles. But on what basis is this distinction to be made? Once again, a scientific approach to phenomena involves interpretation, the correct understanding of signs.

This seems to be Herder's main concern when, in the outline for book 5 of *Ideas*, he comes to sketch out the parameters for the discussion of political revolutions. His main question is twofold: what exactly are political revolutions, and when they occur, what remains? Herder casts the scope of this question very broadly, implying that political revolutions cannot simply be discussed in the register of social and political analysis; they are also environmental events: "what changes? remains unchanged?: land? soil? air? sky? – for the better, for the worse?" And, as environmental events, they are also economic events: "fields? meadows? forests? mines? salt springs? trees? products? method of preparation? application?" Finally, as economic events, they are political and global events: "people? hands? families? skilled trades? classes? dealings with foreigners? sales to them? goods received from them? colonies; commodities; commerce: slaves!!!" This simple list illustrates clearly the entanglement of natural phenomena with economic and political form, and of bodies with imperialism. But again, Herder places these in the context of the natural ubiquity of the revolutionary process and its necessity in the creation of humanity: "Perpetually … Revolutions – from day to day, from year to year, from country to country, from continent to continent; in people, families, factories, crafts, cities, communities, countries, arts; but always unnoticed, quietly, but all the more powerfully, without it no world, no human race." In conclusion, he notes that "the state must not be afraid [of revolutions], but instead take control of them, see them as the motus peristalticus of its nature, build on them in all of its operations, presuppose them, encourage them whenever they stagnate" (*HSW* 13, 649).[36]

The plan was to have this fifth volume of *Ideas* in the bookstores by the winter of 1791–2. Instead, Herder found himself writing this continuation of *Ideas* in the form of the *Letters on Humanity*. By the spring of 1792, Herder is speaking of his *Letters on Humanity* as his latest project, and some time towards the end of the year, he sends Knebel an initial draft containing letters commenting on the latest political developments in France and Germany. In April 1792, Caroline mentioned that her husband was working on a volume with the title *Breife, die Fortschritte der Humanität betreffend* (literally, Letters concerning the Advances of Humanity). In the following months, while closely following the development of the revolution, he completed an initial collection of letters under this title. The manuscript, which was never published, testifies to Herder's sympathy with the revolution and the radical changes he saw accompanying it. The radicalism of the first version is not as apparent in the final published version, the first volume of which appeared in 1793 as *Briefe zu Beförderung der Humanität* (literally, Letters Intended to Advance Humanity). The changed title is telling, since it makes a subtle move from a commentary on humanity's advancement to an aesthetic intervention in support of this advancement. Herder had set himself the task not only of commenting on how, in troubled times, humanity might triumph, but demonstrating how art and philosophy, if they are to remain true to their calling, will join the struggle for humanity. They do this by realizing their potential as a politics of interpretation. Herder's achievement in this book is unique among his contemporaries, in that it does not take sides for or against the revolution, nor does it remain agnostic. Instead, it takes the reader on a journey through the social, cultural, and political issues related to the revolution, showing how, in the act of reading, a call to interpretation is being answered.[37] And in this call lies the calling of the human condition.

As if to prepare the reader for this calling, Herder had an emblem of humanity specially drawn for the *Letters* by Heinrich Meyer, Director of the *Free Institute for Drawing* in Weimar (see figure 6.1). It shows the muse of humanity resting on the zodiac, behind her the sun, and at her feet the earth. In her hand she holds a scroll, an indication that all documents promoting humanity's unified development are safe in the hands of the spirit that guides this development. But they need to be untied and unrolled in acts of interpretation.[38]

It was essential to Herder to place the concept of humanity in this perspective. The message of humanity had to be one of lasting values mediated in print, and inviting interpretation. And the perspective from which this composite emblem of humanity, world, text, and interpretation could be contemplated had itself to be conceived in cosmic terms. And yet, the book was intended to be firmly grounded in the geopolitical circumstances of Herder's times. This reflected Herder's conviction that humanity's development was a matter to be investigated and promoted in historical and geographical research. But more than that, it represented one of the core tenets of his philosophy, according to which, as he wrote in the seventy-third letter, "all natural forces we know of prove themselves in organs. The more noble the force, the

6.1 Frontispiece to *Briefe zu Beförderung der Humanität*, Collection 1, ed. J.G. Herder (Riga: Hartknoch, 1793).

more sophisticated the organ of its realization. As far as I am concerned there are no bodiless spirits" (*HSW* 17, 376). The bodily expression of natural forces provides the link between the idea of humanity and the interpretation of current political events. The first letter begins with the words "It is with joy and concurrence, my friend, that your suggestion for a correspondence on the progress and regress of humanity in ancient and recent times – but mainly in the most recent times – has been welcomed and adopted by all our friends" (*HSW* 17, 5). What this meant for Herder was that the promotion of humanity could not bypass a history of the present, and a history of the present was the story of revolution.

At the same time, his thoughts on the revolution were far from coherent. In the draft chapters he repeatedly weighs up the ambivalent tendencies which the revolution is bringing to the fore: "Europe's states are built upon a system of religious and bellicose conquest. The pillars of this system are still standing, but time is gnawing at them. When they fall, I fear that many states will perish beneath the rubble of their ancient barbarism" (*HFA* 7, 775). The demise of Europe's imperialist states is inherent in their political systems, and in this sense it is natural. But the expression of this demise troubles Herder: "The people [*Volk*], my friends, are to be regarded more with pity and melancholy than with pride and hope. For many long centuries they have remained uneducated, deceived, oppressed, and neglected. They are sleeping the sleep of death, or if they were to wake in a fever, who would not have to be terrified of their feverish fury. I know nothing more hideous than an agitated, crazy people, and the rule of a crazy people. Are we not familiar with the sad examples from ancient times? And how little benefit arose from this for the lasting, continuous good of humanity!" (*HFA* 7, 773–4).

In the initial draft of the *Letters* in 1792, Herder begins the dialogue on the French Revolution in the sixteenth letter, which raises the kinds of criticism the revolution was currently attracting. This letter asks if the political events in France might give rise to hopes that humanity is on the right path to perfection, and ironically goes on to call these events "this horrible, and in its consequences so ghastly, at the very least still very dubious, *French malady*" (*HSW* 18, 313). From this point of view, France is in a state of chaos; it remains unclear just what the nation has achieved, and what lesson the entire process carries for Germany. He then goes on to evaluate the revolution in terms of its fundamental aims and principles. But not before he mocks the German princes for having sought to emulate France. We have to think back to his position on French cultural imperialism to appreciate his *Schadenfreude* when he observes that "since the time of Louis XIV, regents in Germany – almost down to the most insignificant – took pains to be *sovereigns like Louis XIV, and to design their courts in the French manner*" (*HSW* 18, 316). But the real point of Herder's engagement with the revolution is to do justice to what he recognizes as the most important events in recent history. Indeed, he claims that "since the introduction of Christianity and the civilization of the barbarians in Europe, to my knowledge, nothing has happened, save for the scientific renaissance and the reformation, which could equal this event in terms of its memorability and consequences" (*HSW* 18, 314). France has only brought Germany the misfortunes of the imitator, and the linguistic and cultural chasm that separates the two nations is so great that "never, even up until the last great National Assembly of the world on the Day of Judgement, will Germany want to become another France" (*HSW* 18, 317). But it is precisely this chasm that enables the German intellectual "to keep our healthy German intellect intact, to see everything with a critical eye, to make reasonable use of the good, and to justly and appropriately condemn what is condemnable" (*HSW* 18, 316). It is the privileged position of German intellectuals to be sufficiently marginalized by the revolution that they can work towards a genuinely critical position.

When, in the 1792 draft of the eighteenth letter, Herder comes to list the unresolved issues of the revolution, his concerns are simple and to the point: What is the best constitution the French can hope for? Will it be possible to set up a unitary government in a country so large and complex as France? Will France be willing to negotiate its future position in Europe with other European nations? If there is resistance from the rest of Europe, what will France do? What economic system will emerge from the revolution, and will it leave France stronger or weaker as a trading nation? What will French cultural politics look like, and what effects will be felt on both French and German literature? By formulating these questions, Herder is attempting to deflect what he sees as a kind of tabloid fascination with breaking news, the tendency among many of his compatriots to take part in the revolution "only as one might take part in a newspaper rumour" (*HSW* 18, 316). For to do so is to miss the point that these are events of world-political significance, and that the fate of France will also affect the fate of humanity: "We, my friends, are inclined to continue, as we have until now, to abstain from all newspaper gossip about individual events, from whatever country they may come to us, and to pay attention all the more impartially to the principles and consequences of things" (*HSW* 18, 320).

Herder is taking a long view of history, and in doing so he is trying to remove all traces of sensationalism from political reactions to the revolution. It is starting to become clear that the revolutionary events in France can be denounced as a violent overthrow of a defective but still largely functional and legitimate order, or they can be accepted as the natural consequence of this order, and thus as a natural development in the history of the world. The Hobbesian position, which was anathema to Herder's view of society, saw the revolution as a failure of the social order. This position was probably voiced most radically by Schiller when he wrote to Prince Friedrich Christian von Augustenburg on 13 July 1793: "In the lower classes we see nothing but raw, lawless instincts, which, once they have freed themselves from bondage, throw off the chains of civil order and rush with uncontrollable fury toward their animal satisfaction. It was not moral resistance from within, but control from without that has until now prevented such outbursts. These were not free people suppressed by the state; no, they were just wild animals which the state had placed in beneficial chains."[39] In the same letter, Schiller goes on to speak of the "wild despotism of the instincts." This is precisely the problem facing intellectuals in light of the violent developments during the revolution: how to evaluate nature's drives. Are we speaking of the *Bildungstrieb*? Or of something darker, more sinister?

Herder could see neither nature nor society with these Hobbesean eyes. But he was also far from certain of just how he should feel about the events in France. His entire philosophy of history points to the revolution as a cataclysmic natural event that requires political, economic, and cultural interpretation. But at the same time, as he writes in another draft of the *Letters on Humanity*: "My motto therefore remains progressive, natural, reasonable evolution of things; not a revolution" (*HSW* 18, 332). Revolution seems to point in both directions. It demonstrates the shortcomings in the reason of state that legitimated the monarchy, and it demonstrates the failures of the political theories that overthrew the monarchy. It shows how the passions can drive political process, acting as a force of nature, but it shows how reason can pervert the passions in political design. Here the passion of revolution can indeed effect sudden change in the social order, and in doing so it can align itself with human will and the divine. But the passions can also fail as an expression of community if they are not expressed in appropriate political systems. In revolution, Herder saw the opposite of political reason. As reasoned collective action, politics can be seen as the expression of nature's force acting for the benefit of humanity, or it can equally be a stubborn refusal to enact this force. But if it is the latter, is it not also an expression of nature's force?

How is Herder going to solve this problem in political reason? One thing was certain in his mind: Social change follows natural principles and it cannot be forced by abstract human design, a priori systems, avarice, or any other of the various motivations he thought he saw driving so much of contemporary politics.[40] Herder expresses this idea with respect to the revolution by repeatedly invoking the Spirit of the Times, and in the sixteenth letter he writes: "*Time* is a thought-image of successive conditions interlinked with one another; it is a measure of things according to the succession of our thoughts; things themselves are its measured contents. *Spirit of the Times* [*Geist der Zeiten*], therefore, would be the sum of the thoughts, attitudes, strivings, drives, and living forces expressing themselves with given causes and effects in a definite course of events" (*HSW* 17, 80).[41] This notion of spirit at work in time is related to his understanding of force, of *Bildung*. Herder's fundamental conviction that all life is an expression of nature's ability to grow into its appropriate form implies that any attempt to steer this process by the powers of a priori thought leads to disastrous effects.

Revolution presented Herder with the fundamental problem of his entire philosophy – how to understand reason as both deriving from nature, as a component of the Spirit of the Times, while at the same time needing to make room for acts of reason that set themselves apart from natural processes. This is where he turns to aesthetics. Aesthetic activity engages reason in what could be called the self-interpretation of nature. But not in a fatalistic or automatic manner. Interpretation is nature's revelation, but it is also humanity's freedom of thought. And, as we have seen, it is always a politics of interpretation. This is in effect the same aesthetic principle Herder used to try to resolve the problem of political reason. The liberal faith in *Bildung* came naturally to Herder, but in the formulation of his political ideas, this position was less accessible. He certainly did not hold faith in the principle of aesthetic sublimation. Increasingly, he had nothing but scorn for those who saw the aesthetic as a higher realm into which they could withdraw from the messiness of everyday life. If the contradictions in contemporary politics were to be engaged, this would have to happen directly and it would involve the politics of representation and interpretation. This was to take place first and foremost on the level of historical and geographical discourse.

And where these discourses ended, poetic discourse could continue, as set out in the *Letters*.

Imperialism and the Problem of Moral Judgment

In its founding impulse and in its deep structure, the *Letters* never strayed far from the topic of the French Revolution, even if it is often absent from the surface of the text. This is why Herder didn't want to write what Schubart called "a crippled history of the present,"[42] where everything seems to stand in the way of natural development. In the book's wider trajectory, Herder was following the same path he had taken in the *Ideas*, and was exploring the manifestations of humanity, and the obligations the ideal of humanity places on European politics, culture, and philosophy. And, just like in the *Ideas*, the more he develops this trajectory, the more the ideal of humanity becomes bonded to an anti-imperialist aesthetics. But unlike in the *Ideas*, Herder speaks not with a single authorial voice, but with a polyphony of compound positions, fitting to the compound image of humanity's appearance. In the first version, he had presented the letters as a dialogue, a correspondence, with shifting narrative and ideological positions, and as Wolf Köpke has argued, he retains this polyvocal ensemble in all subsequent versions.[43] The intention is to show that humanity will prevail – not through a linear development, but through a diversity of self-expression, and that the reader will enact this diversity in the negotiation of the book's polyphony.

Before addressing the problem of imperialism directly, Herder takes the reader once again through some of his favourite themes. He condemns wars of conquest and defends the rights of any one culture to its own self-realization, unimpeded by another culture's language and mores (10th letter); he reiterates the need to understand humanity historically as a collection of individual spirits (15th letter); he defends his image of society as open and universal, uniting all enlightened peoples in all parts of the world, and he sees print media as the guarantor of this vision (26th letter); he repeats his understanding of nature as attaining fulfilment and self-knowledge in human life, and rendered visible by humanity in art (63rd letter); and he repeatedly confirms the idea of humanity as diversity in unity. And, when he returns to the injustices committed by Europeans in the expanding world economy, he finds himself once again on the same ground he had covered in the *Ideas*.

It takes Herder a long time to get to the section on European imperialism in his book. Not until the tenth and final collection, published in 1797, does he embark on a sustained and impassioned critique of all that has gone wrong in Europe's attempts to spread out into the world and take control of it. But when he does, he arrives at the topic with such sudden determination, with such passion, that the reader immediately realizes Herder has been holding this voice at bay, waiting for its moment of realization. In fact, as the book nears its close, one suspects that the topic of Europe's imperialist and expansionist interference with the rest of the world has been just as important as the French Revolution in setting the direction of the *Letters*. For if the French Revolution is the crisis that gave rise to the *Letters*, and if, as a crisis, it can remain largely unexamined in the final version, the crisis of European imperialism has driven Herder's active critical project so far.

The suppression of the theme of imperialism through most of the book has much to do with Herder's silence on the revolution. It is true, the strict censorship laws of the day made it difficult for writers to directly address the events in France, especially if this involved a positive appraisal. But the problem runs deeper, and it has to do with the fact that, in the hands of the French, revolution is starting to look more and more like the unjust and exploitative expansion of European control into the far parts of the world. It is telling that when Herder introduces the revolution in the initial unpublished version of the *Letters*, he does so by associating the injustices of absolutism with those of imperialism. In the fourteenth of these *Letters*, he addresses the concern that "the barbaric system of wars and conquest is the only, irrevocable basis of all the states of Europe" (*HFA* 7, 777). Reading this in the context of the events of 1792, it is remarkable how Herder blurs the focus of this barbarism to the point where it is not entirely clear what he is referring to. Is it France's besieged nobility? "Europe will find it outrageous to bleed to death for a few families who consider the business of government to be a genealogically owned leasehold" (*HFA* 7, 777). Or is it (as he contemplates in the published version of the twenty-second letter) Europe's destabilization of the rest of the world through its military power? here he considers the proposition that "the barbaric system of wars and conquests" might form "the unshakeable foundation of Europe." This begs the question: "Has it not been troubling itself and the world for long enough? Is not every continent dripping with the blood of those whom it slaughtered? with the sweat of those whom it tormented as slaves?" If there is not hope that this can be changed, the logical conclusion is that "for the good of humanity, Europe should perish." But Herder hopes that Europe can become something other than what it is, and that "Europe will make good the evil that it has perpetrated in the frenzy of passion, beneath the veils of superstition and barbarism, under the yolk of prejudice and despotism; and all humanity will rejoice for its clearer reason, its more balanced justness, its more accurate methods of consideration" (*HFA* 7, 116).

Herder poses these questions in order to demonstrate that nature cannot tolerate a political system dependant on such acts. The challenge he faces is how to define a position distinct from the various political systems that seem to be repeating the errors of European expansionism – including not only the revolution itself, but also the Prussian-Austrian coalition against it. He concludes the draft version of the fourteenth letter asserting his conviction that "the mad, raging system of conquest is not, or at least should not be permitted to be the basic constitution of Europe, nor will it be forever" (*HFA* 7, 778). But in this very formulation, his political theory reveals its weakness. Imperial conquest should not be permitted, which implies an a priori legislative position for intervening in the course of history. And linked to this is the implication that European reason – which he himself tied to injustice and imperialism – will somehow emerge as the guiding light for humanity. Herder seems to be espousing faith in a system that will reform itself of its own accord, and a use of reason that can remove itself from its political misuses. It seems that, if he is to believe that injustice will not always be present, he needs to imagine reason decoupled from power politics in a manner that remains at best confusing. I believe that Herder's problems with his drafts of the letters on revolution and imperialism arise not only through self censorship, but also through the contradictions in the understanding of reason that emerge as he tries to condemn imperialism while at the same time promoting an alternative vision of reason.

In the final published *Letters*, Herder may find it possible to remain silent on the revolution, but not on imperialism. It returns, like the repressed problem of history, to occupy the final discussion of the book. If absolutism, imperialism, and the *French* revolution (as opposed to revolution in general) all appear to perpetuate Europe's barbaric madness, what then is their purpose? This is the question that opens the discussion of imperialism and conquest in the final published version of 1797. He begins the 114th letter by rejecting the hypothesis that when a nation interferes with another, it does so for the sake of the "progressive growth of culture" (*HFA* 7, 671). He immediately responds that "the book of history" tells a very different story, and proceeds to name the conquering and invading nations that have failed to support the improvement of humanity: the Chaldaeans, Attila, "the *Phoenicians*, the *Carthaginians* with their much-praised colonies, even the *Greeks* with their plantations, the *Romans* with their conquests, did they serve this purpose?" Christianity, too, "as soon as it affects other peoples through the machinery of the state, oppresses them terribly; in some cases it has mutilated their character to the extent that a millennium and a half have not been able to restore it." Finally, he asks what is to be said of "the culture that the *Spanish*, *Portuguese*, English and *Dutch* brought to the East and West Indies, to the Negroes of Africa, to the peaceful Islands of the South Seas? Do not all these lands cry out – some more, some less – for revenge?" (*HFA* 7, 671–2).

The sudden and intense indictment of European interference with the New World comes in a context that has become familiar to Herder's readers. In the course of the ninth collection of letters, Herder has prepared this discussion by returning to the question of French cultural imperialism and the negative effects it has on German cultural self-realization. He speaks of "*French propaganda in Germany*" (end of 112th letter; *HFA* 7, 652), of the "blind veneration" for French culture and language in some sectors of German society, the "Gallicomania of the Germans, this most ridiculous of follies that a serious people can discern among itself" (113th letter; *HFA* 7, 655). This is a multidimensional problem. Part of it is Herder's old conviction that Germany is acting in bad faith and against nature when it imitates the French. But a new dimension has been added; as the revolution has so clearly demonstrated, the French courtly manners so readily adopted by the German nobility (and which the upwardly-mobile middle classes have been eyeing with mixed awe and disgust) are themselves but a passing fashion. They have become outdated in France. "Let's wait and see," Herder chides, "if the Germans will hold onto these, or if they perhaps even decide to become republicans *because it is fashionable*. German-French Republicans, female and male! [*Deutsch-Französische Republikanerinnen und Republikaner!*]" (*HFA* 7, 653).

The lesson to be learned from the failure of French cultural imperialism is not one of isolationism, but of common self-determination and mutual aid. It is in this context that Herder hopes for a new identity in the German-speaking world. In the shadow of a failing French cultural imperialism, Germany might find its voice – not as an emergent power to follow in the footsteps of Europe's long history of exploitation, but as a promoter of humanity's true calling. Herder sees the "humble Germans" as a nation that "does not wish to instruct the entire universe, but to learn from every nation from whom we can learn" (*HFA* 7, 655). For Herder (and this was to become a basic ideological tenet of German colonialism a century later), the Germans remain everywhere in the service of Europe's conquering nations, as scientists, philosophers, even as mercenaries:

> Und doch sind sie in ihrer Herren Dienst
> So *hündisch-treu*! Sie lassen willig sich
> Zum Mississippi und Ohiostrom,
> Nach Candia und nach dem *Mohrenfels*
> Verkaufen. (*HFA* 7, 660)

> And yet in their masters' service they are
> As *devoted as dogs*! Willingly sold,
> To the Mississippi and Ohio Rivers,
> To Crete and to the *Rock of the Moors*[44]
> They go.

It follows that, when Herder turns to the crimes against humanity perpetrated by Europeans in their expansionist ambitions, he is asking his German readers to bear in mind at all times that there is a humanitarian opportunity for them, as a critical voice, but also as a voice in pursuit of a practical program for furthering the cause of humanity, and that this opportunity must be thought of in the context of what increasingly appears to be a failed revolution in neighbouring France – failed at least in Herder's humanist sense.

The main point in Herder's critique of Europe's crimes against humanity is that, where Europeans have forced their way into other parts of the world, they have hindered the natural progress of humanity by destroying indigenous cultures. This is an infraction of the natural law of diversity in unity. Wherever European power expands, it has sinned against "undefended and unsuspecting humanity" by way of "unjust wars, greed, deception, oppression, through illness and harmful gifts … Our continent ought not to be called the wise, but the *presumptuous, intrusive, manipulative* part of the earth; it has not cultivated, but destroyed the germs of other peoples' cultures, wherever and however it was able." A forced imposition of culture goes against the rule of nature, in that it "oppresses and deforms, or it casts into the abyss" (*HFA* 7, 672–3).

This forceful imposition of culture is compounded by the ideology of expansionism, which claims that providence has "granted us the power, the cunning and the tools to become the thieves, intruders, agitators, and destroyers of all the world," and so we are only fulfilling providence. This may be true, he counters, but if we are tools in the hands of providence, it is only to ensure that "the poisons we have stolen cause us to die a disgusting, slow death, impoverished amidst the greatest wealth by our restless, infernal activity, tormented by desires, enervated by luxurious sloth" (*HFA* 7, 673). Providence will, he hopes, deal so harshly with our infractions because they upset what for Herder is one of the most important principles of life – the working of divine force in the order of nature. And this order is, as we have seen, founded on the idea of natural diversity. Once again, diversity becomes the guiding idea in the critique of the injustices Europeans have committed in other parts of the world. It is important to realize that Herder is speaking as a scientist proposing a new model for understanding history, geography, and anthropology; and in doing so he hopes to develop guiding principles for international law and human rights. The prerequisite for all of this is philosophical – it has to do with the correct conception of nature and the world. As he had gone to pains to demonstrate in *Ideas*, the basis for this scientific model is "to regard the earth as a sphere, upon which, given all the environments and products of these environments [*mit allen Klimaten und Erzeugnissen der Klimate*], there must be many different kinds of peoples in all circumstances" (*HFA* 7, 689).

Human diversity is a testament to the diverse forms of expression of nature's force. We saw why Herder insists on a model of diversity based on different forms of expression of nature's force according to the different environments in which humanity has developed. And this is established in express opposition to any claims that human diversity is evidence of human inequality. When it comes to evaluating the different circumstances in which the diverse peoples of the earth live, it is necessary to recognize that diversity is not proof of inequality – not inequality of cognition, nor of achievement, of happiness, of social systems, of life fulfilment, and so on. Cultural diversity is not proof of different levels of human development in different parts of the world; it testifies to the richness of environmental diversity. In the *Letters*, he reiterates that idea, but he does so in order to make a number of points concerning the ideological function of scientific inquiry. Herder is interested not in the absolute truth of humanity; his studies have led him to the point where he understands science as model-formation. "The archetype, the prototype of humanity is not to be found in one nation and one part of the world. It is the derived concept [*der abgezogne Begriff*] of all specimens of human nature in both hemispheres" (*HFA* 7, 699). This extremely important statement is often overlooked in Herder, and it provides an important clue to understanding how universality functions in his theory of humanity. Humanity can lay claim to universality only to the extent that it is a derived concept of that which humanity in all its diverse manifestations has in common. This is why "faithful travelogues provide a much more reliable means to acknowledge what is human in humans than systems" (*HFA* 7, 701). And as such, he requires those concepts that can be responsibly derived from the empirical evidence at hand, and that at the same time promote the larger goal – the self-realization of humanity. And the point is: the act of responsible derivation (read, scientific accuracy of model formation) is itself the guarantee that the larger goal is being served. This goal cannot be specified, beyond describing the process from which it is derived.

The name Herder gives this process and the appropriate scientific discourse is, as we have seen, a natural history of humanity. In the tenth collection of letters, he gives voice to a number of European writers, philosophers, and travellers he sees representing this discourse, writers such as Bartolomé de las Casas, François de Salignac de la Mothe-Fénelon, Charles-Irénée Castel, the Abbé de Saint-Pierre, Jacques-Henri Bernardin de Saint-Pierre, William Penn, Reinhold Forster, Montesquieu, Giambattisto Vico, and others. These are the European voices that have spoken out against injustice, whose "basic principles do not aim at contempt but the appreciation and the happiness of all nations of humanity" (*HFA* 7, 689). For Herder, history works on two levels – it uncovers the tradition of a European critical discourse aimed against injustice and exploitation, but more than that, it proposes a model that displaces questions of truth onto questions of hermeneutics – the scientist inquires not about the single, unchanging, true nature of humanity, but about the changing ways in which different societies have expressed nature's force in different world environments.

This hermeneutic quest for nature's force and nature's diversity can be developed in a number of directions, and Herder outlines these in the final collection of the *Letters*. One of these is a poetics of human diversity. Why a *poetics* of human diversity? The reason has to do with the transmission of historical events. In the 117th letter, Herder investigates the uses and abuses of history in the ideology of conquest. The justification for "most wars and conquests in all parts of the world" lies presently with "the crusades and campaigns against heretics, the activities of Europeans against shamans and Jews, and their conduct in both Indies" (*HFA* 7, 707). The transmission of this justification has to do not only with historiography, but with popular culture; in the eulogies to the conquerors, the line between poetics and historiography begins to blur. And just as the discourses that once praised the St Bartholomew's Day massacres and the pogroms against the Jews have been discredited, so should the "thieves and murderers of other peoples" be discredited in a "pure *history of humanity*" (*HFA* 7, 707).

Herder has already provided some sample sketches of this poetics of diversity in the 114th letter. Drawing on anecdotes showing the brutality of Europeans in the New World, and how European injustice has met with noble behaviour on the part of peoples from indigenous cultures, he composes a number of free-verse poems he calls "Negro Idylls." These poems – neither idylls nor anti-idylls[45] – are intended, as Samuel Knoll observes, to prepare the way for Herder's justification of self-defence of the less powerful in the face of inhumanity on the part of the powerful.[46]

In these, he retells a number of episodes taken from St John de Crèvecoeur's *Letters of an American Farmer* (1782), a strong indictment of slavery, dedicated to Raynal.[47] The first of these, "Fruit on the Tree," has an anonymous witness describe how he finds a black man in a cage hanging from a tree.

Ich sah den Menschenwidrigsten
Anblick. Ein Neger, halb zerfleischt,
Zerbissen; schon Ein Auge war
Ihm ausgehackt. Ein Wespenschwarm
An offnen Wunden sog aus ihm
Den letzten Saft. Ich schauderte. (*HFA* 7, 674–5)

I saw the most inhuman sight
A negro, half mutilated,
And mauled; one eye
Had been hacked from the socket. A swarm of wasps
Drew from open wounds
His last juices. I shuddered.

In conversation, it transpires that the victim had dared protest when one of the settlers tried to seduce his bride, and this is his punishment.

In another verse, a white slave-owner condemns one of his slaves to death in a moment of rage. When another slave, an African prince, protests, the "white devil" announces that the prince is to carry out the execution. Rather than perform this deed, he cuts off the hand "which is to carry out the executioner's task" and hands it to the slave owner, then proceeds to die of his wounds. In "The Brothers" a white slave-owner and a black slave have grown up together, "nourished by the same breast." When, as an adult, Quassi the slave realizes that he is subject to the cruel whims of his brother/owner, he reminds the white man of their common childhood – but to no avail. When this leads them to fight, Quassi ends up stabbing himself rather than kill the other. And the longest of the idylls, "Zimeo," tells of a man who has joined one of the free republics founded by escaped slaves in Jamaica in the first half of the eighteenth century.[48] Zimeo has joined a group of insurgents, not to have revenge, but to remind them of their obligation to respect the humanity even of those who have done them injustice:

Denn meiner Brüder Qual
Rief vom Gebürge mein Geschlecht herab
An Tigern sie zu rächen. Aber ich
Begleitet' sie, sie einzuhalten; wo
Ich irgend Milde fand, verschont' ich. Ich
Verschmähte, selbst mit schuldger Weißen Blut
Mich zu beflecken. (*HFA* 7, 680)

For the sufferings of my brothers
Called my tribe from the mountains
To avenge them with tigers. But I
Joined them, to restrain them; wherever
I found any clemency I spared them. I
Disdained the shedding even of the blood of
Guilty whites.

These poems are all designed to speak to our deepest sense of outrage at the conduct of European settlers and soldiers in the New World and to awaken our admiration for the victims; and they draw on a whole array of melodramatic devices to have the desired effect. The most crass violations of human rights need to be displayed to the reader, since they point to a future where human rights will be actualized. In the fifteenth book of *Ideas* he had stated: "There can be no doubt that what has not yet come to pass on earth shall in the future come to pass: for the rights of humanity do not lapse and the powers God has invested in humanity cannot be effaced" (*HMA* 3/1, 584). In this sense, the "Negro Idylls" seek to establish an alternative discourse of human rights to augment the anecdotal narratives on which they are based. For, as Herder explains in the 117th letter, a discourse of human rights cannot depend on the same authority that perpetuated the crimes they are to remedy. The brutality of past times means that historical precedent cannot draw on a regime of morality outside of history in order to determine what is and is not a legitimate use of force. The historiographer has to establish an alternative *narrative* authority. The "written histories of the wars and conquests of peoples" cannot legitimately be used to derive the "principles according to which they acted and wrote." Wherever it is tied to a legitimation of power, history will present a false moral code to posterity. "Violence and power may be able to hold sway over that which they command, but not over *the principles of what is just and unjust in the history of humanity*" (*HFA* 7, 708). If we are to establish a code of human rights outside the power structures of a specific time and place, we need to draw on all the devices and discourses at our disposal, one of which is the shared poetic sensibility of the day. Poetry points to what is universal in human experience, and in this case the idyll is the genre of youthful idealism and hope for a better future.[49]

But it would be wrong to derive from this nothing more than a sentimental appeal to a vague sense of common humanity. Herder understands that this is the surface effect of his statement (in fact, of many of his statements). But primarily, it is intended as a scientific finding on human nature, formulated in the most appropriate register. What is missing from the discourses of his day is the ability to effectively evaluate uneven power relations based on the principles driving the interactions of cultures and peoples. This inability is a symptom of a disturbed relationship to rationality. As Herder laments at the beginning of the 117th letter, not even historiography is immune. In fact, the idea of common human principles can even be (and has been) used to avoid any condemnation of imperialist Europe's relationship to "Negros and Savages" (*HFA* 7, 706). If a common principle guides human action, then surely all cultures should be judged by the same measures. This, Herder points out, reveals a lack of historical awareness. He lists the "wars and conquests of all parts of the world" as examples of imperialist inhumanity which was once eulogized but is now condemned. This historical consciousness brings with it an awareness of the way the present is misread by historians and poets alike: "Who, Spaniards and

Portuguese excepted, would dare to compose an epic poem praising as heroic the deeds of *Cortez, Pizzaro*, or the great *Albuquerque* at *Suez, Hormuz, Calcutta, Goa, Malacca*? Who would dare praise today the principles that were valid *then*? The eulogists of the St Bartholomew's Day massacre or of the murder of the Jews have been heaped with disgrace. It is to be hoped that the plunderers and murderers of other nations, in spite of their proven heroism, will, in the future, also be disgraced, purely and simply on the basis of an unadulterated *history of humanity*" (*HFA* 7, 707). He then makes the decisive point that will later found the critique of ideology, warning against judging "all the documented histories of the nations, their wars and conquests, their negotiations, their plans for trade, according to the same principles of action and documentation" (*HFA* 7, 708). At the heart of historiography lies this problem, that historical documents perform the truth and the moral values that authorized them in the first place. Against this play of power and knowledge in representation, the historiographer must pursue the principle of human rights. Or as Herder puts it: "Violence and despotism can command the things they have power over, but not the *principles of rights and their infringements* [*Grundsätze des Rechts und Unrechts*] *in the history of humanity*" (*HFA* 7, 708).

To prove his point, Herder switches discourses and concludes this letter with six anecdotes in unrhymed, free verse. These are intended as fables to demonstrate correct action in situations where basic legal principles are at stake: In the case of wars fought in the name of religion, a political leader should not commit his people to war when his own personal property is at risk, but only when their shared property is affected ("The Prince of the Huns"). When evoking God to direct the course of war, a sovereign should not pray for victory, but justice ("The Prayer of War"). When meting out justice, a king should ensure blindness towards the perpetrator, thus guaranteeing the equality of all before the law ("The Law of War"). If a party is acting as a mediator between warring nations, he should be protected, regardless of the outcome of mediation ("The Deceived Mediator"). "The Prince of the Huns" describes how, faced with the threat of war, the prince decides to give up his horse and his favourite concubine to avoid plunging his people into conflict with the Tartars; but he decides to fight rather than yield his land.

"Nein!" Sprach der Fürst, "so lang' es *mich* nur galt,
Mein *Pferd*, die *Sklavin*, gerne gab ichs hin
Des Volkes Blut zu schonen; doch mein *Land*,

Des Staates Eingentum muß ich als Fürst
Verwalten, nicht verschenken. Auf! Zur Schlacht" (*HFA* 7, 709).

"No!" spoke the Prince, "as long as only *I* was affected,
My *horse*, the *slave woman*, I gladly gave them up
To spare the blood of the people; but my *land*,
The property of the state it is my duty as prince
To administer and not give away. Onward! To battle!"

In "War Justice," the Sultan of India personally executes a high-ranking officer whom a poor man has accused of extortion. The officer is not named by his accuser, but the sultan is well aware that his favourite officers, and his own sons, are most capable of such a deed. In order to ensure blind justice, he extinguishes the lights so as not to recognize who he is about to execute. And in "The Deceived Negotiator" a missionary convinces the chiefs of the Iroquois to attend peace negotiations with the French. The French put them in chains and send them to the galleys. The nation of the Iroquois are in uproar, but the Eldest warns the missionary that his life is in danger, and saves him.

... "Wir haben Dir vertraut,
Und sind mit unerhörtem Schimpf betrogen.
Ich weiß, Du bist nicht Schuld daran; Du meintest
Es redlich; doch nicht jeder Jüngling denkt
In unsrer Nation wie ich. Drum flieh!
Flieh, Fremder! Eher laß ich nicht von Dir,
Bis ich Dich sicher weiß" – Er ließ ihn über
Die Grenze hin geleiten. – Edler Mann! (*HFA* 7, 713)

... "We trusted you
And have been deceived in the most disgraceful way.
I know that you are not at fault; your intentions
Were good. But not every young man
Among my people feels the same. Thus flee!
Flee stranger! I will not leave you
Until I know you are in safety" – he had him
Escorted over the border. – Noble man!

It is easy to fault Herder on these poems. In each case, the protagonist appears to be acting according to a priori moral principles, thereby demonstrating the Kantian categorical imperative. But on closer examination, all the moral choices are questionable. And what is more, their apparent timelessness contravenes Herder's own dictates on human rights. In the place of fundamental principles of rights and their infringements, he presents a set of situations where the reader's sentiments are aligned with decisions based on morally disputable, historically contingent notions of right and wrong. Was it really right for the Prince of the Huns to give away his horse and "his woman" to avoid war, but to fight for the community's land? Was the Sultan of India really right in killing a high-ranking officer without trial, even though he had extinguished the lights before seeing who it was, in order to ensure blind justice (his sons were also officers). Even the tale of the Iroquois and the missionary is open to moral debate. The missionaries were complicit in the situation described, even if this particular missionary meant well.

Each time, the narrative voice seems deeply invested in moral judgment. But it cannot have been Herder's intention to demonstrate the absolute validity of the judgments in question, even if some of them seem to accord well with what he regards as fundamental moral principles. They are intended as fables to demonstrate correct action in situations where basic legal principles are at stake, but the poems are called upon to display the contingency of morality, its historical specificity, and to appeal to the reader to understand that this – not the categorical imperative – is the essence of morality. With this understanding of morality, Herder repeats his challenge to Kantian reason: its inability to disentangle itself from the political interests of the day; its propensity to speak about history as if it were a set of facts rather than a set of representations; its devaluing of happiness; and the fundamental contradiction between its progressive view of history and its admission that the knowledge of what drives history must escape reason.[50] At the same time, he points to his hopes for an alternative to this struggle for transcendental principles. It is in the formulations of the historiographer and the poet that the distance between historical analysis and the principles of political critique open up. In Herder's ideal of aesthetic practice, the sentimentality of the poet is matched by the impartiality of the scientific observer; both together should provide the guarantee of natural human development. The interpretation of empirical evidence on the improvement of humanity needs to be augmented with the aesthetic production of truly human situations – not through acts of scientific description, but through poetic challenges to the moral horizon of the reader.

In the following letter, which presents the short sketch "Zum ewigen Frieden. Eine Irokesische Anstalt" (Perpetual Peace. An Iroquois Institution), Herder again throws down the gauntlet to Kant. The idea of Perpetual Peace, as it interested Herder, goes back to the three-volume work of Charles-Irénée Castel, Abbé de Saint-Pierre, *Projet pour rendre la paix perpétuelle en Europa* (1713–17),[51] but his immediate point of reference is Kant's essay of 1795 *Zum ewigen Frieden. Ein philosophischer Entwurf* (Perpetual Peace. A Philosophical Sketch). This short article is one of Kant's best known and most commented political works, and in it he interrogates the possibility and conditions of eternal peace. It is divided into a main part, consisting of two sections (the preliminary and definitive articles of perpetual peace between nations), followed by two supplements (on the guarantee and the secret article of perpetual peace), and two appendices (explaining the incompatibility of morality and politics, and proposing a solution).

The preliminary articles set out clearly the conditions necessary for peace. These salient and perceptive observations have not lost their force today. Standing armies are to be abolished, peace treaties are to be clearly distinguished from ceasefires, no state shall forcefully interfere with the internal politics of another state, dishonest and immoral acts of war undermine subsequent peace arrangements and should be outlawed, and so on. Because these conditions are valid in all cases, it is possible to generalize the mechanisms that can prevent war, and Kant does this in the definitive articles. He begins with the Hobbesean tenet that the state of nature is a state of war, and that peace among nations should not be confused with nature (*KPW* 98). Instead, nature has given humans the capacity and the urge to overcome nature, and when it comes to war and peace, this is expressed in fundamental principles of constitutional and international law. All states should be constituted as republics, there should be a federation of states as the basis for international law, and national citizens should also enjoy certain cosmopolitan rights or rights associated with world-citizenship.

In the supplements, Kant goes on to explore how these transcendental principles of law might come to be realized. But first, the larger question must be addressed: if nature is best described by Hobbes's *bellum omnium contra omnes*, what is it about nature that has lifted and will continue to lift human society out of this condition? Much like Rousseau before him, Kant argues anthropologically, claiming that nature seeks to populate the earth through migration and conflict, which in turn lead to settlement, mutual cooperation, and law. States are the result of this natural process of development. Like Montesquieu, Kant then explains how commerce acts as an analogous process on an international scale, promoting peace between states. "For the spirit of commerce sooner or later takes hold of every people, and it cannot exist side by side with war" (*KPW* 114). With this, Kant's anthropology has led him to the same place Herder found himself when he interrogated the idea of *doux commerce* and discovered that history does not validate it. As we saw, he concluded that imperialism, and not a federation of states, seems to be the natural consequence of international commerce. The task of the philosopher-historian is to understand the relationship between natural processes and the history of wars, and thereby gain a better understanding of how the ideal of *doux commerce* fails and imperialism gains the upper hand. What is it about human nature that stands in the way of its own development?

Kant takes a completely different tack. Assuming that the natural principle of mutual cooperation among individuals, communities, and states is a stronger principle than that of total war, but that the sovereign, immersed in power politics, is unable to see this – or is at least unable to act accordingly – he then asks how the rationality of peace can be brought to bear against the rationality of war. This question is addressed in the second supplement, where he distinguishes between the public use of reason by the state and the secret counsel it receives from the philosopher. The state needs the philosopher as a figure who formulates generally valid principles according to universal reason and morality, and for this reason it should encourage the public pronouncements of the philosopher. But in the case of power politics directed at warfare, the principles of universal reason and morality are at odds with the reason of state – which, Kant is quick to point out, is more powerful than philosophy. The only way to resolve this apparent split in reason is for the sovereign to take secret counsel from the philosopher, while presenting to the public the face of absolute power. This is how power becomes enlightened.

But for the philosopher this does not solve the problem of the opposition between morality and politics, between a practical reason directed purely towards political goals and a practical reason guided by the principle of pure reason. Morality is the domain of pure reason and it must have priority over the aims of politics. And just to press the point home, Kant repeats the formal principle of practical reason: "Act in such a way that you can wish your maxim to become a universal law (irrespective of what the end in view may be)" (*KPW* 122). And he ends this section by concluding that "a true system of politics cannot therefore take a single step without first paying tribute to morality" (*KPW* 125). In the case of perpetual peace, this means that it cannot be seen as a political end to be attained through any means and through any cynical use of reason. Instead, it must be linked as an immediate goal of political action to transcendental principles of morality. In the final section, the second appendix, Kant explains how this can be achieved through the concept of public right, which he calls a transcendental concept. If politics is to be brought in line with morality, its reasoning will have to become public. Since political action is ideally aimed at increasing the public good, and since this is morally desirable, then the reasoning behind political action must at all times be open to the public. This is why Kant declares that if a maxim requires publicity in order to attain a specified goal, then it is in agreement with both politics and morality (*KPW* 130).

When it comes to the necessary conditions for avoiding war, history has proved Kant right. Without the principles outlined above, and without the attendant international legislation, peace is not to be attained. Even in Kant's own time, it would have been hard to object to his argument. But Herder could not be satisfied with the idea that there are transcendental principles that could align morality with politics. Even though he agreed with the principles Kant named, he could not bring himself to agree with their universality. In his own tale of Perpetual Peace, Herder relates an anecdote which he had read about in Georg Heinrich Loskiel's *Geschichte der Mission der evangelischen Brüder under den Indianern in Nordamerika* (History of the Mission of Evangelical Brothers among the Indians of North America, 1789).[52] As Loskiel recounts it (and Herder quotes and paraphrases him at length), when the Europeans began to settle in Philadelphia, their presence displaced the indigenous peoples, leading to conflict between various nations. This exacerbated a long-standing dispute between the Iroquois and the Delaware, leading to open warfare. The Iroquois, realizing that they were the weaker party, offered to play the part of what Herder calls the "Woman of Peace" (*Friedensfrau*; *HFA* 7, 716). As Loskiel explains, this was a strategic response to European colonialism, since the driving force of peace negotiations was the realization that war would lead to the destruction of the Indian nations.[53] Herder then goes on to explain in detail what the arrangements of the Woman of Peace with the other warring nations involved: she incorporates the passive, peace-making principle, assigning to the other, "male" nations the role of protectors of the peace. But she is also the voice of practical reason. She is to remind them in times of conflict: "You men, what are you doing, fighting like that? Consider that your women and children will have to die if you do not stop. Do you want to erase yourselves from the face of the earth?" (*HFA* 7, 714). Then, again following Loskiel, Herder details the symbolic and allegorical moves that the Indian nations make in order to cement their peace in tradition. What emerges is an aesthetic negotiation of conflict to create a temporary and not very stable peace.

What made Herder turn to this anecdote in response to Kant? It was precisely the aesthetic principle at work in the determination of a peace settlement that Herder wanted to show. This principle appeared eternal, even though it couldn't be. The aesthetic principle reinforces the idea that peace cannot be established on the basis of preconceived political ideas, such as reciprocity of action, a secret pact between philosopher and sovereign, or moral imperatives. It has to be derived strategically from each and every political system. Humanity is not forced to pursue transcendental moral principles through its propensity to conflict, and human development is not driven by philosophical and social responses to Hobbesean belligerence – Kant's "unsocial sociability" (Fourth Proposition of the *Idea for a Universal History*; *KPW* 44). The natural inclination of peoples is peaceful, and it is the conflicting uses of reason that introduce conflict into social life. This is not an article of faith, but a matter of good historical understanding. Herder's example of perpetual peace is a good illustration of this. At first glance it seems to provide a perfect example for Kant's unsocial sociability. The Delaware and the Iroquois, the Europeans and the Indians found themselves in conflict, prompted by their natural desire for their own advantage. But their sociability guided them to a peaceful solution. Herder wants to show something different. The pursuit of perpetual peace by the Delaware and Iroquois was not prompted by an understanding of the need to apply transcendental moral values to a situation of conflict. This was not the freedom of thought pitted against man's natural propensity for aggression. The war between the two nations was initiated by and was a rational response to a specific historical development, namely, European imperialism. And imperialism itself is a form of rationality – albeit a failed rationality based on instrumental ideas, as Herder has been at pains to show throughout his writing. Loskiel explains how, in the initial stages of European settlement, Indians and Europeans dwelt peacefully side by side in

Philadelphia. The conflict only began after Europeans started settling in large numbers, expanding their agricultural holdings and their trading grounds, driving the Indians further into the woods to pursue the game which the Europeans had displaced. Then, the Europeans began attacking those Indians who had remained in the colonial settlements, forcing them to leave. "In this way, the arrival of Europeans caused migrations of entire peoples. One displaced nation ousted the next, scattering it or restricting its territory."[54] This is such a familiar scenario of European colonialism that Kant's faith in migration as the natural guarantor of peace (outlined in the first supplement) begins to look like pure fantasy. No wonder Herder thought that a correct understanding of history discredited the metaphysician's faith in moral principles of pure reason.

This is a more serious claim than simply that Kant didn't understand the history of imperialism. It begins to open his philosophy to the suspicion that his ability to identify transcendental moral principles is hampered by the fact that the methodology that leads to these principles is historically contingent, and that they are themselves determined by his own socio-historical situation. Kant would counter this with the argument that historical contingency always stands between the moral individual and the unknowable essence of moral agency, and that history itself is a process of clarification, whereby historical contingency itself becomes increasingly transparent to moral principles. But even if he is right, Herder's claim carries considerable weight: that the forms whereby historically situated individuals and groups represent moral principles are also historically contingent, and therefore the medium that presents transcendental moral principles is just as historically tainted as is the consciousness and thought processes of individuals. The effect of this is the illusion that historically contingent representations of morality will somehow bring one closer to transcendental moral principles than the use of reason would. This is why, in pitting his female protagonist, "the great artist *Nature* herself" (*Die große Künstlerin Natur*; *KPW* 108), against Herder's Woman of Peace, Kant seems to imply that, contrary to his own claims, he can indeed know what nature is and what it wants: it is a woman and it wants peace. Herder sees this problem and he chooses to focus on the use of aesthetic devices not as a bridge to morality but as an enactment of the production of moral principles out of specific historical situations. Against Kant's gendered nature, Herder suggests gender as a role play performed by what Schultz calls his "Indian transvestites" for the purpose of assigning distinct social functions to the warring parties.[55]

Finally, the "perpetual" in perpetual peace needs to be examined. Kant begins his essay by noting the discrepancy between the sovereign's practical reliance on war and the philosopher's blissful "dream of perpetual peace" (*KPW* 93). The temporality of thought is split between the practical and the ideal, making the peaceful development of humanity something like a regulative concept, whose timeless validity appears to be at odds with the temporality through which it reveals itself. Two years after *Perpetual Peace*, in *The Metaphysics of Morals*, Kant stated that the concept of perpetual peace requires us to act "as if it could really come about (which is perhaps impossible)" (*KPW* 174). This is what Pauline Kleingeld calls the "atemporality problem": the fact that "his notion of rational development, especially the notion of 'moralization,' seems to run counter to his thesis that moral agency is noumenal and hence atemporal."[56] In a way, Kant's entire essay is circling around the problem of how to bring the timelessness of regulative concepts to bear on the temporal contingencies that embed practical reason in history. Herder uses temporality in a completely different way – more like Derrida uses it. Time is a function of human cognition: it does not exist apart from human life and the life of the senses. On the contrary – and we recognized this as one of the innovations of his theory of language – human temporality is a by-product of the delay between sense perception and language/reason. This is why it makes no sense to see the perpetuality of peace in ideal terms. Perpetuality can only be understood as the negation of time, and time can only be understood as part of human life. This, incidentally, offers a serious alternative to Kant's discussion of the antinomies of time and space in the *Critique of Pure Reason*. For a philosopher to assume that his conception of eternity is universal is to fundamentally misunderstand Crusius's insight that time (like space) defines bodies as distinct from God. When it comes to morality, the gap between time itself and moral atemporality is too large to be bridged by acts of reason. Or as Michel Despland explains, the distinction between objective and subjective uses of practical reason is undermined by the philosophy of history. "The philosophy of history shows how the 'objective' moral law was 'subjectively' learned by the race, or by some in it, only at some point in the process of history." What this means is that morality itself is "embedded in the historical process, related to, say, historical experience." As soon as morality is temporalized in this way, it stands "in tension with the rather timeless standpoint of the *Critique of Practical Reason*."[57] Kant would, as Kleingeld suggests, have an answer to this – morality in its timeless validity is not created in moments of historical insight, but is being discovered by humanity in a long process.[58]

This is the point of Herder's objection. Morality cannot be discovered, it can only be created. What looks like the discovery of morality is in fact only the production of aesthetic media capable of transmitting ideas that appear to have transcendental validity. What needs to be at issue is not morality but the aesthetic media themselves and the means of their production. Perpetual peace, like eternity itself, is always only hinted at through the distorted representations of human time. Perpetual peace is an idea derived analytically from the arrangements that can be made to create peaceful situations out of specific moments of conflict. In this view, Kant's distinction between the practical statesman (for whom time is measured by actions and strategic thoughts about actions) and the dreaming philosopher (for whom time is something to be destroyed) begins to break down. If we examine temporality carefully and in the terms Herder is asking us to, the concept of time itself will not withstand this distinction.

But if time lies at the heart of Kant's philosophy, where it unsettles his founding ideas, it does something similar in Herder. Like the rise and fall of cultures, peace comes and goes, but the historian-philosopher sees in this kaleidoscope of failed peace an idea which might be called perpetual peace. This means that eternity, if it is not a regulative concept, is to be grasped in terms that might be called the mystification of the aesthetic – like epiphany or transubstantiation, the eternal can indeed be perceived by way of analogy in the present. Political arrangements that hold onto a tenuous peace, such as the one between the Iroquois and the Delaware, cannot be eternal in the sense that they will last forever. History does not work like that. Cultures rise and fall, civilizations blossom and disappear, peace is arranged and fails. European imperialism displaces indigenous peoples and forces them into conflict, they make peace, only to find once again that their efforts are at odds with the fact of imperialism. Loskiel tells how the peace between the Indian nations collapsed when they were forced once again into war with the settlers. But in these moments of harmony, Herder wants to see an eternal principle at work, mediated and revealed through the aesthetic. This is the paradox of aesthetics against imperialism. Aesthetic practice lays claim to timelessness when it confronts images in time. And it sees its own embeddedness in temporality whenever it glimpses the timeless. But – and this is Herder's wager – in the aesthetic production of individuals and their cultures, humanity works on nature, forming it, giving it expression, and negotiating which models of nature are the most expedient for the self-realization of humanity.

Conclusion: Herder, Postcolonialism, and the Antinomy of Universal Reason

The scholarship has long since known that in Herder's aesthetics and his politics, all paths lead to contradiction. How are we to reconcile his promotion of diversity with his unified vision for all humanity? How can he hope for general moral values and aesthetic principles without violating the integrity of individual cultures? How can history be diverse and cyclical while at the same time humanity is advancing towards an unspecified goal? How can he deny racial difference and still speak as if it exists? What are we to do with his sustained opposition to Kant, itself based on the position Kant himself thought he needed to move beyond with his critical theory? What about the formulations that made it possible for the Nazis to court him briefly, passionately, unsuccessfully?[1] What is it in his writing that allows scholars to continue to misunderstand his ideas on nationalism?[2]

At the heart of Herder's thought lies a set of apparently contradictory positions around language, history, humanity, and free will. I say that they are apparently contradictory, because they are intended to point towards a resolution that lies not in the matter itself, but in the methodology with which they can be analysed. Herder himself was explicit on this point in his later writings, particularly in his metacritique of Kant. I will mention the contradictions as succinctly as possible (since they are apparent from the preceding chapters), adding some of Herder's own later observations where relevant. We have already encountered the most important of these basic contradictions:

Language restricts the world for the thinking individual, but it is possible to think the world beyond this limitation.

All languages are equally valuable as different vehicles for conceptualizing the world. Seen this way, individual languages are "precious entities whose multiplicity and variety is the wealth of the human mind."[3] The mother tongue provides the context for conceptualizing the world, but to conceptualize the world in the mother tongue is to represent the world as incomplete. But Herder also believed (following the incipient ethnolinguistics of the day) that some languages are more developed than others; they are more complex, more conceptually inclined, more given to abstraction. This introduces a fundamental contradiction between the position that individual languages provide a unique way of being in the world, an essential component of the human experience, and the position that some of these ways of being in the world are more advanced than others. This is compounded by the implication that there is a common conceptual ground that allows communication across languages, elevating the relative development of a language as if from outside of language. This contradiction is intensified by the fact that, the closer we look at linguistic diversity, the more we must recognize that the multiplicity of languages breaks down into a multiplicity of dialects, sociolects, idiolects, to the point where it begins to look as if there are as many languages as there are individuals in the world (*HFA* 1, 792).

History is cyclical and finite, but it is also possible to conceive of history as linear and infinite.

History is moving humanity towards some kind of final goal, but at the same time, history is cyclical, diverse, and intelligible only within a limited cultural horizon. One of the consequences of this contradiction is what Bob Chase calls Herder's "attempts, on the one hand, to distance himself from Eurocentrism, and, on the other, to acknowledge Europe's alleged preeminence in the world."[4] But the contradiction itself is more deep-seated in his thought. Its effect is noted in his discussion (in the *Metacritique of the Critique of Pure Reason*, 1799) of Kant's first antinomy of pure reason, which states on the one hand that the world is spatially finite and has a beginning in time, but on the other hand that it has to be considered to be spatially infinite and temporally without beginning. Herder displaces this contradiction (he refuses to call it an antinomy of reason) onto different faculties of cognition. The imagination conceives of the world as infinite, the understanding can only function in a finite world, and reason sees the limits of the understanding in the unboundedness of the cosmos (*HSW* 21, 226–7). With this, reason takes account of the contradiction that founds historical time (and Herder lends reason a voice, addressing the understanding): "In the epitome of your thoughts on the being of things, the measure of their duration and the beginning of every emerging thing in the cosmos [*jedes Emporkommenden im Weltall*] you have, in every moment, beginning and end, apparent emergence and demise, but always the progress of time. But time itself has everywhere and nowhere a beginning and an end; like space, it is only a determinate measure within the immeasurable" (*HSW* 21, 227). This leaves history both finite and infinite, depending on how it is conceptualized. And since conceptualization itself is rooted in history, the contradiction remains.

Humanity is both diverse and singular.

The contradiction of humanity's diversity and its singularity is a direct result of the contradictions of language and history: Humanity is an organic whole, and it is possible to develop a historical metanarrative of humanity;[5] but at the same time, humanity can only flourish if it is promoted as a set of "integral wholes distinct from one another."[6] This contradiction in turn points to the problem of the one and the many, which is reflected in Kant's second antinomy of pure reason: that all things are either in themselves simple, or they are composed of simple things; but all things can just as well be considered complex, and there is nothing simple in the world. In his critique of Kant's antinomies, Herder sees the problem of the one and the many in terms of the singularity and multiplicity of forces (*HSW* 21, 228). This allows him to bypass the paradox of the one and the many (which had occupied the Presocratics), and displace it onto his theory of force. But it does not resolve the contradiction that arises when he attempts to understand humanity as both diverse and unitary.

Free will is an act of individual volition, but it is also an expression of a natural force outside the cognitive processes of the individual.

Everything in Herder's philosophy points to the idea that individuals have free will and can make free choices. But free will is the freedom to unfold one's inner potential and thereby actualize immanent natural forces. This actualization is called history. In the historical unfolding of the world, the force that drives history acts collectively through the diverse forms of human reason. This makes individual and collective acts of reason little more than an expression of a larger natural force towards self-fulfilment. To state that individual acts of reason are free is to state that they are determined by the forces of nature at work on the organism. As reason reprimands fantasy in the *Metacritique*: "In nature, everything is free; only through this freedom can the forces of nature take effect" (*HSW* 21, 228). The laws of nature result from the relationships that emerge when different free forces encounter one another. When reason speaks to the understanding, it reminds it that "freedom, even the wildest freedom, is a force of nature; if it opposes the laws [of nature] they will take revenge, and the highest force we know in nature, self-determination, is only free when, by its own force, as self-determination, it obeys the highest laws of nature" (*HSW* 21, 229). This leads directly to the problem of interpretation: "Self-determination in accordance with the laws of nature, not outside of these laws, is the highest freedom, in that it creates and organizes laws in accordance with the laws of nature" (*HSW* 21, 229). By making freedom into a self-regulating determination of natural law, Herder has everything hinge on the interpretation of individual actions. This casts him back into the contradictions surrounding language, since language is the medium of interpretation. Consequently, language reveals the free will as culturally determined, but needs to conceive of freedom as determined by those forces that work within the organism, pushing thought beyond the culturally specific, towards the universally human.

It is easy to dismiss Herder as a writer hopelessly mired in contradiction, unable to live up to his own insights into some of the founding problems of philosophy. Robert Young, for example, in his otherwise perceptive pages on contradiction in Herder, concludes that he "speaks with a forked tongue: offering on the one hand rootedness, the organic unity of a people and their local, traditional culture, but also on the other hand the cultural education of the human race whereby the achievements of one culture are grafted onto another, sometimes occurring via revolution, or change of state (for example, the end of the Roman empire) or through migration, which Herder acknowledges as an historical tendency. In this way he resolves the anthropological question of how the unity of the human race squares with its inherent diversity."[7] The point of my book has been to argue that, if we read him this way, we are missing an important opportunity to understand the anti-imperialist project – not only Herder's own particular brand of anti-imperialism, but some of the dominant ideas in postcolonial theory. This is not to decry the project itself. I wrote this book on the assumption that the opposition to imperialism is one of the most important impulses in the academic world today. My intention has been to show how Herder developed an anti-imperialist stance alongside his shift from a critique of rationalist philosophy to a philosophy of history, anthropology, and aesthetics. His self-conscious development of this trajectory offers an understanding of some deep systemic problems in postcolonial theory. My analysis of his writings has, I hope, offered insight into the kind of moves that need to be made if these problems are to be addressed. I hope it will have become clear in these pages that Herder's problems persist in discourses of anti-imperialism today, whenever these discourses approach the problem of imperialism as a problem of form – of how cultural difference leads to differences in expression, and how formal analysis can do justice to these formal differences. I have asked the reader to follow me through a detailed discussion of Herder's anti-imperialism, but to hold in mind the strong arguments being made today for aesthetics against imperialism.

Once the epistemological genesis of Herder's anti-imperialism is recognized, it becomes apparent that his path from an anti-rationalist epistemology to a critique of imperialism sets important markers for the postcolonial project. These markers are visible wherever contradiction appears in Herder's work. And contradiction points in one direction – to the problem of universal reason. At the heart of Herder's project lies an antinomy which I am calling the antinomy of universal reason. It can be stated like this:

There is a universal capacity for reason that makes humans human; human biology (or to be more precise, neurology)[8] ensures that reason is a shared human capacity for cognizing life.[9] *Abstraction and reflection are what makes thought human.[10] This innate structural organization of reason provides the universal ground on which human thought develops.*

BUT

There is no such thing as universal reason; reason exists only in the plural, and the plurality of reason ensures that life will be cognized in countless different ways. *The diversity of reason follows the diversity of languages, sociolects, idiolects, cultural communities, and individuals. Herder speaks of "the* **human** *paths" to reason in the plural.[11]*

Neither Herder nor the theorists of postcolonialism have been able to formulate this antinomy with any degree of clarity. Herder himself did not believe there was such a thing as antinomies of reason.[12] But even the terms in which he attempts to dismiss the idea show how close his epistemological problems are to those of postcolonial theory – in order to speak against pure reason, he has to fragment the faculties, assigning them their own voices and jurisdictions.

I believe it would be possible to show, through detailed analysis, that Herder passed this antinomy on genealogically to postcolonial theory. The channels of this transmission are convoluted, but would be worth reconstructing. They would lead through Goethe, Hegel,[13] and Marx[14] to the Frankfurt School and the post-structuralist reaction to French Marxian theory; through Romantic psychology to Freud and the psychoanalytic dimension of post-structuralism; from the experiments of the German Romantics[15] to the rediscovery by Nietzsche[16] and Derrida[17] of how writing strategies structure truth. These channels are almost entirely unknown today, but I am convinced that careful research would reveal a genealogy linking postcolonialism directly to the figure who was once seen as one of the most important intellectuals of his time – and until this research is done, I can offer nothing more than this speculative assertion. But even without the genealogical link, there is a clear structural affinity between Herder's antinomy of universal reason and the general project of postcolonial theory. I realize this is a generalization, but I believe it is a fair one, and I will try to support it in the paragraphs that follow – although they cannot be much more than a gesture towards postcolonialism's own version of Herder's antinomy of universal reason.

Dipesh Chakrabarthy, for example, understands the project of "provincializing" Europe as resting on the antinomy of universal reason. His stated aim (in the foreword to the 2007 edition of *Provincializing Europe*) is "to find out how and in what sense European ideas that were universal were also, at one and the same time, drawn from very particular intellectual and historical traditions that could not claim any universal validity."[18] The challenge here is to explain how this fractured universality relates to modernity. Chakrabarthy does this by pointing out how the historicist project has recast particular, non-universal intellectual and historical traditions encountered in the colonized world as the same kind of experiences Europe has overcome in the universalizing process of modernization. This is what makes historical reason (to use his term) elitist, furthering the imperialist cause.[19] Chakrabarthy proves perceptive in formulating the challenge facing historiography in the context of postcolonialism: "to hold in a state of permanent tension a dialogue between two contradictory points of view." These are "the Enlightenment promise of an abstract, universal but never-to-be-realized humanity" and the "diverse ways of being human, the infinite incommensurabilities through which we struggle – perennially, precariously, but unavoidably – to 'world the earth' in order to live within our different senses of ontic belonging."[20] This is a precise formulation of the challenge Herder's antinomy poses for postcolonial historiography. But Chakrabarthy takes it a step further and pronounces the problem that Herder never completely managed to exorcise from his encounter with universal reason. When it comes to morality, Kant, it seems, was right. In Chakrabarthy's words: "We need universals to produce critical readings of social injustices." And yet, Herder's criticism of Kant is equally valid in recognizing that (again in Chakrabarthy's words) "the universal and the analytical produce forms of thought that ultimately evacuate the place of the local."[21] But to this must be added Herder's hope that the universal of Kantian morals is not the same thing as analytic method – and that, despite the strong argument Chakrabarthy makes connecting analytic method to a priori universals, analytic method can somehow inflect universals with the ontic belonging out of which they arose. This was the hope he invested in the work of aesthetics. And, as I will argue later, it may indeed be here that Herder has something to offer postcolonialism in understanding methodology.

The sustained hope that the aesthetic can counter a priori universalism, perhaps even producing an alternative path to universalism subtly inhabits Achille Mbembe's *On the Postcolony*. Mbembe uses the antinomy of universal reason to explore what can be said about modernity once it is wrenched from the grasp of the "West."[22] This wrenching cannot help but confront the claims to universal reason that drove modernity in Europe: "What a certain rationality, claiming to be universal but in reality mired in the contingent and the particular, has never understood is that all human societies participate in a complex order, rich in unexpected turns, meanders, and changes of course, without this implying their necessary abolition in an absence of center."[23] Mbembe sees the necessity of uncovering the heterogeneity of those societies excluded by Enlightenment rationality, and he sees this as opposing those theories whose roots lie in disciplines that sought legitimacy by stressing their "capacity to construct universal grammars."[24] The points at which Mbembe encounters this problem are roughly the same as the ones Herder traced in his critique of imperialism, and Mbembe also restates Herder's shift from rationalist philosophy to the aesthetic, in so many words.

Mbembe's starting point is the dilemma facing African subjectivity in the wake of slavery and colonization. The "re-affirmation of African humanity" has left Africans with a choice that seems to reside at the heart of the project of African nationalism and that is characterized by the split between emancipation and assimilation: either to accept "a tragic duality and an inner twoness," or to assert "the absoluteness of the African self."[25] The problem with this is that, either way, it involves a development of African reason in relationship to the universal reason whose domain is the "uncompromising nature of the Western self."[26] These attempts to identify "the essence, the distinctive genius, of the black 'race'" implied also the identification of a specifically African form of reason in history, but the realization of this genius was "its fusion in the crucible of the universal."[27] Consequently, the African finds himself engaged in the paradoxes of negation and self-negation described by Fanon.

What Mbembe is describing is the difficulty in finding a specific form of reason that refuses the dialectical relationship to the universal. In assuming that the forms of African reason do indeed need to refuse the relationship to the universal, we are on well trodden ground, but Mbembe undermines his own project by his unwillingness to ask what the consequences should be for his own acts of theorization. The result is a wavering between the assumption of a homogeneous African subject who is capable of autonomy and of differentiated thought and action – in spite of having been defined as homogeneous through a history of subjugation – and an African characterized by autochthonous figures of reason. I understand why Mbembe sees the need to speak of the African subject as if it were indeed possible or even desirable to generalize using the register of economic development ("Sub-Saharan Africa"),[28] and why at the same time he wants to investigate the contingencies of everyday life in Africa that work against this generalization. If the dilemma of reason in Africa is to be understood, it needs to be shown to rest on a distinction between how Africans can be spoken of in a register of universal reason and how their acts of reason can also be investigated empirically, while resisting their integration into universal systems – in the way Chakrabarthy pointed out. But if the ideological dismissal of Africa (the place where, as Hegel told his students, the rationality of history fails) is to be countered, we need to realize that the failure of rationality is inherent in rationality itself, and not tied to geographical place, that its failure has been repeated time and again in acts of political violence, not just under colonialism, not just in Africa.

Mbembe is at his most interesting when he understands the dilemma of reason in Africa as the distinction between reason as process, system, or structure, and reason as form – and here he comes close to following Herder's distinction between humanity and its cultural manifestations, and to understanding the work of critique as aesthetic work. Confronting universal reason as a process, Mbembe finds himself trying to "state in the most productive possible way, some general questions suggested by concepts drawn from social theory." And where this fails – "where these concepts were manifestly incapable of describing the particular figures of reason in African history and the practices of our time, I have invented different modes of discourse, *a different writing*."[29] In other words, aesthetic work is offered in opposition to the universalizing discourses of imperialism. This is laudable, but as we see in the unfolding of his book, not as easy as Mbembe seems to assume. The reason is that he seems uncertain about what exactly the aesthetic – the invention of new forms for writing the particularity of African reason – has to offer in resistance to universal reason, and how this relates to the material context of his own discourse. Let me briefly discuss two points: time and dehumanization.

Mbembe arrives at the question of time via the same observation Herder had taken from Crusius: that it is a human thing.[30] As Mbembe puts it: "There is a close relationship between subjectivity and temporality," or in other words, "in some way, one can envisage subjectivity as temporality."[31] To say as much is, as Herder explored at length, to open the way for a discussion of subjective time as caught up in the language/reason system, and to ask how historical time relates to universal and to contingent forms of reason. Mbembe begins to follow up on this when he notes that "every age, including the postcolony, is in reality a combination of several temporalities."[32] There are different ways of understanding this statement. If time is a human thing, then the phenomenology of time would make way for multiple temporalities within a single event. The multiplicity of time would relate to the multiplicity of sensory perception and to how disparate sensory impressions are resolved in common sense. Where more than one individual is involved, the multiplicity of time is compounded by the multiplicity of resolutions. Multiplicity now becomes a problem of social time and the temporality of production. Then there is the question of representation, or narratives of time and, eventually, of history. It is at this point that Mbembe intends to intervene. What he calls the "time of African existence" sets itself apart from the universal temporality in which the dominant narratives of history are inscribed: "To think relevantly about this time that is appearing, this passing time, meant abandoning conventional views, for these only perceive time as a current that carries individuals and societies from a background to a foreground, with the future emerging necessarily from the past and following that past, itself irreversible."[33] As an alternative, Mbembe offers a picture of time that is not linear, not predictable, and not irreversible. The only way to make sense of this alternative picture of time is to see it as represented time. Where it seems he wants to talk about a politics of phenomenology, he is in fact evoking the politics of representation (whose importance he explains later).[34] It is in this failed connection of temporality to the politics of representation that the missed opportunity lies. The observation that "the contemporary African experience"[35] is distinguished by the apparent closure of the future and the apparent receding of the horizon of the past could have been an important comment on the politics of representation, but as it stands, it seems to want to claim a common human experience of time as the distinguishing mark of African existence, a claim that returns him to the antinomy of universal reason.

A similar process is at work when it comes to dehumanization. The question of dehumanization is introduced via an oblique passage on what I take to be the same distinction Herder makes between *aisthesis* (Mbembe speaks of "living in the concrete world"), and *aesthesis* ("the subjective forms that make possible any validation of its contents").[36] Mbembe raises the fascinating and important point that the aesthetic formalization of *aisthesis* sets the particularity of reason in a relationship with violence. This is, incidentally, no different from Herder's attempts to set up a constellation of reason, form, and violence in the so-called *Negro-Idylls* of 1797.[37] But as Mbembe's attention turns to strategies of dehumanization in the exercise of colonial power, he becomes distracted and begins to lose sight of the problem of reason that, in Herder's analysis, founds the universality of *aisthetic* processes and the particularity of *aesthetic* form. Instead (in chapter 1, "On Commandment"), he sidesteps the problem of reason's universality, concentrating on the cynical alignment of reason with power and interest. It is a well-known story that the question whether Africans think like Europeans or not was swept off the table by the powerful interests of the slave traders and the trading companies. But much more interesting than the sweeping itself is how to bring the question back in a way that does justice to the fact that African reason, like reason itself, is both universal and particular. In many respects, Mbembe's book can be read as an attempt to do just that, and in many respects points towards interesting ways that this can be accomplished. What I find noteworthy, however, is that, where it falls down, it does so by failing to address the antinomy of universal reason.

An instructive attempt to address the problems of writing across the gap between universal reason and local formulations of reason is Gayatri Spivak's *Critique of Postcolonial Reason*. This is, I think, the intention of her central figure of the native informant, and it seems to be the guiding idea that leads to her valuable uncovering of the marks left by imperialism on the writings of Kant, Hegel, and Marx. I'm hesitant here, since Spivak's unwillingness to address the core of her intent in plain language leaves her open to the suspicion that what she is writing is not a critique of postcolonial reason, but an enactment of its *aporia*. I'll give her the benefit of the doubt; perhaps she is right that this enactment is the only way to set out her own position between the various subject positions she explores in her book and the universal discourse in which she writes. Read like this, Spivak displays the challenge facing postcolonial theory: how to adopt writing strategies that uncover the ways the native informant is incorporated into aesthetic practices and into theory formation while at the same time making interventions that are effective within the discourses that effect this incorporation. In her discussion of Kant, this display (she calls it a "performance") is intended to indicate the "nascent axiomatics of imperialism" that authorized his universalism.[38] At the same time, she understands the methodological difficulty this raises for her own work: in exposing the centrality of imperialism through what she calls her "tropological analysis," she has to avoid the possible objection that her own reading of Kant, by placing it into a wider frame of world history, or of the advancement of scholarship, itself reclaims the universality at issue. It is instructive to see how this works against statements concerning the antinomy of universal reason. To decry the universalism that makes the native informant's statements useful and necessary to philosophy seems to imply a position that itself can lay claim to universality – unless it be inscribed rhetorically with markers of its own refusal.

This is the problem of reason that the Enlightenment has bequeathed to postcolonialism, and Spivak acknowledges it when she notes the contradictory historical positions that threaten the integrity of postcolonial studies: "Colonial Discourse studies, when they concentrate only on the representation of the colonized or the matter of the colonies, can sometimes serve the production of current neocolonial knowledge by placing colonialism/imperialism securely in the past, and/or by suggesting a continuous line from that past to our present."[39] What Spivak is addressing is the same contradiction at work when Herder addresses teleology in history: if we are to do justice to the past, it has to be understood as irrevocably past, and the logic that drove it has to be understood historically; but in order for this understanding of the historical past to present itself as understanding (that is, as an analysis of texts that lay claim to rendering past events comprehensible in terms that exceed the historical moment in which they occurred), there needs to be an idea of a plan, a direction for history, and an attendant universal mode for accessing this plan. As Michael Mack notes, the recognition of these two contradictory moments will allow Herder to develop an understanding of historiography as a dialectical affirmation of the fact that "the present incorporates the non-presence of the past."[40] Spivak repeatedly alludes to the coupling of this historiographical contradiction with the antinomy of universal reason. The problem is evident in her lengthy footnote on Kant's mention of the New-Hollanders and the Fuegeans in paragraph 67 of the *Critique of Judgment*. Spivak hopes to sustain these "two proper names of peoples" (New Hollanders and Fuegeans) as representations of how the supposedly inhuman inhabitants have entered and authorized the philosophical discourse of modernity, of how in the act of naming, an alternative way of being in the world is acknowledged and immediately dismissed. Spivak wants these names to "invaginate" her text.[41] But how is this to happen? She describes how the pursuit of Aboriginal languages (following Herder, a pursuit of their specific mode of reason)[42] stalled her manuscript for years. What stalled it was the discovery of their heterogeneity. But here the problem of universal reason reappears in its link to the universality of capitalism: "In the process I found, of course, that, like any people on earth, the Koorie today is also class heterogeneous, and divided in its ambitions. I realized that, as for all peoples who are not the felicitous subject of the European Enlightenment, their perennially blocked path to 'modernity' has been hybrid, not 'European.' (Indeed, if one understands hybridity as an absolute, the so-called European path of modernity is hybrid as well.)"[43] Looking from a European perspective at the heterogeneity of non-European languages means at the same time looking at the heterogeneity of modes of conceptualizing the world, the heterogeneity of reason. But the scholar's perspective is still one of universality. There is a logic to the way the Koorie live their lives and speak of their lives that is accessible to the inquisitive scholar in the late-capitalist world. In this respect, I have to read her reference to the "felicitous subject of the European Enlightenment" as hypocatastasis, the unspoken subject position being the universal subject position from which she speaks. The heterogeneity of hybrid subjects would seem to confirm the homogeneity of the European subject – until one turns the same gaze on the European subject and discovers there too a heterogeneity, a hybridity that calls into question the very opposition Spivak started with. Adorno named this problem nicely: "The universal that compresses the particular until it splinters, like a torture instrument, is working against itself, for its substance is the life of the particular; without the particular, the universal declines to an abstract, separate, eradicable form."[44] But does this make the particular an alternative to the universal? That would be a misunderstanding of the opposition out of which both arise.

Spivak reveals this insight in her discussion of Fredric Jameson's *Postmodernism, or the Cultural Logic of Late Capitalism*, in which she identifies "a desire to obliterate the subject-position implied by our everyday as we speak about 'our world.'"[45] But this desire itself casts the writing subject in a structural contradiction between the empirical observations it can make (since the invocation of the empirical "vitiates the generality of our argument") and the "deduced experience of a general U.S. ideological subject."[46] Spivak proves remarkably perceptive in locating the antinomy of universal reason at the heart of attempts to rephrase philosophical arguments as analyses of culture.

I could continue with this attempt to engage the writers of postcolonial theory with Herder's problem of universal reason. I believe it is a crucial undertaking – even if it serves only as a kind of therapy for the difficulty of reading postcolonial theory. To understand the antinomy I have discussed is to grasp the unenviable position in which readers of postcolonial theory are often placed: of having to decide whether to give the writer the benefit of the doubt and assume that the radical message their texts seem to be formulating can be reconstructed as a *clear* radical message without buying into the same corrupt regime of signification the author claims to be writing against. The alternative is to accept the strategies of semiological deviance as a radical refusal to enter into complicity with the universal regime of reason that carries epistemological violence – and refuse a shared standard that would permit the radicalness of the message to be evaluated. It is as if we hear the writer saying: "I speak to you in the language of universal reason, but my rhetoric shows that this language is nothing but a hollow shell. You, dear reader, must choose whether you want to join ranks with the imperialists and measure my statements on the scale of universal reason, or if you want to join the forces of liberation and accept the formal encapsulation of incommensurability as a performance of universal reason's impossibility." Clearly, this choice balances on the fence dividing universal reason from embodied and local forms of reason, and clearly the antinomy it marks cannot be resolved by displacing the burden of responsibility onto the reader. The problem lies with the simple projection of the antinomy of universal reason onto the opposition to or support of imperialism. Of course, you can speak against imperialism in the language of universal reason just as effectively as you can in the language of conceptual particularity. The point is, as Chakrabarthy points out, it's not a matter of choosing one discursive register over the other, but one of articulating the two together.

So what is to be done?

What is interesting and instructive methodologically in Herder is how and at what moments in his argument he tries and fails to come to terms with the antinomy of universal reason. At these moments he invariably takes recourse to poetic language to mark the limits not only of rationalist discourse, but also to radicalize the methodology that in his day seems most promising in challenging rationalism: the dialogical and dialectical structure of argument.

Throughout his works, Herder uses the dialogical structure of argument to confront the antinomy of universal reason. This was a common device at the time, and its intention was to display the close connection between what could be said about a matter and who was speaking.[47] Presiding over dialogue for Herder is the death of Socrates.[48] With the voice gone that will guide the interlocutors on the path to truth, truth becomes an absent position to which all the others point. Instead of rolling out homogenizing or hegemonic discourses of truth, Herder proposes allegorizing dialogues. Dialogue cannot offer truth, since "the provision of nature is poetically and intellectually inexhaustible."[49] But it can provide insight into how various inclinations towards truth fail to reach it, and in failing, indicate what truth might and might not be.

Herder's dialectics emerge from his dialogics. If there is a way to think the relationship between an utterance and its truth value in dialogue, it is in the discrepancy between different dialogical positions. What emerges in Herder's dialectic is that the discrepancy between truth and its representation is not only due to the limitations in individual cognition; it resides objectively in the human condition itself, as it resides in social arrangements and in the nature of things.[50] The methodological emphasis on the dialectic arose from the centrality of historical development and of representation in Herder's thought. This establishes the crucial role of the historian in matters of philosophy. As a historian, Herder is caught up in the dilemma of wanting to reawaken things whose vitality is suspended in writing.[51] Writing, like conversation, bears within itself the structural markings of its own distance from truth. As a result, Herder's relationship to writing is driven by the promise that the discrepancy between written statements and truth can be investigated historically. The ensuing historical dialectic leads to a search for origins, a historical negation of the negation of truth in writing, or a determinate negation of the sign. What Herder's historical dialectic will uncover is not the lost truth of the Golden Age, not even the fact that it is lost; it will discover the way writing preserves the marks of its own genesis, and how the diversity of concepts is both preserved and concealed in writing.

In general, postcolonial theory has had a nuanced relationship to the dialectic, and one of its covert struggles has involved addressing the problems in dialectical method pointed out by Foucault, Derrida, and others. In its more sophisticated moments, postcolonial theory articulates well its subtle debt to dialectical method. Spivak is probably the most careful thinker of the dialectic in the postcolonial context, and her comments on the dialectic in "Scattered Speculations on the Question of Value" (1985) still deserve careful consideration.[52] Here, it is understood that the challenge is how to come to terms with the question of whether difference is situated in the discourses (and disciplines) that formulate it, or in the human condition itself, or in the relationship between the two. This is, in many respects, Herder's question, and to recognize it as such is to take a step towards understanding the conceptual universe out of which postcolonial theory arose. The methodological and rhetorical strategies he developed represent a serious attempt to forestall the complicity of reason and exploitation against which postcolonial theory has set itself. Herder's methodology provides an example of how aesthetics and rhetoric can be solicited in this process. But in his writings we also see the shortcomings of his method. I believe an engagement with his writings can help bring conceptual clarity to a set of problems which are urgent today and which Herder witnessed in the making.

Notes

Introduction

1 I have written on this subject in John K. Noyes, "The World Map and the World of Goethe's *Weltliteratur*," *Acta Germanica* 38 (2010): 128–45; "Goethe on Cosmopolitanism and Colonialism: Bildung and the Dialectic of Critical Mobility," *Eighteenth-Century Studies* 39/4 (2006): 443–65; and "Commerce, Colonialism, and the Globalization of Action in Late Enlightenment Germany," *Postcolonial Studies* 9/1 (2006): 81–98. See also Karl S. Guthke, *Goethes Weimar und "Die große Öffnung in die weite Welt,"* Wolfenbütteler Forschungen 93 (Wiesbaden: Harrassowitz, 2001); Karl S. Guthke, *Die Erfindung der Welt: Globalität und Grenzen in der Kulturgeschichte der Literatur* (Tübingen: Francke, 2005); Michael Jaeger, *Fausts Kolonie: Goethes kritische Phänomenologie der Moderne* (Würzburg: Königshausen und Neumann, 2004); and Susanne Zantop, *Colonial Fantasies: Conquest, Family, and Nation in Precolonial Germany, 1770–1870* (Durham and London: Duke University Press, 1997).

2 Dimas Figueroa, *Philosophie und Globalisierung* (Würzburg: Königshausen und Neumann, 2004), 10.

3 See A.G. Hopkins, *Globalization in World History* (New York: Norton, 2002); A.G. Hopkins, *Global History: Interactions between the Universal and the Local* (New York: Palgrave-Macmillan, 2006); Jürgen Osterhammel and Niels P. Petersson, *Globalization: A Short History* (Princeton: Princeton University Press, 2005); and Figueroa, *Philosophie und Globalisierung*, 13–14.

4 Immanuel Wallerstein, *The Modern World System III: The Second Era of Great Expansion of the Capitalist World Economy 1730–1840's* (San Diego, London: Academic Press, 1989).

5 Reinhard Koselleck, *Critique and Crisis: Enlightenment and the Pathogenesis of Modern Society* (Oxford: Berg, 1988), 6, translation modified ("Ihr Aktionsfeld war die eine Welt des Globus").

6 For an excellent discussion of how world trade and imperialism were assimilated in current legal and political debates see Istvan Hont, *Jealousy of Trade: International Competition and the Nation-State in Historical Perspective* (Cambridge, MA: Belknap Press, 2005), introduction.

7 Ibid., chapter 7.

8 See the excellent outline of Herder's relativism in relation to his universalism in Sonia Sikka, *Herder on Humanity and Cultural Difference: Enlightened Relativism* (Cambridge: Cambridge University Press, 2011), chapter 1.

9 Robert Norton, *Herder's Aesthetics and the European Enlightenment* (Ithaca and London: Cornell University Press, 1991), 5.

10 See "Abbreviated Titles" list at beginning of Bibliography for abbreviations.

11 Emphasis in citations from Herder's works are in the original. Herder makes frequent use of textual emphasis in his writings, shown in the print versions using print letter spacing. I have placed these sections in italics.

12 Christopher A. Bayly, "The First Age of Global Imperialism c. 1760–1830," *Journal of Imperial and Commonwealth History* 26/2 (1998). Bayly notes that "imperialism – territorial expansion within and outside Europe – was centrally driven by the scissors effect which rising military expenditure and stagnant or falling cash revenues put on all the larger regimes, European and non-European. Imperatives of military finance had driven states to strengthen internal control and to projects of external conquest throughout history. But these forces now worked with a global reach and they were reinforced by ways of deploying men, knowledge, and control over physical resources. This speeding up of quantitative changes became, in the later eighteenth century, the forcing house of qualitative change" (32).

13 Barbara Bush, *Imperialism and Postcolonialism* (Harlow, UK: Pearson Longman, 2006), 1–2.

14 Gayatri Chakravorty Spivak, *A Critique of Postcolonial Reason: Toward a History of the Vanishing Present* (Cambridge: Harvard University Press, 1999), 3.

15 V.G. Kiernan, *Imperialism and Its Contradictions*, ed. Harvey J. Kaye (New York: Routledge, 1995), 46.

16 Herder, note 245 to the 116th of the *Letters on the Advancement of Humanity* (*HPW* 396–7).

17 This is in keeping with d'Alembert's observation that the study of human diversity is facilitated by the study of empires. "One of the principal rewards of the study of empires and their revolutions lies in the examination of how men, having been separated into various great families, so to speak, have formed diverse societies, how these different societies have given birth to different types of governments, and how they have tried to distinguish themselves both by the laws that they have given themselves and by the particular signs that each has created in order that its members might communicate more easily with one another." Jean Le Rond d'Alembert, "Preliminary Discourse," *The Encyclopedia of Diderot & d'Alembert Collaborative Translation Project*, trans. Richard N. Schwab and Walter E. Rex (Ann Arbor: Michigan Publishing, University of Michigan Library, 2009), at http://quod.lib.umich.edu/d/did/did2222.0001.083?view=text;rgn=main.

18 Isaiah Berlin, *Vico and Herder* (London: The Hogarth Press, 1976), 164, 160.

19 Isaiah Berlin, "Herder and the Enlightenment," in *The Proper Study of Mankind: An Anthology of Essays*, ed. Henry Hardy and Roger Hausheer (London: Chatto and Windus, 1997), 373.

20 F.M. Barnard, *Herder on Nationality, Humanity and History* (Montreal: McGill-Queen's University Press, 2003), 5.

21 Ingeborg H. Solbrig, "American Slavery in Eighteenth-Century German Literature: The Case of Herder's 'Neger-Idyllen,'" *Monatshefte* 82/1 (1990): 40. I believe, for reasons that will become apparent, that it is misleading to speak of Herder's anti-colonialism.

22 John Tomlinson, *Cultural Imperialism: A Critical Introduction* (London: Continuum, 1991), 5–6.

23 Tod Kontje, *German Orientalisms* (Ann Arbor: University of Michigan Press, 2004), 74.

24 Michael L. Frazer, *The Enlightenment of Sympathy: Justice and the Moral Sentiments in the Eighteenth Century and Today* (Oxford: Oxford University Press, 2010), 148.

25 Sankar Muthu, *Enlightenment against Empire* (Princeton: Princeton University Press, 2003), 121.

26 Ibid., 278, 212.

27 Samson B. Knoll, "Beyond the Black Legend: The Anticolonialism of Johann Gottfried Herder," *North Dakota Quarterly* 57/3 (1989): 57.

28 Ibid., 58.

29 Ibid., 61–2.

30 Vicki A. Spencer, *Herder's Political Thought: A Study on Language, Culture, and Community* (Toronto: University of Toronto Press, 2012),17, 153.

31 Ibid., 145.
32 Ibid., 216.
33 Nicholas Robinette, "The World Laid Waste: Herder, Language Labor, Empire," *New Literary History* 42 (2011): 193. Robinette's otherwise excellent article is flawed by his reading of Herder's later works as a conservative slide into romanticization of the native (194), and by his attempts to distinguish a radical semiotician in the early works from an increasingly reactionary anthropologist in the later ones.
34 Ibid., 198–9.
35 Ibid., 198.
36 Sikka, *Herder on Humanity*, 99–100.
37 Ibid., 15.
38 See ibid., 18.
39 Ibid., 21.
40 Ibid., 85.
41 Ibid., 259.
42 Ibid., 4–5.
43 Daniel Carey and Lynn Festa, eds., *Postcolonial Enlightenment* (Oxford: Oxford University Press, 2009), 8.
44 See the excellent introduction to Carey and Festa, *Postcolonial Enlightenment*.
45 Carey and Festa compare Enlightenment to Postcolonialism in this regard: they share "a kinship to the extent that both simultaneously describe a period, a kind of political order, a cluster of ideas, a theoretical purchase point, and a mode of thinking." *Postcolonial Enlightenment*, 7.
46 This is spelled out in the introduction to Muthu, *Enlightenment against Empire*. See also Graeme Garrard, *Counter-Enlightenments: From the Eighteenth Century to the Present* (London: Routledge, 2006).
47 Dipesh Chakrabarty, *Provincializing Europe: Postcolonial Thought and Historical Difference* (Princeton: Princeton University Press, 2000), 4.
48 Spivak, *A Critique of Postcolonial Reason*, 3–4.
49 Pheng Cheah, *Spectral Nationality: Passages of Freedom from Kant to Postcolonial Studies* (New York: Columbia University Press, 2003), 2.
50 Ibid., 2.
51 Sikka, *Herder on Humanity*, 58.
52 "His metaphysics involves an attempted synthesis of Spinoza and Leibniz, combining the former's thesis that nature (or God) is a single substance with the latter's conception of reality as composed of dynamic centers of self-organizing activity." Sikka, *Herder on Humanity*, 56.
53 Cheah, *Spectral Nationality*, 40.

54 Ibid., 7.
55 Ibid., 39.
56 Ibid., 8.
57 See the excellent discussion in Sikka, *Herder on Humanity*, 211–18.
58 Spencer, *Herder's Political Thought*, 166, 176.
59 Theodor W. Adorno and Max Horkheimer, *Dialectic of Enlightenment*, trans. John Cumming (London: Verso, 1979).
60 Donna Haraway, "A Cyborg Manifesto: Science, Technology, and Socialist-Feminism in the Late Twentieth Century," in *Simians, Cyborgs and Women: The Reinvention of Nature* (New York: Routledge, 1991), 153.
61 Ibid., 157.
62 This is argued by Gayatri Spivak in "Can the Subaltern Speak?" in *Marxism and the Interpretation of Culture*, ed. Cary Nelson and Lawrence Grossberg (London: MacMillan, 1988), 271–313.
63 Sumit Sarkar, "Orientalism Revisited: Saidian Frameworks in the Writing of Modern Indian History," *Oxford Literary Review* 16/1 (1994): 205–24.

1. From Epistemology to Aesthetics

1 Herder writes in an opaque prose, giving the impression that the word *Versuch* is to be read in the sense of an experiment, not just an essay.
2 In his biography of Herder, Rudolf Haym reads this essay as a recapitulation of some premises that Kant was putting forward in his lectures around the time Herder was studying in Königsberg. Rudolf Haym, *Herder nach seinem Leben und seinen Werken*, vol. 1 (Berlin: Rudolph Gaertner, 1880), 44. Haym mentions Herder's rejection of the Lockean position on Being and knowledge, as well as that of Descartes, Crusius, Wolff, and Baumgarten. All of these philosophers were discussed in Kant's lectures on metaphysics. Adler believes that Herder's essay is in the first instance a commentary on Kant's lectures on Metaphysics, a point which he supports by referring to Herder's extensive notes on the lectures. He speaks of "Kant's critical presentation of rationalist metaphysics, seen through Herder's prism." Hans Adler, *Die Prägnanz des Dunklen: Gnoseologie, Ästhetik, Geschichtsphilosophie bei Johann Gottfried Herder* (Hamburg: Meiner, 1990), 52. Adler refers to the lasting bias introduced by Haym's Kantian tilt, whereby Herder has been continually burdened with the label of an unphilosophical thinker, or simply a derivative of Kant. *Die Prägnanz des Dunklen*, 51. In *Kant, Herder, and the Birth of Anthropology* (Chicago: University of Chicago Press, 2002, 410n78), John Zammito repeats the opinion of Marion Heinz, that Herder

is attempting to establish his own philosophical status by engaging critically with the core ideas of his teacher; *Sensualitischer Idealismus: Untersuchungen zur Erkenntnistheorie des jungen Herder* (Hamburg: Meiner, 1994), 1. More recent readings suggest a more striking originality in the essay. For example, Heinz herself, writing with Heinrich Clairmont, speaks of Herder's stance against Kant's claim that philosophy could be a demonstrative science ("Herder's Epistemology," in *A Companion to the Works of Johann Gottfried Herder*, ed. Hans Adler and Wulf Koepke [Rochester: Camden House, 2009], 46). Ulrich Gaier describes the project in the essay as a "transcendental philosophy of sensory, existential experience," and places this in direct opposition to Kant (*Herders Sprachphilosophie und Erkenntniskritik* [Stuttgart-Cannstatt: frommann-holzboog, 1988], 35); and in his notes to the critical edition, Gaier claims that Herder is anticipating Kant's own position on the proof of the existence of God which he later takes in the critical writings (*HFA* 1, 845).

3 "For this reason, Descartes was wrong when he stated: I think therefore I am. So was Crusius when he stated: I am conscious of myself, therefore I am. Both deduced existential being from ideal being " (*HMA* 1, 587).

4 In *Träume eines Geistersehers* (Dreams of a Spirit-Seer, 1766), he puts it like this: "The second advantage of metaphysics is more consonant with the nature of the human understanding. It consists both in knowing whether the task has been determined by reference to what one can know, and in knowing what relation the question has to the empirical concepts, upon which all our judgements must at all times be based. To that extent, metaphysics is a science of the *limits of human reason*. A small country always has a long frontier; it is hence, in general, more important for it to be thoroughly acquainted with its possessions, and to secure its power over them, than blindly to launch on campaigns of conquest. Thus, the second advantage of metaphysics is at once the least known and the most important, although it is also an advantage which is only attained at a fairly late stage and after long experience." Immanuel Kant, *Theoretical Philosophy 1755–1770*, trans. and ed. David Walford and Ralf Meerbote (Cambridge: Cambridge University Press, 1992), 354.

5 Norton has shown how the problem of method arose out of the debates around empiricism in the eighteenth century in *Herder's Aesthetics*, chapter 1.

6 He stated this clearly in his "Prize Essay" of 1763, *Untersuchungen über die Deutlichkeit der Grundsätze der natürlichen Theologie und der Moral* (Inquiry Concerning the Distinctness of Natural Theology and Morality), the first paragraph of which bears the title "Mathematics arrives at all its

definitions synthetically, while philosophy arrives at them analytically" (Kant, *Theoretical Philosophy 1755–1770,* 248). This is repeated in "M. Immanuel Kant's Announcement of the Programme of His Lectures for the Winter Semester 1765–1766," in which he notes that the science of metaphysics "remains so imperfect and uncertain, in spite of the great efforts of scholars, because its unique method has not been recognized, that is to say that it is not synthetic, as that of mathematics, but analytic" (ibid., 299).

7 Zammito, *Kant, Herder, and the Birth of Anthropology,* 150.

8 Willem de Jong, "How Is Metaphysics as a Science Possible? Kant on the Distinction between Philosophical and Mathematical Method," *Review of Metaphysics* 49/2 (1995): 260–1.

9 Christian Wolff, *Vernünftige Gedanken von Gott, der Welt und der Seele der Menschen, auch alle Dingen überhaupt* (Frankfurt and Leipzig: Rengerische Buchhandlung, 1738), para. 10, p. 6

10 See Heinz and Clairmont, "Herder's Epistemology," 44.

11 Gaier, *HFA* 1, 858.

12 See Kant, *Untersuchung über die Deutlichkeit der Grundsätze der natürlichen Theologie und der Moral* (Inquiry concerning the Distinctness of the Principles of Natural Theology and Morality, 1764): "And Crusius is also right to criticise other schools of philosophy for ignoring these material principles and adhering merely to formal principles. For on their basis alone it really is not possible to prove anything at all. Propositions are needed which contain the intermediate concept by means of which the logical relation of the other concepts to each other can be known in a syllogism. And among these propositions there must be some which are the first. But it is not possible to invest some propositions with the status of supreme material principles unless they are obvious to every human understanding." Kant, *Theoretical Philosophy 1755–1770,* 268–9.

13 See Zammito, *Kant, Herder, and the Birth of Anthropology,* 151.

14 "Once it is appreciated that the whole of our cognition ultimately resolves itself into unanalysable concepts, it will also be understood that there will be some concepts which are almost unanalysable; in other words, there will be some concepts where the characteristic marks are only to a very small degree clearer and simpler than the thing itself. Such is the case with our definition of existence." Kant, *Theoretical Philosophy 1755–1770,* 119.

15 See Heinz and Clairmont, "Herder's Epistemology," 45.

16 Zammito discusses the problems in Herder's easy association between "the *givenness of the real,* as Kant developed in his lectures" and the idea

that Being as the most sensory (or given) of concepts provides certainty. Zammito sees Herder sidestepping "the problematic question about the reality of a congeries of givens" in order to espouse "the determinate ontological notion of a simple, unitary reality (being)"; *Kant, Herder, and the Birth of Anthropology*, 152. I think that Herder would come to realize in the following decades that he needed the concept of a simple unitary being in order to pursue the congeries of givens, for this is the direction that his studies will take him in the 1770s.

17 F.M. Barnard, *Herder's Social and Political Thought: From Enlightenment to Nationalism* (Oxford: Clarendon Press, 1965), 40.

18 Sikka, *Herder on Humanity*, 204.

19 See Norton, *Herder's Aesthetics*, 33.

20 See Adler's excellent survey of Baumgarten's project in *Die Prägnanz des Dunklen*, chap. 1. Heinz and Clairmont call his *Metaphysica* "the most advanced position of rationalistic gnoseology, where the marginal area of 'confused cognition' is circumscribed as an independent complex that was later developed by Baumgarten in his *Aesthetica* into a systematic complement of distinct cognition." "Herder's Epistemology," 43.

21 Herder accuses him of *petitio principii*, and of abandoning the method proper to philosophy (*HMA* 1, 580), and he declares Baumgarten in error when he understands Being on the basis of a logical concept of nothingness (*HMA* 1, 583).

22 See Norton's discussion of the context of Baumgarten's ideas and their importance for Herder in *Herder's Aesthetics*, chapter 1.

23 See Norton, 33.

24 Zammito, *Kant, Herder, and the Birth of Anthropology*, 157.

25 See Gaier, "Myth, Mythology, New Mythology," in Adler and Koepke, *Companion to the Works of Johann Gottfried Herder*, 174–5.

26 See Robert Sommer, *Grundzüge einer Geschichte der deutschen Psychologie und Aesthetik von Wolff-Baumgarten bis Kant-Schiller* (Amsterdam: E.J. Bonnet, 1966), 89–90.

27 Adler, *Die Prägnanz des Dunklen*, 49.

28 Gaier, *Herders Sprachphilosophie und Erkenntniskritik*, 35.

29 Wolfgang Pross, "Anhang," in *HMA* 2, 871.

30 In this sense, the *Fourth Critical Grove* can be read as a continuation of his critical studies of Baumgarten. See Gaier, *Herders Sprachphilosophie*, 70.

31 Friedrich Justus Riedel, *Theorie der schönen Künste und Wissenschaften. Ein Auszug aus den Werken verschiedener Schriftsteller* (Jena: Cuno, 1767), 7, cited in Herder, *HFA* 2, 250.

32 This begs a question that will later be explored by Goethe: given the ability of individuals and cultures to express a particular manifestation of ideal beauty, and thus to derive an understanding of the ideal itself, is it possible to find forms that express the ideal, not in its particularity, but as an essential form? See Richards, *The Romantic Conception of Life*, 395–6.
33 Leibniz and Wolff ascribed to animals lower orders of cognition, which they share with humans, such as memory, anticipation, association, etc. These orders function as *analoga rationis*, in that they are able to link separate facts of cognition without understanding the causes. See Leibniz, *Monadology*, para. 26, 28 and *Theodicy*, Preliminary Dissertation, para. 65; and Wolff, *Psychologia empirica*, para. 506, *Philosophia rationalis*, para. 766, and *Vernünfige Gedanken*, 1, para. 872.
34 Sommer shows the importance of contemporary work on animal psychology for Herder's understanding of the organic nature of sensation. See his chapter on Reimarus in *Grundzüge einer Geschichte der deutschen Psychologie und Aesthetik*, 89–136.
35 See Heinz and Clairmont, "Herder's Epistemology," 49–50.
36 Ibid., 46–7.
37 Baumgarten's disregard for this distinction caused him to believe that aesthetics could be, as he wrote in the first paragraph of *Aesthetica*, not only a theory of art but also an epistemology of lower cognition, the art of reasoning by analogy, and the art of beautiful thinking. Later, in the *Fourth Critical Grove*, Herder will expand on this criticism of Baumgarten, *HFA* 2, 267–8.
38 Herder's critique of Baumgarten will be sharpened by Kant in his *Critique of Pure Reason*, where he points out that Baumgarten's fundamental flaw was to confuse judgments of cognition with those of taste. "The Germans are the only ones who now employ the word 'aesthetics' to designate what others call the critique of taste. The ground for this is a failed hope, held by the excellent analyst Baumgarten, of bringing the critical estimation of the beautiful under principles of reason, and elevating its rules to a science. But this effort is futile." Kant, *Critique of Pure Reason*, ed. and trans. Paul Guyer and Allen Wood (Cambridge: Cambridge University Press, 2000), 173.
39 Zammito, *Kant, Herder, and the Birth of Anthropology*, 157–8.
40 See Norton, *Herder's Aesthetics*, chap. 1.
41 See Pross, *HMA* 1, 845.
42 Norton, *Herder's Aesthetics*, 235.
43 This is how I interpret his note: "Geschichte der Menschheit nicht der Menschen (Politik. Geschichte. Bruchstücke)" (History of humanity, not of humans – Politics, History, Fragments); *HFA* 1, 131.

44 Kant followed Crusius in holding that if something exists it is bound in time and space (Zammito, *Kant, Herder, and the Birth of Anthropology*, 151–2).
45 Robert T. Clark, "Herder's Conception of 'Kraft,'" *PMLA* 57/3 (1942): 737.
46 See the excellent discussion in Clark, "Herder's Conception of 'Kraft'"; also Norton, *Herder's Aesthetics*, 141–53.
47 Sommer, *Grundzüge einer Geschichte der deutschen Psychologie und Aestehtik*, 90.
48 Jeffrey Edwards, *Substance, Force, and the Possibility of Knowledge: On Kant's Philosophy of Material Nature* (Berkeley: University of California Press, 2000), 67.
49 Ibid., 67–8.
50 Norton, *Herder's Aesthetics*, 142–3.
51 Sommer, *Grundzüge einer Geschichte der deutschen Psychologie und Aestehtik*, 104.
52 Clark, "Herder's Conception of 'Kraft,'" 740.
53 For this reason Sommer claims that "Reimarus provides the connection between Leibniz's world view and Herder's view of nature," *Grundzüge einer Geschichte der deutschen Psychologie und Aestehtik*, 96.
54 Ibid., 98.
55 Ibid., 107.
56 Robert T. Clark, *Herder: His Life and Thought* (Berkeley and Los Angeles: University of California Press, 1955), 97.
57 Ibid., 97–8.
58 Sikka, *Herder on Humanity*, 57. The citation refers to *HFA* 6, 636.
59 Cited in Martin Kessler, "Herder's Theology," in Adler and Koepke, *Companion to the Works of Johann Gottfried Herder*, 252. As Kessler notes, the coupling of goodness and wisdom with the organic forces of creation is Herder's way of paraphrasing "God" (251).
60 Around the time Herder arrived in Königsberg, Kant's announcements of his forthcoming classes almost always included physical geography. Some of Herder's handwritten notes on Kant's geography lectures are to be found in the Berlin Akademie Archiv under AA-Kant: 29 0069–71 NL.-Kant Nr. 15; NL.-Adickes U 4; and also in Berlin, Staatsbibliothek Preußischer Kulturbesitz, Haus II: NL.-Herder: XXV, 44; XXV, 44a. Looking back on his career shortly before his death in 1800, Kant observes that over the course of thirty years he had been careful to include courses on both anthropology and physical geography in his duties as a teacher of philosophy. He is explicit in stating that these two disciplines complement one another in imparting "Weltkenntniß"

(knowledge of the world). Kant, *Anthropology from a Pragmatic Point of View*, ed. Robert B. Louden, (Cambridge: Cambridge University Press, 2006), note to page 6.

61 See John Headley, *The Europeanization of the World: On the Origins of Human Rights and Democracy* (Princeton: Princeton University Press, 2008), 113–16.

62 This is the position of J.A. May in *Kant's Concept of Geography and Its Relation to Recent Geographical Thought* (Toronto: University of Toronto Press, 1970); see esp. p. 113.

63 In the report on the plan of his lectures for the winter semester 1765–6, the year after Herder left Königsberg, Kant suggests a threefold conception of the discipline that would include "physical, moral and political geography." The basis of this threefold geography is "the natural relationship which holds between all the countries and seas of the world," as well as the basis of their interconnection. Kant calls this basis "the real foundation of all history," without which "history is scarcely distinguishable from fairy tales." The second step is to investigate "humanity according to the variety of its natural properties," with the aim of acquiring "a comprehensive map of the human species." Finally, the interaction of these two aspects allows a study of "the condition of the *states* and nations throughout the world." Kant, "M. Immanuel Kant's Announcement," in Kant, *Theoretical Philosophy 1755–1770*, 299. By the mid-1770s he is referring to geography as "the preliminary exercise in the *knowledge of the world*," and it lends a pragmatic aspect to all other forms of knowledge and skills. Kant, "Of the Different Races of Human Beings," in Immanuel Kant, *Anthropology, History and Education*, ed. Günter Zöller and Robert Louden (Cambridge: Cambridge University Press, 2007), 97.

64 Karl Menges, "Identity as Difference: Herder's 'Great Topic' and the 'Philosophers of Paris,'" *Monatshefte* 87/1 (1995): 8.

65 Stefan Greif, "Herder's Aesthetics and Poetics," in Adler and Koepke, *Companion to the Works of Johann Gottfried Herder*, 143. See also Menges, "Particular Universals," 193.

66 See the tabular representation of this in Norton, *Herder's Aesthetics*, 201.

67 Zammito, *Kant, Herder, and the Birth of Anthropology*, 160.

68 Ibid.

69 I am following Gaier in understanding the word *Volk* as "a new mythic category" referring to "original mankind, which receives inspiration through its nature and anthropological essence"; Gaier, "Myth, Mythology, New Mythology," in Adler and Koepke, *Companion to the Works of Johann Gottfried Herder*, 170.

70 Elias Palti, "The 'Metaphor of Life': Herder's Philosophy of History and Uneven Developments," *Eighteenth-Century Natural Sciences* 38/3 (1999), 322–47.

71 Marion Heinz, *Sensualistischer Idealismus: Untersuchungen zur Erkenntnistheorie des jungen Herder (1763–1778)* (Hamburg: Meiner, 1994).

72 Heinz and Clairmont, "Herder's Epistemology," 49.

73 Ibid., 49–50.

74 Ibid., 52.

75 See ibid. Gaier speaks of Herder's "brand-new systems theory of cognition"; "The Problem of Core Cognition in Herder," *Monatshefte* 95/2 (2003): 295. See also Ulrich Gaier, "Herders Systemtheorie," *Allgemeine Zeitschrift für Philosophie* 23/1 (1998): 3–17.

76 "Über die Bildung einer Sprache," in *Über die neuere deutsche Literatur, Fragmente, Werke*, vol. 1, ed. Wolfgang Pross (Munich: Hanser, 1984), 154.

77 Norton, *Herder's Aesthetics*, 40.

78 In 1765, Herder will draw on Blackwell's studies of Homer as evidence of the fact that "in everyday life, poetry is older than prose. This is also the reason why the first writers were poets, the first νόμοι were songs, and the oldest religions were mythologies, all of which spoke the sensory language of the people" (*HFA* 1, 133). Thomas Blackwell, *An Enquiry into the Life and Writings of Homer* (London: n.p., 1735).

79 See Michael Morton, *Herder and the Poetics of Thought* (University Park and London: Pennsylvania State University Press, 1989), 8. I follow Morton in using the Suphan edition of Herder's essay, which is the version he published in the *Gelehrte Beiträge* (*HSW* 1, 1–7), and I cite Menze's translation in *HEW*, which also follows the Suphan edition.

80 Gaier, *HFA* 1, 870. See also Herder's comments in *Journal meiner Reise* (*HSW* 4, 388ff.).

81 In *Herder and the Poetics of Thought*, Morton doesn't mention *Versuch*, but he uncovers a wealth of themes that relate directly to that study, themes which Herder will continue to develop in the following decades. Morton argues for the germinal nature of Herder's *On Diligence*. But in failing to link *On Diligence* to *On Being*, he misses its position in the development of Herder's studies in history out of his epistemology. Pross makes a similar move when, in volume 1 of *HMA*, he decides to place *On Being* directly before *This Too a Philosophy*. The latter work is, he claims, the most immediate realization of the principle of evidence postulated in *On Being* (*HMA* 1, 845). This is probably correct, but *On Diligence* needs to be read as an important intermediate statement between Herder's two essays.

82 See the discussion in Katie Terzakis, *The Immanent Word: The Turn to Language in German Philosophy, 1759–1801* (New York and London: Routledge, 2007), chap. 1. Spencer claims that scholars have overestimated Hamann's influence on Herder. *Herder's Political Thought*, 62.
83 Hamann, *Aesthetica in nuce*, in *Classic and Romantic German Aesthetics*, ed. J.M. Bernstein (Cambridge: Cambridge University Press, 2003), 12.
84 Terzakis, *The Immanent Word*, 40.
85 Hamann, *Aesthetica in nuce*, 2.
86 Ibid., 3, translation modified.
87 Ibid., translation modified.
88 "Speak, that I may see Thee! This wish was answered by the Creation, which is an utterance to created beings through created beings (*an die Kreatur durch die Kreatur*), for day speaketh unto day, and night proclaimeth unto night. Its word traverses every clime to the ends of the earth, and its voice can be heard in every dialect." Hamann, *Aesthetica in nuce*, 4; translation modified.
89 Ibid., 16.
90 Ibid., 2.
91 Ibid., 12, translation modified.
92 See Gaier's comments in *HFA* 1, 987.
93 As Norton points out, this is the same sentiment Herder had expressed in *On Being* when he alluded to Hamann as one of those "few fine minds who perceived the end of philosophy and the endless efforts of the philosophers" and who respond by reviling philosophy, instead of demonstrating, as Herder was attempting to do, how the task of philosophy emerges out of "the impossibility of analyzing the concept [of Being]" (*HFA* 1, 13). *Herder's Aesthetics*, 67.
94 "We contemporaries of the templates for letters concerning recent literature are all the happy ones privileged to be schooled by taste, which becomes a mathematical teacher of the aesthetic average, building in the playful caprice of its declamations and of the most recent literature on foundations which no eye has seen and no ear heard"; Hamann, *Hamburgische Nachricht aus dem Reiche der Gelehrsamkeit. Nach dem ein und sechzigsten Stücke des Jahres 1762*, in Johann Georg Hamann, *Hamann's Schriften*, 8 vols., ed. Friedrich von Roth (Berlin: Reimer, 1821), 2: 492–3.
95 Gaier notes that Diderot made the same observation in *Lettre sur les aveugles, à l'usage de ceux qui voient* (Letter on the Blind, for the Use of Those Who Can See, 1749).

96 This is the famous problem of synthetic judgment a priori which Kant will tackle in *Critique of Pure Reason*, and which Herder will address in his *Metakritik zur Kritik der reinen Vernunft* (Metacritique of the Critique of Pure Reason, 1799).
97 This is the "actual relationship between poetic and discursive language" of which Morton speaks; *Herder and the Poetics of Thought*, 12.
98 Ibid., 30.
99 See the comments by Menze and Menges in *HEW* 238–9.
100 See Helmuth Kiesel, "Das nationale Klima. Zur Entwicklung und Bedeutung eines ethnographischen Topos von der Renaissance bis zur Aufklärung," in *Rom – Paris – London: Erfahrung und Selbsterfahrung deutscher Schriftsteller und Künstler un den fremden Metropolen. Ein Symposion*, ed. Conrad Wiedemann (Stuttgart: Metzler, 1988), 123–34; and Jan Golinski, *British Weather and the Climate of Enlightenment* (Chicago: University of Chicago Press, 2007), chap. 6.
101 Gaier, "Core Cognition," 303.
102 In 1755 Kant had published his *Allgemeine Naturgeschichte und Theorie des Himmels* (Universal Natural History and Theory of the Heavens), in which he argues the unity of diverse phenomena on a cosmic scale. In his reading of this idea, Herder emphasized the notion of a *Kette der Wesen* (chain of beings, *HSW* 4, 381), which would later form the basis for his inquiries into the geographical distribution of diversity across a world characterized by human unity.
103 Russell Arben Fox, "J. G. Herder on Language and the Metaphysics of National Community," *Review of Politics* 65/2 (2003): 247.
104 Morton, *Herder and the Poetics of Thought*, 36.
105 See ibid., 42.
106 See Fox, "Herder on Language."
107 In the first collection of the *Fragments*, Herder continually returns to the inadequacy of translation in conveying the nuances of the original. See *Fragments* 8–10 (*HEW* 118–28).
108 Herder repeats this in the first collection of *Fragments*: "Our nursemaids, who train (*bilden*) our tongues are our first teachers of logic" (*HEW* 102).

2. From Organic Life

1 Heinz and Clairmont, "Herder's Epistemology," 47–8.
2 Ibid., 49.
3 Kelly Barry, "Natural Palingenesis: Childhood, Memory, and Self-Experience in Herder and Jean Paul," *Goethe Yearbook* 14 (2006): 1–25.
4 Morton, *Herder and the Poetics of Thought*, 36.

5 It is not certain whether Herder used this term or not. It is attributed to him by Friedrich Wilhelm Kantzenbach in *Johann Gottfried Herder* (Reinbek bei Harnburg: Rohwohlt, 1970), 27.

6 See Hans Adler, "Herder's Concept of Humanität," in Adler and Koepke, *Companion to the Works of Johann Gottfried Herder*, 99.

7 Johann Gottfried Herder, "On Recent German Literature: Fragments," in *Selected Early Works, 1764–1767: Addresses, Essays, and Drafts; Fragments on Recent German Literature*, ed. Ernest A. Menze and Karl Menges, trans. Ernest A. Menze with Michael Palma (University Park: Pennsylvania State University Press, 1992), 85–233.

8 As Menges notes, "The occasion for the writing of the *Literaturbriefe* was the Seven Years' War (1756–63) in which a friend of Lessing's, Ewald Christian von Kleist, had been severely wounded." Karl Menges, "Particular Universals: Herder on National Literature, Popular Literature, and World Literature," in Adler and Koepke, *Companion to the Works of Johann Gottfried Herder*, 189. In his introduction of 1759, Lessing explains that the *Letters* are written in response to a request by a friend who was injured in the battle of Zorndorf and wishes to be kept abreast of the latest developments in literature since the beginning of the Seven Years' War. The popular poet Kleist would, on 24 August 1759, succumb to wounds he had received at the battle of Kunersdorf on 12 August. Herder had already cited him in his essay *On Diligence*.

9 In his history of the Seven Years' War (1789), the historian and publisher J.W. von Archenholz describes it as a war that "was fought in all parts of the world"; *Geschichte des Siebenjährigen Krieges in Deutschland* [1789] 12th ed. (Leipzig: Amelang, 1866). It was also the first war in which conflicts over colonial territories were played out on European soil, and the war that set the stage for the "ruin" of the French empire and Britain's domination of international trade, as described by Immanuel Wallerstein in *The Modern World System*, 3: 81–5. And it played a central role in the intellectual formation of some of the major figures of the time. On Lessing and the Seven Years' War see John Whiton, "Tellheim and the Russians: Aspects of Lessing's Response to the Seven Years' War in Minna von Barnhelm," *Lessing-Yearbook/Jahrbuch* 17 (1985): 89–108. Kurt Stavenhagen claims in *Kant und Königsberg* (Göttingen: Deuerlich, 1949) that the war was more important in Kant's development than had been portrayed by Vorländer. For Lessing's importance to Herder see Wulf Köpke, "Herder's Views on the Germans and Their Future Literature," in Adler and Koepke, *Companion to the Works of Johann Gottfried Herder*, 215–32; also Norton, *Herder's Aesthetics*, chap. 4.

10 Morton, *Herder and the Poetics of Thought*, 6
11 His letters around the time of publication refer to the need for a new, unknown author to remain anonymous with his first publication. In a letter to Nicolai (19 February 1767) he writes that readers would find his *Fragments* unbearable if he did not write anonymously. The anonymity of his *Fragments* allows him to send them out into the world, like an explorer or a scout (*Vorläufer*), and he remarks that he will never be able to adopt them as children (*HBG* 1, 70). Nicolai would later criticize anonymity, warning "German youth" against "the foolishness of premature and excessive writing, above all anonymous writing, which brings lies and indigestibility into circulation and renders German sense rare and the paper mills expensive." *Immannuel Kant's Kennzeichen der Philosophie, oder Weisheitsliebe im reinen Sinne des Worts* (Frankfurt and Leipzig: n.p., 1796), 29.
12 See Haym, *Herder*: 1: 214–15.
13 In 1769 he published a declaration in Nicolai's *Allgemeine Deutsche Bibliothek* (General German Library), insisting once again that he was not the author: "We have seen the anonymous publication of *Critical Groves*, commenting on Klotz's works. – Who can have written them? According to Mr Klotz and his followers, none other than I myself, and yet again, I, regardless of the fact that I have long disputed this in public. This provides the opportunity to insult my office, my rank, my lifestyle (*Aufenthalt*), and to expose them to abuse, without concern for honour, the public, and human rights. I protest once again the *Critical Groves*, whose tone I find just as disagreeable as does Mr. Klotz. But I object in the strongest terms before the impartial public to such personal attacks and insults." *Allgemeine Deutsche Bibliothek* 9/2 (1769): 306.
14 Herder relied heavily on the migrations of the Jewish people in his establishment of a model for the proper place, movement, and settlement of a culture (see Barnard, *Herder on Nationality, Humanity and History*).
15 Johann David Michaelis, *Fragen an eine Gesellschaft Gelehrter Männer, die auf Befehl Ihro Majestät des Königes von Dännemark nach Arabien reisen* (Frankfurt/M.: J.G. Garbe, 1762).
16 See the excellent discussion of this expedition in Jonathan M. Hess, *Germans, Jews and the Claims of Modernity* (New Haven and London: Yale University Press, 2002), chap. 2.
17 Michaelis, *Fragen an eine Gesellschaft Gelehrter Männer*, 350ff.
18 Montesquieu, *Persian Letters*, trans. Margaret Mauldon (Oxford: Oxford University Press, 2008).

19 See Gaier, "Myth, Mythology, New Mythology," in Adler and Koepke, *Companion to the Works of Johann Gottfried Herder.*

20 See Jürgen Trabant, "Herder and Language," in Adler and Koepke, *Companion to the Works of Johann Gottfried Herder*, 119–21.

21 Menges, "Particular Universals," 191.

22 In response to the danger of identifying private speech with the passions and public speech with authority, Kant will later (in the essay *What Is Enlightenment?* 1784) demand of private speech (as an expression of the private use of reason) that it conforms to the limitations placed by existing structures of authority on the speaker's profession, while public speech (as public reason) is called on to challenge the limitations coming from authority.

23 This is the position taken by the Swiss philosopher of aesthetics, Johann Jakob Breitinger, whom Herder cites: "As long as a language was the dialect of a sensual people, it remained introspective and imperfect; it was thinking, philosophizing, and the fine arts that brought it to perfection." Johann Jacob Breitinger, *Critische Dichtkunst*, vol. 2 (Zurich: Conrad Orell, 1740), cited in *HFA* 1, 184–5; it is not clear whether Herder's citation is correct or not.

24 Herder laments how, in his popular *Kurzer Begriff aller Wissenschaften und anderer Theile der Gelehrsamkeit* (Brief Compendium of All Sciences and Other Components of Scholarship, 1745), the Swiss philosopher Johann Georg Sulzer proposes a number of reforms aimed at cleansing language of its poetic blemishes for the purpose of a clearer philosophical language. This would involve, among other things, slimming down conceptual language to prevent ambiguity and misunderstanding, promoting syntactic flexibility where necessary for the sake of precision, and so forth. These impulses could be seen as developments of Leibniz's logical calculus, which sought (in *De Arte Combinatorio*, 1666) to relate logical operations to mathematics, thereby legitimating them as a universal scientific language.

25 Gaier, "Myth, Mythology, New Mythology," 169–70.

26 Ibid., 170.

27 Menges, "Particular Universals," 195.

28 Gaier, "Myth, Mythology, New Mythology," 176.

29 "Do We Still Have the Public and Fatherland of Yore?" (*HEW* 53–64). Menze and Menges see in this address not just a rhetorical piece, but "the sketch of a modern social theory" (*HEW* 253).

30 See Harold Mah's discussion of this aspect of Herder's speech in *Enlightenment Phantasies*, 27–30.

31 Menges, "Particular Universals," 199.
32 See the discussion in Dominic Eggel, Andre Liebich, and Deborah Mancini-Griffoli, "Was Herder a Nationalist?" *Review of Politics* 69/1 (2007): 48–78.
33 Menges, "Particular Universals," 199.
34 Barnard, *Herder on Nationality*, 58.
35 In Charles Taylor's view, Herder's great achievement (Taylor speaks of the "Herder revolution") was to clear the way for understanding language as embodied thought, a "stance" that implies "bodily attitudes or actions on or toward objects." Charles Taylor, "The Importance of Herder," in *Philosophical Arguments* (Cambridge, MA: Harvard University Press, 1995). 91–3.
36 Menges, "Particular Universals," 198.
37 The original meaning of the word was *imago*, and this is retained in its eighteenth-century usage. However, it is overlaid with the stronger meaning of process, i.e., form-giving, even poetic production: *poeisis*. Added to this sense of process is then the idea of assisted development and education. To this day, the education authorities in German-speaking countries are called institutions of *Bildung*. Depending on the context, I will be translating the word *Bildung* alternatively as development, self-development, education, formation, self-formation. As Koselleck points out, Shaftesbury's term "self-formation" is probably closest to the discussions around *Bildung* in the eighteenth century. See Reinhard Koselleck, *Begriffsgeschichten* (Frankfurt: Suhrkamp, 2010), 109.
38 The link between the idea of common humanity, globalization, and the emergence of dissent in Western Europe is examined in Headley, *The Europeanization of the World*. See also Koselleck, *Critique and Crisis*.
39 This is described by Garlieb Helwig Merkel in his 1796 volume *Die Letten, vorzüglich in Liefland am Ende des philosophischen Jahrhunderts. Ein Beitrag zur Völker und Menschenkunde* (Leipzig: Gräf, 1796; Wedemark: Hischheydt, 1998), chap. 4.
40 Cited in Haym, *Herder*, 1: 105.
41 See, for example, the short review of the writings of Simon-Nicholas Henri Linguet, "Ueber Herrn Linguet, die Knechtschaft überhaupt, und die Rußische insonderheit" (On Linguet, Servitude in General, and Russian Servitude in Particular), written by State Councillor Müller in Moscau, *Magazin für die neue Historie und Geographie* 18 (1784): 73–82.
42 Garlieb Merkel described in 1796 the atrocities of the German landowner, noting that "hatred, combined with bitter repulsion is the only passionate emotion of which downtrodden spirits are capable. The Latvian expresses

this towards his oppressor in a thousand different ways. In his private language, German means everything that is arrogant, greedy, evil, all that is repulsive." Merkel, *Die Letten*, 25.

43 Menges, "Particular Universals," 205–6.

44 Clark questions this date (the one provided by Haym and Suphan), noting that the essay "bears traces of the Riga period"; *Herder*, 59.

45 "In Herder the problem of the irretrievability of the origins became linked to questions not merely of an epistemological nature, but of a fundamentally ontological one." Palti, "The Metaphor of Life," 328.

46 Ibid.

47 Ibid.

48 Ibid., 324.

49 H.B. Nisbet, *Herder and the Philosophy and History of Science* (Cambridge: Modern Humanities Research Association, 1970), 31.

50 As Wolfgang Pross observes, the fundamental experience of the non-analysability of Being, the non-analysable perception of self, is manifest in the "tendency of humans to use signs in which the conflict between consciousness and the external world is documented" (*HMA* 2, 874).

51 See Pross, ibid.

52 As Hans Adler notes, this obscure idea is the same certainty of Being Herder expounded in the *Essay on Being*, a certainty which is itself constitutive of subjectivity and provides the only truth which the inner sense can immediately grasp. *Die Prägnanz des Dunklen*, 66.

53 The expression is Royal J. Schmidt's; "Cultural Nationalism in Herder," *Journal of the History of Ideas* 17/3 (1956): 407–17.

54 Barnard, *Herder on Nationality*, 149.

55 Ibid.

56 Sikka, *Herder on Humanity*, 245; Richard White also claims that "even though Herder does emphasize the diversity of different cultures and their radical incommensurability with each other, he frequently writes as if each particular culture is largely homogeneous and embodies a single way of life"; "Herder: On the Ethics of Nationalism," *Humanitas* 18 (2005): 176.

57 Spencer, *Herder's Political Thought*, 68.

58 Palti, "The Metaphor of Life," 328.

59 Ibid., 330.

60 François Duchesneau, "Charles Bonnet's Neo-Leibnizian Theory of Organic Bodies," in *The Problem of Animal Generation in Early Modern Philosophy*, ed. Justin E.H. Smith (Cambridge: Cambridge University Press, 2006), 285.

61 C.W. Bodemer, "Regeneration and the Decline of Preformation in Eighteenth-century Embryology," *Bulletin of the History of Medicine* 38 (1964): 23. See also Gould, *Ontogeny and Phylogeny*, 20.
62 Gould, *Ontogeny and Phylogeny*, 22.
63 Epigenetic theory in the 1760s stood in a complex relationship of interdependence with preformationism and vitalism. For an excellent overview, see Shirley Roe, *Matter, Life, and Generation* (Cambridge: Cambridge University Press, 1981).
64 Zammito, *Kant, Herder, and the Birth of Anthropology*, 232.
65 Palti, "The Metaphor of Life," 331–2. The citation is from Herder, *This Too a Philosophy of History*. See *HPW* 306–7.
66 "Über den Begriff der Geschichte," in *Illuminationen* (Frankfurt: Suhrkamp, 1977), 258.
67 Palti, "The Metaphor of Life," 333.
68 This earlier view is explained by Kant in 1747 in "Gedanken von der wahren Schätzung der lebendigen Kräfte" (Thoughts on the True Estimation of Living Forces), in *Natural Science*, ed. Eric Watkins (Cambridge: Cambridge University Press, 2012), 1–155.
69 Kant, "Dreams of a Spirit-Seer Elucidated by Dreams of Metaphysics," in *Theoretical Philosophy 1755–1770*, 301–59.
70 See Gaier, "Myth, Mythology, New Mythology."
71 Palti, "The Metaphor of Life," 335.
72 Ibid.
73 Zammito, *Kant, Herder, and the Birth of Anthropology*, 173, 418n218.
74 Ibid., 174.
75 For the way Herder's early work prefigured his later criticism of Kant see Paul Guyer, "Free Play and True Well-Being: Herder's Critique of Kant's Aesthetics," *Journal of Aesthetics and Art Criticism* 65/4 (2007): 353–68.
76 Zammito, *Kant, Herder, and the Birth of Anthropology*, 175.
77 Writing to Hamann in April 1768, he tells of this discontent with Rousseau: "I never succeeded, even while I was still a keen Rousseauian, in discovering his solution to the central knot, 'How did it come about that man passed from the state of nature into the world's present malaise? If his nature contained the locked treasure-trove of abilities, of inclinations and so forth, which had to remain locked for the sake of his felicity, why did God give him this germ of potential error? How did it begin to sprout?' I remember having asked Kant, the great student of Rousseau, about this once; but he responded like Uncle Toby Shandy" [In vol. 3, chap. 41, Sterne writes: "There is no cause but one, replied my uncle *Toby*, – why one man's nose is longer than another's, but because

that God pleases to have it so." Lawrence Sterne, *The Life and Opinions of Tristram Shandy, Gentleman* (New York: Derby and Jackson, 1857), 199.]; *HBG* 1, 97.

78 *Kant, Herder, and the Birth of Anthropology*, 175. In the fourth of the polemical essays on aesthetics, *Critical Groves*, which Herder commenced in Riga in 1769 and continued to work on in France, he can still read Kant in this light. He praises Kant as "altogether a social observer," who in his essay on the beautiful and the sublime takes "the formable [*bildsam*] nature of humans, the social side of our nature in its finest hues and shades as the field of his observations" (*HFA* 2, 420, cited in Zammito, ibid., 172.

79 See Gaier, *HFA* 1, 994.

80 Gaier, *Herders Sprachphilosophie*, 70.

81 See Hans Georg Gadamer's discussion of *sensus communis* in antiquity and in Vico; *Truth and Method* (New York: Continuum, 2006), 18–20.

82 Ibid., 19.

83 Ibid., 24.

84 Herder, "An den Herrn Direktor der Historischen Gesellschaft in Göttingen," *Ausgewählte Werke in Einzelausgaben: Schriften zur Literatur 2/1: Kritische Wälder*, 687; cited in John Zammito, "Herder and Historical Metanarrative: What's Philosophical about History?" in Adler and Koepke, *Companion to the Works of Johann Gottfried Herder*, 71.

85 This was one of Herder's complaints against Voltaire's historical studies. See Zammito, "Herder and Historical Metanarrative," 67.

86 This is spelled out in the draft to the 1766 essay "On the Change of Taste" (*HPW* 255).

87 Gaier, *HFA* 1, 857.

88 Menges, "Identity as Difference," 15.

89 Menges refers to the *Fragments: On the Most Recent German Literature*, whose supplementary nature is reflected not only in their form, but also in their subtitle: *Eine Beilage zu den Briefen, die neueste Literatur betreffend* (A Supplement to the Letters concerning the Most Recent German Literature); "Identity as Difference," 15.

90 Michael Mack, *Spinoza and the Specters of Modernity: The Hidden Enlightenment of Diversity from Spinoza to Freud* (London: Continuum, 2010), 70.

91 Menges, "Identity as Difference," 15.

92 Spivak, "Can the Subaltern Speak?" 87.

93 Ibid., 89. The reference is to Jacques Derrida, *Of Grammatology*, trans. Gayatri C. Spivak (Baltimore: Johns Hopkins University Press, 1976), 93; the emphasis on *historical* is Derrida's.

3. From Human Restlessness

1 F.M. Barnard, *Herder on Nationality, Humanity and History* (Montreal and Kingston: McGill-Queen's University Press, 2003), 74, 78. See also Barnard, *Herder's Social and Political Thought*, 99–100.

2 As Gerrit Steunebrink puts it, "Because humanity is an abstract concept for Herder, cosmopolitanism is a kind of empty humanity. The heart of a cosmopolitan is a house for nobody according to Herder." "*Sensus communis* and Modernity as a Common Horizon: A Contribution to the Theory of Intercultural Communication," in *Sensus Communis in Multi- and Intercultural Perspective: On the Possibility of Common Judgments in Arts and Politics*, ed. Heinz Kimmerle and Henk Oosterling (Würzburg: Könighausen and Neumann, 2000), 41.

3 Barnard, *Herder on Nationality*, 40.

4 See Sankar Muthu, *Enlightenment against Empire* (Princeton: Princeton University Press, 2003), 226.

5 Writing to Nicolai in 1768, Herder states that he wants to be like Lessing: "a citizen of the world (*Weltbürger*), … A man like that can enlighten Germany" (27 December 1768, *HBG* 1, 125).

6 John Hawkesworth, *An Account of the Voyages undertaken by order of his present Majesty for making Discoveries in the Southern Hemisphere* (London: W. Strahan and T. Cadell, 1773), 2: 142. See James Cook, *Captain Cook's Journal during His First Voyage round the World*, ed. W.J.L. Wharton (London: Elliot Stock, 1893), 146.

7 When the Tahitians brought a 90-pound hog to the ship for barter, they would settle for nothing less than a carpenter's broad axe in exchange. Cook was unable to part with this, and they left again with the hog. Those very people, Cook writes in his journal, "who but 2 years ago prefer'd a spike Nail to an Axe of any Sort, have so far learnt the use of them that they will not part with a Pig of 10 or 12 pounds weight for anything under a Hatchet, and even those of an inferior or small sort are of no great esteem to them."*Captain Cook's Journal*, 133.

8 Berman's claim that "Cook's concern is the strategic assertion of a sign system," is certainly correct, though it is not entirely accurate to see Cook as "hostile to speech and communication" in favour of acts of writing (*Enlightenment or Empire: Colonial Discourse in German Culture* [Lincoln: University of Nebraska Press, 1998], 35, 39). Cook seems to have chosen writing or speech, assertion or adoption of sign systems depending on the situation. In this respect, Cook's understanding of scientific knowledge was indeed skewed towards "instrumental rationality"

(ibid., 40), but it demonstrates a higher level of scientific canny than Berman credits him with.

9 This is even more pronounced in the journal of Joseph Banks: *The* Endeavour *Journal of Joseph Banks, 1768–1771,* 2 vols., ed. J.C. Beaglehole (Sydney: Angus and Robertson, 1963).

10 Hawkesworth, *An Account of the Voyages,* 2: 81.

11 Parallel to the *Journal,* Herder wrote "Thoughts on Reading Montesquieu," which remained unpublished, and it is there he refines exactly what it is he agrees and disagrees with in the works of his French colleague (*HSW* 4, 464–8).

12 Montesquieu, *The Spirit of the Laws,* trans. and ed. Anne Cohler, Basia Miller, and Harold Stone (Cambridge: Cambridge University Press, 1989), 338.

13 Anthony Pagden, "The Effacement of Difference: Colonialism and the Origins of Nationalism in Diderot and Herder," in *After Colonialism: Imperial Histories and Postcolonial Displacements,* ed. Gyan Prakash (Princeton: Princeton University Press, 1995), 130. Similarly, Berman refers to Cook's material exchange with the native New Zealanders as one "between shrewd equals engaged in complicated negotiations with much attention to details and nuances" (*Enlightenment or Empire,* 33). This may be true in the individual act of exchange, but time and again it is clearly evident in Cook's descriptions of trade that equal trade takes place within a broader context of unequal power relations.

14 *Laissez-faire* doctrines of trade were easily combined with radical politics. As late as 1791, the American revolutionary Thomas Paine wrote in *The Rights of Man* that commerce is "the greatest approach toward universal civilisation that has yet been made by any means not immediately flowing from moral principles. Whatever has a tendency to promote the civil intercourse of nations by an exchange of benefits, is a subject as worthy of philosophy as of politics." Paine went on to observe that commerce is a logical alternative to war, since it allows a cheaper and more commodious procurement of scarce commodities from another part of the world than by force. Thomas Paine, *The Rights of Man; Being an Answer to Mr. Burke's Attack on the French Revolution,* in *The Political Works of Thomas Paine* (Chicago and New York: Belford, Clarke & Co., 1887), 302.

15 Hawkesworth, *An Account of the Voyages,* 1: preface.

16 Wallerstein, *The Modern World System,* 3: 200.

17 David Mackay, *In the Wake of Cook: Exploration, Science, and Empire: 1780–1801* (London: Croom Helm, 1985), 29.

18 This concern is clearly shown by Samson Knoll, "Beyond the Black Legend: The Anticolonialism of Johann Gottfried Herder," *North Dakota Quarterly* 57/3 (1989): 55–64.

19 Montaigne had written in his essay *On Coaches*: "So many cities razed, so many nations exterminated, so many millions of people put to the sword, and the richest and most beautiful part of the world turned upside down, for the traffic in pearls and peppers." Michel de Montaigne, *The Complete Essays*, trans. Donald M. Frame (Stanford: Stanford University Press, 1965), 695.

20 Cited and translated by Knoll, "Beyond the Black Legend," 59.

21 Mah believes that Herder's puritanical mistrust of luxury causes his politics to remain vague and unfocused; *Enlightenment Phantasies*, 7. This may be true, but at the same time it gave him insight into the emerging structures of power in the world economy. It is probably more accurate to say that Puritanism itself was shaping its politics in response to the same economic developments Herder was observing.

22 This idea was expressed forcefully in the widely read report of Joseph François Lafitau, *Moeurs des sauvages amériquains comparées aux moeurs des premiers temps* (Customs of the American Indians Compared with the Customs of Primitive Tribes) (Paris: Saugrain l'aîné & C.-E. Hochereau, 1724). Lafitau had observed the peoples he wrote about first hand as a missionary to the Iroquois from 1711 to 1717, and his book argued for a relativist approach to Native American customs based on knowledge of their language, and not through measuring them on a European scale of values. At the same time, however, he saw them on a historical continuum that linked them to Western antiquity. Anthony Pagden reviews this idea in chapter 4 of *European Encounters with the New World* (New Haven and London: Yale University Press, 1993). As he puts it: "To Lafitau, the Huron and the Iroquois he had encountered during his years as a missionary in northern Canada, seemed culturally to be another form of Spartan or Lycian" (148).

23 Herder is referring to Forster's comments on Hodges. See *HWS* 13: 251, note.

24 This work was translated in 1800 by T. Churchill; it is also available in a version heavily edited by Frank E. Manuel, on which I rely in the first instance, and reference it as *HRP*. I also provide the reference to the original German from the Suphan edition of Herder's works (*HSW*). Where Manuel does not translate the original, translations are by John Koster, and the reference is *HSW*. Translations are modified as indicated.

25 Herder uses the term *Humanität* to refer to his concept of unitary humanity. Where he refers to humankind as a collection of cultures, he prefers the term *Menschheit*, though he sometimes also speaks of *Humanität* in this context.

26 Adler, "Herder's Concept of *Humanität*," 106.

27 Johann Gottfried Herder, *Journal meiner Reise im Jahr 1769*, translated in 1952 by John Francis Harrison as "Journal of My Travels in the Year 1769" (PhD diss., Columbia University). A rather random collection of extracts is translated in F.M. Barnard, *J. G. Herder on Social and Political Culture* (Cambridge: Cambridge University Press, 1969), 63–114.

28 Mah, *Enlightenment Phantasies*, 30. Harrison compares it to Aristotle's *Poetics*, both being "essentially collections of notes, fully intelligible only to their authors," but this exaggerates the hermetic quality of the text; Introduction to "Journal of My Voyage," 42. The methodology of the *Journal* tends to work against the form of the book. It is both larger than a single book, being the plan or the abstract or the summary of several books – and less than a single book, since its fragmentary quality does not want to ripen into anything like a book. It is instead, in Katherine Mommsen's words, a collection of "reflections, self-observations, dreams, visions, associations of ideas ..."; "Nachwort," in *Journal meiner Reise im Jahr 1769* (Stuttgart: Reclam, 1976), 189.

29 This plan would soon come to fruition, spurred on by his visit to the impressive collection of Greek and Roman copies at Versailles. Herder's notes are published in Suphan's edition as *Studien und Entwürfe zur Plastik* (*HSW* 8, 88–115). These notes would eventually lead to the publication of *Plastik* (Riga: Hartknoch, 1778), translated by Jason Gaiger as *Sculpture: Some Observations on Shape and Form from Pygmalion's Creative Dream* (Chicago: University of Chicago Press, 2002).

30 Harrison, "Journal of My Voyage," "Introduction," 123.

31 Pauline Phemister, "Monads and Machines," in *Machines of Nature and Corporeal Substances in Leibniz*, ed. Justin E.H. Smith and Ohad Nachtomy (Dordrecht: Springer, 2011), 49.

32 Herder's early adoption and interpretation of Leibniz is recorded in "Über Leibnizens Grundsätze von der Natur und Gnade" (*HSW* 32, 225–7). For a more detailed discussion of Herder's reading of Leibniz see Günter Arnold's excellent essay "'... der größte Mann den Deutschland in den neuern Zeiten gehabt' – Herders Verhältnis zu Leibniz," *Studia Leibnitiana* 37/2 (2005): 161–85.

33 Christian Adolph Klotz, *Epistolae homericae* (Altenburgi: Ex officina Richteria, 1764).

34 Herder appears to have taken the word *Hondatkonsonas* for Iroquois "spirits of all kinds" from Balthasar Ludwig Eskuche, *Erläuterungen Heiliger Schrift aus morgenländischen Reise-Beschreibungen* (Lemgo: Johann Heinrich Meyer, 1750), 359.

35 Sikka, *Herder on Humanity*, 129.

36 Later (in the seventh book of *Ideas*) he will be more precise in insisting that "species" cannot be used in the plural when applied to humanity: "The human race is but *one and the same species on this earth*" (*HSW* 13: 255, emphasis in original).

37 Barnard discusses Herder's view of the nation as a living thing, in opposition to the machine-like quality of the state (*Herder's Social and Political Thought*, 31). By attempting to naturalize community in relation to the sea, Herder is taking a stance on what has been called the politicization of oceanic space. See Elizabeth Mancke, "Early Modern Expansion and the Politicization of Oceanic Space," *The Geographical Review* 89 (1999): 225–36.

38 See Harrison's discussion of Herder's responses to French literature in his introduction to "A Journal," 69–75.

39 This political critique as a critique of aesthetics was a common German response to the powerful cultural hegemony which France retained in German-speaking lands following the Treaty of Paris in 1763, which dealt the final blow to French political rule in North America and India. French cultural domination had been answered with vehement rejection by a small group of German intellectuals, at least since the beginning of the Seven Years' War. Lessing had written in his "Abhandlungen von dem weinerlichen oder rührenden Lustspiele" (Treatises on Tearful or Moving Comedy, 1754): "The Frenchman is a creature who always wants to seem greater than he is"; Lessing, "Abhandlungen von dem weinerlichen oder rührenden Lustspiele," in *Werke*, 4: 13. And in a letter to Nicolai of 18 December 1756, he had stated: "But I hate French tragedies, which never manage to wring a few tears from me until the end of the fifth act"; Lessing, *Briefwechsel über das Trauerspiel* (Correspondence on Tragedy, in *Werke*, 4: 187). Lessing is objecting to what Herder would later pejoratively call a "French talent for representation," meaning a penchant for superficiality. This he found in "nearly all their intellectual works, even scientific ones: their judicial speeches and their sermons, their academies and elogia, even their affairs and principles of state; everywhere justice, devotion, learnedness, praise, politics, and science appear as *representing*" (*HSW* 18, 55). Harrison links Herder's critique of French classicism to his conviction that poetry is, as Baumgarten had

claimed, the gateway to the lower faculties. The Aristotelian tradition that found its way into French classicism ignores "the psychology of irrational sensation," confining itself instead to external objects. "This is striking at the root of French neoclassical aesthetics with a vengeance, as Herder apparently realized." Harrison, "Introduction," 69.

40 Guillaume Thomas Raynal, *L'Histoire philosophique et politique des établissements et du commerce des Européens dans les deux Indes* (Amsterdam: Chez E. van Harrevellt and D.J. Changuion, 1770). The first German translation began to appear in 1774 under the title *Philosophische und politische Geschichte der Besitzungen und des Handels der Europäer in beiden Indien* (Hanover: In der Hofbuchhandlung der Gebrüder Helwing, 1774–8).

41 Gianluigi Goggi, "Quelques remarques sur la collaboration de Diderot à la première édition de l'Histoire des deux Indes," *Studies on Voltaire and the Eighteenth Century* 286 (1991): 17–52. Although it is commonly assumed that Diderot's contribution to the *Histoire* only commenced after the appearance of the first edition, Goggi presents convincing evidence that Diderot was already working together with Raynal in the summer of 1769. In the eighth book of the *History of the Two Indias*, Diderot attempts to outline some fundamental principles of colonization, according to which it is permissible for inhabitants of one nation to settle in another land. His stance cannot be called anti-colonial; on the contrary, he begins by stating that "reason and equity permit the establishment of colonies, but they also mark out the principles from which one must not stray when founding them." Denis Diderot, *Political Writings*, ed. and trans. John Hope Mason and Robert Wokler (Cambridge: Cambridge University Press, 1992), 175.

42 Kant, *Metaphysics of Morals*, ed. Mary Gregor (Cambridge: Cambridge University Press, 1996), 121–2.

43 As Anthony Pagden observes, Diderot understood that "one of the consequences of modern colonization and the new trade routes that it had helped create was that the metropolis could never be fully insulated from the consequences of the process of overseas expansion that it had itself initiated"; "The Effacement of Difference," 138.

44 "Livonia, thou province of barbarism and luxury, of ignorance and pretended taste, of freedom and slavery, how much would there be to do in thee! How much to do to destroy barbarism, to root out ignorance, to spread culture and freedom, to become a second Zwingli, Calvin and Luther to this province! Can I do this? Do I have the disposition, the opportunity, the talents? What must I do to attain this end? What must

I destroy in myself? – Why do I still ask that? Give up writing useless criticisms and pursuing dead researches; raise myself above disputations and literary fame; dedicate myself to the benefit and the education of the living world; win the confidence of the administration, the imperial government and the court; travel through France, England, Italy and Germany with this in mind and acquire the French language and *savoir-faire*, the English sense of reality and freedom, the Italian taste for subtle invention, the German thoroughness and knowledge, and finally, where it is necessary, Dutch erudition; arouse others to a high opinion of me and myself to great plans; conform to the age in which I live and acquire the spirit of legislation [*Geist der Gesetzgebung*], of commerce and polity; dare to examine everything from the point of view of politics, the state and finances" (*HJV* 235–6, translation modified).

45 Herder, "An den Herrn Direktor der Historischen Gesellschaft in Göttingen" (1768), cited in Zammito, "Herder and Historical Metanarrative," 70.

46 "That superb fitness for his own moment made Herodotus all the more problematic for imitators in later times." Zammito, ibid., 70.

47 See Zammito, *Kant, Herder, and the Birth of Anthropology*, 338.

48 As Zammito observes, one of the central sociological hinges that ties the new mobility to the cosmopolitan principle of improvement was reading. "Reading was essential to identity formation: that one read, how one read, what one read – all these marked one as *gebildet*. Reading was for self-discovery or self-formation (*Bildung* had that sense at its core), but it was also for orientation to the world (*Weltkenntnis*, a term of decisive importance for Kant). Through these first two processes, reading was expected to lead to the achievement of urbanity, a self-confident sense of attunement to and participation in current affairs, in the 'public sphere.'" Zammito, *Kant, Herder*, 31.

49 "Besides, true laughter has, happily, vanished from the delicate modern French comedy as completely as true feeling from the tragedy. Everything is performance, sobbing, wringing of hands, declamation, set scenes, the [correct] connection of scenes, etc. For this last, and for the sense of probability afforded by the unities of time and place, etc., they do have the feeling of which the German has less and the Englishman nothing. And in fact this thing which they make their chief concern is nothing but the etiquette of the theater … How much freer a nature the English have in these matters, although with them it is exaggerated! And what a fine middle path we Germans could take!" (*HJV* 263–4).

50 Already in Riga he had written an essay which he did not publish, "Haben wir eine französische Bühne?" (Do We Have a French Stage?) sketching out the lamentable state of German theatre with its fixation on the French style: "How can Germany have a Paris, when the art critic himself admits of differences in taste and mores among the provinces? The plays of this law-giving theatre would therefore still be *foreign models* for its vassals, and would bring forth clumsy imitators and a skewed taste" (*HSW* 2: 212–13).

51 See Harrison, "Introduction," 74. As he details, using the example of Montesquieu, the *Encyclopédie*, Diderot, and Voltaire, there was a well-developed intellectual tradition in eighteenth century France which was "keenly aware that their own age was substantially different from that of Louis XIV, and were not at all reluctant to criticize either or both." Ibid., 75.

52 Ibid., 90.

53 Johann Georg Hamann, *Kreuzzüge des Philologen*, in *Sturm und Drang: Kritische Schriften*, ed. Erich Löwenthal (Heidelberg: Lambert Schneider, 1972), 111.

54 See Ingeborg Nerling-Pietsch, *Herders literarische Denkmale: Formen der Charakteristik vor Friedrich Schlegel* (Münster: Lit, 1997) for a more detailed discussion of Herder's views on Winckelmann.

55 Zammito, *Kant, Herder*, 335–6

56 In the 40th and 41st *Letters on the Advancement of Humanity* (1794), Herder cites at length (with minor editing) the German Enlightenment writer Gabriel Wagner on the national status of Germany. Wagner wrote under the pseudonym Realis de Vienna, was a protégé of Leibniz and an outspoken critic of academic philosophy and of all forms of cultural imitation – primarily the current fad for imitating French culture. What seems to interest Herder as a point of departure is Wagner's claim that "God wished to impart cleverness to the world through two peoples, prior to Christ's birth the Greeks, and after Christ the Germans." Realis de Vienna, *Nachricht von Realis' de Vienna Prüfung des europäischen Verstandes durch die weltweise Geschicht, von derselben Inhalt und Beschaffenheit; wobei sonderlich erwogen wird die Frage von der Nachahmung. Wider des Sammlers unehrlichen Bericht, der 1714 in sogenannten unparteiischen Gedanken alle Bücher-Auszüge zu sammeln and auszuziehen angefangen* (Frankfurt, 1715). Cited in *HFA* 7, 215.

57 J.J. Winckelmann, *Monumenti antichi inediti*, 2nd ed., ed. Pietro Paolo Montagnani-Mirabili (Rome: A spese dell'autore, 1821), vol. 2, pt. 1, no. 40. From Winckelmann, *History of the Art of Antiquity*, trans. Harry Francis Mallgrave (Los Angeles: Getty Research Institute, 2006).

58 Menges, "Particular Universals," 200.
59 See Muthu, *Enlightenment against Empire*, 229–30.
60 See Anthony J. La Vopa, "Herder's Publikum: Language, Print, and Sociability in Eighteenth-Century Germany," *Eighteenth Century Studies* 29 (1995): 5–24.
61 See Barnard, *Herder on Nationality*, 146.
62 Zammito, *Kant, Herder*, 310.

4. From the Location of Language

1 Herder, "Auszug aus einem Briefwechsel über Ossian und die Lieder alter Völker," *Von Deutscher Art und Kunst* (1773); *HSW* 5, 164.
2 Zammito, "Herder and Historical Metanarrative," 67.
3 Heinrich Gottlob Franke (1705–81) was professor of morals, politics, and state law in Leipzig.
4 As Michael Mack observes, this will lead to the recognition that "the present incorporates the non-presence of the past." *Spinoza and the Specters of Modernity: The Hidden Enlightenment of Diversity from Spinoza to Freud* (London: Continuum, 2010), 70.
5 See the overview provided by Wolfgang Pross in his commentary on Herder's *Treatise* in *HMA* 2, 895–919; Norton, *Herder's Aesthetics*, chap. 3; Hans Aarsleff, "The Tradition of Condillac: The Problem of the Origin of Language in the Eighteenth Century and the Debate in the Berlin Academy before Herder," in *Studies in the History of Linguistics*, ed. Dell Hymes (Bloomington: Indiana University Press, 1974), 93–156; and Jürgen Trabant, "Herder and Language," in *A Companion to the Works of Johann Gottfried Herder*, ed. Adler and Koepke, 117–19.
6 Maupertuis had published his *Dissertation sur les différens moyens dont les hommes se sont servis pour exprimer leurs idées* as a volume of the academy's papers in 1756; in *Oeuvres* (Lyon: Chez Jean-Marie Bruyset, 1756), 3: 437–68. At the beginning of book 3 of the *Essay Concerning Human Understanding*, Locke had stated that "if we could trace them to their sources, we should find, in all languages, the names, which stand for things that fall not under our senses, to have had their first rise from sensible ideas"; *Essay Concerning Human Understanding, Philosophical Works and Selected Correspondence of John Locke*, ed. Mark C. Rooks (Charlottesville: InteLex Corporation, 1995), 1: 4.
7 Johann Peter Süßmilch, *Versuch eines Beweises, daß die erste Sprache ihren Ursprung nicht vom Menschen, sondern allein vom Schöpfer erhalten habe* (Berlin: Im Buchladen der Realschule, 1766); see Norton, *Herder's Aesthetics*, 106–7.

8 The scholarship has demonstrated that Herder's position is not nearly as far away from Süssmilch's as he gave to believe. For a valuable discussion of the ways Herder misrepresented Süssmilch, see Bruce Kieffer, "Herder's Treatment of Süssmilch's Theory of the Origin of Language in *Abhandlung über den Ursprung der Sprache*: A Re-evaluation," *Germanic Revue* 53/3 (1978): 96–104; Michael N. Forster, "Herder's Philosophy of Language, Interpretation, and Translation: Three Fundamental Principles," *Review of Metaphysics* 56/2 (2002): 323–56. Spencer's chapter on language is also instructive: *Herder's Political Thought*, 29–31.

9 Locke, *Concerning Human Understanding*, 60.

10 In 1703, Louis-Armond de Lahontan had published dialogues with a "savage of good sense, who has traveled," portraying the critical perspective of Adario, a Huron, on some aspects of French civilization. *Nouveaux voyages de Mr. le baron de Lahontan dans l'Amérique Septentrionale* (La Haye: Chez les fréres l'Honoré, 1703). Lahontan's book was translated the same year into English: *New voyages to North America … also a dialogue between the author and a general of the savages … to which is added a dictionary of the Algonkine language which is generally spoke in North-America* (London: H. Bonwicke, 1703). These dialogues may have been partially or completely fictitious, but they proved immensely popular, and had an important influence on writers such as Leibniz, Rousseau, and Voltaire, and thus on the idea of the noble savage. Pagden claims that "almost every bon sauvage of Canadian origin created by succeeding writers owes something, and frequently everything, to Adario [Lahontan's Huron interlocutor]"; *European Encounters with the New World* (New Haven and London: Yale University Press 1993), 121. Adario's pronouncements pointed to the weaknesses of the contemporary French – and, by extension, "civilized" – economic, political, and moral systems. At the same time, they postulated savagery as a realm uncorrupted by luxury and sophistication. "'Tis an uncontested Truth, that the Nations which are not debauch'd by the Neighbourhood of the *Europeans*, are Strangers to the Measures of *Meum* and *Tuum*, and to all Laws, Judges, and Priests … Now this being granted, we ought not to scruple to believe, that these are such wise and reasonable People. I take it, that a Man must be quite blind, who does not see that the Property of Goods (I do not speak of the ingrossing of Women) is the only Source of all the Disorders that perplex the *European* Societies"; Lahontan, *New voyages to North America*, preface. Sankar Muthu points out that this celebration of the noble savage in Lahontan

is accompanied by an aggressive argument against any form of political self-determination: "The *Realpolitik* of many of Lahontan's analyses of French imperial policies demonstrates that a noble savage celebration of Amerindian life not only sits alongside aggressive colonial schemes, but without as much contradiction as one might originally have thought"; *Enlightenment against Empire*, 31.

11 In the *Supplément au voyage de Bougainville* (1772), Diderot has one of the interlocutors explain that Autourou, a Tahitian man who was taken back to Paris by Bougainville, "had such a slight grasp of things here, and will not find terms in his language that correspond to the meagre impressions he formed." The gap between the two worlds is both linguistic and developmental: "The life of the savage is so simple, and our societies are such complicated machines. The Tahitian is close to the origins of the world and the European near its old age. The gulf between us is greater than that separating the new-born child from the decrepit dotard." "Supplement to the Voyage of Bougainville, or Dialogue between A and B on the Inappropriateness of Attaching Moral Ideas to Certain Physical Actions that do not Accord with them," in *Political Writings*, ed. and trans. John Hope Mason and Robert Wokler (Cambridge: Cambridge University Press, 1992), 40.

12 See note 10.

13 See his discussion in *European Encounters with the New World*, chap. 4.

14 In this connection, Pagden speaks of the "anti-lexica," i.e., the "lists of terms which savages did *not* have," claiming that these "could be used either to reflect on the poverty of the savages' cultures or on the unnecessary, and malign richness of ours. But they were always used in the same way. Words were matched against things." Pagden, *European Encounters with the New World*, 127–8.

15 "If physiology should ever get to the point where it's demonstrated the science of the soul – which I very much doubt that it will, however – then it would cast many a ray of light on this phenomenon [that the struck string calls forth a sympathetic echo] from the dissection of the nerve structure" (*HPW* 66).

16 See Mack, *Spinoza and the Specters of Modernity*.

17 Ibid., 65; see also Michael Frazer, *The Enlightenment of Sympathy: Justice and the Moral Sentiments in the Eighteenth Century and Today* (New York: Oxford University Press, 2010), 206n14. Also Daniel Whistler, "The Discipline of Pious Reason," in *Moral Powers, Fragile Beliefs: Essays in Moral and Religious Philosophy*, ed. J. Carlisle, J. Carter, and D. Whistler (London: Continuum, 2011), 53–81.

18 Sikka, "Herder's Critique of Pure Reason," *Review of Metaphysics* 61/1 (2007): 47.

19 *Besinnen* comes from the Middle High German; it builds on the word for sense in the dual meaning of responding to stimulus and knowing, *sapere* and *excogitare,* and it can be both transitive and intransitive. *Besonnen* is the past participle, and the suffix *heit* substantiates it.

20 Trabant, "Herder and Language," 124. For this reason, Herder would later see *Besonnenheit* as a real alternative to Kant's pure reason. See Sikka, "Herder's Critique of Pure Reason," 36–7.

21 Trabant, "Herder and Language," 126.

22 Herder's theory of language points to a missing part in Kant's philosophy: a plausible account of how the kind of consensus is reached on which transcendental idealism is based; i.e., if transcendental idealism depends both on a cognitive idealism and a representational transcendentalism, what is the mechanism of transmission of representations between individuals? (e.g., when Kant speaks of "us" in para. 49 of *Critique of Judgment*).

23 Trabant compares Herder's idea of reason to Augustine's *appetitus noscendi,* the appetite of the mind for gaining knowledge. Trabant, "Herder and Language," 125.

24 Menges, "Herder's 'Great Topic,'" 12.

25 "Even 'relativist' writers such as Helvetius and Montesquieu never doubted that 'man in general has always been what he is,' as Voltaire had remarked. When Hume wrote that 'mankind are so much the same, in all times and places,' that, therefore, the chief task of the historian was 'only to discover the constant and universal principles of human nature,' he merely expressed what practically everyone else took for granted." Barnard, *Herder's Social and Political Thought*, 132. The reference to Voltaire is footnoted: *Oeuvres*, ed. Lequiquieu, (Paris, 1820), vol. XI, p. 19; the Hume reference is from *An Enquiry concerning Human Understanding*, vol. 37, part 3, ed. Charles W. Eliot (New York: P.F. Collier & Son, 1909–14), 7.

26 In their translation of the *Treatise*, Moran and Gode justify omitting the second part altogether, since its central theme is "no longer the origin of language as such but the evolution of it in diverse forms." *On the Origin of Language: Jean-Jacques Rousseau, Essay on the Origin of Languages; Johann Gottfried Herder, Essay on the Origin of Language*, trans. John H. Moran and Alexander Gode (New York: Ungar, 1966), 173.

27 Trabant compares the four natural laws to the *lingua adamica*, the speech of Adam and Eve, the story of Babel, and finally the Pentecostal speaking in tongues (Trabant, "Herder and Language," 130).

28 Spinoza makes this distinction in part 1, paragraph 30 of *Ethics*.

29 See Steven Nadler, "Spinoza and Consciousness," *Mind* 117/467 (2008): 575–601.

30 Herder made this point as early as 1766 in his *Outline of a History of Lyric Poetry*: "To be sure, all human races on this earth are of one blood; however, transmigrations have so much deprived them of any knowledge of their fathers that we encounter each people by itself in that most miserable and deprived state that compelled it to invent for itself all necessities as if it never had possessed them before. Now, since all peoples have the same kinds of needs and the same kinds of capacities to provide for these needs, it is indeed natural that one should seek to find among them what, on the basis of deductions so facile and uncertain, one gathers from other favorite realms, like pepper from India. If it is so that even a wild people may have poets, and must have them to begin with, then poetry may have its origins anywhere; now, if this origin *in the case of one people is supernatural, then it is divine in the case of all*" (*HEW* 76–7).

31 Trabant, "Herder and Language," 131–2.

32 In this sense, David Pan is quite right to speak of restlessness as promoting multiculturalism in Herder's view. David Pan, "J.G. Herder, the Origin of Language, and the Possibility of Transcultural Narratives," *Language and Intercultural Communication* 4/1–2 (2004): 10–20.

33 See Pagden, *European Encounters with the New World*, 117.

34 Herder, *Eine Metakritik zur Kritik der reinen Vernunft* (Leipzig: Hartknoch, 1799); *HSW* 21, 1–339. See the excellent discussion in Marion Heinz, "Herders Metakritik," in *Herder und die Philosophie des deutschen Idealismus*, 89–106. In "Herder's Critique of Pure Reason," Sikka makes a convincing case for reading the *Metacritique* not as a misunderstanding of Kant's critical philosophy, but as a strong challenge to it.

35 Zammito, "Herder and Historical Metanarrative," 75.

36 This is what leads to Zammito's appraisal that Herder was "a pioneer in the endeavor to weave together naturalism and historicism." "Herder and Historical Metanarrative," 76.

37 "A man who could [influence the course of events in advance] would be more than a Bacon, greater in prophesy than Newton; but he would have to observe with the spirit of a Montesquieu, write with the fiery pen of a Rousseau and have Voltaire's good fortune in catching the ear of the great" (*HJV* 307).

38 Mack, *Spinoza*, 126. This same realization presides over Walter Benjamin's *Theses on the Philosophy of History*.

39 Zammito is right to warn against reading a radical relativism into Herder's historical method; "Herder and Historical Metanarrative," 65. Herder had already developed a critique of relativism of taste in his rejection of Riedel in the *Fourth Critical Grove* (see Norton, *Herder's Aesthetics*, 172). Sikka explains the limits to Herder's relativism in *Herder on Humanity*.
40 As Michael Mack states, "Recognition of prejudice means the realization of limits. The study of history reveals such limits. History, in Herder's view, shows that the center does not hold. The national center is the starting point for the recognition of transnational interdependence." Mack, *Spinoza*, 111.
41 See the excellent comparison between Herder's and Kant's understanding of happiness in Sikka, *Herder on Humanity*, chap. 2.
42 Menges, "Particular Universals," 197.
43 See Mack, *Spinoza*, 70.
44 Herder's critique of Voltaire is focused on the introduction to the extremely popular *Essai sur les moeurs et l'esprit des nations* (*An Essay on Universal History, the Manners, and Spirit of Nations, from the Reign of Charlemaign to the Age of Lewis XIV*, 1756). But he had also read Voltaire's praise of the present in previous works, such as *Essai sur l'histoire du siècle de Louis XIV* (1739). It spoke against everything Herder stood for when he read Voltaire's opening claim in the latter work that the age of Louis XIV was "the most intelligent age in the annals of time," and that, "among the four ages [of world history], this perhaps is that which comes the nearest to perfection. Enriched with the discoveries of the other three, it made a more considerable progress in one article than the three put together." *An Essay on the Age of Lewis XIV*, trans. Mr. Lockman (London: Knapton, 1739), 1, 3–4. See Harrison, Introduction to "A Journal of My Voyage," 8–9.
45 See the excellent discussion in Sikka, *Herder on Humanity*, "The Progress of What?" 87–106.
46 Menges, "Identity as Difference," 8.
47 Mack, *Spinoza*, 18. Herder gives his most coherent account of perfectibility much later in the *Letters on the Advancement of Humanity*. Here perfectibility is the process, not the goal (*HSW* 17, 115). See also Barnard, *Herder's Social and Political Thought*, 133.
48 Sikka, *Herder on Humanity*, 99–100.
49 See Menges, "Identity as Difference," 6–7.
50 Mack, *Spinoza*, 104–5.
51 Palti, "The Metaphor of Life," 326.

52 In the words of Trabant, Herder objected to "Voltaire's *philosophie de l'histoire* and other teleological universalist conceptions of the history of mankind as a history of the victory of the one – European, that is, French or enlightened rationalist – 'progressive' cultural model"; Trabant, "Herder and Language," 122. It is certainly correct that Herder "adopted the macro-structure of the historical blueprint" from Voltaire (as well as Iselin and Hume), as Pross states in the notes to the essay (*HMA* 1, 850), but his interpretation of the model through which this blueprint should be read deviates so strikingly from his predecessors as to make for a thorough methodological break.

53 See Menges, "Identity as Difference."

54 "Influenced by Lucretius, Boyle, and Spinoza, Herder develops a concept of composition and decomposition which is transferred from the history of nature to the history of humanity" (Pross, *HMA* 1, 853). Pross cites two letters of 1769 to Moses Mendelssohn in which this point is emphatically made (*HMA* 1, 851–2).

55 Zammito, "Herder and Historical Metanarrative," 67.

56 For Herder's search for a model for organic development in *This Too a Philosophy of History* see Edgar Schick, *Metaphorical Organicism in Herder's Early Works: A Study of the Relation of Herder's Literary Idiom to His World-View* (The Hague, Paris: Mouton, 1971), chap. 2.

57 "Just as in all probability the human species [*Geschlecht*] constitutes a single progressive whole with a single origin in a single great household-economy, likewise all languages too, and with them the whole chain of civilization [*Bildung*]"; *Treatise on the Origin of Language* (*HPW* 154). In *On the Change of Taste*, history is described as a "chain of changes, that has run around many centuries in such a regular manner" (*HPW* 254).

58 Schick notes how Herder uses arboreal imagery alongside "fermentative, seminal, and vegetable figures; *Metaphorical Organicism*, 67. Pross claims that Herder was influenced by the tree metaphor in Diderot, who used it to describe the natural process of continual growth and decay (*HMA* 1, 851).

59 "The stem of the tree grown to its greater height strove to bring peoples and nations under its shade, into twigs" (*HPW* 290);

60 "Certain, several, collected, abstracted, fermented ideas, inclinations, and conditions spread themselves out over the world – how the one ancient, simple tribal stem of the human species broke out into branches and twigs!" (*HPW* 312).

61 Nisbet makes this point in *Herder and the Philosophy and History of Science*, 36.

62 See ibid., 32–3.

63 Kant, *Prolegomena zu einer jeden künftigen Metaphysik, die als Wissenschaft wird auftreten können* (Berlin: Hartknoch, 1783).
64 Heinz and Clairmont, "Herder's Epistemology," 51.
65 See Nisbet, *Herder and the Philosophy and History of Science*, 33–5.
66 Menges, "Herder's 'Great Topic,'" 8.
67 In the words of Heinz and Clairmont: "Since the mind is irrevocably tied to the body and conditioned by the perceptions received at the lower levels of the vital process, bodily and environmental conditions become factors that mold the soul to each specific shape. This imprint manifests itself in the appropriation of the world, that is, in the way in which representations, concepts, languages are formed." Heinz and Clairmont, "Herder's Epistemology," 52.
68 In his 12 November 1783 letter to Jacobi he states: "It is another stroke of good fortune in my life that the wretched clouds, which for so long separated Herder from me, finally had to dissipate, and I am convinced that they have done so for good" (*GWA* 4/6, 211).
69 As Reinhard Koselleck points out, one of the great driving forces of the Enlightenment was the dual-pronged struggle of politics and philosophy to overcome the political hold exercised by the theologians' monopoly on morality. *Critique and Crisis*, 20–2.
70 See Michael N. Forster, "Herder and Spinoza," in *Spinoza and German Idealism*, ed. Eckart Förster and Yitzhak Y. Melamed (Cambridge: Cambridge University Press, 2012).
71 Ibid., 69. Forster cites "four poetic works in the years 1770–3: "Charlemagne" (1770), "Eagle and Worm" (1771), the first draft of the poetic drama "Brutus" (1772), and "Origin, Condition, Purpose, and History of Monarchy" (1773)."
72 See Étienne Balibar, *The Philosophy of Marx*, trans. Chris Turner (London: Verso, 2007), 40–1.
73 Forster, "Herder and Spinoza," 70.
74 In 1781, although Goethe had been complaining about Herder's tendency to make enemies, he tells Knebel that "with Herder I have entered into a relationship which promises me all the best for the future" (*GWA* 4/5, 195). And in December 1783 he writes to the Swiss pastor and author Johann Caspar Lavater: "One of the most exquisite joys of my life is that Herder and I no longer have anything between us keeping us apart. If I were not such a stubborn mute, everything would have been resolved earlier, but this way it's also once and for all, and for me a happy prospect" (*GWA* 4/6, 232). It is at times touching to read between the lines of Goethe's letters just how much he relied on the continued

companionship with Herder: for example, when he tells Charlotte von Stein that moves are potentially afoot to offer Herder a position as chief pastor in Hamburg, adding: "I would lose much if he goes, for without you and him I would be alone here" (*GWA* 4/7, 247). And Herder reciprocated Goethe's attachment, albeit with a great deal more ambivalence.

75 Friedrich Schlegel, *Dialogue on Poetry and Literary Aphorisms*, trans. Ernst Behler and Roman Struc (University Park: Pennsylvania State University Press, 1968).

76 Herder, *The Spirit of Hebrew Poetry*, trans. James Marsh (Naperville, IL: Aleph Press, 1971), 13.

77 Ibid., 15; translation modified.

78 Gaier, "Myth, Mythology, New Mythology," in *Companion to the Works of Johann Gottfried Herder*, ed. Adler and Koepke, 185.

79 Goethe appears to have taken on this view. Writing to his friend Carl Ludwig von Knebel in 1785, he observed that "humans are so closely related to the places in which they reside that contemplation of these must also give us some insight into the people who live there" (*GWA* 4/7, 152).

80 Schubart, "Voltaire und Raynal," in *Gesammelte Schriften*, 8: 332.

81 Guillaume-Thomas (Abbé) Raynal, *A philosophical and political history of the settlements and trade of the Europeans in the East and West Indies*, trans. J.O. Justamond (London: W. Strahan & T. Cadell 1783), 1: 1–2.

82 On 5 May 1782, he describes to Carl Ludwig von Knebel how he is occupied with reading Raynal's book; *GWA* 4/5, 319.

83 Koselleck seems to agree with Herder: "Raynal was a typical philosophe *de l'histoire* who had hardly a single original idea, but as a popular figure of the Paris salons he was a zealous collector of the wisdom of others." *Critique and Crisis*, 175.

84 Ibid., 171.

85 Hence Raynal's polemic against Frederick II in *History of the Two Indias*, together with his plea for a *roi citoyen*. See Kosellek, *Begriffsgeschichten*, 295–7.

86 Raynal, cited in Koselleck, *Critique and Crisis*, 174.

87 Arnd Bohm, "Herder and Politics," in *Companion to the Works of Johann Gottfried Herder*, ed. Adler and Koepke, 279.

88 Cited in Bohm, "Herder and Politics," 279.

89 Translated as Frederick II, King of Prussia, *Anti-Machiavel, oder, Prüfung der Regeln Nic. Machiavells von der Regierungskunst eines Fürsten: mit historischen und politischen Anmerkungen* (Göttingen: Verlag der Königlichen Universitäts-Buchhandlung, 1741).

90 Voltaire, *Anti-Machiavel, ou, Essai de critique sur le Prince de Machiavel* (La Haye: Pierre Paupie, 1740).
91 Diderot, Letter to Princess Dashkoff, 3 April 1771, in *Oeuvres complètes*, vol. 20, ed. J. Assézat and Maurice Tourneux (Paris: Garnier, 1877), 28, cited in Koselleck, *Critique and Crisis*, 172.
92 This is probably most clearly expressed by Diderot in his "Supplément au Voyage de Bougainville" (1771–3), in *Political Writings*, ed. John Hope Mason and Robert Wokler (Cambridge: Cambridge University Press, 1992).
93 Koselleck, *Critique and Crisis*, 176.
94 Georg Forster, *Cook der Entdecker*, in *Cook der Entdecker: Schriften über James Cook von Georg Forster und Georg Christoph Lichtenberg*, ed. Klaus-Georg Popp (Leipzig: Reclam, 1981), 57.
95 George Forster (1777), *A Voyage round the World*, ed. Nicholas Thomas and Oliver Berghof (Honolulu: University of Hawai'i Press, 2000), 1: 9.
96 See Russell Berman's excellent discussion of this point in *Enlightenment or Empire*, chap. 1.
97 See his letters in *Aus Herders Nachlass*, ed. Heinrich Duentzer (Frankfurt: Meidinger, 1856–7), 2: 387, 395ff., 402, 420.

5. *From Human Diversity*

1 Stuart Hampshire, *Spinoza and Spinozism* (Oxford: Clarendon Press, 2005), xxix.
2 See Don Garrett, "Spinoza's conatus Argument," in *Spinoza: Metaphysical Themes*, ed. Olli Koistinen and John Biro (Oxford: Oxford University Press, 2002), 127–58.
3 Mack, *Spinoza and the Specters of Modernity*, 54.
4 Bernard Mandeville, *The Fable of the Bees: Or, Private Vices, Publick Benefits* (1732), vol. 1, ed. F.B. Kaye (Oxford: Clarendon, 1924), 344. Cited in Jonathan Lamb, *Preserving the Self in the South Seas, 1680–1840* (Chicago: University of Chicago Press, 2001), 32.
5 Lamb, *Preserving the Self*, 32.
6 Barbara Cassin, ed., *Dictionary of Untranslatables. A Philosophical Lexicon*, trans. Steven Rendall et al. (Princeton: Princeton University Press, 2014), 115. Cassin observes that in Herder's work "*Bildung* acquires a status that allows it to include the reference both to the biological and organic development of forms and to intellectual education and the refinement of manners" (113).
7 See Robert J. Richards, *The Romantic Conception of Life: Science and Philosophy in the Age of Goethe* (Chicago and London: University of Chicago Press, 2002).

8 As Suphan notes, these include "the history of culture, literature and states, geography, social sciences, ethnography, astronomy, meteorology and travel, language and customs, physiology and anatomy, and the many forms of the natural sciences in general" (*HSW* 14, 679). In his correspondence with friends and associates during these years, he is constantly requesting books, maps, and essays about far-off places; or he is mining his networks of cosmopolitan intellectuals for observations and opinions about distant lands. He asks Daniel Gotthilf Moldenhawer, librarian in Copenhagen, for Africa travelogues for his friend August von Einsiedel (20 August 1784); he borrows books from Christian Gottlob Voigt describing travels throughout the world (August 1788); he writes to the university librarian in Göttingen, Friedrich Ludwig Wilhelm Meyer, requesting the "Memoirs" of the "East-India Society" in Calcutta, headed by the Orientalist scholar and founder of the Asiatic Society in Calcutta in 1784, Sir William Jones. Herder also requests "everything poetical and fairytale-like from the Ganges to the Nile" (*HBG* 5, 58, 317, 239). When Karl Ludwig von Knebel writes to Herder on 14 January 1785, he muses: "After I retired on the last evening I saw you, I delighted in the prints which Bernoulli publishes in Berlin, based, I believe, on drawings and sketches by Father [Joseph] Tiefenthaler. There is nothing extraordinary in their presentation of a number of cities, palaces, regions and buildings in India. Yet I was nonetheless pleased to peruse the style and spirit of this people, whose architecture displays the same quiet simplicity, seriousness, unique exaltation and withdrawn inner being which are manifest in its other works."

9 Leibniz, "On the Doctrine of Malebranche. A Letter to M. Remond de Montmort, containing Remarks on the Book of Father Tertre against Father Malebranche," in *The Philosophical Works of Leibnitz*, trans. George Martin Duncan (New Haven: Tuttle, Morehouse & Taylor, 1890), 234.

10 See Richards, *The Romantic Conception of Life*, 225.

11 J.F. Blumenbach, *De generis humani varietate nativa liber* (Gottingae: Vandenhoeck, 1775). This study was written under the supervision of Christian Wilhelm Büttner (1716–1801), whose reports of travels and discoveries in the far-flung corners of the world proved particularly inspiring to his student. Büttner lived in Weimar in the 1780s, where he was one of Goethe's important interlocutors on matters of scientific theory.

12 Blumenbach, "Üeber den Bildungstrieb (Nisus formativus) und seinen Einfluß auf die Generation und Reproduction," *Göttingisches Magazin der Wissenschaften und Litteratur* 1/5 (1780): 247–66.

13 Blumenbach, *Über den Bildungstrieb und das Zeugungsgeschäft* (Göttingen: Dieterich, 1781); *An Essay on Generation*, trans. A. Crichton (London: T. Cadell, 1792).
14 See Richards, *The Romantic Conception of Life*, chap. 5, for an excellent discussion of Blumenbach's theories and their context.
15 Blumenbach, "Über den Bildungstrieb," 250.
16 Blumenbach, *Über den Bildungstrieb*, 24. Blumenbach is referring to Charles Bonnet's *Considérations sur les corps organizés, ou l'on traite de leur origine, de leur développement, de leur réproduction* (Amsterdam: Rey, 1762).
17 Blumenbach, "Über den Bildungstrieb," 259.
18 See Timothy Lenoir's description of how Bildung relates to race in "Kant, Blumenbach, and Vital Materialism in German Biology," *Isis* 71/1 (1980): 77–108.
19 Blumenbach, "Über den Bildungstrieb," 260.
20 Ibid., 261.
21 Blumenbach, "Einige zerstreute Bemerkungen über die Fähigkeiten und Sitten der Wilden," *Göttingisches Magazin der Wissenschaften und Litteratur* 2/6 (1782): 409–25.
22 Richards, *The Romantic Conception of Life*, 227.
23 Ibid.
24 Menges, "Particular Universals," 206–7.
25 This point is made by Bondeli, "Von Herder zu Kant," in *Herder und die Philosophie des deutschen Idealismus*, 212.
26 Palti, "The 'Metaphor of Life,'" 336.
27 Writing to Knebel in December 1784, Herder asked him to send him copies of both Blumenbach's *Über den Bildungstrieb* and Wolff's *Theoria generationis* (*HBG* 5, 84).
28 "No force can be destroyed; for what does that mean: a force is destroyed? In nature there is no example for this, and in our minds there is no concept … It is hardly possible for a single atom to be destroyed or lost, and it is even less possible in the case of the invisible force acting in this atom" (*HMA* 3/1, 156).
29 Herder was not yet prepared to go as far as Adorno would when, in 1932, he described the task of analysing natural history: "to grasp historic being in its utmost historical determination [*Bestimmtheit*], in the place where it is most historic, as natural being, or to grasp nature, in the place where it seems most deeply, inertly natural, as historic being"; T. Adorno, "Die Idee der Naturgeschichte" (Idea of Natural History,1932), cited in *Negative Dialectics*, trans. E.B. Ashton (London: Routledge, 2004), 359. Or, as he later put it, "to see all nature, and

whatever would install itself as such, as history, and all history as nature"; *Negative Dialectics*, 359.

30 Marx will put this same idea more radically in his *Ökonomisch-philosophische Manuskripte aus dem Jahre 1844* (Economic and Philosophic Manuscripts of 1844) when he writes: "Neither nature objectively nor nature subjectively is immediately given in a form adequate to the human being. And as everything natural has to have its genesis, man too has his act of genesis – history – which, however, is for him a known history, and hence as an act of genesis it is a conscious self-sublating act of genesis. History is the true natural history of man." Karl Marx, *Economic and Philosophic Manuscripts of 1844*, ed. Dirk J. Struik, trans. Martin Milligan (New York: International Publishers, 1964), 182 [translation modified].

31 Sonia Sikka notes that "Herder's attitude towards natural desire is strikingly different from that of Kant." Herder's belief that human self-awareness brings humanity closer to the forces of nature and to divinity makes it easy for him to align desire with the holy. *Herder on Humanity*, 57.

32 Isaiah Berlin, *Three Critics of the Enlightenment: Vico, Hamann, Herder* (London: Pimlico, 2000), 181.

33 See John M. Headley, *The Europeanization of the World: On the Origins of Human Rights and Democracy* (Princeton: Princeton University Press, 2008), 37–40.

34 St Augustine, *The City of God against the Pagans*, trans. Eva Matthews Sanford and William McAllen Green, vol. 5 (Cambridge: Harvard University Press, 1965), 51.

35 See Robert Young, *Colonial Desire: Hybridity in Theory, Culture and Race* (London and New York: Routledge, 1995). Young reads Herder – incorrectly, I believe – as paving the way for nineteenth-century racism through his linking of localism to diversity (39).

36 Polygenesis is, according to this view, the result of a deficient sense of history and a disregard for the empirical evidence; this amounts to an inability to read the signs of human nature and society. Headley discusses how the idea of common humanity relates to the monogenesis debates in *The Europeanization of the World*, chap. 2.

37 Herder's reference is not clear. Voltaire was the most prominent proponent of polygenesis. Samuel Thomas Sömmering, professor of anatomy in Mainz, also cast doubt on monogenesis in his book *Über die körperliche Verschiedenheit des Mohren vom Europäer* (Frankfurt and Leipzig, 1785). According to Bernasconi, "Kant advocated the value of the scientific concept of race for natural history primarily as a support for

monogenesis against the assault of Voltaire, Henry Home [Lord Kames], and others"; *Race* (Oxford: Wiley-Blackwell, 2001), 155.

38 Sikka, *Herder on Humanity*, 129. See also p. 139.

39 See Heinz Stolpe, "Anmerkungen," in *Ideen zur Philosophie der Geschichte der Menschheit*, vol. 1 (Berlin and Weimar: Aufbau, 1965), 481–7. According to Stolpe, this position was shared by a number of leading anthropologists and natural historians of the time; he mentions Buffon, Peter Simon Pallas, and Eberhardt August Wilhelm Zimmermann.

40 *Pongo* is the genus of the orang-utan; with *longimanus* Herder is referring to the gibbon.

41 This is clearly outlined in Sara Eigen, ed., *The German Invention of Race* (Albany: SUNY Press, 2006).

42 Published in J.J. Engel's journal *Der Philosoph für die Welt* 2 (1777): 125–64; Kant, "On the Different Races of Humankind," trans. J.M . Mikkelsen, in *The Idea of Race*, ed. R. Bernasconi and T. Lott (Indianapolis: Hackett Publishers, 2000), 8–22. Kant had published this essay two years earlier as an announcement of his lectures in physical geography for the summer semester 1775.

43 In particular, his "Bestimmung des Begriffs der [einer] Menschenrace" ("Determination of the Concept of a Human Race" [1785], trans. Holly Wilson and Günter Zöller, in *Anthropology, History and Education*, ed. G. Zöller, R.B. Louden, et al. [Cambridge: Cambridge University Press, 2007], 145–59); "Über den Gebrauch teleologischer Prinzipien in der Philosophie" ("On the Use of Teleological Principles in Philosophy" [1788], trans. Günter Zöller, in *Anthropology, History and Education*, 195–218); and "Anthropologie in pragmatischer Hinsicht" (*Anthropology from a Pragmatic Point of View* [1798], trans. Robert B. Louden [Cambridge: Cambridge University Press, 2006]). See the chapter "Who Invented the Concept of Race? Kant's Role in the Enlightenment Construction of Race," in Bernasconi, *Race*.

44 Georg Forster, "Noch etwas über die Menschenraßen," *Der Teutsche Merkur*, October/November 1786, 62.

45 Ibid., 63.

46 "I am by no means prepared to answer the question whether there are several original branches of humanity with a decisive yes … at least I cannot consider it incomprehensible or improbable that two distinct branches, and perhaps in each a considerable number of individuals emerged as autochthones in different regions of the world"; ibid., 161. According to Ulrich Enzensberger, Forster privately shared Sömmering's belief that the negro is more closely related to apes than to whites; *Georg*

Forster: Ein Leben in Scherben (Frankfurt am Main: Eichborn, 1996), 158. Sikka points to the mutual influence of Sömmering and Herder, but I believe she is too quick to find agreement between their views on the position of the "negro" with relation to the apes; *Herder on Humanity*, 136.

47 Forster, "Noch etwas über die Menschenraßen," 161. Blumenbach, too, insisted on the empirical foundation of any distinction in human physiological types, and although he spoke of five different "races" of humanity, he appears to have understood these strictly in terms of his theory of *Bildung*. That is, climate effected physiological changes in homogeneous groups derived from the single original family of humanity. Like Kant, he saw this project in opposition to the racial theories of polygeneticism, most notably the theories of Lord Kames. Zammito, *Kant, Herder*, 304.

48 The sense that eyewitness accounts of travellers were able to overturn common preconceptions about other cultures would gain a significant boost when the letters of Alexander von Humboldt began to appear in German journals at the turn of the century. Humboldt's vividly descriptive and evocative letters were read with great interest by the public. Among many other observations, he lists evidence for the complex language and high culture of the indigenous inhabitants of the Spanish colonies in South America. In a letter published in the *Neue Berlinische Monatschrift* in August 1803, he takes issue with the French explorer and mathematician Charles Marie de la Condamine, who spent ten years in South America (1735–44). He denounces Condamine's claim that the native languages of South America are impoverished. On the contrary, Humboldt encounters languages that combine "richness, strength, and subtlety." They also possess expressions for abstract concepts. In particular, the Inca language is "so rich in manifold turns of phrase that young men who want to whisper sweet nothings to their ladies usually switch to Inca when they have exhausted the wealth of Castilian." Following Herder's lead, Humboldt sees language as the key to a culture's complexity and sophistication; Alexander von Humboldt, "Beschluß der neuesten Reiseberichte des Herrn Oberbergraths von Humboldt," *Neue Berlinische Monatschrift* 5 (1803): 86. For an overview of this topic see Eigen, ed., *The German Invention of Race*; also Sikka, *Herder on Humanity*, chap. 4.

49 Zammito, *Kant, Herder*, 332.

50 Kant too seems to have responded in a similar manner to Montesquieu's innovations. According to Vorländer, he was one of the first proponents of Montesquieu in Prussia in the 1760s (and perhaps already in the late

1750s); Karl Vorländer, *Immanuel Kant: Der Mann und das Werk* (1924), 2nd ed. (Hamburg: Meiner, 1977), 2: 211. In his lectures on geography, he justifies the geographical foundation of peoples and states in terms reminiscent of Montesquieu, and similar to those that will become important for Herder. Peoples and states must be explained on the basis of permanent underlying principles such as "the lay of their lands, the products, manners, commerce, trade and population" (Curriculum Outline of 1765–6, cited in Vorländer, ibid., 212).

51 Charles-Louis de Secondat, Baron de Montesquieu, *The Spirit of the Laws*, trans. and ed. Anne M. Cohler, Basia Carolyn Miller, and Harold Samuel Stone (Cambridge: Cambridge University Press, 1989), 232–3.

52 In chapter 3 of book 7 of *Ideas*, he makes direct reference to Montesquieu's physiological theories. Although he is prepared to accept the scientific validity of Montesquieu's observations, he is not willing to use these limited empirical observations to draw general conclusions about "entire peoples or regions of the world" (*HSW* 13, 267). His dedication to Montesquieu probably prevents him from direct criticism, but he chides his great forerunner indirectly, noting that "even the great Montesquieu has been accused of basing his climatic spirit of the laws on a deceptive experiment with a mutton's tongue" (*HSW* 13, 268) – an experiment Montesquieu saw as proof of the direct physiological impact of climate on organisms. Montesquieu describes the experiment as follows: "I have observed the place on the surface tissue of a sheep's tongue which appears to the naked eye to be covered with papillae. Through a microscope I have seen the tiny hairs, or a kind of down, on these papillae; between these papillae were pyramids, forming something like little brushes at the ends. It is very likely that these pyramids are the principal organ of taste. I had half of the tongue frozen; and, with the naked eye I found the papillae considerably diminished; some of the rows of papillae have even slipped inside their sheaths: I examined the tissue through the microscope; I could no longer see the pyramids. As the tongue thawed, the papillae appeared again to the naked eye, and, under the microscope, the little brushes began to reappear. This observation confirms what I have said that in cold countries, the tufts of nerves are less open; they slip inside their sheaths, where they are protected from the action of external objects. Therefore, sensations are less vivid." Montesquieu, *The Spirit of the Laws*, 233.

53 Bernard, *Herder's Social and Political Thought*, 122.

54 Ibid., 121.

55 I think Sikka is too quick to claim that this passage shows Herder's support for European centrality and expansionism in the realm of reason and humanity (*Herder on Humanity*, 25). Too much of his writing militates against this idea. The cited passage clearly states that Europe has not yet achieved humanity and reason, making its domination of the world something unnatural.

56 See also "Von der Annehmlichkeit, Nützlichkeit und Nothwendigkeit der Geographie" (On the Advantages, Usefulness, and Necessity of Geography), *HSW* 30, 96–103. Suphan tentatively dates this speech to 1784.

57 Peter Kalm, "*Beschreibung der Reise die er nach dem nördlichen Amerika … unternommen hat*," in *Göttingische Sammlung neuer und merkwürdiger Reisen zu Wasser und zu Lande*, vols. 9 and 10 (Göttingen: Verlag der Witwe Abrams Vandenhoek, 1754, 1757).

58 Ibid., 10: 187.

59 See ibid., 10: 243.

60 Ibid., 10: 326.

61 Ibid., 10: 284–5.

62 Ibid., 10: 558, 315–18.

63 This was a growing theme in writings on settler colonization. See, for example, H. Williamson, "Versuch die Ursachen von der Veränderung des Klima zu erklären, welche in den, in dem innern Theil des mitternächtlichen Amerika belegenen Kolonien bemerkt worden," *Berlinische Sammlungen* 7 (1775): 5–21.

64 "Even just considered as a tool it would seem that the Roman *spirit of conquest* had to *precede* in order to open paths everywhere, to establish a *political connection* between peoples which was previously unheard of, to set in motion on precisely this path *tolerance, ideas of international law among peoples* previously unheard of on that scale!" (*HPW* 304).

65 "The incorporation of tradition into the life of a people can be named Culture after the tilling of the soil or Enlightenment after the image of light; regardless of the name, the chain of culture and enlightenment reaches to the ends of the earth." This includes "the Californian and the Fire-lander" (*HSW* 13, 347–8).

66 In this, Herder was strongly influenced by Lavater. See Palti, "The 'Metaphor of Life,'" 335.

67 Zammito, "Herder and Historical Metanarrative," 77.

68 Herder is referring to the "Tabula mundi geographico zoologica" published around 1760 in Augsburg by the geographer and professor of mathematics in Braunschweig, Eberhard Zimmermann. Herder

apparently didn't realize that the French geographer Robert de Vaugondy had already published an anthropological map of the world in 1778 ("Mappe-Mond suivant la projection des cartes reduites" [Paris: Delamarche]).

69 See John K. Noyes, "Nomadic Landscapes: Producing Landscapes of Mobility in German Southwest Africa," *Ecumene* 7/1 (2000): 47–66.

70 Sikka, *Herder on Humanity*, 117.

71 See Bondeli, "Von Herder zu Kant," 212–14.

72 Ibid., 214.

73 Later, Kant would address this with his discussion of *sensus communis* in paragraph 40 of the *Critique of Judgment*, where he develops the idea of *sensus communis* as "a power to judge that in reflecting takes account (a priori), in our thought, of everyone else's way of presenting [something], in order *as it were* to compare our own judgment with human reason in general," *Critique of Judgment*, trans. Werner Pluhar (Indianapolis: Hackett, 1987), 160.This concession to Herder's criticism (if that's what it was) is even more striking when he notes that the *sensus communis* is better understood as operating via aesthetic, not intellectual judgments.

74 Menges, "Particular Universals," 208.

75 Pross speaks of the "major mistake" in Kant's criticism, his failure to recognize the larger scientific context that legitimated Herder's views; *HMA* 3/2, 431. See Pross's excellent discussion of Herder's engagement with the latest scientific debates; *HMA* 3/2, 430–7.

76 Karl Leonard Reinhold, "Schreiben des Pfarrers zu *** an den H des T. M. Ueber einee Recension von Herders Ideen zur Philosophie der Geschichte der Menschheit," *Der Teutsche Merkur*, 1st quarter (1785): 148–74. See Bondeli's excellent discussion of the exchange in "Von Herder zu Kant," 214–19.

77 Bondeli, "Von Herder zu Kant," 215. Bondeli is citing Herder's letter to Wieland, who edited the *Teutsche Merkur*, January 1785; *HBG* 5, 102.

78 Sikka, *Herder on Humanity*, chap. 2: "Happiness and the Moral Life." As she notes: "The opposition between Kant and Herder on the subject of happiness is more complex than one might think, touching upon a host of questions in metaphysics, epistemology, and ethics. Kant and Herder hold sharply contrasting views of the relation between mind and body, between reason and perception, and between means and ends within various spheres of teleological understanding. They also differ on the nature and role of the emotions, and on the status of the 'natural' as a category applying both to an aspect of human subjectivity and to the objective world. All of these differences are implicated in the dispute

between them on the character and value of happiness, in relation to morality, a dispute which has serious consequences for social and political practice" (49).

79 In the *Nicomachean Ethics* (1097b, 22) Aristotle states that happiness is "something final and self-sufficient, and is the end of action." *Basic Works*, 942.

80 Sikka makes this point; *Herder on Humanity*, 50.

81 Kant will explain this later in *Die Religion innerhalb der Grenzen der blossen Vernunft* (Religion within the Limits of Reason Alone, 1793), where he gives section 3: 1/2 the heading: "Man shall exit the ethical state of nature, in order to become a member of an ethical body politic."

82 "Before Kant, no-one qualifies the necessity of the institution of the state as founded in pure reason of law. No theory of the state of nature but the Kantian one interprets the results of this, which are shared by all, as the contents of an a priori obligation toward the law." Wolfgang Kersting, *Wohlgeordnete Freiheit: Immanuel Kants Rechts- und Staatsphilosophie* (Berlin and New York: De Gruyter, 1984), 199–200.

83 "Kant does not argue merely that a civil order is morally permissible, considered perhaps as a rational cooperation problem *consistent* with one's moral standing as a free, rational being. Rather, anyone willing to remain in a pre-civil state is not just an irrational noncooperator, but thereby does '*wrong* in the highest degree' ('*unrecht ... im hochsten Grad*') (6:308; 86) and such a civil condition must be understood as some sort of *requirement* of pure practical reason. (It is practically necessary, not just permissible.)" Robert B. Pippin, "Mine and Thine? The Kantian State," in *Cambridge Companion to Kant and Modern Philosophy*, ed. Paul Guyer (Cambridge: Cambridge University Press, 2006), 416–46, 417.

84 Kant stated this position clearly two decades later, in 1797, when he published his *Metaphysik der Sitten* (The Metaphysics of Morals). Here he explained the obsolescence of government based on hereditary right, and the need to replace it with institutions that guaranteed the separation of the powers of government, the foundation of government in public law, and the concentration of government in the hands of the people. Government appears to Kant as the opposite of violence, the bond of law that founds society. Law holds violence at bay, and as a result, the condition of nature looks increasingly like one of lawlessness, if not raw violence. The state allows human society to emerge from nature's lawlessness by joining under the auspices of openly declared laws. *Metaphysics of Morals*, trans. Mary Gregor (Cambridge: Cambridge University Press, 1991), part 2: "Public Right," 123–77.

85 This was reiterated in a short essay entitled "Muthmaßlicher Anfang der Menschengeschichte" (Conjectures on the Beginning of Human History), which Kant published in the *Berliner Monatsschrift* in 1786, the year following his review of Herder's *Ideas*, and presumably under the influence of his reading of Herder. Here, he imagines the workings of reason that allowed the first humans to go through the process of individuation described in Genesis, and to reach the point where their natural instincts had been overcome by reason, indeed where they were then in a position to dominate nature. For Kant, it is in overcoming the voice of nature (which he identifies with the instincts, *KPW* 223) that humanity tastes freedom and has the right to be treated as a free being. Reason acts like Mephistopheles in *Faust*, as a restless drive that pushes individuals beyond the self-satisfied fulfilment of natural urges: "In the future, the hardships of life would often arouse in him [the human being] the wish for a paradise created by his imagination, a paradise where he could dream or idle away his existence in quiet inactivity and everlasting peace. But restless reason, irresistibly driving him on to develop his innate capacities, stands between him and that imagined seat of bliss, and does not allow him to return to the state of rude simplicity from which it had originally attracted him" (*KPW* 226).

86 See Sikka, *Herder on Humanity*, 58–70.

87 Ibid., 157.

88 Sikka believes Herder's challenge to Kant on this point "calls into question the entire framework of Kant's practical philosophy, its most basic categories, distinctions, and value judgements. In spite of recent attempts to defend and rehabilitate Kant's ethical thought, these criticisms remain valid." Ibid., 49.

89 Sikka speaks of Herder's "strong" relativism when it comes to the theory of happiness. Ibid., 34.

90 As Pross points out, Herder is siding with Spinoza, who, in paragraph 20 of the *Tractatus theologico-politicus*, argues "on the basis of the inviolable law of freedom of choice of individuals, the purpose of the state cannot be the subjugation of individuals and citizens" (*HMA* 3/2, 542).

6. *The Aesthetics of Revolution*

1 Bondeli refers to Herder's letters to Hamann and Jacobi of February 1785. "Von Herder zu Kant," 215n39.

2 Wulf Koepke, "Klarheit und Wahrheit: Herders 'Wende' nach 1787," *Monatshefte* 95/2 (2003): 273–93.

3 See the excellent analysis of the positions taken by Kant and Herder on the state in Sikka, *Herder on Humanity*, chap. 2.
4 Ulrich Gaier, "Poesie oder Geschichtsphilosophie? Herders erkenntniskritische Antwort auf Kant," in *Johann Gottfried Herder: Geschichte und Kultur*, ed. Martin Bollacher (Würzburg: Königshausen und Neumann, 1994), 2.
5 Bohm, "Herder and Politics," 291.
6 Cited and trans. by Sikka, *Herder on Humanity*, 72.
7 Koepke, "Klarheit und Wahrheit," 276.
8 As Koepke summarizes, this short sketch outlines a "participatory community body, in other words an 'organic state,' in which unity and diversity remain balanced and the 'national welfare' (national well-being) is the measure of all actions. A clear linguistic and historical consciousness are the preconditions, for without the knowledge of tradition there is no orientation toward the future." Koepke, "Klarheit und Wahrheit," 277.
9 Gaier, "Poesie oder Geschichtsphilosophie?" 2. The essay has been translated as "On Image, Poetry, and Fable," in *HAW*, 357–82.
10 Clark, *Herder*, 348.
11 According to Gaier, the essay explores object creation in the poetic process. Gaier, "Myth, Mythology, New Mythology," in *Companion to the Works of Johann Gottfried Herder*, ed. Adler and Koepke, 171.
12 Norton, *Herder's Aesthetics*, 43.
13 See Koepke, "Klarheit und Wahrheit," 286.
14 Ibid., 276.
15 F.H. Jacobi, *Über die Lehre des Spinoza in Briefen an Herrn Moses Mendelssohn* (Breslau: Gottlieb Löwe, 1785).
16 Klaus Hammacher regards Jacobi's doctrine of a personal God as a truly original contribution to theological debates at the time; "Herders Stellung im Spinozastreit," in *Herder und die Philosophie des deutschen Idealismus*, ed. Marion Heinz,168.
17 David Janssens, "The Problem of the Enlightenment: Strauss, Jacobi, and the Pantheism Controversy," *Review of Metaphysics* 56/3 (2003): 609–10.
18 Clark, *Herder*, 339.
19 Janssens, "The Problem of the Enlightenment," 611.
20 When Jacobi's *Spinoza* appeared in 1785, Goethe found himself unwilling to plainly state his objections to the book. In a letter of 9 June (sounding very much like Herder), he tells Jacobi: "You recognize the supreme reality which is the basis of all Spinozism, the foundation and source of everything. He does not prove the existence of God; existence is

God" (*Letters from Goethe*, trans. M. von Herzfeld and C. Melvil Sym [Edinburgh: Edinburgh University Press, 1957], 157). And yet he was clearly unhappy with Jacobi's refusal to draw the full consequences of this recognition; instead, Jacobi appeared to be making exactly the same error Goethe had written about in 1773 when he spoke of those people "who call themselves philosophers and play a downright ridiculous character in the world. There is nothing more dismal than hearing people speak incessantly of reason while behaving according to prejudice alone" (*Letter from the Pastor of* ***, *GBA* 17, 277). In a letter to Jacobi in October, Goethe is still more outspoken in his criticism. He writes that he does not share Jacobi's opinions, and that Spinozism is in no way to be equated with atheism. He then states that, if he had to name a book that came closest to describing his own views of nature, it would be the *Ethics*. Finally, he takes issue with Jacobi's use of the word *glauben*: "I still can't let you get away with this usage; it's only appropriate for sophists of faith who must find it extremely convenient to obscure all certainty of knowledge, and suffuse it with the nebulae of their wavering ethereal kingdom, seeing as they cannot in fact shake the foundations of truth" (*GWA* 4/7, 110). But Goethe was less interested in the metaphysical implications of Jacobi's Spinoza. This he felt better left to Herder. In July he had told Jacobi: "Forgive me – as one who has never laid claim to the metaphysical mode of inquiry – for not writing more, and nothing better, after so long a time. I am going to admonish Herder today and I hope he shall do it better" (*GWA* 4/7, 64).

21 Sikka puts this well when she notes that "the ultimate ground and explanation of reality, which Herder defines as force or power, *Kraft*, is not merely, for him, an indication of God, but *is* God"; *Herder on Humanity*, 224.

22 Herder is alluding to Montesquieu's *Spirit of the Laws*, though the source of the citation is unclear.

23 In the dialogues on God, Herder has Theophron observe that "in the matter of tolerance, our states have been disposed to take almost no other direction than that which Spinoza in his day anticipated to the hatred of all." Herder, *God, Some Conversations*, trans. Frederick H. Burckhardt (Indianapolis: Bobbs-Merrill, 1940), 80.

24 The strongest statement of Herder as a Spinozist is probably Michael Mack's *Spinoza*, who bases this among other things on Herder's adoption of *conatus*. According to Clark, in contrast, "it is patent" that Herder's system "is not the pantheism of Spinoza, from which it borrows only a modified form of Spinoza's 'immanence' and almost nothing of Spinoza's method"; *Herder*, 346.

25 Koepke, "Klarheit und Wahrheit," 276.
26 Ibid., 281.
27 Ibid., 278.
28 Undated letter to Karl Ludwig von Knebel, in *Knebels Literarischer Nachlaß und Briefwechsel*, vol. 2 (Leipzig: Reichenbach, 1840), 310; cited by Suphan, *HSW* 18, 524.
29 Clark implies that Herder self-censored in reaction to the Terror, but I see nothing in his comments to indicate that he had changed his position on revolution in general, or on the French Revolution. *Herder*, 369.
30 Sikka makes this point in *Herder on Humanity*, 45.
31 "Ueber die Fähighkeit zu sprechen und zu hören," *Neue Deutsche Monatsschrift* 2 (1795): 60; *HSW* 18, 387.
32 I agree with Robert Norton that Herder's political position is misrepresented by Isaiah Berlin, who deduces an anti-revolutionary position from Herder's supposed anti-Enlightenment stance.
33 See his prize-winning essay *Vom Einfluß der Regierung auf die Wissenschaften, und der Wissenschaften auf die Regierungen* (On the Influence of Government on the Sciences, and of Science on Government), submitted to the Berlin Academy der Sciences, and published in 1780; *HSW* 9, 307–407.
34 *On the Influence of Government*, *HSW* 9, 375.
35 George Müller, *Aus dem Herder'schen Hause* (Berlin: Weidmann'sche Buchhandlung, 1881), 109; cited by Suphan, *HSW* 18, 524.
36 I have altered Herder's punctuation for ease of reading.
37 This point is made by Wolf Köpke, "Humanität in Goethes Weimar: Herder nach der französischen Revolution," *"Verteufelt human?"* In *Zum Humanitätsideal der Weimarer Klassik*, ed. Volker C. Dörr and Michael Hofmann (Berlin: Erich Schmidt Verlag, 2008), 53–4.
38 See the excellent analysis by Hans Dietrich Irmscher in *HFA* 7, 844–5.
39 *Schillers Werke* (*Nationalausgabe*), vol. 26, ed. Edith Nahler and Horst Nahler (Weimar: Böhlau, 1992), 263.
40 This is similar to the position taken by the British statesman and author Edmund Burke, though Burke reaches quite different conclusions. In his pamphlet *Reflections on the Revolution in France*, which was to become a bestseller in France and Germany, Burke spoke out sharply against the idea that the social order could be adequately engineered by a sudden radical change based on a priori doctrines of political life. Against this, he invoked the hidden rationality of tradition. Neither Goethe nor Herder seem to have been particularly interested in Burke; Herder possessed a copy of Burke's observations on the revolution (Johann Friedrich

Vieweg sent it to him early in 1793), but he does not take issue with the Englishman. Edmund Burke, *Reflections on the revolution in France, and on the proceedings in certain societies in London relative to that event: In a letter intended to have been sent to a gentleman in Paris* (London: Dodsley, 1790), trans. as *Betrachtungen über die französische Revolution: In Zwei Theilen* (Berlin: Vieweg, 1793).

41 Cited and trans. by Clark, *Herder*, 369.

42 "If all the world is a chain, with one ring attached to the next, we are much to be deplored, that in this mighty chain we see so few that are equal. Each annalist takes his fatherland as a starting point, squinting with a crooked eye at other provinces, lets himself be tricked and fooled by rumours, this whore of all the world, then sits down and writes a crippled history of his time. We see so little and think we see so much. We know nothing and sit in judgment over all things." C.F.D. Schubart, "Weltschau," in *Gesammelte Schriften*, vol. 8 (Stuttgart: Scheible, 1840), 122–3.

43 Köpke, "Humanität in Goethes Weimar," 51–2.

44 The meaning of *Mohrenfels* is not clear. Irmscher reads it as a reference to Cape Town's Table Mountain (*HFA* 7, 1104).

45 Gerhard Sauder, "Herder's Poetic Works, Translations, and Views on Poetry," in *A Companion to the Works of Johann Gottfried Herder*, ed. Adler and Koepke, 313.

46 Knoll, "Beyond the Black Legend," 60.

47 J. Hector St John de Crèvecoeur, *Letters from an American farmer describing certain provincial situations, manners, and customs, not generally known* (London: Thomas Davies and Lockyer Davis, 1782). See Irmscher's commentary in *HFA* 7, 1109. Also Philip Allison Shelley, "Crèvecoeur's Contribution to Herder's 'Neger-Idyllen,'" *Journal of English and Germanic Philology* 37/1 (1938): 48–69.

48 This is a retelling of a story from Johann Ernst Kolb, *Erzählungen von den Sitten und Schicksalen der Negersklaven: Eine rührende Geschichte fur Menschen guter Art* (Bern: Haller, 1789).

49 Sauder, "Herder's Poetic Works," 313.

50 On this last point see Sikka, *Herder on Humanity*, 72–3.

51 Charles-Irénée Castel, Abbé de Saint-Pierre, *Projet pour rendre la paix perpétuelle en Europa* (Utrecht [Paris]: Chez A. Schouten, 1713–17).

52 Georg Heinrich Loskiel, *Geschichte der Mission der evangelischen Brüder under den Indianern in Nordamerika* (Leipzig: Paul Gotthelf Kummer, 1789), 160–2.

53 Ibid., 161.

54 Ibid., 160.
55 Karla Lydia Schultz, "Herders indianische Friedensfrau," *Monatshefte* 81/4 (1989): 413.
56 Pauline Kleingeld, "Kant, History, and the Idea of Moral Development," *History of Philosophy Quarterly* 16/1 (1999): 59.
57 Michel Despland, *Kant on History and Religion. With a Translation of Kant's "On the failure of all attempted philosophical theodicies"* (Montreal: McGill-Queen's University Press, 1973), 68.
58 Kleingeld, "Kant, History, and the Idea of Moral Development," 68.

Conclusion

1 Sikka probably presents the most balanced discussion of what linked the Nazis to Herder, concluding that "his relation to the concept of race could not be more distant from that of the National Socialists." *Herder on Humanity*, 158; see also 147–50.
2 Fredric Jameson cites Herder as an example of "that organic populism or nationalism which articulated the rather different historicity of the central and Eastern European peoples," an idea he dismisses as "discredited under [its] hegemonic embodiment … in nationalism"; *The Political Unconscious: Narrative as a Socially Symbolic Act* (Ithaca: Cornell University Press, 1981), 19. Homi Bhabha calls Herder's sense of the nation "morally arbitrary"; "Unsatisfied: Notes on Vernacular Cosmopolitanism," in *Text and Nation: Cross-Disciplinary Essays on Cultural and National Identities*, ed. Laura Garcia-Moreno and Peter C. Pfeiffer (Columbia, SC: Camden House, 1996), 196. In *After Globalization* (Chichester: Wiley-Blackwell, 2013), Eric Cazdyn and Imre Szeman refer to Herder's ideas on the nation as "nonsense," which have managed, "not only to stand the test of time, but to become even more popular as the years pass by" (48). This appraisal is odd, since many of their own views on community and globalization are – unwittingly, I can only assume – close to those of Herder, including a theological dimension they appear not to recognize.
3 Trabant, "Herder and Language," 122.
4 Chase, "Herder and the Postcolonial Reconfiguring of the Enlightenment," 186.
5 Zammito, "Herder and Historical Metanarrative," 83.
6 Sikka, *Herder on Humanity*, 120.
7 Young, *Colonial Desire*, 42.
8 In his *Treatise on the Origin of Language* (1774), Herder argues that there is a "language of nature," a neurological substratum, a somatic system

comprising the "internal nerve structure" of the body and the organs of speech. The sympathetic cries (speech is saying too much) aroused in the nervous system are no more than "the natural law of a sensitive machine," and have little or nothing to do with the moment of language acquisition. The neurological system already evokes a certain sociability in the expressive individual, since expression assumes the resonance of another sympathetic being (intended in a purely biological sense). This is the sociability of the organism, not of the reasoning human. But as a shared process for structuring the sensitivity to the external world, it guarantees the universality of reason. See Herder, *HPW*, 73–4.

9 In 1774 he notes that "reason is no compartmentalized, separately effective force but an orientation of all forces that is distinctive to his [i.e., the human being's] species." *Treatise on the Origin of Language*, 85.

10 "Versuch über das Sein," *HFA* 1, 10.

11 Ibid.

12 In a section of his *Metacritique of the Critique of Pure Reason* of 1799, entitled "Von Antinomien der Vernunft" (On Antinomies of Reason), he states that there may be antinomies in law, but not in reason, for "to assume two pure reasons which contradict themselves means to reduce the examiner to quarrel [*eris*] and to change the office of reason into the art of quarrel [*eristic*]" (*HSW* 21, 223). Herder rejects Kant's use of the antinomies of pure reason, arguing that they are situated in psychological capacities of relating to the world, and their opposition is resolved within reason itself. Thus, as Nisbet observes, "all conflicts are ultimately reconcilable, and never absolute, for Herder." H.B. Nisbet, *Herder and the Philosophy and History of Science* (Cambridge: Modern Humanities Research Association, 1970), 72.

13 "Hegel implicitly acknowledges that he is indebted to Herder for several of his own mature positions (including his neo-Spinozist monism and his concept of *Geist*) in a neglected and much misunderstood section of the Phenomenology of Spirit of 1807 which turns out to be entirely concerned with Herder's standpoint: 'The Spiritual Animalkingdom [*Das geistige Tierreich*].'" Michael N. Forster, *German Philosophy of Language: From Schlegel to Hegel and Beyond* (Oxford: Oxford University Press, 2011), 147.

14 Herder's biographer Robert T. Clark noted that Herder's historical writing is "not the talk of a Romanticist; it sounds more like the economic determinism of a forerunner of Marx, and some commentators have pointed out that Herder anticipated Marx's delineation of the class struggle. This, like various other ideas accorded Herder by later writers, is an exaggeration; but it is clear that the germ of economic determinism,

of the materialist interpretation of history, lies in Part IV of the *Ideas*." *Herder*, 333–4.

15 "Herder's interest in politics was but an aspect of a much wider interest which encompassed not only art and literature but also a distinct cosmology and philosophy of history. For it was this close association of political, historical, poetical, and religio-cosmological thinking that was to characterise the comprehensive, 'ideological' style of political thought from the Romanticists to the Marxists." (Barnard, *Herder's Social and Political Thought*, 31.

16 Sonia Sikka notes Herder's "role in shaping the thought of later German philosophers, such as Nietzsche, Hegel, and Heidegger." *Herder on Humanity*, 5. See also chapter 6 in her book.

17 Jürgen Trabant, "Language and the Ear: From Derrida to Herder," *Herder Yearbook* 1 (1992): 1–22.

18 Dipesh Chakrabarty, *Provincializing Europe: Postcolonial Thought and Historical Difference* (Princeton: Princeton University Press, 2008), xiii.

19 "Reason becomes elitist whenever we allow unreason to stand in for backwardness, that is to say, when reason colludes with the logic of historicist thought." Ibid., 238.

20 Ibid., 254.

21 Ibid.

22 Mbembe frames his book by questioning what Enlightenment's promise of universality means for Africa (*On the Postcolony*, 11), and by observing how "Africa" exists only in the contiguous, the peripheral, the ephemeral (p. 242).

23 Ibid., 8.

24 Ibid., 9.

25 Ibid., 12.

26 Ibid.

27 Ibid.

28 Ibid., 14.

29 Ibid.

30 Herder distinguishes between Being or God, which cannot be positioned in time and space, and the being of bodies, which can be located and described in terms of Crusius's *ubi* (where?) or *quando* (when?). And mediating between Being and bodies is *per*, the concept of force. *Versuch über das Sein* (*HMA* 1, 586).

31 Mbembe, *On the Postcolony*, 15.

32 Ibid.

33 Ibid., 16. This reads as remarkably similar to Herder's attacks on the idea of progress in history. "Humankind is destined to undergo a progression

of scenes, of forms, of mores: woe betide the person who dislikes the scene in which he is to appear, act, and live out his life! But woe betide also the philosopher of humanity and mores whose own scene is the only one, and who also always mistakes the first one for the worst. If all belong together to the whole of the advancing play: in each one a new, quite remarkable side of humanity is manifest." Herder, "Auszug aus einem Briefwechsel über Ossian und die Lieder alter Völker," in *Von Deutscher Art und Kunst* (1773), *HSW* 5, 164.

34 Mbembe's anaysis is moved by the desire to counter what he regards as undue emphasis placed on representation by social theory (*On the Postcolony*, 6), while at the same time acknowledging the centrality of representation in civil society (39) and in political action (142–3).

35 Ibid., 16–17.

36 Ibid., 17. It is unclear whether "its" refers to "the concrete world" or "living in the concrete world." Either way, the point is the same: form gives content to experience.

37 As Samson Knoll observes, these poems are intended to prepare the way for Herder's justification of self-defence of the less powerful in the face of inhumanity on the part of the powerful. "Beyond the Black Legend: The Anticolonialism of Johann Gottfried Herder," *North Dakota Quarterly* 57/3 (1989): 60.

38 Spivak, *A Critique of Postcolonial Reason*, 19.

39 Ibid., 1.

40 Mack, *Spinoza*, 70.

41 Spivak, *Critique of Postcolonial Reason*, 27.

42 "Without language the human being has no reason, and without reason no language." *On the Origin of Language*, 91.

43 Spivak, *Critique of Postcolonial Reason*, 28.

44 Adorno, *Negative Dialectics*, 346.

45 Spivak, *Critique of Postcolonial Reason*, 312.

46 Ibid., 312, 319.

47 He did this most clearly in *God, Some Conversations* (1787), in which the positions of the interlocutors are at least intended to point to, if not replicate, those of Herder's friends who were involved in the debates around Spinoza in the year 1783 (Herder, Goethe, Jacobi, Lessing, Mendelssohn). Again and again, we find him structuring his works around the dialogical principle. We find it, for example, in his short piece "Über die Seelenwanderung. Drei Gespräche" (On Metempsychosis. Three Conversations, 1782); in the early fragment "Ein Gespräch Zweifel. Zu Mendelssohns Phädon" (A Conversational Doubt. On Mendelssohn's

Phaedon, 1768); in some of the *Letters on the Advancement of Humanity*; and in the pieces he wrote for the *Journal von Tiefurt* in 1781–2: "Verstand und Herz. Ein Hausgespräch am langen Winterabend" (Understanding and Heart. A Domestic Conversation on a Long Winter Evening), "Die heilige Cäcilia oder wie man zu Ruhm kommt. Ein Gespräch" (St Cecilia, or On How One Attains Renown. A Conversation), and "Ob Malerie oder Tonkunst größere Wirkung gewähre. Ein Göttergespräch" (On Whether Painting or Music Provides the Greater Effect. A Conversation among the Gods).

48 See the note to Hamann accompanying the conversation on Mendelssohn's *Phaedon*: "Socrates is dead, and his disciples are celebrating his communion; a Simmias among them ruminates on the doubts that refuse to leave me upon reading Moses's *Phaedon*" (*HSW*, 32, 200).

49 Clark, *Herder*, 351.

50 Nisbet's pages on the dialectical method in Herder's writings are worth noting, although I find he tries a little too hard to distance Herder's dialectic from the historical materialism of the Marxian dialectic. *Herder and the Philosophy and History of Science*, 72–85.

51 As Menges points out, "Writing is a symptom of the aging of a culture, as is the preference for prescriptive rules, academic decorum, and imitative entertainment. These symptoms are indicative of a loss of sensual perception in the process of modernity and its accelerating descent into an ever-more differentiated rational but also impersonal and alienating life-world. Herder's general interest in questions of origin is a reflection of this dialectic of Enlightenment." Karl Menges, "Particular Universals: Herder on National Literature, Popular Literature, and World Literature," in *Companion to the Works of Johann Gottfried Herder*, ed. Adler and Koepke, 195.

52 Spivak, "Scattered Speculations on the Question of Value," *Diacritics* 15/4 (1985): 73–93.

Bibliography

Abbreviations

GBA Goethe, Johann Wolfgang von. 1960–78. *Poetische Werke. Kunsttheoretische Schriften und Übersetzungen*. 22 volumes. Berlin and Weimar. *Berliner Ausgabe.*

GHA Goethe, Johann Wolfgang von. 1961–4. *Werke.* 14 volumes. Textkritisch durchgesehen und mit Anmerkungen versehen von Erich Trunz et al. Hamburg: C. Wegner. *Hamburger Ausgabe.*

GWA Goethe, Johann Wolfgang von. 1987. *Goethes Werke.* Edited on Commission of Großherzogin Sophie von Sachsen. 143 volumes. Weimar: H. Böhlau, 1887–1918. *Weimarer Ausgabe.*

HAW Herder, Johann Gottfried. 2006. *Selected Writings on Aesthetics.* Translated and edited by Gregory Moore. Princeton: Princeton University Press.

HBG Herder, Johann Gottfried. 1977. *Briefe. Gesamtausgabe 1763–1803.* 10 volumes. Edited by Karl-Heinz Hahn et al. Weimar: Böhlau.

HEW Herder, Johann Gottfried. 1992. *Selected Early Works, 1764–1767: Addresses, Essays, and Drafts; Fragments on Recent German Literature.* Edited by Ernest A. Menze and Karl Menges. Translated by Ernest A. Menze with Michael Palma. University Park: Pennsylvania State University Press.

HFA Herder, Johann Gottfried. 1985–. *Werke.* 10 volumes. Edited by Martin Bollacher, Jürgen Brummack, Ulrich Gaier, Gunter E. Grimm, Hans Dietrich Irmscher, Rudolf Smend, Johannes Wallmann. Frankfurt: Deutscher Klassiker Verlag.

HJV Herder, Johann Gottfried. 1952. "A Journal of My Voyage in the Year 1769." Translated, with introduction and notes, by John Francis Harrison. PhD diss., Columbia University.

HMA Herder, Johann Gottfried. 1984–. *Werke*. 3 volumes. Edited by Wolfgang Pross. Munich: Hanser.

HPW Herder, Johann Gottfried. 2002. *Philosophical Writings*. Edited and translated by Michael N. Forster. Cambridge: Cambridge University Press.

HRP Herder, Johann Gottfried. 1968. *Reflections on the Philosophy of the History of Mankind*. Edited by Frank Manuel. Chicago: University of Chicago Press.

HSW Herder, Johann Gottfried. 1967–8. *Sämtliche Werke*. 33 volumes. Edited by Bernhard Suphan. Hildesheim: G. Olms.

KPW Kant, Immanuel. 1970. *Political Writings*. Edited by H. Reiss. Translated by H.B. Nisbet. Cambridge: Cambridge University Press.

Works

Aarsleff, Hans. "The Tradition of Condillac: The Problem of the Origin of Language in the Eighteenth Century and the Debate in the Berlin Academy before Herder." In *Studies in the History of Linguistics*, edited by Dell Hymes, 93–156. Bloomington: Indiana University Press, 1974.

Adler, Hans. *Die Prägnanz des Dunklen: Gnoseologie, Ästhetik, Geschichtsphilosophie bei Johann Gottfried Herder*. Hamburg: Meiner, 1990.

Adler, Hans, and Wulf Koepke. *A Companion to the Works of Johann Gottfried Herder*. Rochester, NY: Camden House, 2009.

Adorno, Theodor W. "Die Idee der Naturgeschichte" (1932). In *Gesammelte Schriften 1: Philosophische Frühschriften*. Suhrkamp: Frankfurt am Main, 1973.

Adorno, Theodor W. *Negative Dialectics* (1966). Translated by E.B. Ashton. London: Routledge, 2004.

Adorno, Theodor W., and Max Horkheimer (1944). *Dialectic of Enlightenment*. Translated by John Cumming. London: Verso, 1979.

Adler, Hans. *Die Prägnanz des Dunklen: Gnoseologie, Ästhetik, Geschichtsphilosophie bei J. G. Herder*. Hamburg: Meiner, 1990.

d'Alembert, Jean Le Rond. 1751. "Discours Préliminaire." In *Encyclopédie ou Dictionnaire raisonné des sciences, des arts et des métiers*, volume 1. Paris: Briasson, David l'aîné, Le Breton, and Durand, i–xlv. "Preliminary Discourse." In *The Encyclopedia of Diderot & d'Alembert Collaborative Translation Project*. Translated by Richard N. Schwab and Walter E. Rex. Ann Arbor: Michigan Publishing, University of Michigan Library, 2009.

Archenholz, J.W. von. *Geschichte des Siebenjährigen Krieges in Deutschland* (1789). 12th edition. Leipzig: Amelang, 1866.

Aristotle. *The Basic Works of Aristotle*. Edited by Richard McKeon. New York: Random House, 1941.

Arnold, Günter. "'... der größte Mann den Deutschland in den neuern Zeiten gehabt' – Herders Verhältnis zu Leibniz." *Studia Leibnitiana* 37/2 (2005): 161–85.

Augustine. *The City of God against the Pagans*. Translated by Eva Matthews Sanford and William McAllen Green. Cambridge: Harvard University Press, 1965.

Balibar, Étienne. *The Philosophy of Marx*. Translated by Chris Turner. London: Verso, 2007.

Banks, Joseph. *The* Endeavour *Journal of Joseph Banks, 1768–1771*. 2 volumes. Edited by J.C. Beaglehole. Sydney: Angus and Robertson, 1963.

Barnard, F.M. *Herder on Nationality, Humanity and History*. Montreal: McGill-Queen's University Press, 2003.

Barnard, F.M. *Herder's Social and Political Thought: From Enlightenment to Nationalism*. Oxford: Clarendon Press, 1965.

Barnard, F.M. *J. G. Herder on Social and Political Culture*. Cambridge: Cambridge University Press, 1969.

Barry, Kelly. "Natural Palingenesis: Childhood, Memory, and Self-Experience in Herder and Jean Paul." *Goethe Yearbook* 14 (2006): 1–25.

Baumgarten, Alexander Gottlieb. *Aesthetica*. 2 volumes. Frankfurt/Oder: Johannes Christian Kleybl, 1750–8.

Bayly, Christopher A. "The First Age of Global Imperialism c. 1760–1830." *Journal of Imperial and Commonwealth History* 26/2 (1998): 28–47.

Benjamin, Walter. "Über den Begriff der Geschichte" (1941). In *Illuminationen*. Frankfurt: Suhrkamp, 1977.

Berlin, Isaiah. "Herder and the Enlightenment." In *The Proper Study of Mankind: An Anthology of Essays*, edited by Henry Hardy and Roger Hausheer. London: Chatto and Windus, 1997.

Berlin, Isaiah. *Three Critics of the Enlightenment: Vico, Hamann, Herder*. London: Pimlico, 2000.

Berlin, Isaiah. *Vico and Herder*. London: Hogarth Press, 1976.

Berman, Russell. *Enlightenment or Empire: Colonial Discourse in German Culture*. Lincoln and London: University of Nebraska Press, 1998.

Bernasconi, Robert. *Race*. Oxford: Wiley-Blackwell, 2001.

Bhabha, Homi. "Unsatisfied: Notes on Vernacular Cosmopolitanism." In *Text and Nation: Cross-Disciplinary Essays on Cultural and National Identities*, edited by Laura Garcia-Moreno and Peter C. Pfeiffer. Columbia, SC: Camden House, 1996.

Blackwell, Thomas. *An Enquiry into the Life and Writings of Homer*. London: n.p., 1735.

Blumenbach, Johann Friedrich. *De generis humani varietate nativa liber*. Gottingae: Vandenhoeck, 1775.

Blumenbach, Johann Friedrich. "Einige zerstreute Bemerkungen über die Fähigkeiten und Sitten der Wilden." *Göttingisches Magazin der Wissenschaften und Litteratur* 2/6 (1782): 409–25.

Blumenbach, Johann Friedrich. "Über den Bildungstrieb (Nisus formativus) und seinen Einfluß auf die Generation und Reproduction." *Göttingisches Magazin der Wissenschaften und Litteratur* 1/5 (1780): 250; reprinted as *Über den Bildungstrieb* (see below).

Blumenbach, Johann Friedrich. *Über den Bildungstrieb und das Zeugungsgeschäft*. Göttingen: Dieterich, 1781. *An Essay on Generation*. Translated by A. Crichton. London: T. Cadell, 1792.

Bodemer, C.W. "Regeneration and the Decline of Preformation in Eighteenth-century Embryology." *Bulletin of the History of Medicine* 38 (1964): 20–31.

Bondeli, Martin. "Von Herder zu Kant, zwischen Kant und Herder, mit Herder gegen Kant – Karl Leonhard Reinhold." In *Herder und die Philosophie des deutschen Idealismus*, edited by Marion Heinz, 203–34. Amsterdam: Rodopi, 1997.

Bonnet, Charles. *Considérations sur les corps organizés, ou l'on traite de leur origine, de leur développement, de leur réproduction*. Amsterdam: Rey, 1762.

Breitinger, Johann Jacob. *Critische Dichtkunst*. 2 volumes. Zürich: Conrad Orell, 1740.

Burke, Edmund. *Reflections on the revolution in France, and on the proceedings in certain societies in London relative to that event: In a letter intended to have been sent to a gentleman in Paris*. London: Dodsley, 1790. Translated as *Betrachtungen über die französische Revolution: In Zwei Theilen*. Berlin: Vieweg, 1793.

Bush, Barbara. *Imperialism and Postcolonialism*. Harlow, UK: Pearson Longman, 2006.

Carey, Daniel, and Lynn Festa, editors. *Postcolonial Enlightenment*. Oxford: Oxford University Press, 2009.

Cassin, Barbara, ed. *Dictionary of Untranslatables. A Philosophical Lexicon*. Translated by Steven Rendall, Christian Hubert, Jeffrey Mehlman, Nathanael Stein, and Michael Syrotinski. Princeton: Princeton University Press, 2014.

Castel, Charles-Irénée, Abbé de Saint-Pierre. *Projet pour rendre la paix perpétuelle en Europe*. Utrecht [Paris]: Chez A. Schouten, 1713–17.

Cazdyn, Eric, and Imre Szeman. *After Globalization*. Chichester: Wiley-Blackwell, 2013.

Chakrabarty, Dipesh. *Provincializing Europe: Postcolonial Thought and Historical Difference*. Princeton: Princeton University Press, 2000.

Chase, Bob. "Herder and the Postcolonial Reconfiguring of the Enlightenment." *Bucknell Review* 41/2 (1998): 172–96.

Cheah, Pheng. *Spectral Nationality: Passages of Freedom from Kant to Postcolonial Studies*. New York: Columbia University Press, 2003.

Clark, Robert T. "Herder's Conception of 'Kraft.'" *PMLA* 57/3 (1942): 737–52.

Clark, Robert T. *Herder: His Life and Thought*. Berkeley and Los Angeles: University of California Press, 1955.

Cook, James. *Captain Cook's Journal during his First Voyage round the World made in H. M. Bark "Endevour" 1768–71*. Edited by W.J.L. Wharton. London: Elliot Stock, 1893.

Cook, James. *A Voyage to the Pacific Ocean. Undertaken, by the Command of His Majesty, for Making Discoveries in the Northern Hemisphere, to Determine the Position and Extent of the West Side of North America; Its Distance from Asia; and the Practicability of a Northern Passage to Europe. Performed under the Direction of Captains Cook, Clerke, and Gore, in His Majesty's Ships the Resolution and Discovery, in the Years 1776, 1777, 1778, 1779, and 1780*. 3 volumes and atlas volume. London: Printed for John Stockdale, Scatcherd and Whitaker, John Fielding, and John Hardy, 1784.

Crèvecoeur, J. Hector St John de. *Letters from an American farmer describing certain provincial situations, manners, and customs, not generally known*. London: Thomas Davies and Lockyer Davis, 1782.

De Jong, Willem. "How Is Metaphysics as a Science Possible? Kant on the Distinction between Philosophical and Mathematical Method." *Review of Metaphysics* 49/2 (1995): 235–74.

Derrida, Jacques. *Of Grammatology*. Translated by Gayatri C. Spivak. Baltimore: Johns Hopkins University Press, 1976.

Despland, Michel. *Kant on History and Religion. With a Translation of Kant's "On the failure of all attempted philosophical theodicies."* Montreal: McGill-Queen's University Press, 1973.

Diderot, Denis. *Political Writings*. Edited and translated by John Hope Mason and Robert Wokler. Cambridge: Cambridge University Press, 1992.

Diderot, Denis. *Oeuvres complètes*. Edited by J. Assézat and Maurice Tourneux. Paris: Garnier, 1875–7.

Duchesneau, François. "Charles Bonnet's Neo-Leibnizian Theory of Organic Bodies." In *The Problem of Animal Generation in Early Modern Philosophy*, edited by Justin E.H. Smith. Cambridge: Cambridge University Press, 2006.

Düntzer, Heinrich, and F.G. von Herder, editors. *Aus Herders Nachlass. Ungedruckte Briefe von Herder und dessen Gattin, Goethe, Schiller, Klopstock, Lenz, Jean Paul, Claudius, Lavater, Jacobi und andern bedeutenden Zeitgenossen*. 3 volumes. Frankfurt: Meidinger, 1856–7.

Edwards, Jeffrey. *Substance, Force, and the Possibility of Knowledge: On Kant's Philosophy of Material Nature*. Berkeley: University of California Press, 2000.

Eggel, Dominic, Andre Liebich, and Deborah Mancini-Griffoli. "Was Herder a Nationalist?" *Review of Politics* 69/1 (2007): 48–78.

Eigen, Sara, editor. *The German Invention of Race*. Albany: SUNY Press, 2006.

Einsiedel, August von. *Ideen*. Edited by Wilhelm Dobbek. Berlin: Akademie Verlag, 1957.

Enzensberger, Ulrich. *Georg Forster: Ein Leben in Scherben*. Frankfurt am Main: Eichborn, 1996.

Eskuche, Balthasar Ludwig. *Erläuterungen Heiliger Schrift aus morgenländischen Reise-Beschreibungen*. Lemgo: Johann Heinrich Meyer, 1750.

Figueroa, Dimas. *Philosophie und Globalisierung*. Würzburg: Königshausen und Neumann, 2004.

Förster, Eckart, and Yitzhak Y. Melamed, editors. *Spinoza and German Idealism*. Cambridge: Cambridge University Press, 2012.

Forster, George. 1777. *A Voyage round the World*. 2 volumes. Edited by Nicholas Thomas and Oliver Berghof. Honolulu: University of Hawai'i Press, 2000.

Forster, Georg. *Cook der Entdecker: Schriften über James Cook von Georg Forster und Georg Christoph Lichtenberg*. Edited by Klaus-Georg Popp. Leipzig: Reclam, 1981.

Forster, Georg. "Noch etwas über die Menschenraßen." *Der Teutsche Merkur*, October/November 1786, 57–86.

Forster, Michael N. *German Philosophy of Language: From Schlegel to Hegel and Beyond*. Oxford: Oxford University Press, 2011.

Forster, Michael N. "Herder's Philosophy of Language, Interpretation, and Translation: Three Fundamental Principles." *Review of Metaphysics* 56/2 (2002): 323–56.

Fox, Russell Arben. "J. G. Herder on Language and the Metaphysics of National Community." *Review of Politics* 65/2 (2003): 237–62.

Frazer, Michael. *The Enlightenment of Sympathy: Justice and the Moral Sentiments in the Eighteenth Century and Today*. New York: Oxford University Press, 2010.

Frederick II, King of Prussia. *Anti-Machiavel, oder Prüfung der Regeln Nic. Machiavells von der Regierungskunst eines Fürsten: mit historischen und politischen Anmerkungen*. Göttingen: Verlag der Königlichen Universitäts-Buchhandlung, 1741.

Gadamer, Hans-Georg. *Truth and Method*. New York: Continuum, 2006.

Gaier, Ulrich. "Herders Systemtheorie." *Allgemeine Zeitschrift fiir Philosophie* 23/1 (1998): 3–17.

Gaier, Ulrich. *Herders Sprachphilosophie und Erkenntniskritik*. Stuttgart-Cannstatt: frommann-holzboog, 1988.

Gaier, Ulrich. "Poesie oder Geschichtsphilosophie? Herders erkenntniskritische Antwort auf Kant." In *Johann Gottfried Herder: Geschichte und Kultur*, edited by Martin Bollacher, 1–17. Würzburg: Königshausen und Neumann, 1994.

Gaier, Ulrich. "The Problem of Core Cognition in Herder." *Monatshefte* 95/2 (2003): 294–309.

Garrard, Graeme. *Counter-Enlightenments: From the Eighteenth Century to the Present*. London: Routledge, 2006.

Garrett, Don. "Spinoza's Conatus Argument." In *Spinoza: Metaphysical Themes*, edited by Olli Koistinen and John Biro, 127–58. Oxford: Oxford University Press, 2002.

Goethe, Johann Wolfgang. *Letters from Goethe*. Translated by M. von Herzfeld and C. Melvil Sym. Edinburgh: Edinburgh University Press, 1957.

Goggi, Gianluigi. "Quelques remarques sur la collaboration de Diderot à la première édition de l'Histoire des deux Indes." *Studies on Voltaire and the Eighteenth Century* 286 (1991): 17–52.

Golinski, Jan. *British Weather and the Climate of Enlightenment*. Chicago: University of Chicago Press, 2007.

Gould, Stephen Jay. *Ontogeny and Phylogeny*. Cambridge, MA: Harvard University Press, 1977.

Greif, Stefan. "Herder's Aesthetics and Poetics." In *A Companion to the Works of Johann Gottfried Herder*, edited by Hans Adler and Wulf Koepke, 141–64. Rochester, NY: Camden House, 2009.

Guthke, Karl S. *Die Erfindung der Welt: Globalität und Grenzen in der Kulturgeschichte der Literatur*. Tübingen: Francke, 2005.

Guthke, Karl S. *Goethes Weimar und "Die große Öffnung in die weite Welt."* Wolfenbütteler Forschungen 93. Wiesbaden: Harrassowitz, 2001.

Guyer, Paul. "Free Play and True Well-Being: Herder's Critique of Kant's Aesthetics." *Journal of Aesthetics and Art Criticism* 65/4 (2007): 353–68.

Hamann, Johann Georg. *Aesthetica in nuce* (1760). In *Classic and Romantic German Aesthetics*, edited by J.M. Bernstein. Cambridge: Cambridge University Press, 2003.

Hamann, Johann Georg. *Hamann's Schriften*. 8 volumes. Edited by Friedrich von Roth. Reimer: Berlin, 1821–43.

Hamann, Johann Georg. *Kreuzzüge des Philologen* (1762). In *Sturm und Drang: Kritische Schriften*, edited by Erich Löwenthal, 93–144. Heidelberg: Lambert Schneider, 1972.

Hampshire, Stuart. *Spinoza and Spinozism*. Oxford: Clarendon Press, 2005.

Haraway, Donna. "A Cyborg Manifesto: Science, Technology, and Socialist-Feminism in the Late Twentieth Century." In *Simians, Cyborgs and Women: The Reinvention of Nature*, 149–81. New York: Routledge, 1991.

Hawkesworth, John. *An Account of the Voyages undertaken by order of his present Majesty for making Discoveries in the Southern Hemisphere*. 4 volumes. London: W. Strahan and T. Cadell, 1773.

Haym, Rudolf. *Herder nach seinem Leben und seinen Werken*. 2 volumes. Berlin: Rudolph Gaertner, 1880–5.

Headley, John M. *The Europeanization of the World: On the Origins of Human Rights and Democracy*. Princeton: Princeton University Press, 2008.

Heinz, Marion. *Sensualitischer Idealismus: Untersuchungen zur Erkenntnistheorie des jungen Herder*. Hamburg: Meiner, 1994.

Heinz, Marion, editor. *Herder und die Philosophie des deutschen Idealismus*. Amsterdam: Rodopi, 1997.

Heinz, Marion, and Heinrich Clairmont. "Herder's Epistemology." In *A Companion to the Works of Johann Gottfried Herder*, edited by Hans Adler and Wolf Koepke. Rochester, NY: Camden House, 2009.

Herder, Johann Gottfried. *God, Some Conversations*. Translated by Frederick H. Burckhardt. Indianapolis: Bobbs-Merrill, 1940.

Herder, Johann Gottfried. *Ideen zur Philosophie der Geschichte der Menschheit*. Edited by Hans Stolpe. 2 volumes. Berlin and Weimar: Aufbau, 1965.

Herder, Johann Gottfried. *Journal meiner Reise im Jahr 1769*. Edited by Katherine Mommsen. Stuttgart: Reclam, 1976.

Herder, Johann Gottfried. *On the Origin of Language: Jean-Jacques Rousseau, Essay on the origin of languages; Johann Gottfried Herder, Essay on the origin of language*. Translated by John H. Moran and Alexander Gode. New York: Ungar, 1966.

Herder, Johann Gottfried. *Plastik*. Riga: Hartknoch, 1778.

Herder, Johann Gottfried. *Sculpture: Some Observations on Shape and Form from Pygmalion's Creative Dream*. Translated by Jason Gaiger. Chicago: University of Chicago Press, 2002.

Herder, Johann Gottfried. *The Spirit of Hebrew Poetry*. Translated by James Marsh. Naperville, IL: Aleph Press, 1971.

Hess, Jonathan M. *Germans, Jews and the Claims of Modernity*. New Haven and London: Yale University Press, 2002.

Hont, Istvan. *Jealousy of Trade: International Competition and the Nation-State in Historical Perspective*. Cambridge, MA: Belknap Press, 2005.

Hopkins, A.G. *Globalization in World History*. New York: Norton, 2002.

Hopkins, A.G. *Global History: Interactions between the Universal and the Local*. New York: Palgrave-Macmillan, 2006.

Humboldt, Alexander von. "Beschluß der neuesten Reiseberichte des Herrn Oberbergraths von Humboldt." *Neue Berlinische Monatschrift* 5 (1803): 81–9.

Jacobi, F.H. *Über die Lehre des Spinoza in Briefen an Herrn Moses Mendelssohn.* Breslau: Gottlieb Löwe, 1785.

Jaeger, Michael. *Fausts Kolonie: Goethes kritische Phänomenologie der Moderne.* Würzburg: Königshausen und Neumann, 2004.

Jameson, Fredric. *The Political Unconscious: Narrative as a Socially Symbolic Act.* Ithaca: Cornell University Press, 1981.

Janssens, David. "The Problem of the Enlightenment: Strauss, Jacobi, and the Pantheism Controversy." *Review of Metaphysics* 56/3 (2003): 605–31.

Kalm, Peter. *Beschreibung der Reise die er nach dem nördlichen Amerika … unternommen hat. Göttingische Sammlung neuer und merkwürdiger Reisen zu Wasser und zu Lande.* Volumes 9 and 10. Göttingen: Verlag der Witwe Abrams Vandenhoek, 1754, 1757.

Kant, Immanuel. *Anthropologie in pragmatischer Hinsicht* (1798/1800). In *Gesammelte Schriften*, volume 7. Edited by the Königlich-Preussischen Akademie der Wissenschaften zu Berlin. Berlin: Akademie der Wissenschaften, 1917.

Kant, Immanuel. *Anthropology from a Pragmatic Point of View.* Edited by Robert B. Louden. Cambridge: Cambridge University Press, 2006.

Kant, Immanuel. *Critique of Judgment* (1790). Translated by Werner S. Pluhar. Indianapolis: Hackett, 1987.

Kant, Immanuel. *Critique of Pure Reason* (1781/87). Edited and translated by Paul Guyer and Allen Wood. Cambridge: Cambridge University Press, 2000.

Kant, Immanuel. "Determination of the Concept of a Human Race" (1785). Translated by Holly Wilson and Günter Zöller. In *Anthropology, History and Education*, edited by G. Zöller, R.B. Louden, et al. , 145–59. Cambridge: Cambridge University Press, 2007.

Kant, Immanuel. *Gesammelte Schriften.* 23 volumes. Berlin: Akademie der Wissenschaften, 1902–.

Kant, Immanuel. *Metaphysics of Morals* (1797). Translated by Mary Gregor. Cambridge: Cambridge University Press, 1991.

Kant, Immanuel. "On the Different Races of Humankind" (1775). Translated by J.M. Mikkelsen. In *The Idea of Race*, edited by R. Bernasconi and T. Lott, 8–22. Indianapolis: Hackett Publishers, 2000.

Kant, Immanuel. "On the Use of Teleological Principles in Philosophy" (1788). Translated by Günter Zöller. In *Anthropology, History and Education*, edited by G. Zöller, R.B. Louden, et al., 195–218. Cambridge: Cambridge University Press, 2007.

Kant, Immanuel. *Philosophy of Material Nature*. Translated by James W. Ellington. Indianapolis: Hackett, 1985.

Kant, Immanuel. *Religion within the Limits of Reason Alone* (1793). Translated by Theodore M. Greene and Hoyt H. Hudson. San Fransisco: Harper Torchbooks, 1960.

Kant, Immanuel. *Theoretical Philosophy 1755–1770*. Translated and edited by David Walford and Ralf Meerbote. Cambridge: Cambridge University Press, 1992.

Kant, Immanuel. "Thoughts on the True Estimation of Living Forces and Assessment of the Demonstrations that Leibniz and Other Scholars of Mechanics have made Use of in this Controversial Subject" (1746–9). Translated by Jeffrey B. Edwards and Martin Schönfeld. In *Natural Science*, edited by Eric Watkins, 1–155. Cambridge: Cambridge University Press, 2012.

Kant, Immanuel. "Von den verschiedenen Racen der Menschen" (1775). In *Gesammelte Schriften*, volume 2. Berlin: Akademie der Wissenschaften, 1905.

Kantzenbach, Friedrich Wilhelm. *Johann Gottfried Herder*. Reinbek bei Hamburg: Rohwohlt, 1970.

Kersting, Wolfgang. *Wohlgeordnete Freiheit: Immanuel Kants Rechts- und Staatsphilosophie.* Berlin and New York: De Gruyter, 1984.

Kieffer, Bruce. "Herder's Treatment of Süssmilch's Theory of the Origin of Language in *Abhandlung über den Ursprung der Sprache*: A Re-evaluation." *Germanic Review* 53/3 (1978): 96–104.

Kiernan, V.G. *Imperialism and Its Contradictions*. Edited and introduced by Harvey J. Kaye. New York: Routledge, 1995.

Kiesel, Helmuth. "Das nationale Klima. Zur Entwicklung und Bedeutung eines ethnographischen Topos von der Renaissance bis zur Aufklärung." In *Rom – Paris – London: Erfahrung und Selbsterfahrung deutscher Schriftsteller und Künstler un den fremden Metropolen. Ein Symposion*, ed. Conrad Wiedemann, 123–34. Stuttgart: Metzler, 1988.

Kleingeld, Pauline. "Kant, History, and the Idea of Moral Development." *History of Philosophy Quarterly* 16/1 (1999): 59–80.

Klotz, Christian Adolph. *Epistolae homericae*. Altenburgi: Ex officina Richteria, 1764.

Knebel, Karl Ludwig von. *Knebels Literarischer Nachlaß und Briefwechsel*. Leipzig: Reichenbach, 1840.

Knoll, Samson B. "Beyond the Black Legend: The Anticolonialism of Johann Gottfried Herder." *North Dakota Quarterly* 57/3 (1989): 55–64.

Koepke, Wulf. "Klarheit und Wahrheit: Herders 'Wende' nach 1787." *Monatshefte* 95/2 (2003): 273–93.

Koepke, Wolf. "Humanität in Goethes Weimar: Herder nach der französischen Revolution." In *"Verteufelt human?": Zum Humanitätsideal der Weimarer Klassik*, edited by Volker C. Dörr and Michael Hofmann, 47–68. Berlin: Erich Schmidt Verlag, 2008.

Koistinen, Olli, and John Biro, editors. *Spinoza: Metaphysical Themes*. Oxford: Oxford University Press, 2002.

Kolb, Johann Ernst. *Erzählungen von den Sitten und Schicksalen der Negersklaven: Eine rührende Geschichte für Menschen guter Art*. Bern: Haller, 1789.

Kontje, Tod. *German Orientalisms*. Ann Arbor: University of Michigan Press, 2004.

Koselleck, Reinhard. *Begriffsgeschichten* (1926). Frankfurt: Suhrkamp, 2010.

Koselleck, Reinhard. *Critique and Crisis: Enlightenment and the Pathogenesis of Modern Society* (1959). Oxford: Berg, 1988.

Lafitau, Joseph-François. *Moeurs des sauvages ameriquains, comparées aux moeurs des premiers temps*. Paris: Saugrain l'aîné & C.-E. Hochereau, 1724.

Lahontan, Louis Armand de Lom d'Arce, Baron de. *Nouveaux voyages de Mr. le baron de Lahontan dans l'Amérique Septentrionale*. La Haye: Chez les fréres l'Honoré, 1703. Translated as *New voyages to North America … also a dialogue between the author and a general of the savages … to which is added a dictionary of the Algonkine language which is generally spoke in North-America*. London: H. Bonwicke, 1703.

Lal, Vinay. "The Politics of Culture and Knowledge after Postcolonialism: Nine Theses (and a Prologue)." *Continuum: Journal of Media & Cultural Studies* 26/2 (2012): 191–205.

Lamb, Jonathan. *Preserving the Self in the South Seas, 1680–1840*. Chicago: University of Chicago Press, 2001.

La Vopa, Anthony J. "Herder's Publikum: Language, Print, and Sociability in Eighteenth-Century Germany." *Eighteenth Century Studies* 29 (1995): 5–24.

Leibniz, Gottfried Wilhelm. "On the Doctrine of Malebranche. A Letter to M. Remond de Montmort, containing Remarks on the Book of Father Tertre against Father Malebranche" (1715). In *The Philosophical Works of Leibnitz*, translated by George Martin Duncan, 233–7. New Haven: Tuttle, Morehouse & Taylor, 1890.

Lenoir, Timothy. "Kant, Blumenbach, and Vital Materialism in German Biology." *Isis* 71/1 (1980): 77–108.

Lessing, Gotthold Ephraim. *Werke*. Edited by Herbert G. Göpfert, Karl Eibl, et al. 8 volumes. Munich: C. Hanser, 1970–.

Locke, John. *Essay Concerning Human Understanding* (1690). In *Philosophical Works and Selected Correspondence of John Locke*. Edited by Mark C. Rooks. 4 volumes. Charlottesville: InteLex Corporation, 1995.

Loskiel, Georg Heinrich. *Geschichte der Mission der evangelischen Brüder under den Indianern in Nordamerika.* Leipzig: Paul Gotthelf Kummer, 1789.

Mack, Michael. *Spinoza and the Specters of Modernity: The Hidden Enlightenment of Diversity from Spinoza to Freud.* London: Continuum, 2010.

Mackay, David. *In the Wake of Cook: Exploration, Science, and Empire: 1780–1801.* London: Croom Helm, 1985.

Mah, Harold. *Enlightenment Phantasies: Cultural Identity in France and Germany 1750–1914.* Ithaca and London: Cornell University Press, 2003.

Mancke, Elizabeth. "Early Modern Expansion and the Politicization of Oceanic Space." *The Geographical Review* 89 (1999): 225–36.

Mandeville, Bernard. *The Fable of the Bees: Or, Private Vices, Publick Benefits* (1732). Edited by F.B. Kaye. 2 volumes. Oxford: Clarendon Press, 1924.

Marx, Karl. *Economic and Philosophic Manuscripts of 1844.* Edited by Dirk J. Struik. Translated by Martin Milligan. New York: International Publishers, 1964.

Maupertuis, Pierre-Louis Moreau de. *Dissertation sur les différens moyens dont les hommes se sont servis pour exprimer leurs idées.* In *Oeuvres.* 4 volumes. Lyon: Chez Jean-Marie Bruyset, 1756.

May, J.A. *Kant's Concept of Geography and Its Relation to Recent Geographical Thought.* Toronto: University of Toronto Press, 1970.

Mbembe, Achille. *On the Postcolony.* Berkeley, Los Angeles, London: University of California Press, 2001.

Menges, Karl. "Identity as Difference. Herder's 'Great Topic' and the 'Philosophers of Paris.'" *Monatshefte* 87/1 (1995): 1–16.

Menges, Karl. "Particular Universals: Herder on National Literature, Popular Literature, and World Literature." In *A Companion to the Works of Johann Gottfried Herder,* edited by Hans Adler and Wulf Koepke, 189–213. Rochester, NY: Camden House, 2009.

Merkel, Garlieb Helwig. *Die Letten, vorzüglich in Liefland am Ende des philosophischen Jahrhunderts. Ein Beitrag zur Völker und Menschenkunde.* Leipzig: Gräf, 1796; Wedemark: Hischheydt, 1998.

Michaelis, Johann David. *Fragen an eine Gesellschaft Gelehrter Männer, die auf Befehl Ihro Majestät des Königes von Dännemark nach Arabien reisen.* Frankfurt: J.G. Garbe, 1762.

Montaigne, Michel de. *The Complete Essays.* Translated by Donald M. Frame. Stanford: Stanford University Press, 1965.

Montesquieu, Charles de Secondat, baron de. *Persian Letters* (1721). Translated by Margaret Mauldon. Oxford: Oxford University Press, 2008.

Montesquieu, Charles de Secondat, Baron de. *The Spirit of the Laws* (1748). Translated and edited by Anne M. Cohler, Basia Carolyn Miller, and Harold Samuel Stone. Cambridge: Cambridge University Press, 1989.

Morton, Michael. *Herder and the Poetics of Thought: Unity and Diversity in* On Diligence in Several Learned Languages. University Park and London: Pennsylvania State University Press, 1989.

Müller, George. *Aus dem Herder'schen Hause*. Berlin: Weidmann'sche Buchhandlung, 1881.

Müller, Herr. "Ueber Herrn Linguet, die Knechtschaft überhaupt, und die Rußische insonderheit." *Magazin für die neue Historie und Geographie* 18 (1784): 73–82.

Müller-Michaels, Harro. "Herder in Office: His Duties as Superintendent of Schools." In *A Companion to the Works of Johann Gottfried Herder*, edited by Hans Adler and Wulf Koepke, 373–90. Rochester, NY: Camden House, 2009.

Muthu, Sankar. *Enlightenment against Empire*. Princeton: Princeton University Press, 2003.

Nadler, Steven. "Spinoza and Consciousness." *Mind* 117/467 (2008): 575–601.

Nerling-Pietsch, Ingeborg. *Herders literarische Denkmale: Formen der Charakteristik vor Friedrich Schlegel*. Münster: Lit, 1997.

Nicolai, Friedrich. *Immanuel Kant's Kennzeichen der Philosophie, oder Weisheitsliebe im reinen Sinne des Worts*. Frankfurt and Leipzig: n.p., 1796.

Nisbet, H.B. *Herder and the Philosophy and History of Science*. Cambridge: Modern Humanities Research Association, 1970.

Norton, Robert. *Herder's Aesthetics and the European Enlightenment*. Ithaca and London: Cornell University Press, 1991.

Noyes, John K. "Commerce, Colonialism, and the Globalization of Action in Late Enlightenment Germany." *Postcolonial Studies* 9/1 (2006): 81–98.

Noyes, John K. "Goethe on Cosmopolitanism and Colonialism: Bildung and the Dialectic of Critical Mobility." *Eighteenth-Century Studies* 39/4 (2006): 443–65.

Noyes, John K. "Nomadic Landscapes: Producing Landscapes of Mobility in German Southwest Africa." *Ecumene* 7/1 (2000): 47–66.

Noyes, John K. "The World Map and the World of Goethe's *Weltliteratur*." *Acta Germanica* 38 (2010): 128–45.

Osterhammel, Jürgen, and Niels P. Petersson. *Globalization: A Short History*. Princeton: Princeton University Press, 2005.

Pagden, Anthony. "The Effacement of Difference: Colonialism and the Origins of Nationalism in Diderot and Herder." In *After Colonialism: Imperial Histories and Postcolonial Displacements*, edited by Gyan Prakash, 129–52. Princeton: Princeton University Press, 1995.

Pagden, Anthony. *European Encounters with the New World*. New Haven and London: Yale University Press, 1993.

Paine, Thomas. *The Rights of Man; Being an Answer to Mr. Burke's Attack on the French Revolution* (1791). In *The Political Works of Thomas Paine*, 233–448. Chicago and New York: Belford, Clarke & Co., 1887.

Palti, Elias. "The 'Metaphor of Life': Herder's Philosophy of History and Uneven Developments." *Eighteenth-Century Natural Sciences* 38/3 (1999): 322–47.

Pan, David. "J.G. Herder, the Origin of Language, and the Possibility of Transcultural Narratives." *Language and Intercultural Communication* 4/1–2 (2004): 10–20.

Phemister, Pauline. "Monads and Machines." In *Machines of Nature and Corporeal Substances in Leibniz*, edited by Justin E.H. Smith and Ohad Nachtomy. Dordrecht: Springer, 2011.

Pippin, Robert B. "Mine and Thine? The Kantian State." In *The Cambridge Companion to Kant and Modern Philosophy*, edited by Paul Guyer, 416–46. Cambridge: Cambridge University Press, 2006.

Prakash, Gyan, editor. *After Colonialism: Imperial Histories and Postcolonial Displacements*. Princeton: Princeton University Press, 1995.

Raynal, Guillaume Thomas (Abbé). *L'Histoire philosophique et politique des établissements et du commerce des Européens dans les deux Indes*. 10 volumes. Amsterdam: Chez E. van Harrevellt & D.J. Changuion, 1770.

Raynal, Guillaume Thomas (Abbé). *Philosophische und politische Geschichte der Besitzungen und des Handels der Europäer in beiden Indien*. Hanover: In der Hofbuchhandlung der Gebrüder Helwing, 1774–8.

Raynal, Guillaume Thomas (Abbé). *A philosophical and political history of the settlements and trade of the Europeans in the East and West Indies*. Translated by J.O. Justamond. 8 volumes. London: W. Strahan & T. Cadell, 1783.

Reinhold, Karl Leonard. "Schreiben des Pfarrers zu *** an den H des T. M. Ueber eine Recension von Herders Ideen zur Philosophie der Geschichte der Menschheit." *Der Teutsche Merkur*, 1st quarter (1785): 148–74.

Richards, Robert J. *The Romantic Conception of Life: Science and Philosophy in the Age of Goethe*. Chicago and London: University of Chicago Press, 2002.

Robinette, Nicholas. "The World Laid Waste: Herder, Language Labor, Empire." *New Literary History* 42 (2011): 193–203.

Roe, Shirley. *Matter, Life, and Generation*. Cambridge: Cambridge University Press, 1981.

Rousseau, Jean Jacques. *On the Origin of Language: Jean-Jacques Rousseau, Essay on the origin of languages; Johann Gottfried Herder, Essay on the origin of language*. Translated by John H. Moran and Alexander Gode. New York: Ungar, 1966.

Sarkar, Sumit. "Orientalism Revisited: Saidian Frameworks in the Writing of Modern Indian History." *Oxford Literary Review* 16/1 (1994): 205–24.

Schick, Edgar. *Metaphorical Organicism in Herder's Early Works: A Study of the Relation of Herder's Literary Idiom to His World-view*. The Hague, Paris: Mouton, 1971.

Schiller, Friedrich. *Werke*. Im Auftrag des Goethe- und Schiller-Archivs, des Schiller-Nationalmuseums und der Deutschen Akademie. Edited by Julius Petersen and Gerhard Fricke. Weimar: H. Böhlaus Nachfolger, 1943–.

Schlegel, Friedrich. *Dialogue on Poetry and Literary Aphorisms*. Translated by Ernst Behler and Roman Struc. University Park: Pennsylvania State University Press, 1968.

Schmidt, Royal J. "Cultural Nationalism in Herder." *Journal of the History of Ideas* 17/3 (1956): 407–17.

Schubart, Christian Friedrich Daniel. *Gesammelte Schriften*. 8 volumes. Stuttgart: Scheible, 1839–40.

Schultz, Karla Lydia. "Herders indianische Friedensfrau." *Monatshefte* 81/4 (1989): 413–24.

Shelley, Philip Allison. "Crèvecoeur's Contribution to Herder's 'Neger-Idyllen.'" *Journal of English and Germanic Philology* 37/1 (1938): 48–69.

Sikka, Sonia. "Herder's Critique of Pure Reason." *Review of Metaphysics* 61/1 (2007): 31–50.

Sikka, Sonia. *Herder on Humanity and Cultural Difference: Enlightened Relativism*. Cambridge: Cambridge University Press, 2011.

Smith, Justin E.H., editor. *The Problem of Animal Generation in Early Modern Philosophy*. Cambridge: Cambridge University Press, 2006.

Smith, Justin E.H., and Ohad Nachtomy, editors. *Machines of Nature and Corporeal Substances in Leibniz*. Dordrecht: Springer, 2011.

Solbrig, Ingeborg H. "American Slavery in Eighteenth-Century German Literature: The Case of Herder's 'Neger-Idyllen.'" Monatshefte 82/1 (1990): 38–49.

Sommer, Robert. *Grundzüge einer Geschichte der deutschen Psychologie und Aesthetik von Wolff-Baumgarten bis Kant-Schiller*. Amsterdam: E.J. Bonnet, 1966.

Sömmering, Samuel Thomas. *Über die körperliche Verschiedenheit des Mohren vom Europäer*. Frankfurt und Leipzig, 1785.

Spencer, Vicki A. *Herder's Political Thought: A Study on Language, Culture and Community*. Toronto: University of Toronto Press, 2012.

Spinoza, Benedict de. "The Ethics" (1677). *On the Improvement of the Understanding. The Ethics. Correspondence*. Translated by R.H.M. Elwes. New York: Dover, 1955.

Spivak, Gayatri Chakravorty. "Can the Subaltern Speak?" In *Marxism and the Interpretation of Culture*, edited by Cary Nelson and Lawrence Grossberg, 271–313. London: MacMillan, 1988.

Spivak, Gayatri Chakravorty. *A Critique of Postcolonial Reason: Toward a History of the Vanishing Present*. Cambridge: Harvard University Press, 1999.

Spivak, Gayatri Chakravorty. "Scattered Speculations on the Question of Value." *Diacritics* 15/4 (1985): 73–93.

Stavenhagen, Kurt. *Kant und Königsberg*. Göttingen: Deuerliche Verlagsbuchhandlung, 1949.

Sterne, Lawrence. *The Life and Opinions of Tristram Shandy, Gentleman* (1759–69). New York: Derby and Jackson, 1857.

Steunebrink, Gerrit. "*Sensus Communis* and Modernity as a Common Horizon: A Contribution to the Theory of Intercultural Communication." In *Sensus Communis in Multi- and Intercultural Perspective: On the Possibility of Common Judgments in Arts and Politics*, edited by Heinz Kimmerle and Henk Oosterling, 31–52. Würzburg: Könighausen and Neumann, 2000.

Sulzer, Johann Georg. *Kurzer Begriff aller Wissenschaften und anderer Theile der Gelehrsamkeit*. Leipzig: Johann Christian Langenheim, 1745.

Süssmilch, Johann Peter. *Versuch eines Beweises, daß die erste Sprache ihren Ursprung nicht vom Menschen, sondern allein vom Schöpfer erhalten habe*. Berlin: Im Buchladen der Realschule, 1766.

Taylor, Charles. *Philosophical Arguments*. Cambridge, MA: Harvard University Press, 1995.

Terzakis, Katie. *The Immanent Word: The Turn to Language in German Philosophy, 1759–1801*. New York and London: Routledge, 2007.

Tomlinson, John. *Cultural Imperialism: A Critical Introduction*. London: Continuum, 1991.

Trabant, Jürgen. "Language and the Ear: From Derrida to Herder." *Herder Yearbook* 1 (1992): 1–22.

Voltaire, François-Marie Arouet. *An Essay on the Age of Lewis XIV*. Translated by Mr. Lockman. London: Knapton, 1739.

Vorländer, Karl. *Immanuel Kant: Der Mann und das Werk* (1924). 2nd edition. Includes volumes 1 and 2. Hamburg: Meiner, 1977.

Wallerstein, Immanuel. *The Modern World System*. Vol. 3: *The Second Era of Great Expansion of the Capitalist World Economy 1730–1840's*. San Diego, London, etc.: Academic Press, 1989.

Whistler, Daniel. "The Discipline of Pious Reason." In *Moral Powers, Fragile Beliefs: Essays in Moral and Religious Philosophy*. Edited by J. Carlisle, J. Carter, and D. Whistler. London: Continuum, 2011.

White, Richard. "Herder: On the Ethics of Nationalism." *Humanitas* 18/1–2 (2005): 166–81.

Whiton, John. "Tellheim and the Russians: Aspects of Lessing's Response to the Seven Years' War in Minna von Barnhelm." *Lessing-Yearbook/Jahrbuch* 17 (1985): 89–108.

Wiedemann, Conrad, editor. *Rom – Paris – London: Erfahrung und Selbsterfahrung deutscher Schriftsteller und Künstler un den fremden Metropolen. Ein Symposion*. Stuttgart: Metzler, 1988.

Williamson, H. "Versuch die Ursachen von der Veränderung des Klima zu erklären, welche in den, in dem innern Theil des mitternächtlichen Amerika belegenen Kolonien bemerkt worden." *Berlinische Sammlungen* 7 (1775): 5–21.

Winckelmann, Joachim Johann. *Gedanken über die Nachahmung der griechischen Werke in der Malerei und Bildhauerkunst*. 2nd edition. Dresden: Walther, 1756.

Winckelmann, Joachim Johann. *History of the Art of Antiquity*. Translated by Harry Francis Mallgrave. Los Angeles: Getty Research Institute, 2006.

Winckelmann, Joachim Johann. *Monumenti antichi inediti*. 2nd edition. Edited by Pietro Paolo Montagnani-Mirabili. Rome: A spese dell'autore, 1821.

Wolff, Christian. *Vernünftige Gedanken von Gott, der Welt und der Seele der Menschen, auch alle Dingen überhaupt*. Frankfurt und Leipzig: Rengerische Buchhandlung, 1738.

Young, Robert J.C. *Colonial Desire: Hybridity in Theory, Culture and Race*. London and New York: Routledge, 1995.

Zammito, John H. "Herder and Historical Metanarrative: What's Philosophical about History?" In *A Companion to the Works of Johann Gottfried Herder*, edited by Hans Adler and Wulf Koepke, 65–91. Rochester, NY: Camden House, 2009.

Zammito, John H. *Kant, Herder, and the Birth of Anthropology*. Chicago: University of Chicago Press, 2002.

Zantop, Susanne. *Colonial Fantasies: Conquest, Family, and Nation in Precolonial Germany, 1770–1870*. Durham and London: Duke University Press, 1997.

Zimmermann, Eberhardt August Wilhelm. *Geographische Geschichte des Menschen und der allgemein verbreiteten vierfüßigen Tiere*. 3 volumes. Leipzig: Weygand, 1778–83.

Zöller, Günter. *Anthropology, History and Education*. Edited by Günter Zöller, Robert B. Louden, et al. Cambridge: Cambridge University Press, 2007.

Index

Abbt, Thomas, 86, 174
Access to the Songs of Foreign Peoples, 133
action, and poetic instinct, 123
Adler, Hans, 30, 106
Adorno, Theodor W., 20, 201, 309
aesthetic acts, 182
aesthetic drive, 46
aesthetic humanity, 221, 253
aesthetic judgement, 243
aesthetic production, 193
aesthetic reflection, 43
Aesthetica (Baumgarten), 28, 34
Aesthetica in nuce (Hamann), 49, 50
aesthetics, artificial, 34, 35; of cultural difference, 226–38; factors in, 33; as field of enquiry, 29; fundamental, 252; and imperialism, 60, 244; importance of, 28–35; and language, 20; as metaphysics of fine arts, 29; as metatheory, 28; natural, 34, 35; and philosophy, 35, 251; and poetry, 43; as science, 29; and truth, 34
African subjectivity, and slavery, 304–7
aisthesis/aesthesis distinction, 244–5, 306
aisthetic perception, 43, 117
d'Alembert, Jean de Rond, 119
allegorization, of dialogues, 310; of the mind, 251–2
analogical thought, 174–5
analogon rationis, 60
analysis, and philosophy, 25, 34
Anderson, Benedict, 74
animal/human continuity, 40
animate matter, 110
Another Philosophy of History, 156
Anthropology, 43
anti-colonialism, 13
anti-imperialism, 8–10, 12, 13–16, 20–1, 300–1
Anti-Machiavel, 186
anti-racialism, 12
antinomy of universal reason, 301–3, 310–11
Aquinas, Thomas, 174
armchair philosophy, 188
art, beauty in, 30; epistemological status of, 7; and humanity, 254
artistic drives, 205
artistic expression, 7–8
arts, living perception of, 112
astonishment, and understanding, 27

atemporality problem, 294
atheism, 255
Attempt to Introduce the Concept of Negative Magnitudes into Philosophy, 23, 26
August, Carl, 177, 261, 265
Awareness, 141

Barnard, F.M., 12, 27, 82, 96, 146
Baumgarten, Alexander Gottlieb, 24–5, 28–30, 33, 34, 35, 43
Bayly, Christopher, 9
beauty, in art, 30, 35; in body/mind, 115–17; in science, 35; timeless ideal, of 33; universality of, 30–1, 32
Being, 23–8, 30, 33, 41, 43, 51, 52, 157; cultural manifestations, 55; experience/conceptualization gap, 64; and knowledge, 60, 61; nonanalysability of, 51; self-realization of, 57
Being of God, 28
Benjamin, Walter, 87
Berens, Gustav, 95
Berkeley, George, 35
Berlin, Isaiah, 12, 211
Bildung, 19
biological imagery, 84
Blumenbach, Johann Friedrich, 194–5, 196, 197
body-environment system, 227
body-mind distiction, 38
body-soul constitution, 44
body-soul harmony, 84
Bohm, Arnd, 185
Bonnet, Charles, 85
book-learning, 75
botany, 78, 84
Breitinger, Johann Jacob, 70
Buffon, Comte de, 85, 216
Bush, Barbara, 9

capitalist expansion, 4
Carey, Daniel, 17
Castel, Charles-Irénée, 289
categorical imperative, Kant, 244, 288
Catholicism, 118
causality, and understanding, 27, 79
cause and effect, 232–3
censorship, 260
Chakrabarthy, Dipesh, 18, 302–3, 304, 310
Chase, Bob, 298
chattel slavery, 75–7
Cheah, Pheng, 18–19, 20
church/state separation, 73
City of God, 212
Clairmont, Heinrich 33, 44, 61
Clark, Robert T. 40, 250
climate 218
climatic determinism, 219
cognition, 32; and language, 143; sensory, 33, 34
Colonial Discourse studies, 307–8
Colonization, 198–212; and barbarism, 210–11; beneficial, 120–2; and conquest, 207–12; cultivators/cultivated, 210; and cultural interaction, 120, 206; and dehumanization, 306–7; and greed, 209–10; of improvement, 121; and monogenesis, 47, 150, 152, 212–17. *See also* European imperialism/expansion
Columbus, Herder on, 8, 100–1
commercial spirit, 118–19
commercialism, 4
common sense, 91
commonality, 142–3

communal identity, 62
communication, and stimulation, 141
community, nature of, 140–55
complacent Eurocentric presentism, 136
conatus, 192
concepts, and sensory impressions, 251
conceptual contradiction, 77
conceptualization, 35
Condillac, Étienne Bonnot de, 24, 35, 141, 146
Conquest, 207–12; and history, 282–3
conservation of matter/energy, 200
consideration, and understanding, 27
Conversations on the Transmigration of Souls, 248
Cook, Captain James, 97–100, 187
corrupt power, 187
cosmopolitanism, 95–106, 124
creation, Old Testament story, 253
Crèvecoeur, J. Hector St John de, 283
critical analysis, 237
Critical Groves, 30, 31, 35, 40, 64, 69, 81, 83, 90, 113, 114, 115, 151, 246, 252
critical thinking, 236–7
Critique of Judgement, 91, 175, 243, 308
Critique of Postcolonial Reason, 307–10
Critique of Practical Reason, 175
Critique of Pure Reason, 175, 188, 294, 295
Crusius, Christian August, 26
cultural cross-fertilization, 122
cultural difference, aesthetics of, 226–38; representation of, 114–27
cultural diversity, 4, 7, 136, 137, 181, 182, 216, 226, 281
cultural domination, 120
cultural heterogeneity, 82
cultural homogeneity, 153
cultural hybridity, 82
cultural imperialism, 12
cultural improvement, 120
cultural interaction, 120, 213
cultural intercommunication, 212
cultural interdependence, 212
cultural mobility, 207
cultural nationalism, 82
cultural pluralism, 12
cultural relativism, 6–7, 15, 16
cultural specificity, 134
culture, European, 201–2; forced imposition of, 280–1; and humanity, 221; interpretation of nature, 252; and law, 118; and sympathy, 158–9
cultures, exotic, 229; exploitation of, 101; and human intervention, 153; New World, 103; origins of, 199
customs, and morals, 118
Cyborg Manifesto, 21

The Deceived Mediator, 286
The Deceived Negotiator, 287
decolonizing national discourse, 18
dehumanization, and African experience, 306–7
democracy, 71
Demopaedic project, 62
derivative forces, 38
Derrida, Jacques, 93
Despland, Michael, 294
Despotism, 241
development, and change, 66; natural principle of, 244
development theory, 19, 235
developmental problem in history, 77–86

dialectic, of Enlightenment, 20; Herder's, 310–11; historical, 311; postcolonial, 311
Diderot, Denis, 30, 119, 120, 187
Dithyrambic Rhapsody on the Rhapsody of Cabalistic Prose, 50
diversity, and bildung, 191–8; cultural (*see* cultural diversity); European injustices, 281; geographical, 42–6, 127, 156, 169; human (*see* human diversity); as humanization, 264; of language, 45, 48, 49, 55–6, 138, 150, 151, 298; and nature's force, 281; physiological, 213, 214; in social organization, 213; in unity, 62, 124, 157, 161, 268
diversity/unification contradiction, 297
divine plan, 84, 175–6
Do We Still Have the Public and Fatherland of Yore?, 71, 73–4
doux commerce, 100, 120
Dreams of a Spirit-Seer, 87

Earth, creation of, 268
Edwards, Jeffrey, 38
Embryology, 197
empire, cosmopolitanism of, 96; ideology of 7
empiricism, 188
Encyclopédie, 129
Enlightenment, 17–18; anti-rationalist critique, 109; dialectic of, 20; and philosophy of history, 186
entelechy, 110
environment, and humans, 221–6
environmental degradation, 223–4
epigenesis, 194, 197
epistemology, Herder's, 3–4, 7, 33, 43, 48, 60, 77, 183, 221
Epistolae homericae, 114
Essay on Being, 23–8, 29, 30, 31, 32, 33, 36, 37, 46, 48, 51, 54, 57, 61, 64, 67, 77, 89, 107, 109, 110, 143, 154, 227, 250, 256
Essay on Forces, 191
Essay on the History of Lyrical Poetry, 78, 80
eternity, concept of, 295
Eurocentric dogma, 16
Eurocentric universalism, 15
European colonization. *See* colonization
European culture, 201–2
European domination/supremacy, 7, 166
European expansionism, 4, 6, 8–12, 95–106, 115, 187, 211, 222–6, 278–80, 292–3
European humanity/reason, 220
European imperialism, 60, 106–14, 167–8, 205, 263–4, 277–9
European national spirit, 118
European science, 220
European superiority illusion, 208–9
Existence, 27, 41
Existential Being, 23
Expansionism. *See* European expansionism
experience, and logic, 33

The False Subtlety of the Four Syllogistic Figures, 23
Festa, Lynn, 17
First Critical Grove, 40, 151
fish migration, 109
Flachsland, Caroline, 135

force of nature, 200; and diversity, 281
forces, 36–41, 87, 110, 111, 191–2, 232, 258
Forster, Georg, 187–90, 217, 265
Forster, Johann Reinhold, 187
Forster, Michael N., 178
foundations, logical/real, 26
Fourth Critical Grove, 31, 35, 69, 81, 83, 90, 252
Fox, Russell, 56
Fragments: On the Most Recent German Literature, 62–3, 64, 65, 66, 68, 70, 120, 128
France, politics of representation, 127–34
Frazer, Michael, 12
Frederick the Great, 186, 241
free development, 266
free will, 41; Herder's contradictions, 297, 299–300
freedom, history of, 244; and imagination, 204; and nature, 244, 300; progressive realisation of, 253; of thought, 266; to criticize, 204
French cultural imperialism, 273, 279
French Enlightenment, 119, 162
French language, 119
French Revolution, 250, 259–60, 264, 265–7, 272, 276, 277, 278
Friedrich, Carl, 248
fundamental aesthetics, 252
future ideals, 137

Gadamer, Hans-Georg, 91
Gaier, Ulrich, 25, 28, 35, 70, 140, 183, 248, 250
general images/concepts as abstraction, 157
general pragmatic anthropology, 42
Genetic Force Is the Mother of All Formations on Earth..., 232
genetic power, 197
gentle commerce, 99
geographical diversity, 42–6, 127, 156, 169
geographical materialism, 216
German Ideology, 179
Gleim, Johann Ludwig, 266
global awareness/consciousness, 6
globalization, 3, 4, 6
-gnomy suffix, use of, 227
God, existence of, 23, 25, 26, 27, 255–6
God, Some Conversations, 257
Goethe, Johann Wolfgang, 135–6, 177, 179, 183, 194, 260, 265
Gould, Stephen Jay, 85
government, and human diversity, 259; and human nature, 259–64; and philosophy, 176–80; principle of, 262–3; radical critique of, 261–2; and reason, 179
grammatology, 93
Greek art/drama, 130–2

Habituation, 31
Haller, Albrecht von, 85, 194
Hamann, Johann Georg, 49–50, 51, 55, 95, 119, 130, 177, 249, 260
Happiness, 238–9; as cultural struggle, 242; and nature, 264; of single individuals, 239; and state, 242–3; of Tahitians, 243
Haraway, Donna, 21
Harrison, John, 109
Hartknoch, J.F., 124
Hawkesworth, John, 97, 99, 100
heaven and earth, parallelism of, 180–90

Heinz, Marion, 33, 44, 61
Herder, Johann Gottfried, anti-imperialism, 8–10, 12, 13–16, 20–1, 300–1; antinomy of universal reason, 301–3, 310–11; in Bückeburg, 155; contradictions, 297–300; as cosmopolitan, 95–106, 124; early life, 4; French language/culture, 97; and French Revolution, 129; Kant's criticisms of (*see* Kant); Königsberg Sect, 63; methodological/rhetorical strategies, 311; Painboef to Nantes journey, 108; Prussian Academy prize, 138; as public intellectual, 120–1; on religion, 164; in Riga 61–3, 95; turning point, 246; in Weimar, 177
hieroglyphics of creation, 175
historical development, interpretation of, 86–94, 130, 159, 165
historical dialectic, 311
historical knowledge, as process of life, 175
historical migration, 109–10
historical optimism, 235
historical origins, 46–51, 78–80
historical past, 308
historical processes, 234
historical progress, and happiness, 239
historical sympathy, 158–60
historiography, 93; errors in, 158; as poetry, 165; scientific, 118; as theology, 165
history, and antagonism, 249; and anthropology, 53; and collective humanity, 235; and conquest, 282–3; and cosmology, 43; developmental problem in, 77–86; of diverse humanity, 127–8, 157–8; and free will, 299; genesis of, 78, 80; Herder's contradictions, 297, 298–9; interpretation of, 86–94, 130, 159; and language, 250; local, 123; and morality, 240–1, 294; and natural laws, 247–9, 299; and organisms' development, 61; of peoples, 157; and philosophy, 156, 171–2, 176, 185, 186, 198, 204, 233, 238, 262, 294; as single progressive development, 164; teleology in, 308; and theology, 187; of unified humanity, 127–8
History of the Mission of Evangelical Brothers among the Indians of North America, 291
History of the Two Indies, 120, 183, 185
Hobbes, Thomas, 289
Hodopaedia, 189
Holstein-Eutin, Prince of, 135
Home, Henry, 216
Hont, Istvan, 6
Horkheimer, Max, 20
How Does One Force Give Rise to Another?, 191
How Philosophy Can Become More Universal and Useful for the Benefit of the People, 36
human biology, and reason, 301
human cognition, fundamental, 251
human consensus, and language, 154
human creativity, 182
human desire, 259–60
human development, 61, 81, 197–8; ethnographic evidence, 237; monogenetic, 47, 150, 152; unitary theory of, 237; unity of, 169
human dimension, 24

human diversity, 127–8, 157–8, 165–6, 169–70, 203, 206, 219, 227, 227–8, 227–9, 259, 268, 281, 282
human double creature, 173
human existence, ultimate goals, 31, 32
human expression, 15
human form, representation of, 230
human history, constant change, 268
human imagination, 203
human mind, allegorization of, 251; and organic nature, 236; structure of, 203
human nature, preferential perspectives, 202; and problem of government, 259–64; shared, 42–6, 159
human path, 37, 77
human perfectability, 252, 258–9
human responses, 140
human rights, 288
human sensibility, 256
human social order, 262
human soulmap of, 43; youth and aging, 108
human species, history of, 37
human spirit and the creator, 182
human understanding, 176; conceptual apparatus of, 27
humanity, 12, 14; as aesthetic, 221, 253; and art, 254; and, climate 218; common, 134; common plan for, 154; concept of, 106; and culture, 221; destiny of, 156; and the environment, 218, 219, 221–6; Herder's contradictions, 297, 299; and human nature, 258; ideal form of, 244; incest/interbreeding of, 232; natural forces and, 253; natural history of, 198–210, 282; and nature, 253–5; prototype of, 282; self-realization of, 282; tree model, 172–3; unity of, 153, 155, 174; universality of, 282; vision of, 94; Zimmermann's map, 228–9, 230, 231; and the zodiac, 270
humanization, 264
humankind, perfect civil union of, 247
Hume, David, 23, 79, 137, 188
hybrid beings, 30

Idea for the First Patriotic Institute for the Common Spirit of Germany, 248
Idea for a Universal History with a Cosmopolitan Purpose, 246–7, 248
Ideal Being, 23
idealism, dualism of, 69; and logic, 51
Ideas Concerning the Philosophy of the History of Humanity, 41, 111, 176–7, 180, 183, 191, 203, 207, 210, 216, 221, 226, 227, 231, 233, 245, 263, 264, 265, 276
Imagination, 204
immanent organic finality, 196
imperialism, and aesthetics, 60; critique of, 92–3, 263; cultural, 12; European, 60, 106–14; and moral judgement, 276–96
infinitesimal differences, 214
inorganic to organic, 111
institutional space, 72–7
intellectual, as political agent, 201
international commerce, 99, 290
interpretation, of history, 86–94; politics of, 86–94, 255–9
invisible forces, 232, 234

Jacobi, Friedrich Heinrich, 255–7
Jameson, Fredric, 309

Jews, and conquest, 282–3
Journal of My Travels in the Year 1769, 106–14, 117, 125, 126, 127, 128, 130, 133, 156, 168
justice, and natural history, 202

kakistocracy, 202
Kalm, Peter, 222–3
Kant, Immanuel, and analogy, 175; on Being, 25, 27; categorical imperative, 244, 288; critical thinking, 236–7; and force, 87; on force of nature, 231; and Frederick the Great, 241; on God, 25; Herder as student, 4, 23, 63; humanity and Enlightenment, 247; international commerce, 290; on *Metaphysica*, 25; and morality, 162; nature and war, 289; and occult force, 232, 235; organismic ontology, 19; and philosophical enquiry, 233; and physical geography, 42; political optimism, 89; pre-critical philosophy, 24–5, 42; on race, 216; rationality of peace/war, 290; on the state, 238, 249
Kepler, Johannes, 247–8
Kersting, Wolfgang, 240
Kiernan, V.G., 9
Kleingeld, Pauline, 294, 295
Kleist, Ewald Christian von, 58
Klima, 218
Klotz, Christian Adolf, 63–4, 114–15, 246
Knoll, Samson B., 12–13, 283
knowledge, and Being, 60, 61; drive to, 46; imparted to children, 112; shared, 61
Koepke, Wulf, 246, 251–2, 258, 276
Königlich Preussische Academie der Wissenschaften, 138
Königsberg Sect, 63
Kontje, Tod, 12
Koselleck, Reinhard, 4, 6, 185, 186
Kritik und Krise, 6

Lamb, Jonathan, 192
language, abstract, 74, 139–40; and the aesthetic, 20; analytic development, 139; and cognition, 143; and conceptualization, 57; and culture, 20, 155; development process of, 65–71, 148; diversity of, 45, 48, 49, 55–6, 150, 151, 298; diversity of purposes, 138; and divine intervention, 45, 138–9, 144, 145, 147; and environment, 52–3, 147; ethnolinguistics, 140; foreign languages, 51–9; and four natural laws of nature, 147; and free will, 300; French, 119; German, 249; and God's will, 212; and groups, 82, 83; Herder's contradictions, 297–8; heterogeneity of non-European, 308; and history, 250; history of, 67; and human beings in nature, 254; and human consensus, 154; human/animal, 141, 146; and humanization, 264; and individual psyche, 134; and literature, 64; and memory, 67–8; and mind development, 138; mother tongue, 53–4, 58, 70; multilingualism, 56; and naming, 142; of nature, 50, 145–6; non-conceptual, 250; origins of, 135–55; and past/present continuum, 137–8; and philosophy, 261; poetic, 49, 69, 70–1, 87–8; prose, 67, 68–9; of

psychosomatics, 124; publications on, 138; and reason, 144, 155; role of, 52, 61; and self-realization, 147; and semanto-cognitive relationships, 142; shared structures of, 158; as single law of change, 66; and sociability, 149; thought/language system, 142–3; Tower of Babel, 51–2, 55, 151
language acquisition, 141, 143
language labor, 13–14
language purification, 70
language theory, 61
Lavater, Johannes Kaspar, 63
lawand culture, 118; of nature, 252–3
Leibniz, Gottfried Wilhelm, 19, 25, 33, 38–9, 84–5, 110, 196, 254
Lessing, Gotthold Ephraim, 62, 135, 255
Letters of an American Farmer, 283–4
Letters Concerning the Most Recent German Literature, 62, 65
Letters on Humanity, 76, 131, 134, 179, 185–6, 189, 190, 201, 203, 215, 253, 265, 269–70, 274, 276, 282
Letters on Ossian, 263
Lettres Turques, 130
life and death, 110–11
linguistic engineering, 70
Linnaeus, Carl, 86
Livonia mission, 107, 108, 121
Locke, John, 23, 24, 35, 38, 139, 141
logic, and experience, 33; and idealism, 51; rules of, 24; and understanding, 27
Logical Being, 27–8
logical/real foundations, 26
logocentric bias, 93
Loskiel, Georg Heinrich, 291–2, 295
Machiavelli, 186
Mack, Michael, 93, 141, 157, 162, 163, 192, 308
Mackay, David, 99
Mah, Harold, 106–7
Mandeville, Bernard, 192
Manifoldness, 160
map of the human soul, 43
Marx, Karl, 179, 201
Maupertuis, Pierre-Louis Moreau de, 138
Mbembe, Achille, 303–7
mechanical cause and effect, 232–3
Mendelssohn, Moses, 62, 137, 255, 256
Menges, Karl, 42, 65, 69, 70, 77, 93, 133, 143, 163, 235
Menze, Ernest A., 65
Metacritique of the Critique of Pure Reason, 155, 298, 300
Metaphysica, 25
metaphysical speculation, 89
metaphysics, criticism of, 238, 256–7; and the French, 119
Metaphysics of Morals, 120, 249
Meyer, Heinrich, 270
Michaelis, Johann David, 65
Mindfulness, 141
Miscellaneous Remarks on the Abilities and Customs of the Wild Peoples, 196
Mobility, 127
modern statehood, 71
modernization, 120; and moral responsibility, 121
monarchy, 178
monogenesis, 47, 150, 152, 212–17, 232, 236
Montaigne, Michel de, 9
Montesquieu, Charles de Secondat, baron de, 99, 130, 136, 218, 219
moral innocence, 187

moral judgement, and imperialism, 276–96
moral principles, 185
morality, creation of, 295; and history, 240–1, 294; and politics, 177–8; and the spirit, 248
Morton, Michael, 48, 52, 62, 63
mother tongue, 53–4, 58
Müller, Georg, 266
Müller, Johannes, 185
Multilingualism, 56
Muthu, Sankar, 12, 17–18
myth, as heuristic thinking, 70; in history, 88
mythologies, and laws of nature, 252; new mythology, 180; value of, 115

nation states, 82
national culture, 82
national identity, 61
national songs, 199, 200–1
Native Americans, 11
natural development principle, 194
natural forces, 40, 197, 200
natural history, 198–212; of humanity, 198–210, 282; and justice, 202
natural laws, 247–8
natural principle of development, 244
naturalization of spirit, 44
nature, of community, 140–55; differentiation of, 268; freedom and, 244; and God, 255; and reason, 244; of revolution, 265–76; unity of, 127; and war, 289
Negro Idylls, 12, 283–5, 306
negroes, 116, 150, 195, 214, 216, 217, 237
new mythology, 180
New World culture, 103
Newton, Isaac, 247–8
Newton, Robert, 7, 31, 124
Nicholas V, Pope, 202
Nicolai, Christoph Friedrich, 62, 63, 117
No Force of Nature Is without an Organ, 196
nobility, aversion to, 266
noble expansion of the soul, 206
Norton, Robert, 36, 251

observation, and understanding, 27
observation/experimentation, rules of, 24
occult forces, 87, 232, 235
Old Testament story of creation, 253
On the Change of Taste, 123, 169, 170, 243
On Christian Wolff's Writings, 29
On the Difference Races of Humankind, 216
On Diligence in the Study of Several Learned Languages, 1, 48, 50, 51, 52, 53, 55, 58–9, 89, 144, 151, 153
On the Formative Drive and Procreation, 194, 195
On German Style and Art, 131, 238
On the Human Soul's Cognition and Sensation, 41
On Image, Poetic Production and Fables, 250, 258
On the Postcolony, 303
On the Spinozist Doctrine, 255
On the Stages of Life of a Language, 66–7
On Thomas Abbt's Writings, 86, 174
One and the Many, 62

The Only Possible Argument in Support of a Demonstration of the Existence of God, 23, 25, 26, 27
Opposition between Genesis and Climate, 199
organic development, models of, 171; scientific study of, 78–9, 111
organic drive, 196
organic forces, 196–7
organic life cycles, 175
organic nature, and the mind, 236
organic principle, 60–4
organismic ontology, 19
organization, of the peoples of the world, 229
origins, search for, 78–80
Our Earth Is a Star among Stars, 198–9
Outline of a History of Lyric Poetry, 4684

Pagden, Anthony, 140
Palingenesis, 232
Palti, Elias, 43, 86, 87, 196
pan-dynamism, 38
pantheism, 255, 258
parallelism, of heaven and earth, 180–90; philosophy of, 190
patriarchal family, 71
patriotic curiosity, 66
patriotic institutions, 248
perfectability of man, 252, 258
perpetual peace, 289–95
Perpetual Peace: A Philosophical Sketch, 289
Perpetual Peace: An Iroquois Institution, 289
perpetuality, and time, 294
philosopher of progress, 161
philosophical enquiry, 233
philosophical images, 251
philosophy, and aesthetics, 35, 251; and analysis, 25, 34; and anthropology, 36–7; essence of, 32; and government, 176–80; and history, 156, 171–2, 176, 185, 186, 198, 204, 233, 238, 262, 294; and language, 261; and mathematics, 24; and multiplicity of life, 86; and parallelism, 190; and unity, 238
Philosophy for the Benefit of the People, 92
physical geography, 42, 221
physiognomy, 227
physiological determinism, 218–19
physiological development, and reason, 234–5
physiological diversity, 213, 214
Plato Said, 44
poetic discourse, 29–30
poetic images, 251
poetic instinct, and action, 123
poetic language, 49, 69, 70–1, 87–8
poetic spirit, 234
poetics, of human diversity, 282; and laws of nature, 252
poetry, and aesthetic experience, 43; as art of power, 40; and historical origins, 46–51; and historiography, 165; as mother tongue of human race, 50–1; and new lands, 114–15; and philosophy, 238; and prejudice, 160
political aesthetics, 246–55
political honour, 119
political poetics, 65–71
political quietism, 178
political reason, and revolution, 274–5
political revolutions, 269

political sea-dreams, 108, 118
politicians' nature, 179
politics, and morality, 290–1; primary law of, 186
politics of interpretation, 86–94, 255–9, 265–76
politics of representation, 114; France 127–34
politik, 185
possibility, and understanding, 27
postcolonial theory, 16–18, 21, 22, 301–11
postmodernism, 21–2
Postmodernism, or the Cultural Logic of Late Capitalism, 309
power, legitimation of, 11
power relations, 243–4
The Prayer of War, 286
pre-formed mechanical laws, 110
predicate-in-notion principle, 25
preformation, 85–6, 197
prejudice, 160–1, 164; and truth, 161
The Prince of the Huns, 286–7, 288
print media, 72–3, 74
progress, 161–2, 165–76
Prolegomena, 24
Pross, Wolfgang, 23, 40, 47, 185, 191, 229, 242
providence, 263
Provincializing Europe, 18, 302
public decision making, 72

Questions to a Society of Learned Men..., 65

race, 116, 150, 195, 212–17
racist dogma, 16
rational analogy, 33
rationalism/empiricism, 124
rationalists, 19–20, 31
rationality of peace/war, 290
Raynal, Guillaume Thomas, Abbé, 120, 183–5, 187
reading, 125–6
Real Being, 26, 27, 30, 37
reason, antinomy of universal reason, 301–3, 310–11; emancipation of, 241; and forces of nature, 148; and God, 255; and language, 144; multiplicity of, 140–55; and nature, 244; and physiological development, 234–5; primacy of, 7; and revolution, 274–5; universal, 301; universal capacity for, 301
reflection, 141
Reflections on the Imitation of Greek Works in Painting and Sculpture, 131
Reimarus, Hermann Samuel, 38, 39–40
Reinhold, Karl Leonhard, 236
religion, wars of, 10
representation, of cultural difference, 114–27; strategies of, 127
revolution, nature of, 265–76
Richards, Robert J., 196
Riedel, Friedrich Justus, 31, 32, 90
Robinette, Nicholas, 13–14
Rousseau, Jean Jacques, 89–90, 141, 146, 149, 205

Saidian frameworks, 21–2
Saint-Pierre, Abbé de, 289
Sarkar, Sumit, 21–2
Scattered Notes, 250
Scattered Speculations on the Question of Value, 311
Schaumburg-Lippe, Count Wilhelm von, 155
Schiller, Friedrich, 274
Schlegel, Friedrich, 180

Schubart, Christian Friedrich Daniel, 183
Schütz, Christian Gottfried, 231
science, as model-formation, 281–2
scientific drives, 205
scientific historiography, 118
scientific questions, 66
sea travel, 107, 112–14, 122
Second Critical Grove, 64, 113, 114, 115
sedentary life, and imagination, 113
self, 74–5
self-awareness, 146
self-determination, 300
self-discovery, 77
self-expression, 118; of nature, 261
self-formation, 74, 77, 107
self-preservation, 192
self-realization, 77, 146, 147; of humanity, 282
semanto-cognitive relationships, 142
semilogical deviance, 309
semiotics of the soul/body, 124, 133, 175
sensory cognition, 33, 88
sensory experience, 49, 67; and logical formalism, 60; and logical thought, 24
sensory impressions, 91; and concepts, 251
sensory perception, 142–3, 152
sensory sensibility, 46
sensual idealism, 44
sensus communis, 252
serfdom, 75–7
Seven Years' War, and German literature, 62–3
Shaftesbury, Anthony Cooper, 3rd Earl of, 192, 257
Shakespeare, Herder's article on, 131, 238
shared human nature, 42–6
signifying action, 80–1
Sikka, Sonia, 14–15, 19, 28, 41, 82, 117, 162, 214, 238
slavery, abolition of, 167; African subjectivity, 304; and Arab colonialism, 205–6; Atlantic slave trade, 6; baseness of, 210; brutality of, 283–5; chattel slavery, 75–7; New World, 229, 284–6; outsourcing, 167; and unbelievers, 202
sociability, and language, 149
social cohesion, and public institutions, 71
solar system, 267
Solbrig, Ingeborg, 12
Sommer, Robert, 38
Sömmering, Samuel Thomas, 216
soul, and Being, 44; and body, 44
Spectral Nationality, 18–19
speechless wonder, 141
Spencer, Vicki, 13, 20, 82
Spinoza, Benedict de, 19, 41, 45, 148, 162, 178, 192, 196, 255–9
spirit of changes, 170
The Spirit of Hebrew Poetry, 180–1
The Spirit of the Laws, 99, 218
Spirit of the Times, 275
spiritualization of nature, 44
Spivak, Gayatri Chakravorty, 18, 93, 307–9, 311
Stagnation, 241
state power, and happiness, 238–9; and nature, 238–45, 248
states, criticism of, 211–12; and human settlement, 289–90; as immoral institution, 240; and morality, 290–1; and tyranny, 240; unnatural expansion, of 242
statesmen and philosophers, 178
Stolpe, Heinz, 216
structure of the mind, 203

Subaltern Studies Group, 21
Süssmilch, Johann Peter, 138, 139, 144, 145, 147, 149, 151
symbolization, 40–1, 44
system of theories, 140

Tahiti, Captain Cook in, 97–100; happiness of people, 243; purpose of inhabitants, 242
taste, diversity of, 32
temporality, 294, 295
Terzakis, Katie, 49
Theodicy, 84
Theoria generationis, 85
Theory of the Fine Arts and Sciences, 31
Third Critical Grove, 64
This Too a Philosophy of History for the Formation of Humanity, 156, 157, 166, 168, 171, 175, 176, 177, 178, 185, 197, 199, 213, 266
thought/language development, 151
thought/language system, 142–3
thought/matter dualism, 38
time, and African experience, 305–6
time, space and force, 36–41
Tomlinson, John, 12
Tower of Babel, 51–2, 55, 151
Trabant, Jürgen, 141, 142, 147, 151
Tractatus Theologico-Politicus, 178
trade, and cultural exchange, 208
travellers' questionnaires, 65
travelogues, 189
Treatise on the Origin of Language, 138, 139, 145, 146, 148, 151, 156, 183, 193, 250
tree model, of humanity, 172–3
tropological analysis, 307

unconscious reason, 180
unitary mankind, 197
unity-in-diversity, 62, 124, 157, 161, 268
universalism, 14, 15, 16, 303, 307; and logic, 114
universality, analytical path to, 188; concepts of, 33; in human life, 163; and sensitivity, 189; of thought, 60–1
Upon the 14th of July, 1790, 266

vagina hominum, 109
vegetal feeling, 83
Voltaire, François-Marie Arouet, 24, 150–1, 152, 161, 162, 163–4, 166, 185, 186
A Voyage round the World, 188

wa Thiong'o, Ngugi, 14
Wallerstein, Immanuel, 4
What is Enlightenment?, 240
wild peoples, 135–40, 145, 149, 151, 169, 195, 196, 210–11, 224, 237, 263
Williams, Raymond, 14
Winckelmann, Johann Joachim, 116, 131
Wolff, Caspar Friedrich, 85, 197, 232
Wolff, Christian, 24, 25, 26, 29, 33, 38–9
Wolffian logic, 28, 29, 31, 43, 138
Wöllner, J.C., 260
Women of Peace, 291–2
world trade, 6, 10, 118
writing, problem of, 60–4; and truth, 302

Young, Robert, 300

Zammito, John, 24, 89, 90, 131, 134, 136, 156, 165–6, 218, 227
Zimeo, 284
Zimmermann, Eberhard, 228–9, 230, 231

GERMAN AND EUROPEAN STUDIES

General Editor: Rebecca Wittmann

1. Emanuel Adler, Beverly Crawford, Federica Bicchi, and Rafaella Del Sarto, *The Convergence of Civilizations: Constructing a Mediterranean Region*
2. James Retallack, *The German Right, 1860–1920: Political Limits of the Authoritarian Imagination*
3. Silvija Jestrovic, *Theatre of Estrangement: Theory, Practice, Ideology*
4. Susan Gross Solomon, ed., *Doing Medicine Together: Germany and Russian between the Wars*
5. Laurence McFalls, ed., *Max Weber's "Objectivity" Revisited*
6. Robin Ostow, ed., *(Re)Visualizing National History: Museums and National Identities in Europe in the New Millennium*
7. David Blackbourn and James Retallack, eds., *Localism, Landscape, and the Ambiguities of Place: German-Speaking Central Europe, 1860–1930*
8. John Zilcosky, ed., *Writing Travel: The Poetics and Politics of the Modern Journey*
9. Angelica Fenner, *Race under Reconstruction in German Cinema: Robert Stemmle's Toxi*
10. Martina Kessel and Patrick Merziger, eds., *The Politics of Humour in the Twentieth Century: Inclusion, Exclusion, and Communities of Laughter*
11. Jeffrey K. Wilson, *The German Forest: Nature, Identity, and the Contestation of a National Symbol, 1871–1914*
12. David G. John, *Bennewitz, Goethe,* Faust: *German and Intercultural Stagings*
13. Jennifer Ruth Hosek, *Sun, Sex, and Socialism: Cuba in the German Imaginary*

14 Steven M. Schroeder, *To Forget All and Begin Again: Reconciliation in Occupied German, 1944–1954*

15. Kenneth S. Calhoon, *Affecting Grace: Theatre, Subject, and the Shakespearean Paradox in German Literature from Lessing to Kleist*
16. Martina Kolb, *Nietzsche, Freud, Benn, and the Azure Spell of Liguria*
17. Hoi-eun Kim, *Doctors of Empire: Medical and Cultural Encounters between Imperial Germany and Meiji Japan*

18. J. Laurence Hare, *Excavating Nations: Archaeology, Museums, and the German-Danish Borderlands*
19. Patrick O'Neill, *Transforming Kafka: Translation Effects*
20. Jacques Kornberg, *The Pope's Dilemma: Pius XII Faces Atrocities and Genocide in the Second World War*
21. John K. Noyes, *Herder: Aesthetics against Imperialism*
22. James Retallack, *Germany's Second Reich: Portraits and Pathways*

www.ingramcontent.com/pod-product-compliance
Lightning Source LLC
LaVergne TN
LVHW090146080826
844660LV00013B/691/J

* 9 7 8 1 4 4 2 6 5 0 3 8 1 *